American Furniture

AMERICAN FURNITURE 2011

Edited by Luke Beckerdite

Published by the CHIPSTONE FOUNDATION

Distributed by University Press of New England

Hanover and London

Cover Illustration: Detail, chest, painted decoration attributed to Henrich Otto (1733–ca. 1799), Millbach area, Heidelberg Township, Lancaster County (now Millcreek Township, Lebanon County), Pennsylvania, 1783. (Private collection; photo, Gavin Ashworth.)

Design: Wynne Patterson, Pittsfield, VT
Copyediting: Fronia Simpson, Bennington, VT
Typesetting: Aardvark Type, Hartford, CT
Printing: Meridian Printing, East Greenwich, RI

Published by the Chipstone Foundation
Distributed by University Press of New England
1 Court Street
Lebanon, New Hampshire 03766
upne.com

Contents

Editorial Statement

American Furniture is an interdisciplinary journal dedicated to advancing knowledge of furniture made or used in the Americas from the seventeenth century to the present. Authors are encouraged to submit articles on any aspect of furniture history, essays on conservation and historic technology, reproductions or transcripts of documents, annotated photographs of new furniture discoveries, and book and exhibition reviews. References for compiling an annual bibliography also are welcome.

Manuscripts must be typed, double-spaced, illustrated with black-and-white prints, transparencies, or high resolution digital images, and prepared in accordance with the *Chicago Manual of Style*. The Chipstone Foundation will offer significant honoraria for manuscripts accepted for publication and reimburse authors for all photography approved in writing by the editor.

Luke Beckerdite

American Furniture

Figure 1 Chest, Heidelberg Township area, Lebanon or Berks County, Pennsylvania, 1792. Walnut and mixed-wood inlay (including maple, sumac, holly, birch, and possibly mahogany) with white pine and oak; brass, iron. H. 27″, W. 59¼″, D. 24½″. (Private collection; photo, Laszlo Bodo.) The brasses are replaced.

Figure 2 Detail of the interior of the chest illustrated in fig. 1. (Photo, Laszlo Bodo.) The surviving till lid has a molded top and edge. Two large fraktur were once pasted to the underside of the chest lid.

Lisa Minardi

From Millbach to Mahantongo: Fraktur and Furniture of the Pennsylvania Germans

▼ IN 1792 AN EXTRAORDINARY walnut chest with inlaid decoration was made for Maria Elisabeth Miller (fig. 1). Many unusual features distinguish this object, most notably the four external drawers within the main compartment and three lower drawers, two interior tills, and one till drawer (fig. 2). This extravagant construction would have added greatly to the overall cost of the chest, requiring additional labor to build the seven exterior drawers as well the cost of brass locks, escutcheons, and pulls for each. Walnut was also a more expensive choice than tulip poplar or pine, as were the ogee feet, which are more difficult to make than straight bracket or turned feet. Although the exact cost of the Miller chest is unknown, some idea can be derived from the account book of Bucks County joiner Abraham Overholt, who charged £1.10 in 1792 for a pine chest with three drawers, painted brown, and £3 in 1799 for a "walnut chest with three drawers, locks and hardware." The Miller chest has inlaid floral motifs on a large horizontal panel that is attached to a mortise-and-tenoned frame, rather than the more typical single-board façade. Presumably the maker used that construction to accommodate the external drawers flanking the panel. A second panel containing the owner's name, in elaborate German *Fraktur* lettering, is inset within the larger panel (fig. 3). Who was Maria Elisabeth Miller? Why was her chest built and inlaid in such a singular and costly manner, and who made it? Was the elaborate lettering of Maria Elisabeth's name rendered by the maker of the chest or by a professional calligrapher such as a fraktur artist? Although not all of these questions can be definitively answered, the examination of the Miller chest and other related inlaid or painted objects sheds light on the remarkable furniture production of a distinctive cultural region and enables an exploration of the myriad connections between fraktur and furniture.[1]

Figure 3   Detail of the inscription on the chest illustrated in fig. 1. (Photo, Laszlo Bodo.) The "n" after Miller is a suffix applied to women's surnames (both married and unmarried) in German; depending on the surname, an –n, –en/–in or –sen/–sin suffix was used (e.g., Hoffman/Hoffmanin).

The Miller Chest

The identification of Maria Elisabeth Miller is critical for understanding this chest within its original context and exploring its relation to other objects. Maria Elisabeth Miller (1775–1843) was the youngest child of Michael and Maria Elisabeth (Becker) Miller of Millbach, in Heidelberg Township, Lancaster County (now Millcreek Township, Lebanon County). Named after the Mill Creek or *Mühlbach*, the village was home to several families who attained significant wealth through farming and milling. Four miles to the southwest was Schaefferstown, the largest settlement in the area (see fig. 22). In 1746 Maria Elisabeth's paternal grandfather, George Miller, provided an acre of land on which a German Reformed church and schoolhouse were built. Construction of the church began in 1751, and in 1770 Lutheran patriarch Henry Melchior Muhlenberg (1711–1787) described it as "built of massive stones and is furnished with a tower. . . . Lying between trees and open fields, it offers a pleasant prospect."[2]

Figure 4 House of George and Maria Catharina Miller, then Michael and Maria Elisabeth Miller, Millbach, Heidelberg Township, Lancaster County (now Millcreek Township, Lebanon County), Pennsylvania, built in 1752 and expanded by 1760. (Courtesy, Millbach Foundation, Inc.; photo, Laszlo Bodo.) The gable end of the original gambrel-roof house is to the right, and the addition built by Michael Miller, to the left.

Figure 5 Gristmill of Michael Miller, Millbach, Heidelberg Township, Lancaster County (now Millcreek Township, Lebanon County), Pennsylvania, built in 1784. (Courtesy, Millbach Foundation, Inc.; photo, Laszlo Bodo.)

A German immigrant, George Miller (1706–1791) and his wife, Maria Catharina Stump (1711–1787), built a large stone house along the banks of the Mill Creek in 1752 (fig. 4). The house was soon expanded by their son Michael (1732–1815), who subsequently built a new gristmill that was attached to the main house and likely replaced an older mill in the same location (fig. 5). This house-mill combination is particularly associated with the Pennsylvania Germans and is a rare survival of a European house type. Notable is the house's kicked gambrel roof, which provided a large attic well suited for the storage of grain. Two carved date stones (figs. 6, 7) were made for the buildings, one for the house with the inscription "JERG MÜLER / 17 MARIA CATR M 52" and the other for the mill, "1784 / GOTT ALEIN DE EHR (God alone the Honor) / MICHAEL MIELER / M ELISABET MILERN." The interior of the house is equally impressive, with a Germanic floor plan consisting of a large kitchen, stove room, and bedchamber on the first floor. Other distinctive features include elaborately paneled doors and a massive staircase with square-sawn balusters in the German baroque manner (fig. 8).[3]

Figure 6 Date stone from the Miller house, 1752. (Courtesy, Philadelphia Museum of Art.)

Figure 7 Date stone of Michael Miller's gristmill, 1784. (Courtesy, Millbach Foundation, Inc.; photo, Laszlo Bodo.)

Figure 8 Staircase from the Miller house. (Courtesy, Philadelphia Museum of Art, gift of Mr. and Mrs. Pierre S. du Pont and Mr. and Mrs. Lammot du Pont, 1926.) The staircase was removed in 1926 along with other interior woodwork and installed as a period room at the Philadelphia Museum of Art.

In 1753 George Miller transferred the house, mill, and 144 acres to his son Michael. According to the deed, George was then a resident of Rowan County, North Carolina. Records there appear to confirm the family tradition that George left his wife, Maria Catharina, behind in Pennsylvania and moved to North Carolina with a servant girl. In 1754 he applied for a license to keep a tavern on his plantation in Rowan County. Deed books show that George settled on Abbotts Creek, now part of Davidson County, and established a gristmill. In 1773 he transferred three enslaved servants "for natural love & affection to & for services of 20 yrs. to Glory Miller otherwise Glory Lettsler." In his will of 1785, George refers to his wife, "Glory Litsler Miller," as well as four sons, John, Jacob, David, and Frederick. He died in 1791. On the heels of this family scandal, Michael Miller acquired the Millbach property at only twenty-one years of age. He would become one of the wealth-iest men in the community by the time of his death in 1815 and was consis-tently taxed at one of the highest rates of all residents in Heidelberg Township. In addition to expanding the house (probably to provide his mother with independent living quarters) and building a new gristmill, Michael made other improvements, including the construction of a sawmill by 1777. When the federal direct tax was taken in 1798, Heidelberg Town-ship had a total of nine saw- or gristmills, two of which were owned by Michael Miller. His property comprised the large stone house; a two-storey stone gristmill of 50 by 20 feet, with two pairs of stones and described as "in good order, new"; a sawmill of 40 by 12 feet with double gears, "in very good order"; a large barn of 100 by 28 feet; and a log still house of 30 by 20 feet in "good order." The house and mill were assessed at $1,000.00 each; by comparison, the average tradesman's house in Schaefferstown was val-ued at $268 and the average farmhouse at $434.00.[4]

A partial inventory conducted after Michael Miller's death in 1815 lists a table, stove and pipes; a bed and bedstead worth £3.15 and three more bed-steads; "1 Closset" (likely a schrank) worth £4.10; a "spinet" worth £11.5; "1 Conk shell"; a chest, cradle, dough trough, and meal chest; two kitchen dressers; four tables; a corner cupboard; and extensive pewter including a dozen plates, seventeen spoons, seven basins, and five other "large" forms. Also appraised were a still kettle valued at £16.17.6 and "63 vesels the half belonging to the Stillery" valued at £22.10.6. Known furnishings of the Miller house are as Germanic as the architecture. The stove room was heated by a large iron stove, fed through the back of the kitchen hearth, which was supported by an ornately carved stone (fig. 9) inscribed with the date "1757" and initials "MM / MLM" (for Michael Miller and Maria [E]lisabeth Miller), along with symbols of the miller's trade—lower half of the main wooden gear from a gristmill, a square, and dividers. A tall-case clock (fig. 10) with eight-day movement by Jacob Graff (1729–1778) of

Figure 9 Stove support from the Miller house, 1757. Stone. H. 14¾", W. 20½", D. 5½". (Cour-tesy, Pennsylvania Historical and Museum Com-mission, CW74.190; photo, Gavin Ashworth.) The foliate design above the initials is similar to one carved above the entry of the nearby Hein-rich Zeller house, built in 1745 (see fig. 24).

Figure 10   Tall-case clock with movement by Jacob Graff (1729–1778), Lebanon, Lancaster (now Lebanon) County, Pennsylvania, 1750–1760. Walnut and mixed-wood inlays; brass, silvered brass, bronze, iron, steel; glass. H. 98", W. 24¼", D. 12½". (Courtesy, Winterthur Museum, bequest of Henry Francis du Pont, 1965.2261; photo, Laszlo Bodo.)

Figure 11   Detail of the movement of the clock illustrated in fig. 10. (Photo, Laszlo Bodo.)

Lebanon descended in the family until the early twentieth century and, according to tradition, stood in the kitchen. One of the earliest known Pennsylvania German tall-case clocks, it dates to about the time Michael Miller acquired the house. The case's form and construction are overtly Germanic, with ample use of wooden pegs (rather than nails) and a trapezoidal pediment that appears on Continental furniture but is extremely rare in America. The clock's eight-day movement features a moon phase dial, calendar wheel, and day-of-the-week disk (fig. 11). A walnut chest (fig. 12) with paneled lid in the Continental manner and a hanging corner cupboard with raised panel door (fig. 13) are also associated with the Miller house; details such as the notched corners of the raised panels on the chest and the shape of the raised panel of the cupboard door relate closely to the doors and shutters of the house.[5]

One of the most unusual objects associated with the house is an earthenware angel head (fig. 14) that was probably an architectural ornament. In 1765 Michael and Maria Elisabeth Miller were presented with a large New Year's greeting (fig. 15), which is addressed to them as "my dear neighbors

Figure 12 Chest, Millbach area, Heidelberg Township, Lancaster County (now Millcreek Township, Lebanon County), Pennsylvania, 1750–1775. Walnut with tulip poplar; iron. H. 25½", W. 52½", D. 26". (Courtesy, Millbach Foundation, Inc.; photo, Laszlo Bodo.)

Figure 13 Hanging corner cupboard, Millbach area, Heidelberg Township, Lancaster County (now Millcreek Township, Lebanon County), Pennsylvania, 1750–1775. Tulip poplar; iron. H. 34", W. 37", D. 21". (Private collection; photo, Laszlo Bodo.)

Figure 14 Winged angel head, Millbach area, Heidelberg Township, Lancaster County (now Millcreek Township, Lebanon County), Pennsylvania, 1750–1775. Unglazed earthenware. H. 5¾", W. 6¾", D. 2". (Courtesy, Millbach Foundation, Inc.; photo, Gavin Ashworth.)

and friends." The same artist also made a birth and baptismal certificate for the Millers' son Johannes (John), born in 1766 (fig. 16). At the bottom of the New Year's greeting are the initials "CF," which stand for Caspar Feeman (Viehmann), who either made or commissioned this piece. Less than two miles from the Miller house stands the dwelling of Caspar's brother, Valentine Viehmann (1719–1779) and his wife, Susanna, built in 1762 (fig. 17). The Viehmann and Miller houses share such details as massive carved summer beams and large attics. The Viehmanns' attic also included a hoist system and large bin for storing grain. In 1778 Valentine and Susanna sold their property to their son Adam (1747–1815), who remained at that location until 1796.[6]

Figure 15 New Year's greeting for Michael and Maria Elisabeth Miller, attributed to Caspar Feeman Jr. (ca. 1725–1810), Millbach area, Heidelberg Township, Lancaster County (now Millcreek Township, Lebanon County), Pennsylvania, 1765. Watercolor and ink on laid paper. 20½" x 16¼". (Courtesy, Winterthur Museum, bequest of Henry Francis du Pont, 1957.1202; photo, Laszlo Bodo.) The foliate device framing the text is similar to that on the stove support illustrated in fig. 9.

Figure 16 Photograph of a birth and baptismal certificate for Johannes Miller (1766–1848), attributed to Caspar Feeman Jr. (ca. 1725–1810), Millbach area, Heidelberg Township, Lancaster County (now Millcreek Township, Lebanon County), Pennsylvania, ca. 1767. (Courtesy, Winterthur Library, Joseph Downs Collection of Manuscripts and Printed Ephemera, Frederick S. Weiser Collection.)

Figure 17 House of Valentine and Susanna Viehmann (Feeman), Millbach area, Heidelberg Township, Lancaster County (now Millcreek Township, Lebanon County), Pennsylvania, built in 1762. (Photo, Laszlo Bodo.)

Michael Miller married Maria Elisabeth Becker (1736–1801) circa 1755. They had eight sons, four of whom predeceased them, and two daughters. Michael was an active member of the Millbach Reformed Church, serving intermittently as its treasurer, and his children were baptized and likely schooled there. Philip Erpf (1724–1803), a tavern keeper and prominent Schaefferstown resident, sponsored the baptisms of sons John Frederick and Philip; John Schaeffer (eldest son of Schaefferstown founder Alexander Schaeffer) and his wife, Barbara, sponsored son John (1766–1848); and Maria Catharina Miller (Michael's mother) sponsored the youngest child, Maria Elisabeth (1775–1843). An elaborate certificate (fig. 18) made by fraktur artist Henrich Otto commemorated Maria Elisabeth's baptism. Many of the motifs on this document relate to those inlaid on her chest, in particular the pomegranate with ruffled border. Little is known about Maria Elisabeth's life between her baptism and the death of her father in 1815. She married Henry Schultze (born Henrich Christopher Emanuel Schultze; 1774–1824), probably before 1797, when the couple appear as baptismal sponsors for the daughter of Maria Elisabeth's brother Frederick. Maria

Figure 18   Birth and baptismal certificate for Maria Elisabeth Miller (1775–1843), by Henrich Otto (1733–ca. 1799), Millbach, Heidelberg Township, Lancaster County (now Millcreek Township, Lebanon County), Pennsylvania, ca. 1775. Watercolor and ink on laid paper. 12¾" x 16¼". (Courtesy, Rare Book Department, Free Library of Philadelphia.)

Elisabeth and Henry's marriage was a union between two of the most pre-eminent Pennsylvania German families, the Millers being of significant wealth and the Schultzes of significant influence. Henry's father, Emanuel Schultze (1740–1809), was the minister at Christ Lutheran Church near Stouchsburg, Berks County, from 1771 until his death in 1809, and his mother, Eve Elisabeth Muhlenberg (1748–1808), was the eldest daughter of Lutheran patriarch Henry Melchior Muhlenberg. Henry's brother John Andrew Schultze (1775–1852) was a three-term member of the Pennsylvania House of Representatives; the first prothonotary, recorder of deeds, register of wills, and clerk of courts for Lebanon County, from 1813 to 1821; and a two-term governor of Pennsylvania from 1823 to 1829. Maria Elisabeth and Henry Schultze had no children, a fact that would play a role in her inheritance and, ultimately, the chest's line of descent.[7]

Faced with a substantial estate and many heirs, Michael Miller prepared his last will and testament in 1809. In that document he mentioned 194 acres of land in Berks County given to his late son Benjamin; 94 acres in Tulpehocken Township, Berks County, given to his son Michael; 133 acres in Heidelberg Township given to his late son George; and 138 acres in Heidelberg Township given to his son Frederick (who would also predecease him). The elder Michael's son Jonathan, a Philadelphia merchant, was to inherit £650, and his daughter Catherine, wife of Michael Gunckle, was to inherit £800. To his son John Miller, who had already received 300 acres of land along with the house and mill, Michael Sr. left a horse, two wagons, two plows, two harrows, "my Clock with the case," a ten-plate stove and pipes, two still kettles of his choice and half of the distilling vessels, "and all my smith tools" but permitting "my son Fredk. and the heirs of my deceased son George to work with the said Tools in the smith shop." To his youngest child, Maria Elisabeth, Michael bequeathed £150 outright (in addition to £300 that she had already received) and £600 to be put out at interest, for which she was to receive yearly dividends and payments of £150 at increments of eight, eleven, fourteen, and seventeen years after Michael's death. If she was widowed, she was to receive the entire principal of £600 at once, but if her husband outlived her and they had no issue, the principal was to be divided among her siblings. Michael Miller appointed his son John as the sole executor.[8]

The careful wording of the bequest to Maria Elisabeth indicates that her father wanted to protect her inheritance from her husband. Although Henry Schultze came from a distinguished family, the archival record suggests that he was a bit of a ne'er-do-well. When Henry's father, Emanuel Schultze, died in 1809, the inventory of the latter's estate mentioned the sum from his "Family Book," which listed what each of his children had received. Henry Schultze had been given £2,375.9.9—nearly triple the total of what his four siblings had together received. No record of Henry and Maria Elisabeth's marriage has been found, which is surprising given the numerous ministers on his side of the family, nor have any deeds or estate papers for Henry Schultze come to light. Problems pertaining to inheritance began soon after Michael Miller's will was recorded following his death in late 1815. In May

1817 Henry and Maria Elisabeth Schultze, along with her brother Jonathan Miller and his children Jonathan Miller Jr. and Catharine Miller, wife of Jacob Hiester, were named as defendants in a suit filed in the Lebanon County Court of Common Pleas "to try the validity of a Certain Instrument of Writing purported to be the last Will & Testament of Michael Miller." The plaintiffs were John Miller; Catharine (Mayer/Meier) Miller, widow of George Miller (d. 1804); Catharine (Philippi) Miller, widow of Frederick Miller (d. 1811), and her daughter Catharine, wife of Daniel Strickler; and the heirs presumably of Benjamin Miller (d. 1814): Elisabeth Miller, wife of Andrew Kapp; and Catharine Miller, wife of Jonathan Mohr. Complicating matters further was the fact that John Andrew Schultze, Emanuel's brother, not only was Lebanon County's prothonotary and clerk of courts at the time but was also appointed by one of the defendants, Jonathan Miller, as his personal attorney in November 1816. A protracted legal battle ensued in which both sides hired attorneys and filed numerous appeals. Court documents include testimony that on September 28, 1816, all of the heirs discussed the validity of the will and that "John Miller had given the reasons why his brothers & sisters had got so small a portion." The surviving witness to the will testified that he had met with Michael Miller on October 27, 1809, that following dinner Michael gave him instructions in German regarding his will, and that he then prepared Michael's will in English and explained it to him in German. The court found in favor of the plaintiffs, but the defendants' attorney filed a writ of error to move the case to the Supreme Court of Pennsylvania. On October 11, 1817, the Supreme Court upheld the Court of Common Pleas decision and ordered the defendants to pay the plaintiffs $300.00.[9]

The Schultzes responded by filing suit against John Miller, seeking "amicable action in debt." The court referred the case to arbitration, and three men were appointed to meet at Jacob Stouch's tavern in Lebanon to review the case on January 30, 1818. According to the testimony, John Miller and his attorney "appeared at first but shortly thereafter withdrew." The Schultzes then presented their case, arguing that £150 (or $400.00) had been bequeathed to Maria Elisabeth by Michael Miller and was to be paid within two years of his death, that his executor John Miller had "neglected & refused" to do so, for which the Schultzes sought the £150 "with lawful interest." In addition, the Schultzes claimed that Michael Miller was indebted to them "for the work and labor care and diligence of the said Maria . . . as nurse for the said Michael Miller in his lifetime and at his special instance and request in and about the nursing and taking care of him the said Michael Miller whilst he was sick & laboring under divers maladies and diseases." Furthermore, "being so indebted he the said Michael Miller" had promised on September 1, 1815, to pay Maria Elisabeth the sum of $1,500.00 but died before doing so, and John Miller refused to honor the debt. The arbitrators decided in favor of the Schultzes and ordered John Miller to pay them $1,002.50 ($602.50 "for the attendance of Mrs. Shultze upon her father in his sickness" and $400.00 "as the Legacy in the Will what is Due"), plus court costs. On January 31, 1818, John Miller's attorney filed an appeal and the case went before the Lebanon County Court of Common Pleas. No record of the court's decision has been found, but the final administrative accounts of Michael Miller's estate submitted by John Miller indicate that the Schultzes were paid $602.50.[10]

Henry Schultze died in 1824 and was buried at the Millbach Reformed Church. Soon after his death, Maria Elisabeth and her brother John Miller appear to have resolved their differences. Widowed and childless at the age of forty-nine, Maria Elisabeth moved back to Millbach by 1830 to live with John, who since 1808 had been a widower. She is listed in both the 1830 and 1840 censuses directly before his name. In 1827 and again in 1834, she stood as a baptismal sponsor at the Millbach Reformed Church for two of her great-nieces. Maria Elisabeth died in 1843 and was buried at Millbach beside her husband. Her tombstone identifies her as both the wife of Henry Schultze and the daughter of Michael Miller—nearly thirty years after her father's death. The inventory of her estate totaled more than $1,400.00 and indicates a well-appointed household, including carpet and window curtains; three looking glasses; a stove and pipe; numerous books and two pairs of spectacles; twelve silver teaspoons (six of them German) and "Flowered Glass"; five "Profiles"; an orange tree, flowerpots, garden seed, and eleven chickens. Her furniture consisted of two bureaus and a small case of drawers; two dining tables, twelve chairs, and an armchair; three bedsteads; a thirty-hour clock, corner cupboard, and queensware; two dough troughs and a kitchen cupboard; quilting frames, two spinning wheels, and a wool wheel; "1 Trunk" valued at $1.00, and "2 Chests & 1 Box &c &c" valued at $2.00. On February 27, 1843, Maria Elisabeth prepared her will, beginning it with the date and the word "Mülbach." This brief document, written by her own hand in German script, noted, "the household goods my brother Johannes shall keep what he can use," and the leftover items were to be divided into four portions among his three daughters (Catharine, 1792–1869, m. Jacob Weigley; Sara, 1797–1870, m. William Forry; and Martha, 1802–1885, m. George Zeller) and the children of his deceased daughter Maria Magdalena (1789–1841, m. George Becker). The will also bequeathed a $1,200.00 bond to be divided between her brothers John and Jonathan Miller. Most significantly, the administrator's account included a credit of $198.54 "for the Articles bequeathed to the daughters of John Miller & included in the Inventory." One of these items was almost certainly the inlaid chest (fig. 1).[11]

Five years after Maria Elisabeth died in 1843, John Miller passed away and his executors sold the Millbach property to the Illig family. The inventory of John Miller's belongings lists a silver watch and three items that likely represent the same objects in his father Michael's estate: "1 clock & case" (probably the one made by Jacob Graff), a "Pianno Forte" (probably the "spinet"), and "old Blacksmith tools." John Miller's wife, Anna Catharina, had died in 1808, leaving him to finish raising their four daughters. Sara, born in 1797, was the recipient of a birth and baptismal certificate (fig. 19) that shows the family's continued adherence to Germanic cultural traditions. In addition to the certificate made for John Miller (fig. 16), a colorful certificate with trumpeting angels was made for John Miller's wife, Anna

Figure 19 Birth and baptismal certificate for Sara Miller (1797–1870), Millbach, Heidelberg Township, Lancaster County (now Millcreek Township, Lebanon County), Pennsylvania, ca. 1797. Watercolor and ink on laid paper. 15¾" x 12¾". (Courtesy, Rare Book Department, Free Library of Philadelphia.)

Figure 20 Birth and baptismal certificate for Anna Catharina Lescher (1768–1808), attributed to Johann Conrad Gilbert (1734–1812), ca. 1785. Watercolor and ink on laid paper. 8¼" x 12⅝". (Private collection; photo, Winterthur Museum.)

Catharina Lescher, by schoolmaster Johann Conrad Gilbert. Although this certificate documents her birth in 1768 (fig. 20), it was probably not made before the early 1780s, when Gilbert moved to Tulpehocken Township, Berks County. For some time before his death, John Miller shared the house with his daughter Catharine and her husband, Jacob Weigley (1789–1880). The Weigleys had ten children. One of their sons, William M. Weigley (1818–1887), married Anna Rex (1808–1900), great-granddaughter of Schaefferstown founder Alexander Schaeffer. William M. Weigley made a fortune in the mercantile business and in 1883 erected a brownstone mansion in Schaefferstown so grandiose that it was published in *Godey's Lady*

Book. Following Maria Elisabeth's death, the chest likely went to her niece Catharine (Miller) Weigley, although no documentation exists to confirm this. However, the serendipitous discovery of a notation made by a later descendant reveals the subsequent line of descent. The next documented owner was Catharine Miller Weigley's eldest daughter, Mary (1811–1898), who never married. Four years before her death, Mary gave the chest to her niece Emma (b. 1865), daughter of her youngest brother John (b. 1832). This is documented by a note in a ledger kept by Emma's brother Walrow, who, on March 15, 1894, wrote, "Emma got great-grandfather Miller's sister's chest from Aunt Mary." This notation provides conclusive evidence of this line of descent and indicates that the chest was regarded as a family heirloom. Emma Weigley most likely left the chest to her sister Westa (1859–1934), who lived near Millbach in Richland Borough, Lebanon County. The inventory taken of Westa Weigley's belongings in 1935 includes what appears to be a short list of family heirlooms: a "Grandfathers clock" valued at $100.00; sideboard, $7.50; sofa, $3.00; marble-top table, $1.00; teapot and two pitchers, $1.00; and "Trunk" valued at 25 cents.[12]

What happened to the chest after Westa's death in 1934 is unknown, but its history had been forgotten by 1969, when it was offered in the sale of Pennsylvania collector Perry Martin. The auction catalogue described it as an "Extremely rare Chester County Dower Chest with raised panel, inlaid with closed tulips, hearts, daisy, tulip trees, and vines and berries . . . the only known chest of this kind." No doubt the Chester County attribution was based on the style of the inlaid decoration, which bears a resemblance to the line-and-berry inlay used on furniture owned primarily by Chester County Quaker families (fig. 21). The appearance of similar inlay on the Miller chest raises questions about potential cross-cultural influences, possibly introduced by Quakers who began moving into German-speaking areas of Berks County as early as the 1730s, when the Exeter Friends Meeting was founded by Welsh Quakers from the Gwynedd Monthly Meeting. Whatever the inspiration for the inlay, the revelation of Maria Elisabeth Miller's identity enables the chest to be more fully understood as a product of the Tulpehocken Valley—a region long noted for its extraordinary Germanic architecture but heretofore with little known about its furniture.[13]

Figure 21   Detail of the line-and-berry inlay on a drop-leaf table owned by James and Elizabeth Bartram, possibly by James Bartram (1701–1771), Marple Township area, Chester (now Delaware) County, Pennsylvania, 1725. (Courtesy, Winterthur Museum, promised gift of Mr. and Mrs. John L. McGraw; photo, Gavin Ashworth.)

The Tulpehocken Valley

Derived from an Indian word meaning "land of turtles," the Tulpehocken Valley is a fertile region that extends across what is now western Berks and eastern Lebanon Counties, bounded by the Blue Ridge and South Mountains and containing approximately 322 square miles or 206,000 acres (fig. 22). Much of the valley was originally part of Heidelberg Township, Lancaster County. The Tulpehocken Creek, of which Mill Creek is a major tributary, is the largest stream in western Berks County, rising just west of Myerstown and flowing east approximately twenty-six miles to join the Schuylkill River at Reading. Approximately 95 percent of the original

Figure 22 Map of southeastern Pennsylvania showing the location of the Tulpehocken Valley and the counties of Berks, Dauphin, Lancaster, and Lebanon. (Artwork, Nichole Drgan.)

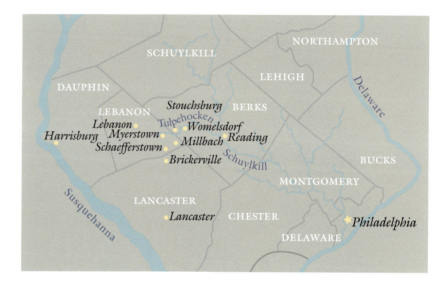

Tulpehocken settlers were of German heritage, a fact that was reflected in the region's early architecture, such as the house built in 1745 for Heinrich Zeller (figs. 23, 24). Many had settled initially in the Schoharie Valley of New York but relocated to the Tulpehocken region in response to an invitation in 1722 by Governor William Keith of Pennsylvania. In 1723 some fifteen to eighteen families from Schoharie traveled southward along the Susquehanna River, then east along the Swatara Creek to its juncture with the headwaters of the Tulpehocken. The early Tulpehocken inhabitants were of diverse religious backgrounds. From 1729 to 1743 Lutheran, Reformed, and Moravian factions competed for influence in a period known as the "Tulpehocken Confusion." The arrival of Lutheran minister Henry Melchior Muhlenberg in 1742, followed by Reformed minister Michael Schlatter in 1746, and their efforts to organize churches and provide ordained ministers helped settle this matter.[14]

Many contemporary observers remarked on the agricultural prosperity and Germanic character of the region. In 1783 German physician Johann David Schoepf wrote, "We crossed Tulpehacken Creek, and passed through a part of the Tulpehacken valley, an especially fine and fertile landscape . . . the inhabitants are well-to-do and almost all of them Germans." The 1790 census reveals that Schoepf was quite accurate in his observation: Berks County was 85 percent German, while Lancaster County was 72 percent and

Figure 23 House of Heinrich Zeller, near New-manstown, Lebanon County, Pennsylvania, built in 1745. (Photo, Laszlo Bodo.) The central chimney and flared kick to the roof are Germanic features.

Figure 24 Detail of the door lintel of the Zeller house. (Photo, Laszlo Bodo.) The foliate device framing the shield is similar to that on the stove support illustrated in fig. 9.

Dauphin County 52 percent. When Theophile Cazenove traveled in 1794 from Womelsdorf to Myerstown, he was astounded by the clothing worn by the local inhabitants, writing, "It seemed to me I saw people coming out of church in Westphalia, so much have all these farmers kept their ancestors' costume." In 1829 Philadelphia antiquarian John Fanning Watson traveled through the "Tulpehocken Country," which he described as "a rich valley country—with high mountains in the distant views. The Cultivation & Scenery always fine. . . . The whole face of the Country looks *German*—All speak that language, & but very few can speak English. Almost all their houses are of squared logs neatly framed—of two stories high. The barns are large & well-fitted,—generally constructed of squared Logs or stone, but all the roofs were of thatched straw." The region's fertile and well drained limestone soil was responsible for the agricultural prosperity, and Tulpehocken Creek supported the development of numerous milling operations

as well as an iron furnace. Founded in 1749 as the Tulpehocken Eisenhammer and later renamed Charming Forge, the site remained in operation until 1895. George Ege acquired the furnace in 1783 and erected a stately mansion with interior woodwork rivaling that of elite Philadelphia town houses (fig. 25). His son Michael Ege married Margaretha Schultze, a sister-in-law of Maria Elisabeth Miller. In the 1820s Tulpehocken Creek became part of the Union Canal system, built to connect the Schuylkill Canal at Reading to the Susquehanna River at Middletown. One of the first canals in the United States, the Union Canal brought great prosperity to Lebanon County before the advent of the railroad.[15]

Millbach, settled in the 1720s, was one of the earliest communities in the Tulpehocken Valley. About four miles to the northwest was Myerstown, founded in 1768. Four miles to the northeast was Womelsdorf (est. 1762), the home of Conrad Weiser (1696–1760), a renowned Indian interpreter and treaty negotiator, justice of the peace, and father-in-law of Henry Melchior Muhlenberg. Just west of Womelsdorf were the town of Stouchsburg and Christ Lutheran Church—one of the most affluent congregations in Pennsylvania in the 1700s and the center of a large parish that was made up of from five to nine congregations in Berks, Lebanon, and Lancaster Counties (fig. 26). Founded in 1743, Christ Lutheran was one of the first churches in Pennsylvania to have an organ, commissioned in 1752 from Moravian Johann Gottlob Clemm of Philadelphia for the staggering amount of £127.3.4 (to which Valentine Viehmann contributed). One of

Figure 26 Christ Lutheran Church, near Stouchsburg, Marion Township, Berks County, Pennsylvania, built in 1786. (Courtesy, Mr. and Mrs. Michael Emery.)

Figure 27 St. Luke Lutheran Church, Schaefferstown, Heidelberg Township, Lebanon County, Pennsylvania, built between 1765 and 1767. (Courtesy, Historic Schaefferstown, Inc.) This photograph was taken before 1884, when the church was remodeled.

the largest settlements in the area was Schaefferstown, laid out in 1758 by Alexander Schaeffer (1712–1786) and initially known as Heidelberg. The illiterate son of a poor German peasant family, Alexander Schaeffer immigrated in 1738 and became a highly successful entrepreneur and landowner by the time of his death. He lived on a farm adjacent to the town, where he built and operated a tavern known as the King George. Schaefferstown grew rapidly after its founding. In 1759 the inhabitants began one of the first public water works in the country, using underground wooden pipes to carry water to two fountains on Market Street. A market house was erected near the center of town, used primarily during the annual cherry fair, which remains in operation to this day. In 1783 the Schaefferstown tax list included a locksmith, blacksmith, nailsmith, mason, miller, tanner, saddler, baker, three carpenters, three tailors, three shoemakers, and six weavers. By 1798 the town's population approached five hundred people.[16]

Soon after Schaefferstown was laid out, the Lutheran and Reformed inhabitants built a log structure to serve as a shared or "union" church and schoolhouse. The arrangement did not last long. In 1765 the Lutheran congregation sold its interest in the log church to the Reformed congregation, which used it until 1795, when it was replaced by a stone church. Between 1765 and 1767 a new Lutheran church was built, later known as St. Luke, using gray limestone with contrasting red sandstone quoins and architraves (fig. 27). This style of stone construction was repeated throughout the Tulpehocken region on other churches as well as prominent houses such as that of the Millers, providing a visual cohesiveness to the region's elite architecture. A unique feature of the new church was the three carved winged angel heads (fig. 28) attached to the cornice, which were likely removed when the building was remodeled in 1884. Dragon heads were also reputed to have been part of the building's woodwork. A committee that included local innkeeper Philip Erpf oversaw the construction, led by master builders

Henry and Philip Pfeffer, who inscribed the sounding board above the wineglass pulpit: "Heinrich Pfeffer, Philip Pfeffer, Schreiner, haben diese Kirche Arbeit gemacht in Juny Monat 1767" (Henry Pfeffer, Philip Pfeffer, Carpenters, have built this church. Made in month of June 1767). Henry Melchior Muhlenberg preached to a large crowd gathered for the dedication of the church in 1769 and described the building as "one of the best in this land, built of massive stones, large, well laid out, and adorned with a tower." In 1770 his son Frederick Muhlenberg (1750–1801) became minister of St. Luke. Arriving in the Tulpehocken region after spending seven years in Germany, Frederick wrote that "the Tulpehocken people may be regarded as quite genteel." In 1771 he married Catharine Schaeffer, daughter of a wealthy Philadelphia sugar refiner. Frederick served as pastor of St. Luke until 1773, when he accepted a call to New York City. He later left the ministry for politics and in 1789 became the first Speaker of the U.S. House. His sister, Eve Elisabeth Muhlenberg, married Lutheran minister Emanuel Schultze, the father-in-law of Maria Elisabeth Miller.

Another renowned Schaefferstown-area inhabitant was ironmaster and glassmaker "Baron" Henry William Stiegel, who emigrated from Germany in 1750 along with his mother and brother Anthony. Stiegel married the daughter of Jacob Huber, owner of the Elizabeth Furnace located some five miles south of Schaefferstown near Brickerville, and engaged in iron manufacture. In 1762 he founded the town of Manheim, Lancaster County, where he established a short-lived glassworks and built a large brick house that is reputed to have had imported Dutch tiles, tapestries and scenic painted landscapes on the walls, and a chapel. In 1769 Stiegel built a seventy-five-foot-tall wooden tower on a hilltop outside Schaefferstown to use for entertaining. Local legend maintains that his visits were heralded by trumpet players and his departures by cannon so the next destination was forewarned to prepare.[17]

The discovery of the Maria Elisabeth Miller chest and its history of ownership provides a starting point from which to explore the furniture of the Tulpehocken Valley. Several other examples of inlaid furniture have been found that relate to the Miller chest, as well as a large group of chests with painted decoration, long associated with the so-called Embroidery Artist. Genealogical research has identified many of the chests' owners and linked them to the Tulpehocken region. Most of the families had ties to the Millbach Reformed Church, St. Luke Lutheran Church, or Christ Lutheran Church. Through an in-depth analysis of this group of furniture, distinctly local patterns of decoration and construction emerge that shed light on the furniture-making traditions of the Tulpehocken Valley.

Related Inlay

Closely related to the Miller chest is another inlaid walnut example made for Magdalena Krall (fig. 29). As on the Miller chest, a separate lightwood plaque that contains the owner's name is set into the façade (fig. 30). Magdalena Krall was the daughter of Christian and Catharine Krall of Elizabeth Township, Lancaster County. Her paternal grandfather, Ulrich Krall, emigrated from Germany in 1729. Tax and probate records reveal that the Kralls were of moderate wealth in comparison with the Miller family. In 1798 Christian Krall's dwelling was assessed as a one-storey log house of 30 by 24 feet, described as "old but in good repair." The inventory taken at the time of his death in 1802 lists a case of drawers valued at £1.2, a clothes-

Figure 29 Chest, Elizabeth Township area, Lancaster County, Pennsylvania, ca. 1790. Walnut and mixed-wood inlay (including sumac, maple, holly, and fruitwood) with white pine; iron, brass. H. 30¼", W. 55¾", D. 24½". (Private collection; photo, Gavin Ashworth.) The lower section, including the drawers, base molding, and feet, is rebuilt.

Figure 30 Detail of the inscription on the chest illustrated in fig. 29. (Photo, Gavin Ashworth.)

Figure 31 Tall-case clock, Berks County, Pennsylvania, ca. 1790. Walnut and mixed-wood inlay (including sumac) with white pine; brass, painted sheet iron, iron, bronze, steel; glass. H. 93½", W. 22¼", D. 12⅛". (Courtesy, John J. Snyder Jr.; photo, Gavin Ashworth.) The feet are replaced.

Figure 32 Detail of the inlay on the chest illustrated in fig. 29 (above) and the clock illustrated in fig. 30 (left). (Photos, Gavin Ashworth.)

The Embroidery Artist Chests

The Miller and Krall chests have several distinctive features of ornament, construction, and hardware that also characterize a group of paint-decorated chests associated with the so-called Embroidery Artist, of which more than twenty examples are known, ranging in date from 1788 to 1805 (fig. 35). Two basic models of painted decoration are found, the first having a large, horizontal panel across the façade, similar to the inlaid walnut chests, in which the owner's name and the date are typically inscribed. The alternative design features a central heart flanked by two arched-head panels. The painted chests are made of tulip poplar or pine and have typical Germanic construction details including the use of wooden pegs to attach the moldings and wedges driven into the end grain of the pins to secure the dovetails. Several more notable construction features are found on the Embroidery Artist chests that help provide a set of defining characteristics. Thirteen of the chests (in addition to the Miller example) have till lids with a stepped molding running down the center, rather than the typical flat board with molded

Figure 35   Chest, Heidelberg Township area, Lebanon or Berks County, Pennsylvania, 1788. White pine; iron, brass. H. 26¾", W. 54", D. 23½". (Private collection; photo, David Bohl.) The feet are replaced.

press at £5, a house clock at £8, a corner cupboard at £7.10, as well as queensware, pewter, grain, and livestock. The total value of his inventory was £1,283.17.10. The Kralls were likely Mennonite, as their name is absent from local church records, and about four miles west of Schaefferstown was the Krall's Mennonite Meetinghouse, founded in 1811. Inlay related to that on the Krall chest appears on another walnut chest with two drawers—inlaid on the façade "1794 / M B" within a rectangular surround from which a pair of undulating vines with leaves and tulips emanates—and several tall-case clocks, including one dated 1789 and another with a history of ownership in the Taylor family of Womelsdorf, Berks County (fig. 31). Inlaid motifs on the pendulum door echo those on the Krall chest, such as heart-shaped leaf and single-berry terminals and flowers consisting of a ring of dots surrounding a single dot (fig. 32). A third clock, with a history of ownership in the Illig family of Millbach, has the initials "PI" (or "PL"), inlaid above the pendulum door and is embellished with line-and-berry motifs, tulips, and stars (figs. 33, 34).[18]

Figure 33   Tall-case clock with movement by Jacob Diehl (d. 1857), Reading, Berks County, Pennsylvania, ca. 1790. Walnut and mixed-wood inlay with pine; brass, painted sheet iron, iron, bronze, steel; glass. H. 96½", W. 21½", D. 12½". (Courtesy, Metropolitan Museum of Art, purchase, Douglas and Priscilla deForest Williams, Mr. and Mrs. Eric M. Wunsch, and The Sack Foundation Gifts, 1976.279; photo, Gavin Ashworth.)

Figure 34   Detail of the inlay on the clock illustrated in fig. 33. (Photo, Gavin Ashworth.)

Figure 36   Detail of the till lid inside the chest illustrated in fig. 48. (Photo, Gavin Ashworth.)

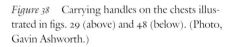

Figure 37   Detail of a crayon mark inside the chest illustrated in fig. 57. (Photo, Gavin Ashworth.)

Figure 38   Carrying handles on the chests illustrated in figs. 29 (above) and 48 (below). (Photo, Gavin Ashworth.)

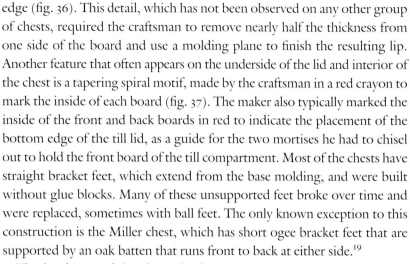

edge (fig. 36). This detail, which has not been observed on any other group of chests, required the craftsman to remove nearly half the thickness from one side of the board and use a molding plane to finish the resulting lip. Another feature that often appears on the underside of the lid and interior of the chest is a tapering spiral motif, made by the craftsman in a red crayon to mark the inside of each board (fig. 37). The maker also typically marked the inside of the front and back boards in red to indicate the placement of the bottom edge of the till lid, as a guide for the two mortises he had to chisel out to hold the front board of the till compartment. Most of the chests have straight bracket feet, which extend from the base molding, and were built without glue blocks. Many of these unsupported feet broke over time and were replaced, sometimes with ball feet. The only known exception to this construction is the Miller chest, which has short ogee bracket feet that are supported by an oak batten that runs front to back at either side.[19]

The hardware of the chests is also unusual and related. Ten chests, including the walnut one made for Magdalena Krall, have identical wrought-iron carrying handles consisting of two quatrefoil backplates and a bale with a pair of incised lines at the center (fig. 38). Another common feature is the locks, eight of which have decorative wrigglework engraving—some with dates and/or initials. Although chest locks are commonly found with decorative filework, locks with wrigglework engraving are highly unusual; thus, the presence of this feature on so many chests in this group is extraordinary. The three locks that are dated correspond closely to the date on the chest. The lock on the Catharina Lebenstein chest, dated

Figure 39   Detail of the lock inside the chest illustrated in fig. 48. (Photo, Gavin Ashworth.)

Figure 40   Details of the lock inside the chest illustrated in fig. 52. This lock is similar to the examples shown in fig. 86.

Figure 41 Detail of pomegranate motifs on the chests illustrated in figs. 1, 48, 52, and 55.

Figure 42 Detail of flower motifs on the chests illustrated in figs. 1 and 52.

1789, is inscribed "HS 1788" (fig. 39). The Henrich Schorck chest, dated 1793, has a lock inscribed with the same date, as does the Susanna Zwally chest with a lock inscribed "17 IS 94." The undated locks range from the lock on the Miller chest, which has a small wrigglework flower between the initials "HS," to that on the Peter Rammler chest, which is embellished with profuse wrigglework on both the top and side and inscribed with the initials "IS" (fig. 40).[20]

The painted ornament on the chests is quite similar. A pomegranate appears inlaid on the Miller chest and on many of the painted examples (fig. 41). Another typical design is a simple flower formed by multiple light-colored dots, surrounding a darker central dot (fig. 42). Because of the elaborate nature of the painted decoration, the overall pattern was laid out first with a compass and straightedge. Many of the designs were then drawn on with a fine brush or pen. Scribe lines were also used to help align the lettering of the names, which were typically rendered in elaborate fashion with many calligraphic flourishes (fig. 43). Fine lines were used to embellish the decoration and inscriptions on many of the chests, such as crosshatching within the pomegranates and between the two vertical strokes of the "1" in the dates.

Variations in the painted decoration and lettering on the chests indicate that three or more decorators may have been involved in their production. Construction differences also help to subdivide the chests further. The largest group (A) is characterized by the use of till lids with a stepped molding, straight bracket feet without glue blocks, and red spiral motifs drawn on the inside of the boards. This group has painted decoration in two different formats, one having a long, horizontal panel with ovolo ends, the other a central heart flanked by arched-head panels. Six of the chests in this group have identical carrying handles, and five retain their original locks with wrigglework ornament. The second group (B) is made up of five chests, each of which has the same type of till lid as group A, along with the additional feature of two small drawers under the till (fig. 44). Only one of the five chests in group B has the iron carrying handles, and none has ornamented locks (although one lock is missing). Group B chests have straight bracket feet, with further embellishment on two examples that have cusps and two with a dentilled base molding. The painted decoration on all five group B chests consists of arched-head panels flanking a central heart but differs from the group A chests in the use of urns within the arched-head panels and the placement of the date flanking the central heart rather than within it. The smallest group (C) includes three chests, which have the same carrying handles as many of the group A chests but differ in that they have flat rather than molded till lids. On the whole, these three groups of chests share a distinctive set of construction details, hardware, and painted deco-

Figure 43 Detail of the inscription on the chest illustrated in fig. 48. (Photo, Gavin Ashworth.)

Figure 44 Detail of the small drawers under the till of the chest illustrated in fig. 76. (Photo, Gavin Ashworth.)

ration—suggesting that they were made in a limited geographic area, if not a single shop, and providing a strong rationale for considering them as one body of evidence. New research on the owners of the chests, none of which has survived with a solid family history, reveals their common origin in the Tulpehocken region and provides a starting point from which to explore the potential makers and decorators of the chests.[21]

GROUP A

The earliest known chest is dated 1788 and bears the name "Maria Stohlern" within the central heart (fig. 45). This chest was recorded by the Index of American Design in 1938 and is one of the most widely published Pennsylvania German examples. Maria Stohler was born in 1761 and grew up on a farm about two miles north of Schaefferstown, near Reistville. Her father, Johannes Stohler (1714–1785), immigrated in 1749 and married Anna Maria Glassbrenner in 1759. Stohler was a wealthy man at the time of his death; his

Figure 45 Detail of the decoration and inscription on the chest illustrated in fig. 35. (Photo, David Bohl.)

inventory lists eighteen pewter plates and dishes; nearly four dozen pewter spoons, half of them new; and extensive linens, including nineteen table-cloths. His daughters Maria and Magdalena were each bequeathed £106—the same as their sisters Ann and Elisabeth had already received, likely when they married. Maria was given an additional £5 and a new side saddle. Three years after her father's death, she received the chest. Circa 1790 Maria married John Shenk (1740–1814), a wealthy Mennonite widower who was twenty-one years her elder. Shenk owned a substantial stone house and several hundred acres in an area of Heidelberg Township known as Buffalo Springs. His estate inventory totaled £3,153, of which £1,678.8 was "Cash in the House." To Maria he bequeathed £1,000 along with the right to use the house, new kitchen and cellar, "Two good Beds and Bedsteads, all my Linen Cloath my two Copper Kettles all my Pewter Ware and Kitchen Furniture, as also all my China Glass Delph and Silver ware in my Corner Cupboard together with the said Cupboard . . . one Cloaths Press . . . House Clock and Case and Ten Plated Stove" and her choice of kitchen furniture. In addition, Maria was to receive an allowance of £36 annually for "cloathing and boarding" his son Christian. John instructed his sons John and Joseph to keep the house in good repair and provide their stepmother with food and firewood and appointed as sole executor "my trusty Friend Samuel Rex," storekeeper in Schaefferstown. Maria outlived her husband by twenty-one years and died in 1835. Her niece Sarah Stohler (1809–1880) was the owner of a small dome-top box with related painted decoration and inscribed with her name and the date, 1828, on the top in elaborate lettering (fig. 46). A closely related flat-top box inscribed for Johanna Kunger and dated 1827 has geometric designs identical to those on the drawers and façade of the Maria Stohler chest (fig. 47).[22]

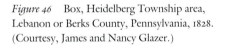

Figure 46 Box, Heidelberg Township area, Lebanon or Berks County, Pennsylvania, 1828. (Courtesy, James and Nancy Glazer.)

Figure 47 Box, Heidelberg Township area, Lebanon or Berks County, Pennsylvania, 1827. (Private collection; photo, Schecter Lee.)

The next chest in the group is dated 1789 and was made for Catharina Lebenstein (1774–1828) (fig. 48). This object retains its original hinges with tulip-shape terminals (fig. 49), carrying handles (fig. 38), and wrigglework-decorated lock bearing the initials and date "HS 1788" (fig. 39). Catharina was born on January 12, 1774, to David Lebenstein Jr. (1736–1789) and Elisabeth Hock, who married in 1762. According to family tradition, her father

Figure 48 Chest, Heidelberg Township area, Lebanon or Berks County, Pennsylvania, 1789. Tulip poplar; iron. H. 23½", W. 53¾", D. 23". (Private collection; photo, Gavin Ashworth.)

Figure 49   Detail of a hinge inside the chest illustrated in fig. 48. (Photo, Gavin Ashworth.)

was born aboard the ship *Princess Augusta* en route from Europe. Immigration records list a David Löebenstein, aged forty, among the ship's passengers, along with such Schaefferstown-area settlers as Gottfried Lautermilch, Bastian Stoler, Durst Thoma; Sebastian, Jean, and Diederich Gackelie; and Hans Zwally. Two David Lebensteins appear in the 1759 tax list for Heidelberg Township, the younger listed as a freeman (single man over age twenty-one). The Lebensteins settled in Millbach, on land next to Michael Miller and the Viehmanns, where they joined a small group of German Baptists or Dunkards (so called for their practice of full-immersion baptism) who in the 1720s established a settlement in Millbach. David Lebenstein Sr. died sometime before 1771, when only David Jr. appears in the tax list. David Jr. died in 1789, having prepared copies of his will in both English and German in which he described himself as "being very Sick and weak in Body." His inventory included farm equipment and livestock; a loom, forty yards of linen and tow; a house clock valued at £6.10; and pewter plates, dishes, and a basin worth £2. To each of his three daughters he bequeathed a £120 share in his estate. Catharina Lebenstein married John Royer (1765–1839) of Heidelberg Township, with whom she had seven

Figure 50   Chest, Heidelberg Township area, Lebanon or Berks County, Pennsylvania, 1790. Pine and tulip poplar; iron. H. 25", W. 54", D. 23½". (Courtesy, Detroit Institute of Arts, USA/The Bridgeman Art Library, 41.127). The feet are replaced.

children. In the 1798 direct tax list, her mother, "Widow Lebenstein," appears as a member of John Royer's household. The tax list also indicates that John Royer was a prosperous farmer and owned nearly two hundred acres of "good limestone land" with a "new and well finished" stone house of 40 by 31 feet along with two smaller hewn-log houses; a small log stable; and a large stone-and-log barn. Catharina died in 1828 and John in 1839; they are buried at the Millbach Brethren Meetinghouse along with her parents. The inventory of John's estate included a weaving loom, anvil and smith tools, farm equipment, and one "Chist"—possibly the one made for Catharina.[23]

A chest bearing the name "Catrina Bicern" was made in 1790 (fig. 50). Although her exact identity remains uncertain, her surname was likely Becker, a prominent local family who intermarried with both the Miller and the Lebenstein families. It is possible that Catharina Bicer/Becker was related to Maria Elisabeth Miller, whose mother was Maria Elisabeth Becker (1736–1801). The composition of the painted designs on the Bicer/Becker chest is similar to those on the Stohler and Lebenstein examples. Another chest, which bears the name "Henrich Schorck" and the date 1793 (fig. 51), is the earliest dated example with a long horizontal panel on the

Figure 51   Chest, Heidelberg Township area, Lebanon or Berks County, Pennsylvania, 1793. Materials and dimensions unrecorded. (Photo, Clarence Spohn.)

façade rather than two arched-head panels flanking a heart. This chest was made for Johann Philip Heinrich Schorck (1772–1842?), son of John George and Salome (Brinsch) Schorck, who were married in 1771 at St. Luke Lutheran Church. Pastor Frederick Muhlenberg baptized Heinrich Schorck there the following year. In the tax list of 1783, George Schorck is identified as a resident of Schaefferstown and a shoemaker. The Schorcks had six other children baptized at St. Luke between 1774 and 1788; thereafter they appear in the records of Christ Lutheran Church near Stouchsburg, Berks County, where Henry was confirmed in 1788 and three of his siblings were baptized in 1796.[24]

An undated chest made for Peter Rammler (1770–1850) has a large horizontal panel like the Schorck chest on both the façade and the lid (figs. 52, 53). Although the panel on the façade has a floral border, the one on the lid, which survives in remarkably good condition, has a zigzag or sawtooth border that may have been inspired by similar panels on stove plates (fig. 54). Peter Rammler was born in 1770 to John and Anna Barbara (Ley) Rammler. John Rammler was born in 1726, shortly after his parents emigrated from Germany. Pastor Emanuel Schultze at Christ Lutheran Church confirmed Peter in 1784. Ten years later he married Eva Uhrig in that church, where four of their children were baptized. The Rammlers moved to East Hanover Township, Dauphin County, where Peter died in 1850 and was buried at Shell's Church, as was Eva, who died in 1869. Peter Rammler's mother grew up just west of Myerstown on a property known as Tulpehocken Manor, which was later acquired by her brother Michael Ley. Michael was one of the few residents in Heidelberg Township with assets comparable in value to those of Michael Miller, and in 1769 Ley and his wife, Eva Magdalena, erected an impressive stone house that rivaled the mass and grandeur of the earlier Miller and Viehmann houses. Built by master joiner Christoph Uhler of Lebanon, the Ley house had a carved pediment above the front door and a pair of date stones on the façade that recall those used on the Miller house and other prominent local buildings. The

Figure 52   Chest, Heidelberg Township area, Lebanon or Berks County, Pennsylvania, ca. 1790. Tulip poplar and pine; iron, brass. H. 26¾", W. 52", D. 23⅛". (Courtesy, a Museum of Fine Arts, Boston trustee and her spouse; photo, Museum of Fine Arts, Boston.)

Figure 53   Detail of the lid of the chest illustrated
in fig. 52.

Figure 54   Stove plate, Elisabeth Furnace, Lancaster County, Pennsylvania, ca. 1765. Iron.
23½" x 25½". (Courtesy, Mercer Museum of the
Bucks County Historical Society.)

interior furnishings included a built-in corner cupboard and massive walnut schrank with sulfur-inlaid decoration. The Leys and Rammlers were consistent supporters of Christ Lutheran Church. In 1772 they were among the highest contributors for the construction of a new parsonage, to which Jacob Rammler and Michael Ley each paid £6 and John Rammler £5. When John Rammler died in 1788, letters of administration were granted to his widow and brother-in-law Michael Ley. The inventory of John Rammler's belongings listed a Bible and eleven other books; "Ward-Rob" and clock; pewter plates, dishes, and spoons; "tea Dishes"; and farm equipment and livestock.[25]

Closely related to the decoration on the Rammler chest is that on one made in 1795 for Catharina Maurer (fig. 55), which also has a similar horizontal panel on the façade and lid, surrounded by floral decoration applied over the blue ground. Catharina Maurer (b. ca. 1775) was likely the daughter of John Philip Maurer Jr. (1746–1786) of Hanover Township, Dauphin County, as she is named in his will and was born circa 1775. Her paternal grandfather, Philip Maurer Sr. (b. 1706), immigrated in 1738 on the *Charming Nancy* and is listed in the Heidelberg Township tax list of 1759. The Maurer and Rammler families were closely intertwined through marriage

Figure 55   Chest, Heidelberg Township area, Lebanon or Berks County, Pennsylvania, 1795. White pine; iron, brass. H. 22¾", W. 50", D. 21½". (Private collection; photo, Gavin Ashworth.) The feet are replaced.

Figure 56 Chest, Heidelberg Township area, Lebanon or Berks County, Pennsylvania, 1796. Tulip poplar; iron. H. 23¾", W. 51½", D. 22⅜". (Private collection; photo, Gavin Ashworth.) The feet are replaced.

Figure 57 Chest, Heidelberg Township area, Lebanon or Berks County, Pennsylvania, ca. 1790. White pine; iron. H. 23½", W. 52", D. 22½". (Private collection; photo, Gavin Ashworth.)

and were frequent baptismal sponsors of each other's children. Philip Maurer Jr. was a first cousin of Peter Rammler; his father, Philip Sr., married Peter's aunt, Anna Catharina Rammler, in 1740.[26]

Horizontal panels like those on the Schorck, Rammler, and Maurer chests can be found on three more chests, two of which have nearly identical decoration, with a single large pomegranate in the center. The only significant difference between the two is that one is dated 1796 (fig. 56) but never had a name, while the other is undated but bears a name, Margaretha Stehlts (fig. 57). Both chests also share an unusual construction feature—the bottom board of the till has a beveled edge, which required the cabinetmaker to chisel out an angled mortise (fig. 58). The unique end panels on the Stehlts chest have S-scrolled floral motifs (fig. 59) similar to those inlaid

Figure 58 Detail showing the underside of the till of the chest illustrated in fig. 57. (Photo, Gavin Ashworth.)

Figure 59 Detail of the end panel of the chest illustrated in fig. 57. (Photo, Gavin Ashworth.)

on the Krall chest and related clock (fig. 32). The third chest was made for Christina Ache (fig. 60), daughter of Henry Ache (1718–1786) and Maria Catharina Filbert/Philbert (1739–1817). Henry Ache (Achey, Aughe) was of French Huguenot ancestry and had a farm outside Schaefferstown. Little is known of Christina, who was born in 1765. She is likely the same Christina Ache of Heidelberg Township who married Henrich Schmidt in 1792 at the Schwartzwald Reformed Church in Exeter Township, Berks County. The chest appears to have descended in the family of her brother Henry Ache Jr. (1761–1807), who married Maria Elisabeth Spengler (1767–1827). Remnants of a birth and baptismal certificate pasted to the underside of the

Figure 60 Chest, Heidelberg Township area, Lebanon or Berks County, Pennsylvania, ca. 1790. White pine and tulip poplar; iron. H. 23½", W. 51⅝", D. 22¼". (Private collection; photo, Gavin Ashworth.) The feet are replaced.

Figure 61 Birth and baptismal certificate for Maria Catharina Ache, attributed to Johann Henrich Goettel (1745–1807), Heidelberg Township area, Lebanon or Berks County, Pennsylvania, ca. 1786. Watercolor and ink on laid paper. 7¾" x 12½". (Courtesy, Sotheby's.)

chest's lid name Elisabeth Spengler as the mother of the child for whom the certificate was made. German émigré and schoolmaster Johann Henrich Goettel prepared an elaborate birth and baptismal certificate for Maria Catharina Ache (b. 1786), daughter of Henry Ache Jr. (fig. 61). Brother Thomas Ache (d. 1826) married Christina Stiegel, niece of Henry William Stiegel, and lived in Schaefferstown. Another Ache sibling, Sophia (b. 1773), was the owner of an undated chest (fig. 62).[27]

Figure 62   Chest, Heidelberg Township area, Lebanon or Berks County, Pennsylvania, ca. 1790. White pine and tulip poplar; iron. H. 22", W. 50", D. 21⅛". (Private collection; photo, Raymond Martinot.)

Another sibling, Samuel Ache (1764–1832), owned a zither (figs. 63, 64) with painted floral decoration and a lengthy inscription that includes his name, the date February 27, 1788, and location of Heidelberg Township, Dauphin County. Also known as a *Zitter*, *Scheitholz*, or dulcimer, the zither was a popular musical instrument among the Pennsylvania Germans, used primarily for secular folk music. Samuel Ache married Elisabeth Albrecht (Albright) circa 1792 and lived about two miles north of Schaefferstown in an area formerly known as Achey's Corner (now Reistville). He was a prominent member of the Reformed Church in Schaefferstown and was elected one of the first county commissioners when Lebanon County was established in 1813. Although Samuel Ache's name on the zither has traditionally been interpreted as that of an owner rather than maker, newly discovered evidence reveals that he made musical instruments and quite possibly furniture as well. His 1833 estate inventory lists two "Carpenter Benches and a lot of old tools," three hundred feet of cherry boards, three grindstones, "1 lott piano paterns," pieces of ivory and ebony wood, "1 ball silver wire and lot piano wire," gold leaf, twelve augers, one crosscut saw, seven hand saws, a lot of chisels and a lot of planes, files, squares, compasses, cramp screws, a vice, and "2 Sets wooden Alphibets." Samuel also owned a "Forte Piano and a House Organ" appraised at $26.00, the highest value of any of his household furnishings. By comparison, the five beds and bedsteads together with forty-five pounds of heckled flax came to $24.50. Based on this inventory, it appears that Samuel was making both keyboard and string instruments, and thus it is reasonable to conclude that the zither inscribed with his name is an example of his work. Although abraded from years of use, the decoration, calligraphic embellishments, and inscription on the

Figure 63   Zither, attributed to Samuel Ache (1764–1832), Schaefferstown, Heidelberg Township, Dauphin (now Lebanon) County, Pennsylvania, 1788. Maple and pine; iron. H. 1⅞", W. 3¾", L. 37⅜". (Courtesy, Colonial Williamsburg Foundation, gift of Mrs. Jeannette S. Hamner, 2000.708.1.) The inscription on the side reads "Das Hertze mein, Soll dir Allein, Ergeben sein, Amen das werde Wahr, wir wollen Singen und Spihlen Ein gantzes jahr / Heydelberg Daunschip Dauphin Caunty 27 Den feberwari SAMUEL ACHE 1788" (This heart of mine shall be given to you alone, Amen. That is true we will sing and play an entire year. Heidelberg Township, Dauphin County 27th of February Samuel Ache 1788).

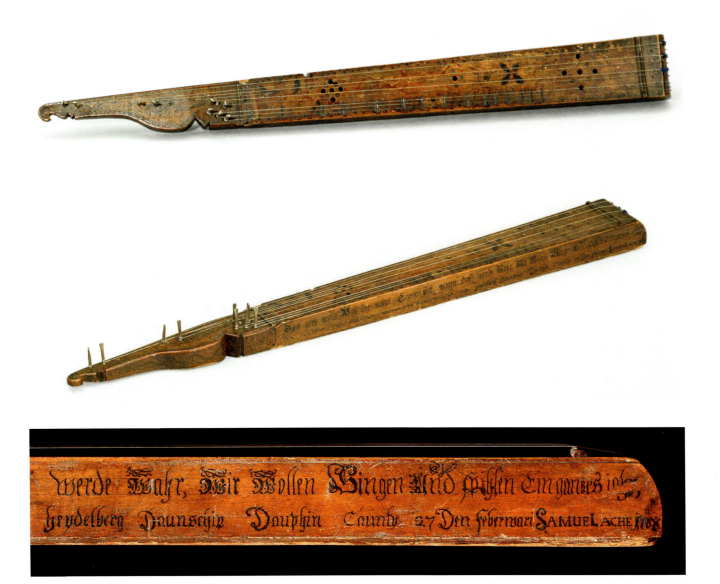

Figure 64   Detail of the inscription on the zither illustrated in fig. 63.

zither relate to those on contemporaneous painted chests. In addition to making a zither for his own use, Samuel Ache may have made a musical instrument for his brother Henry, who had a "Guitar" listed in his estate inventory of 1808. Woodworking and artistic talents may have run in their family. According to family tradition, Samuel's son Jacob taught nephew Peter Ache the carpentry trade. Schoolmaster Hermannus Ache (ca. 1724–1815), who lived in Montgomery County and made several fraktur,

Figure 65 Bookplate for Mary Ache, by Filbert Achey (1812–1832), Schaefferstown, Lebanon County, Pennsylvania, 1829. Watercolor and ink on wove paper. 3¼" x 5½". (Courtesy, Dr. and Mrs. Robert M. Kline; photo, Laszlo Bodo.)

may also have been a relative. Filbert Achey (1812–1832), a nephew of Samuel Ache, also made and signed several fraktur drawings (fig. 65).[28]

If Samuel Ache made the zither, it is possible that he built and decorated some of the Embroidery Artist chests, including the ones owned by his sisters Christina and Sophia. Born in 1764, Samuel was in his mid-twenties by

Figure 66 Schrank, Heidelberg Township area, Lebanon or Berks County, Pennsylvania, ca. 1790. Pine; iron, brass. H. 80", W. 70", D. 21". (Courtesy, Pook & Pook.)

Figure 67   Detail of the tulips on the zither illustrated in fig. 63.

Figure 68   Chest, probably by Moses Pyle (d. 1784), London Grove Township area, Chester County, Pennsylvania, 1747. Walnut and mixed-wood inlay (including sumac, maple, and holly) with white oak, white cedar, and tulip poplar; brass, iron. H. 14¼", W. 21⅛", D. 13½". (Courtesy, Winterthur Museum, partial purchase and partial gift of William R. Smith and sons in memory of Marjorie B. Smith, wife and mother, 2001.19; photo, Laszlo Bodo.) The left drawer is replaced.

1788, when the earliest chest (fig. 35) was made, and was old enough to have acquired the basic skills needed for making such a form. He clearly had woodworking abilities, as evidenced by the two carpenter benches and extensive tools in his probate inventory. A painted schrank (fig. 66) with horizontal tulips similar to those on the zither (fig. 67) relates closely to the preceding chests and may also represent Ache's work. In addition to his ties to owners of the painted chests and his woodworking skills, Samuel Ache also has an intriguing connection to a piece of line-and-berry inlaid furniture through his brother Jacob (1765–1819), who married Lydia Jefferis (1768–1850) of Chester County in 1788. Her mother, Hannah (Darlington) Jefferis (1729–1795), is believed to have been the owner of a small chest-over-drawers inlaid with the initials HD, date 1747, and line-and-berry ornament (fig. 68). It is possible that the decoration on this chest or another similarly decorated object inspired the line-and-berry inlay found on the Miller and Krall chests (figs. 1, 29). Another potential link between Ache and the pro-

duction of inlaid hardwood furniture can be found in the inventory of Maria Elisabeth Miller's father, Michael, who owned a "spinet" when he died in 1815. Valued at £11.5, the spinet was worth more than his bed and bedstead, stove and pipes, and "Closset" (likely a schrank) combined. Michael Miller appears to have acquired his furnishings locally, based on the surviving objects, and very few people in the area were capable of making musical instruments. Thus Samuel Ache, who lived nearby, is a strong candidate to have made the spinet and possibly the chest for Maria Elisabeth Miller as well. Because Michael Miller owned one of the only sawmills in the area, it is likely that the two men also interacted in that regard. It was not unusual for musical instrument makers also to work as joiners or cabinetmakers. David Tannenberg, the renowned Moravian organ builder, worked as a joiner in Bethlehem before making organs. Conrad Doll (1772–1819) of Lancaster was identified in tax records and deeds as a "spinet and organ maker" as well as a "joiner and cabinetmaker." When organ builder Johannes Scheible of New Holland, Earl Township, Lancaster County, died in 1793, the inventory of his estate included an unfinished forte piano and unfinished house organ as well as patterns for clock cases, a painted chest, one chest "not painted without hindges," and "1 unfinished Wallnut Chest." Scheible also had walnut, cherry, and poplar boards; a workbench and lathe; seven new spinning wheels, spinning wheel parts, and bedsteads; tea-table tops and feet; carpenter's tools and unspecified carpentry books; saws, files, bits, chisels, gouges, and thirty-seven molding planes in addition to four "Croofing" or grooving planes, two plough planes, and other molding planes; paintbrushes; and one "Sea Cow Tooth," probably a walrus tusk.[29]

Two other painted chests with horizontal decorated panels similar to those on the Christina and Sophia Ache examples are known. One survives only as a fragment (fig. 69) and has neither name nor date. Unlike the other chests with horizontal panels, this one has a zigzag border rather than floral decoration. The use of a central urn motif from which the floral design springs is similar to the composition of the Miller and Krall chests (figs. 1, 29). The other chest, which is inscribed "Salme 1805 Bahrt" (fig. 70), is the latest of all the examples associated with the Embroidery Artist. She is likely the Salome Barth (1786–1816) who married John Philip Heilman (1781–1856)

Figure 69   Chest façade, Heidelberg Township area, Lebanon or Berks County, Pennsylvania, ca. 1790. White pine; iron. 14½" x 50¾". (Private collection; photo, Gavin Ashworth.) The façade retains its original lock (fig. 86).

Figure 70 Chest, Heidelberg Township area, Lebanon or Berks County, Pennsylvania, 1805. Pine; iron. H. 23½", W. 52½", D. 23". (Private collection; photo, Gavin Ashworth.) The feet are replaced.

and had a son, Samuel, born in 1809. The Barth (Bard) and Heilman families owned adjacent land in Lebanon Township and were prominent members of the Hill Lutheran Church, located about four miles northwest of Lebanon. The decoration on the Bahrt chest may be the work of another hand. The flowers and zigzag border are slightly different from others in the group, and the decoration lacks pomegranates and flowers on the blue ground surrounding the panel. The lettering of the name also appears somewhat different, although the artist took care to use a straightedge for laying out the letters and drew a whimsical face sniffing a flower within the capital "B" of Bahrt; a similar device appears on some contemporary fraktur as well (fig. 71).[30]

Figure 71 Details showing the painted faces on the chest illustrated in fig. 70 and a fraktur. (Private collection.)

Figure 72   Chest, Heidelberg Township area,
Lebanon or Berks County, Pennsylvania, 1790.
Pine; iron, brass. H. 29½", W. 53½", D. 23".
(Courtesy, Christie's.) The feet are replaced.

Figure 73   Pair of date boards on the house of
Johannes and Anna Maria Bollman and their son
George Bollman, Millbach, Heidelberg (now
Millcreek) Township, Lebanon County, 1819.
(Photo, Laszlo Bodo.) The paint is restored,
based on evidence found under a layer of white
overpaint.

Another chest dated 1790 and made for "Susanna Scheblern" or Scheppler (1775–1838)—daughter of Henry Scheppler and Justina Catharina Kraft (b. 1739)—may represent the work of another artist involved in the decoration of group A chests (fig. 72). The pomegranates are rendered very differently from those on the other chests, and the lettering of the name is not as elaborate. Little is known about Susanna's father, but he may be the "Schepler" listed in the account book of Christ Lutheran Church as being paid for sawing wood in 1790 and 1792. Susanna Scheppler's aunt, Anna Margaretha Kraft (b. 1734), married a Johannes Ache in 1754. Susanna married Benjamin Minnich (1766–1832) at Christ Lutheran Church in 1791; her brother Johann married Christina Minnich (1770–1843), Benjamin's sister, at the same time. Benjamin and Christina Minnich's brother Adam owned a chest dated 1796 and painted with black unicorns and lions that bears the location of Bern Township, Berks County. In addition to the chests that feature pomegranate motifs is a pair of wooden date boards (fig. 73) on the house of Johannes Bollman (1755–1836) and his wife, Anna Maria Philippi (1763–1844), later owned by their son George (1790–1829). The Bollmans lived in Millbach and were members of the Millbach Reformed Church, where at least five of their children were baptized—including a son, Samuel, who was sponsored by Samuel Rex of Schaefferstown.[31]

GROUP B

Five chests with closely related decoration and construction seem to be the work of another painter and joiner. With dates ranging from 1792 to 1798, the group B chests appear to have been made at the same time as those in group A. Invariably, the façades of these five chests have a central heart flanked by arched-head panels, each containing a double-handled vase with three tulips. Within the heart is the owner's name, while the date flanks the bottom tip of the heart. The arched-head panels have two types of borders, the first consisting of a black line that zigzags between alternating red and black triangles, the second of S-scrolls and foliate vines. The lids of the chests in this group are typically decorated with a pair of small ovolo-end panels, rather than a single long panel. The chests also have related structural details, such as straight bracket feet without glue blocks and molded till lids, but have the additional feature of two small drawers under the till (fig. 44) and lack the red spiral motif on the inside of the boards. One of the chests has iron carrying handles, and one has a lock with wrigglework engraving.

The earliest chest in group B is dated 1792 and bears the name "Hannes Lautermilch" (fig. 74). The decoration on this example is the most elaborate of the group, with birds, flowers, and compass stars interspersed with the heart and arched-head panels on the façade and sides. Although the chest is missing its feet, remnants of the elaborate dentilled base molding remain (fig. 75). The Lautermilch (Loudermilk) family was among the first to settle in Heidelberg Township. Godfried Lautermilch immigrated in 1736 at the age of twenty-eight on the *Princess Augusta* with other Schaefferstown-area settlers including David Lebenstein. He is listed in the 1751 tax list of Heidelberg Township, along with Wendel and Johannes Lauter-

Figure 74　Chest, Heidelberg Township area, Lebanon or Berks County, Pennsylvania, 1792. Tulip poplar; iron. H. 19½", W. 45½", D. 23". (Courtesy, Renfrew Museum and Park, Waynesboro, Pa.; photo, Gavin Ashworth.)

Figure 75　Detail of the end of the chest illustrated in fig. 74. (Photo, Gavin Ashworth.)

milch, and was appointed one of the overseers of the poor when the township was formed in 1757. The most likely identity of the chest's owner is Godfried's great-grandson Johannes (John) Lautermilch (1770–1854), who was confirmed in 1784, at the same time as his brother Johann Jacob (b. 1768) and Peter Rammler (fig. 52), at Christ Lutheran Church near Stouchs-

Figure 76   Chest, Heidelberg Township area, Lebanon or Berks County, Pennsylvania, 1794. Tulip poplar; iron. H. 24", W. 50", D. 22¾". (Private collection; photo, Gavin Ashworth.)

Figure 77   Detail of the bird drawing on the underside of the till drawer of the chest illustrated in fig. 76. (Photo, Gavin Ashworth.)

burg. The church records identify the two brothers as the sons of Johann Jacob Lautermilch. John Lautermilch married Barbara Meyer of Millbach, a granddaughter of Alexander Schaeffer. Their first son, Henrich, was baptized in 1801 at St. Luke Lutheran Church. Daughter Anna Maria was baptized in 1804 at the Millbach Reformed Church. John Lautermilch had a large farm along the Swatara Creek in East Hanover Township, Dauphin County, when he died in 1854. The inventory of his estate lists three chests.[32]

The next chest is dated 1794 and is inscribed with the name "Susanna Zwaliesin" or Zwally (fig. 76). It is one of two examples with cusps on straight bracket feet. It also has a bird drawn on the underside of one of the small till drawers (fig. 77) that closely relates to the birds on the façades of two other chests in the group (see figs. 79, 80). Susanna Zwally (1777–1860) was the daughter of Christian Zwally Jr. and Sarah Blank. In 1810 her father was named on the list of subscribers for repairs to St. Luke Lutheran Church in Schaefferstown. Susanna married Frantz Seibert (1768–1832) in 1796 at Trinity Tulpehocken Reformed Church. He was the son of Christian Seibert and Catharine Holstine, whose father, Leonard Holstine, was a major contributor to Christ Lutheran Church. Frantz and Susanna had at least six children, two of whom were baptized at the German Reformed Church in Schaefferstown and one at St. Luke. A colorful birth and baptismal certifi-

Figure 78 Birth and baptismal certificate for George Seibert, attributed to Andreas Kessler, Elizabeth Township, Lancaster County, Pennsylvania, ca. 1815. Watercolor and ink on laid paper. 12⅝" x 15⅜". (Private collection; photo, Gavin Ashworth.)

Figure 79 Chest, Heidelberg Township area, Lebanon or Berks County, Pennsylvania, 1795. Tulip poplar and pine; iron. H. 23", W. 50", D. 23". (Courtesy, Peter Tillou; photo, Gavin Ashworth.)

cate made for their son George (fig. 78), born in 1814, documents the family's location as Elizabeth Township, Lancaster County. By the time Frantz died in 1832, they were residents of Heidelberg Township, Lebanon County. The inventory of his estate included livestock and farm equipment along with a corner cupboard, queensware, books, carpet, a clock and case valued at $40, and two chests valued at $3. When Susanna died in 1860, her

worked in Schaefferstown, and brothers Johann Henrich (Henry) and Christopher Frederick Seiler, who emigrated from the northern Alsace town of Wissembourg in 1767. Henry Seiler lived in the town of Lebanon and appears on the tax lists beginning in 1771. In 1779 and 1781 he is iden-

Figure 86 Details showing the tops and inner surfaces of three locks, the center example installed on the chest illustrated in fig. 69, probably by Henry Seiler (d. 1785) or Henry Seiler Jr. (b. 1772), Lebanon, Lebanon County, ca. 1780–1790. (Courtesy, Sidney Gecker and Philip H. Bradley Co.; photo, Gavin Ashworth.)

tified as a locksmith. Although his initials match those on the locks, Henry Seiler died in 1785, leaving a widow, Catharine, and a son, Andreas, who was a clockmaker in Germany. His inventory includes "all kinds of Lock smith Tools," along with "3 Large Chest Locks" valued at 12s. and six small chest locks valued at 6s. Some of these locks may well be the ones that bear his initials and were used in chests built after his death. The locks that postdate his death may be the work of his namesake and nephew, Johann Henrich Seiler, who was baptized at St. Luke in 1772. Henry Seiler's brother Christopher married Maria Elisabeth Kintzel of Lebanon in 1770.

Christopher appears in the Heidelberg Township tax lists beginning in 1775 and is first identified as a locksmith in 1780. He lived in Schaefferstown, where he had a log house and log smith shop. In 1793/94 he made a lock for St. Luke and in 1798 hooks for the market house. When the first jailhouse in Lebanon County was built in 1816, he furnished six locks at a cost of $72.00 and repaired another for $3.00. In 1806 Christopher moved to Swatara Township, Dauphin County, where he died in 1822. His inventory comprised "1 Lot of old Iron & Smith Tools," "1 Chest with Smith Tools and Lockmaker Tools" valued at $20.00, bellows, and an anvil.[39]

The ornate painted decoration on many of the chests also raises the question as to whether the same person who built the chests also decorated them. Clearly the woodworking skills required to construct a chest are quite different from those needed to paint one decoratively. Especially in the case of the Embroidery Artist chests, the highly sophisticated lettering has fueled speculation that a fraktur artist might have been involved in the decoration—a subject that has been debated for years by scholars and collectors alike. In particular, the name of Henrich Otto, who made the baptismal certificate for Maria Elisabeth Miller (fig. 18), has long been associated with painted chests.

Fraktur and Furniture

Early scholars and antiques dealers frequently attributed paint-decorated chests to fraktur artists. In 1925 Esther Stevens Fraser published one of the first articles on painted chests, in which she illustrated a fraktur drawing with four birds flanking a vase of flowers and described it as "a paper pattern, probably a working drawing for a Lancaster chest decoration" (fig. 87). Twelve years later, John Joseph Stoudt reproduced the same drawing, which he attributed to Henrich Otto, and noted that the artist "is believed to have carried this pattern with him as he itinerated to paint chests and illuminate *Taufscheins*" (baptismal certificates). Stoudt illustrated three chests with widely varying decoration, all of which he associated with Otto: the first, dated 1788 and made for Margaret Kern, he described as "believed to be a Chest painted by . . . Otto" (fig. 88). Another chest, made for Jacob

Figure 87 Drawing, attributed to Henrich Otto (1733–ca. 1799), probably Lancaster County, Pennsylvania, 1775–1785. Watercolor and ink on laid paper. 7¾" x 12⅝". (Courtesy, Philadelphia Museum of Art, gift of George H. Lorimer, 25-95-2.)

Figure 88   Chest, probably Alsace or Windsor Township area, Berks County, Pennsylvania, 1788. Tulip poplar; iron, brass. H. 28⅜", W. 50", D. 24". (Courtesy, Winterthur Museum, bequest of Henry Francis du Pont, 1959.2804.) The feet are replaced.

Figure 89   Chest, probably Rapho Township area, Lancaster County, Pennsylvania, 1782. Tulip poplar and pine; iron. H. 23", W. 53½", D. 21⅝". (Courtesy, Philadelphia Museum of Art, gift of George H. Lorimer, 25-95-1; photo, Gavin Ashworth.) The feet are replaced.

Rickert and dated 1782, was "A Heinrich [*sic*] Otto chest" (fig. 89), while the third, dated 1804, was "probably decorated by Otto." The latter chest is similar to the example illustrated in figure 90. The Embroidery Artist chests were also associated with fraktur artists at an early date, although not necessarily Henrich Otto. The chest made for Catharina Maurer (fig. 55) was advertised in 1944 in *Antiques* by Joe Kindig Jr., who noted "the brilliant colors, the delicate and fine quality decoration more closely resemble the Pennsylvania Dutch pen paintings or fraktur work than their heavier, more typical chest decoration." Two years later, the Maurer chest was described

Figure 90   Chest, probably Berks County, Pennsylvania, 1803. Tulip poplar and pine; iron, brass. H. 27", W. 50", D. 22". (Private collection; photo, Pook & Pook.)

by Frances Lichten in her highly influential study *Folk Art of Rural Pennsylvania* as "lettered in such a superior fashion that it points to the work of a fractur-decorator turned chest-ornamenter." She went on to claim that fraktur artist Henrich Otto was also a chest painter and cited the Jacob Rickert chest as evidence that "Decorated chests from his [Otto's] hand show much refinement." Lichten also observed that fraktur was sometimes used as a design source, noting that furniture decorators in the Mahantongo Valley of Northumberland and Schuylkill Counties "liked to paint angels traced from contemporary birth certificates."[40]

Having been linked in these initial studies to fraktur and painted furniture, Henrich Otto became the subject of more and more attributions. In 1950 the *Treasury of American Design* referred to him as a "decorator whose broad interests included not only *Fraktur* work but the painting and decorating of chests and other furniture." The *Treasury* also claimed that Otto designed and carved his own woodblocks as well as printed his fraktur certificates. A small 1956 publication by the Philadelphia Museum of Art noted, "there are several [chests] which are unquestionably from his hand" and illustrated as an example one made for Jacob Dres and dated 1791 (fig. 91). The Dres chest, which is decorated with flowers, birds, and portrait busts, has the initials "J F" on the façade and has since been associated with a joiner named John Flory (fig. 109). In Donald Shelley's 1961 study *The Fraktur-Writings or Illuminated Manuscripts of the Pennsylvania Germans*, he juxtaposed images of fraktur and furniture, including the Margaret Kern chest (fig. 88) with two Henrich Otto fraktur and examples of Mahan-

Figure 84   Chest, Heidelberg Township area, Lebanon or Berks County, Pennsylvania, 1797. White pine; iron. H. 22", W. 50½", D. 21¾". (Courtesy, Olde Hope Antiques; photo, Gavin Ashworth.)

Figure 85   Detail of the decoration and inscription on the chest illustrated in fig. 84. (Photo, Gavin Ashworth.)

in making the chests came from local sources. The native walnut, tulip poplar, and white pine boards used to build them were probably cut at Michael Miller's sawmill. Paint pigments were available in Schaefferstown at the general store kept by Samuel Rex, who regularly stocked lead white, red paint (probably red lead), Spanish white, Prussian blue, and yellow

ochre. Multiple craftsmen were involved in the creation of the chests from start to finish: a joiner, decorator, blacksmith, and possibly locksmith. Subtle variations within the overall group suggest that several workshops and/or decorators were at work simultaneously. Samuel Ache, as discussed above, is one possible candidate for having made some of the chests (particularly those in group A), but several dozen other woodworkers plied their trade in the Tulpehocken Valley region from the mid-1700s to the early 1800s.[37]

The 1783 tax list for Heidelberg Township includes the names of carpenters George Strickler, Leonard Emerd, and Henry Klinger in Newmanstown, and Peter Shwanger, Christian Beck, and Andreas Lap in Schaefferstown. Another source is the 1798 federal direct tax, which lists the owners of three woodworking shops (all built of log) in Heidelberg Township: Samuel Bettz of Newmanstown had a joiner's shop of 18 by 12 feet; Rudy Kinsly of Myerstown had a joiner's shop of 27 by 18 feet; and John Philippi of Schaefferstown had a turner's shop of 24 by 20 feet. Church records are another important source of information. St. Luke, built during the late 1760s, has the names of carpenters Henry and Philip Pfeffer (Pepper) inscribed on the sounding board of the pulpit. It is unclear whether "Henry" refers to Henry Pfeffer Sr., who emigrated from Germany in 1739, settled in Schaefferstown, and died there in 1785, or his son Henry Jr. (1738/39–1808). Henry Jr. may be the more likely candidate. His daughter Maria Magdalena (1763–1807) married Benjamin Miller (1758–1814), son of Michael Miller. Henry Jr. and his wife, Catharina, were also the baptismal sponsors in 1772 for Heinrich Schorck, owner of one of the painted chests (fig. 51). It is unlikely that either Henry Pfeffer Sr. or Jr. was involved with the chests, however, since Henry Sr. died in 1785 and Henry Jr. moved to Philadelphia in 1774. Another woodworker in the area was Christian Kastnitz (1732–1814), who is identified as a carpenter in the 1783 Heidelberg Township tax list but later moved to Bethel Township, Berks County. His name appears numerous times in the account book of Christ Lutheran Church along with his brother-in-law Nicholas Weygand, for carpentry work. Christian's daughter Maria Elisabeth (1776–1844) married organ builder Christian Dieffenbach (1769–1829) in 1796 at Christ Lutheran Church. Together with his father, Jacob Dieffenbach (1744–1803), Christian made at least eight organs between 1796 and 1820 for churches in western Berks and eastern Lebanon Counties, including one for St. Luke circa 1810. As one of the only instrument makers in the area, Christian Dieffenbach is another candidate to have made Michael Miller's spinet in addition to Samuel Ache.[38]

A local blacksmith probably fabricated the wrought-iron hinges and carrying handles for the chests. The superior craftsmanship of the locks, many with ornate wrigglework engraving, suggests that a specialized locksmith made them. Five chests have locks that are dated and/or bear the initials "HS" or "IS" (HS 1788, 1793, 17 IS 94, HS, IS). Other locks that were removed from chests have similar details. One is inscribed "HS" on the top and has a terminal nearly identical to the escutcheon on the Lebenstein chest (fig. 48). Another lock is inscribed "HS 1789" (fig. 86). The Tulpehocken region was home to at least three locksmiths, Philip Brecht (d. 1841), who

Figure 83   Chest, Heidelberg Township area, Lebanon or Berks County, Pennsylvania, 1793. White pine and tulip poplar; iron. H. 22¼", W. 51¼", D. 21¾". (Courtesy, Greg K. Kramer Antiques; photo, Gavin Ashworth.)

the family of Clarence Weimer (1882–1952) of Lebanon County and was likely made for one of his paternal great-great-grandmothers, both of whom were named Catharina. The third chest in group C is dated 1797 and was made for Elisabeth Beinhauer (fig. 84). The decorator of this chest playfully included a face inside the capital "B" in Beinhauer (fig. 85), not unlike a similar device in the chest made for Salome Bahrt (fig. 71). Born in 1772 to Peter and Christina (Weber) Beinhauer, Elisabeth (1772–1849) was baptized by Pastor Frederick Muhlenberg at Emanuel Lutheran Church near Brickerville, Lancaster County. Peter Beinhauer's name appears there between 1772 and 1776 on several lists of communicants, along with John and Rosina Hammer, whose son Benjamin owned the chest illustrated in figure 80. Beginning in 1781 with the baptism of their daughter Susanna, Peter and Christina Beinhauer appear in the records of St. Luke, where four of their nine children were baptized. The Beinhauer family probably lived outside Heidelberg Township, since Peter Beinhauer was not among taxables listed there. He resided in Derry Township, Dauphin County, at the time of his death in 1818. Elisabeth Beinhauer married Johannes Burkholder in 1800 at Zion Lutheran Church in Harrisburg. They later moved to Guilford Township, Franklin County, where Elisabeth died in 1849.[36]

Ranging in date from 1788 to 1805, these twenty-three chests represent a Tulpehocken Valley furniture tradition with distinctive characteristics of construction, hardware, and painted decoration. Most of the materials used

The other "Chest & Sundries" was valued at 47½ cents and was purchased, along with other household furnishings, by his son Moses at the vendue of the estate.[35]

GROUP C

The third group of chests comprises three examples, each of which has the characteristic iron carrying handles. Group C differs from A and B, however, in that the till lid is flat. The earliest chest is dated 1792 and bears the name "Efa Catrina Philipin" (Eva Catharina Philippi) in the central heart (fig. 82). Although the overall decorative scheme of the Philippi chest is very similar to the other two chests in group C, the lettering of the name is quite different. The Philippi (Phillippy) family emigrated from Alsace and settled in Heidelberg Township, where brothers Jacob and Johannes were active supporters of St. Luke Lutheran Church. Jacob Philippi had a daughter Catharina (1775–1845), who is the probable owner of the chest. Catharina married Michael Miller's son Frederick (1765–1811). A second chest, dated 1793, had the owner's name partially removed from the central heart, but traces of the first name, "Catrina," remain (fig. 83). This chest descended in

Figure 82   Chest, Heidelberg Township area, Lebanon or Berks County, Pennsylvania, 1792. Tulip poplar and pine; iron, brass. H. 21⅞", W. 51½", D. 23". (Courtesy, Milwaukee Art Museum, Layton Art Collection, L2000.1; photo, Larry Sanders.)

Figure 81 Chest, Heidelberg Township area, Lebanon or Berks County, Pennsylvania, 1798. Tulip poplar; iron. H. 24⅝", W. 51½", D. 23". (Courtesy, Historical Society of Berks County Museum and Library, Reading, Pa.; photo, Gavin Ashworth.)

sponsors for numerous others between 1772 and 1784. Their names also appear on the lists of communicants from 1773 to 1776. Benjamin Hammer married Eva Catharine Groff (1784–1869). He died in 1852 living in Mifflin Township, Dauphin County, and was interred at St. John's Lutheran Church in Berrysburg. The inventory taken when Eva Catharine died included three chests appraised at $3.25 as well as a corner cupboard, "Clothing Closet" (probably a schrank), and "Large Eight-day Clock" worth $25.00.[34]

The latest chest in group B is dated 1798 and bears the name "Dhiter Gackie" (fig. 81). This example differs from the others in the group by having S-scrolls rather than the typical sawtooth border framing the central heart and arched-head panels. The most likely original owner of this chest was Dietrich Gackley (1777–1845), son of John Gackley Jr. (1755–1820). Dietrich's paternal great-grandfather, Sebastian Gackley/Caquelin (1686–1751), emigrated from the Waldersbach region of Alsace in 1736, sailing on the *Princess Augusta* with Godfried Lautermilch and David Lebenstein. Dietrich married Eva Mohr (1784–1851) and lived in Lower Heidelberg Township, Berks County. Three of their children, Magdalena, Maria, and Moses, were baptized at the Millbach Reformed Church. The inventory of Dietrich Gackley's estate listed three chests, two of which were valued at 50 cents each and were kept by his widow.

inventory listed an eight-day clock, two chests valued at $1.50, and a carriage. Both Susanna and Frantz are buried in the Reformed Church cemetery in Schaefferstown.[33]

Two chests in group B are dated 1795. The one made for Christina Hoffman (fig. 79) has foot cusps like those on the Zwally chest and a dentilled base molding like that on the Lautermilch chest. The original owner was likely Eva Christina Hoffman, born in 1770 to Jost and Maria Catharina Hoffman and baptized at the Millbach Reformed Church. Caspar and Eva Christina Feeman/Viehmann were her baptismal sponsors, while Michael and Maria Elisabeth Miller were the sponsors of her sister (no name given) in 1757. In 1807 Eva Christina Hoffman married widower John Peter Brossman at Christ Lutheran Church near Stouchsburg. She died in 1861 and was buried at St. Luke Lutheran Church in Schaefferstown. The other chest dated 1795 (fig. 80) was made for Benjamin Hammer (1772–1852), who was born in 1772 to John and Rosina Hammer and baptized by Pastor Frederick Muhlenberg at Emanuel Lutheran Church near Brickerville, in northern Lancaster County. John and Rosina Hammer were active members of this church, having nine of their children baptized there and acting as baptismal

Figure 80   Chest, Heidelberg Township area, Lebanon or Berks County, Pennsylvania, 1795. Tulip poplar and pine; iron, brass. H. 26¾", W. 51½", D. 23¾". (Private collection; photo, Milly McGehee.)

tongo furniture with printed certificates depicting similar angels, birds, and flowers. Subsequent studies continued to associate painted furniture with Otto. In Monroe Fabian's 1978 study *The Pennsylvania-German Decorated Chest*, he noted the close relationship of the decoration on the Kern chest to Otto's fraktur: "no decorator followed the example of Henrich Otto more closely than the person who painted this chest." Fabian did not, however, attribute the chest to Otto: "the motifs and the colors are closely copied from Henrich Otto's work," but "the lettering . . . is not like his." Indeed, a comparison between the chest and Otto's fraktur confirms the validity of that statement. The decorative motifs, in particular the pomegranate, tulips, and star-shaped flowers, are similar to Otto's fraktur, but the lettering is unrelated. Fabian also illustrated the Maria Stohler chest (fig. 35), observing, "the lettering is worthy of one of the better Fraktur-writers of the period." In describing the decoration on the Stohler chest, Fabian wrote, "the decorator of this chest, a painter of great capability and patience . . . was fond of painting patterns of flowers and tendrils so like some of the needlework of the period that we could call him an embroiderer in paint"— thus giving rise to the Embroidery Artist nickname for this group of chests. When the chest made for Peter Rammler (fig. 52) appeared at the Philadelphia Antiques Show in 2001, *Maine Antique Digest* reported, "there was discussion about whether it was painted by a fraktur artist or by a decorator who copied a fraktur artist's style." To address the question of whether Pennsylvania German fraktur artists ever applied their talents to decorating painted furniture, a closer look at Henrich Otto and his fraktur is needed.[41]

One of the earliest fraktur artists to make birth and baptismal certificates, and likely the first to have them printed, Henrich Otto is widely considered one of the most significant Pennsylvania German artists. Renowned fraktur scholar Frederick S. Weiser noted that Otto "was destined to influence all Fraktur more than any other" and that his birds and flowers became the standard that others copied. Born February 5, 1733, in Schwartzerden, Germany, Johann Henrich Otto immigrated to Pennsylvania at the age of twenty, arriving in Philadelphia aboard the *Edinburgh* on October 2, 1753. Two years later, he advertised in Christopher Sauer's Germantown newspaper that he was prepared to do weaving and identified himself as living in Tulpehocken. Otto married Anna Catharina Dauterich, daughter of Jacob Dauterich, circa 1755. The couple had nine or more children, including three daughters and six sons. Like many other fraktur artists, Henrich was a schoolmaster. He worked in northern Lancaster County, the Tulpehocken Valley of Berks and Lebanon Counties, and, later in life, Northumberland County. Although his elaborate manuscript fraktur have attracted the greatest attention among scholars and collectors, Otto also filled out and decorated large numbers of printed certificates and broadsides from the printshop at Ephrata. Details about his life aside from his fraktur are scarce. He is absent from tax records, likely because as a schoolmaster he was exempt from paying taxes so long as he did not own property (the same applied to ministers). A Henrich Otto is listed in the 1790 census as a resident of Northumberland County; no township is specified, though it was probably Mahoney Township, where Otto is thought to have taught school at the St. Peter's Lutheran and Reformed Church, built on a bluff overlooking the juncture of the Mahoney and Schwaben Creeks, near the small town of Red Cross. It is also possible, however, that the Henrich Otto listed in the census is the artist's son Henrich Jr., born in 1766. Henrich Sr. is thought to have died sometime before 1800, based on two fraktur that have been attributed to his hand dating to 1797 and 1799. No probate record is known, nor is there any record of his death or burial.[42]

The earliest fraktur attributed to Otto is a birth and baptismal certificate for Johannes Merkie, born in 1769. Two printed broadsides, one about a great comet that appeared in 1769 and one on a suicide that occurred in 1772, are also attributed to Otto. By the mid-1780s Otto began using printed birth and baptismal certificates from the Ephrata printshop and also decorated printed broadsides such as house blessings and spiritual mazes. He continued to make hand-drawn fraktur as well, including bookplates, certificates, and fanciful drawings. Because his designs were copied by many of his contemporaries, great care must be taken when making attributions of unsigned examples. Fraktur signed by him are the most reliable benchmark for comparing his work with painted furniture. The earliest signed and dated, hand-drawn fraktur by Otto is a bookplate made in 1772 for Elisabetha Beck (fig. 92). Otto made a number of hand-drawn birth and baptismal certificates for children born between the late 1760s and early 1780s, including the one for Maria Elisabeth Miller (fig. 18). One of his most elaborate fraktur

Figure 92 Bookplate for Elisabetha Beck, by Henrich Otto (1733–ca. 1799), probably Lancaster County, Pennsylvania, 1772. Watercolor and ink on laid paper. 6⅛" x 13½". (Courtesy, Schwenkfelder Library & Heritage Center, Pennsburg, Pa.; photo, Gavin Ashworth.) The tapering spiral motif after Otto's signature, which he often used for embellishment or to fill space, is related to similar designs used to mark the inside of some chests (see fig. 37).

was made for Johannes Schaeffer (b. 1782), the eldest son of Henry Schaeffer of Schaefferstown and his first wife, Eva (fig. 93). This certificate features many of the distinctive hallmarks of Otto's fraktur, including his typical flowers, pomegranates, and birds; elaborate penmanship with calligraphic flourishes; and the tapering spiral motif that follows his signature. The mermaids and seahorse or hippocampus motifs in the four corners are unusual and give a sense of Otto's creativity. Through his documented fraktur, Otto can be established as working in the Schaefferstown and Millbach area and that he made fraktur for prominent local families, such as the Millers and Schaeffers. Did he ever make the transition from working on

Figure 93 Birth and baptismal certificate for Johannes Schaeffer, by Henrich Otto (1733–ca. 1799), Schaefferstown, Heidelberg Township, Lancaster (now Lebanon) County, Pennsylvania, ca. 1782. Watercolor and ink on laid paper. 12⅝" x 15¾". (Courtesy, Metropolitan Museum of Art, gift of Mrs. Robert W. de Forest, 1933, 34.100.66; photo, Gavin Ashworth.)

paper to wood, such as the Embroidery Artist chests? There is a resemblance between some of the motifs on the fraktur and chests, in particular the pomegranate with ruffled edges that appears on many of the painted chests in group A and is inlaid on the Miller chest. The inlaid pomegranates also have fine penwork lines that echo those on the fraktur and painted chests (fig. 41). The tapering spiral design that appears inside many of the group A chests (fig. 37) also relates to the flourishes used by Otto on his fraktur. Despite these similarities, the letters and numerals on the painted and inlaid

Figure 94   Details of the pomegranate motifs on the chest illustrated in fig. 48 and the fraktur illustrated in fig. 18.

Figure 95   Chest, painted decoration attributed to Henrich Otto (1733–ca. 1799), Earl Township area, Lancaster County, Pennsylvania, 1780. Tulip poplar with oak and walnut; iron. H. 23", W. 50½", D. 21¼". (Courtesy, State Museum of Pennsylvania, Pennsylvania Historical and Museum Commission, 73.163.83; photo, Gavin Ashworth.)

chests do not match those of Henrich Otto. It is more likely that Otto's frak-tur were a design source for the ornament on the chests than Otto decorated any of the Embroidery Artist chests himself. This does not mean, however, that he did not decorate furniture. Several newly discovered painted chests provide convincing evidence that he did.[43]

The first chest is dated 1780 and inscribed with the name "Barbara Gles" (fig. 95). Born to Friedrich and Anna Catharina Gless (Clös/Kless) of Earl Township, Lancaster County, Barbara (1759–1835) was their eldest child, baptized in 1759 at Trinity Lutheran Church in New Holland. Circa 1780 she married John Garman (1760–1822). They lived in Earl Township until sometime between 1800 and 1810, when they moved to Dauphin County. Barbara died in 1835 and was buried at Shoop's Lutheran and Reformed Church in Lower Paxton Township. The façade of the Gless chest is adorned with flowers and clusters of leaves (fig. 96), that spring from a small vase.[44]

The second chest is dated 1783 and bears the name "Johannes Miller" (figs. 97, 98). Although this name was relatively common in the period, the most likely candidate is Johannes/John Miller, brother of Maria Elisabeth

Figure 96   Detail of the floral motifs on the chest illustrated in fig. 95. (Photo, Gavin Ashworth.)

Miller, who lived from 1766 to 1848. In 1783 he would have been seventeen years old—the same age as Maria Elisabeth when she received her chest in 1792. Moreover, the birth and baptismal certificate made by Henrich Otto for Johannes Schaeffer circa 1782 (fig. 93) documents Otto's presence in the area at this time. An extraordinarily unusual pair of camels—unknown on any other painted chest—dominates the façade of the Miller chest, while the

Figure 97 Chest, painted decoration attributed to Henrich Otto (1733–ca. 1799), Millbach area, Heidelberg Township, Lancaster County (now Millcreek Township, Lebanon County), Pennsylvania, 1783. Tulip poplar; iron. H. 23⅛", W. 49¾", D. 22⅛". (Private collection; photo, Gavin Ashworth.) The feet are replaced.

Figure 98 Detail of the lid on the chest illustrated in fig. 97. (Photo, Gavin Ashworth.)

Figure 99   Chest, painted decoration probably by Henrich Otto (1733–ca. 1799), Earl Township area, Lancaster County, Pennsylvania, 1772. Tulip poplar; iron. H. 24⅝", W. 52⅛", D. 22½". (Private collection; photo, Gavin Ashworth.)

lid has a pair of horses, parrots, and a vase with flowers similar to that on the Gless chest. The Miller chest has a narrow beaded molding running along the inside edge of the four sides—a distinctive construction detail that may suggest it was not built by the same craftsman as the Gless chest.[45]

A third chest, dated 1772 and inscribed "GORG DAVID SCHORCK" (fig. 99), may be an earlier example of Henrich Otto's work. Born in 1750, George David Schorck was the eldest son of David and Margaret (Huber) Schorck of Earl Township, Lancaster County. His father was an elder in the Cocalico Reformed Church, where in 1774 George David Schorck married Susanna Schaeffer. By 1779 they had settled in the town of Lebanon, where he died in 1783. The inventory taken after his death in 1783 included farm equipment as well as "a Chest with Drawers" valued at £1.17.6 and "1 Chest" valued at £1.5. In addition to having related lettering and numerals, the Schorck chest has similar flowers and clusters of leaves emanating from vases. A schrank with related floral decoration (fig. 100) may also be the work of the same hand but has no inscription to allow a handwriting comparison.[46]

Figure 100   Schrank, painted decoration probably
by Henrich Otto (1733–ca. 1799), probably Earl
Township area, Lancaster County, Pennsylvania,
ca. 1775. Tulip poplar; iron, brass. H. 82", W. 64",
D. 19". (Private collection; photo, Gavin Ashworth.)

Several factors strongly suggest that Henrich Otto decorated the Gless
and Miller chests, and probably the Schorck example and the schrank as
well. The ornament on these objects has numerous motifs that correspond
directly to those on signed Otto fraktur, such as the flaring tulips flanking
the escutcheon on the Gless chest; the large starburst-shape flowers with
alternating white, yellow, and green petals; a cluster of leaves radiating from
a vase; and an unusual flower with tightly clustered seeds. The small bud-
like flowers and fine red lines used to accent many of the larger petals on the
furniture are also frequently seen on Otto fraktur (figs. 101, 102). The elon-
gated, teardrop-shape eyes of the camels are identical to those on his parrots, and the undulating ground underneath the camels and horses is also a
device typically used by Otto. The most important clues, however, are the
inscriptions. The letters on the Gless and Miller chests are identical to cor-

Figure 101 Details showing the flowers on the chests illustrated in figs. 95, 97, 99; schrank in fig. 100; and fraktur in figs. 92 and 93.

responding calligraphy on the bookplate Otto made for Elisabeth Beck in 1772 (fig. 103). Although Otto did not often use capital Roman letters, his signature on this bookplate and another certificate with similar letters confirms his authorship. Moreover, the date numerals on the chests, in particular the distinctive manner in which the "1" is rendered, are identical to those in Otto's fraktur. The lettering and numerals on the Schorck chest are

Figure 102 Details showing flowers on the fraktur illustrated in fig. 93 and the chest illustrated in fig. 95.

also related, as is the use of a "#" symbol between the numerals. The original paint on the Schorck chest was quite worn and subsequently was enhanced; this may account for the slight differences when the details are closely scrutinized. Some of the flowers on the Schorck chest appear to have been accented with smalt, or ground cobalt glass. An unusual choice for painting furniture, smalt has a beautiful, glistening blue color and is more typically found on fraktur.[47]

Assuming that Henrich Otto is the decorator of these chests, it is therefore unlikely that he was also the decorator of the Embroidery Artist chests. Who, then, might have decorated them? In addition to Samuel Ache, other fraktur artists were at work in the Millbach and Schaefferstown area, including Karl Münch, Georg Friedrich Rick, and Friedrich Speyer (fig. 104). Unfortunately, their handwriting, design motifs, and/or date of arrival preclude them from having decorated the Embroidery Artist chests. Fraktur artist Henrich Dulheurer, whose handwriting appears on a number

Figure 103 Details showing the letters and dates on the fraktur illustrated in fig. 92 and the chests illustrated in figs. 95 and 97.

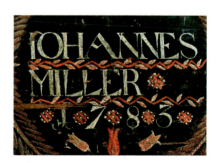

Figure 104 Birth and baptismal certificate for Johann Michael Moor (b. 1776) by Friedrich Speyer (act. ca. 1774–1801), Millbach, Lebanon County, Pennsylvania, 1784. Watercolor and ink on laid paper. 13" x 16". (Private collection; photo, Irwin Richman.) The certificate is signed by Speyer and inscribed "Schulmeister au der Mühlbach" (Schoolmaster on the Mill Creek).

of printed certificates with decoration often attributed to Henrich Otto, was a gifted calligrapher but because he moved to Baltimore circa 1785, he too was probably not associated with the chests. One possible candidate is Johann Christoph Schmidt (1742–1816), who was the schoolmaster at the Warwick (now Brickerville) Church from at least 1774 to 1777 and at Christ Lutheran Church from 1783 to 1803. Schmidt emigrated from Germany in 1764 and signed his name in an elegant, legible hand, and he kept the baptismal and communicant lists at Warwick as well.[48]

Although the identity of the Embroidery Artist decorator(s) may remain a mystery, the idea of a fraktur artist painting a chest or lettering the name on it is not unlike the practice of clockmakers and musical instrument makers who often hired artists to paint clock dials and name boards. The account book of Lancaster painter Jacob Eichholtz (1776–1842) lists payments from piano maker John Wind for "painting a frontis piece" (or name board) and organ builder Conrad Doll for a "frontispiece" in 1809. Eichholtz also recorded several payments from clockmaker George Hoff for "painting his name." Although few account books from Pennsylvania German cabinet-makers survive, those that do include payments for painting furniture that was not necessarily built by the same person. The account book of joiners Johannes Bachman and his son Jacob of Strasburg, Lancaster County, has entries ranging in date from 1773 to 1827 for painting furniture they did not build, including two chests, a bedstead, and two kitchen cupboards. Extant account books also suggest that cabinetmakers primarily painted furniture one or two colors and contain only limited references to more decorative painting. During the 1790s wood turner and joiner Abraham Overholt of Bucks County recorded such entries as: "I made a poplar chest . . . and

Figure 105 Birth and baptismal certificate for William Heiser (b. 1843), infill by Conrad Otto (ca. 1770–1857) on a form printed by Gustav S. Peters in Harrisburg, Dauphin County, Pennsylvania, ca. 1840. Watercolor and ink on wove paper. 16½" x 12⅞". (Courtesy, Philip and Muriel Berman Museum of Art at Ursinus College, Pennsylvania Folklife Society Collection, PAG1998.218; photo, Glenn Holcombe.)

Figure 106 Writing sample, by Jacob Otto (ca. 1762–ca. 1825), Rapho Township, Lancaster County, Pennsylvania, 1795. Watercolor and ink on laid paper. 16¾" x 21". (Private collection; photo, Winterthur Library, Joseph Downs Collection of Manuscripts and Printed Ephemera, Frederick S. Weiser Collection.)

painted it red with two drawers," "I made Martin Oberholtzer a poplar chest with three drawers and blue speckled," and "I made a chest with three drawers, I painted it blue and the mouldings red." In 1807 Peter Ranck of Jonestown, Lebanon County, charged Magdalena Walborn five shillings for "pinting one Chist." Many cabinetmakers may have found it difficult to execute elaborate painted decoration or lettering, which required a different skill set from building chests, and thus might have outsourced this work. The use of separate panels bearing the name and date on the Miller and Krall chests, along with the highly ornate and accomplished nature of the lettering, suggests that they were executed by a skilled calligrapher and then set into the chest façade by the cabinetmaker. Many fraktur artists, Henrich Otto among them, were itinerant schoolmasters who made fraktur as a means of earning extra money. Painting furniture would have provided another source of income.[49]

Information linking several of Henrich Otto's sons to both fraktur and the cabinetmaking trade supports the theory that some fraktur artists also made furniture. Based on signed examples of their work, Conrad, Jacob, William, and Daniel Otto were fraktur artists. Little is known of Conrad (ca. 1770–1857) other than his marriage to Barbara Seiler (1769–1857) and burial at St. Peter's Church in Northumberland County, where he worked as a schoolmaster and laborer. Known fraktur by Conrad are limited to printed certificates, which he filled out and, occasionally, further embellished (fig. 105). More is known about Jacob, William, and Daniel.[50]

JACOB OTTO

Jacob Otto (ca. 1762–ca. 1825) married Dorothy Walther of Rapho Township, Lancaster County, in 1787 at First Reformed Church in Lancaster. In the 1790 census, he is listed as a resident of Mount Joy Township; in 1800 he appears in Rapho Township. Several of his fraktur are known, including a hand-drawn *Vorschrift*, or writing sample, dated 1795 (fig. 106), which shows that he favored floral motifs used by his father and had a strong, sure hand, albeit not as elaborate as that of Henrich. Jacob also filled out and decorated printed certificates from Ephrata, including one for Maria Breneise (b. 1770) (fig. 107) and one for Barbara Danner, both of Earl Township, Lancaster County. Another printed certificate with handwriting and freehand decoration attributed to Jacob Otto was made for Catharina Schaeffer (b. 1774), daughter of Henry and Eva Schaeffer of Schaefferstown (fig. 108). Hand-drawn motifs on the certificate, such as the vase with foliage at the top, show Henrich Otto's influence, but the handwriting matches that on the fraktur signed by Jacob Otto.[51]

Jacob appears in the tax lists of Rapho Township from 1793 to 1825, and his occupation is listed as joiner in five of those years. In 1822 he was exonerated from paying taxes because of poverty. He may be related to the John Otto of neighboring West Hempfield Township, Lancaster County, who died in 1824 possessed of farm equipment, two looms, and "Joiner tools & sundrys." An intriguing group of paint-decorated chests from the Rapho Township area may be associated with Jacob Otto's residency based on

Figure 107 Birth and baptismal certificate for Maria Breneise (b. 1770), infill and decoration by Jacob Otto (ca. 1762–ca. 1825) on a form printed at Ephrata, Lancaster County, Pennsylvania, 1784. Watercolor and ink on laid paper. 13⅜" x 16⅝". (Courtesy, Philadelphia Museum of Art, gift of J. Stogdell Stokes, 28-10-91.)

Figure 108 Birth and baptismal certificate for Catharina Schaeffer (b. 1774), infill and decoration attributed to Jacob Otto (ca. 1762–ca. 1825) on a form printed at Ephrata, Lancaster County, Pennsylvania, ca. 1787. Watercolor and ink on laid paper. 12½" x 15¾". (Courtesy, Philip and Muriel Berman Museum of Art at Ursinus College, Pennsylvania Folklife Society Collection, PAG1998.156.) The vase with cluster of leaves is similar to that on the chest illustrated in fig. 95. Although the flowers on this fraktur are quite similar to those on examples signed by Henrich Otto, there is a slightly heavier feel to them, suggesting that Jacob Otto both infilled and embellished this work.

relationships between their ornament and that on Henrich Otto's fraktur. A distinguishing feature of most of these chests is a large inscription across the front that reads "Diese Kist Gehert Mir" (this chest belongs to me), followed by the owner's name (fig. 109). Known examples include Johannes Flori (1788), Rael (Rahel) Hummer (1788), Abraham Brubacher (1788), Jacob Dres (1791), Rahel Friedrich (1791), Daniel Rickert (1791), Pedrus Schneider (1791), Abraham Gisch (1792), Anna Herr (1792), Susanna Badrof (1792), Bastian Keller (1793), Christian Lang (1793), Jacob Ober

(1794), Veronica Ober (1794), Barbara Stauffer (1799), Mary Mauer (1799), and Maria Witmer (1800).[52]

This group of chests has long been associated with a joiner named John Flory, based on the initials "JF" or "Jo Fl" that appear on the façades of several examples. Tax records for Rapho Township list a John Flory from 1789 to 1824 as a carpenter and joiner. Two John Florys lived in Rapho Township and were cousins, one who lived from 1754 to 1831 and the other from

Figure 109   Chest, probably by John Flory (1767–1836), Rapho Township, Lancaster County, Pennsylvania, 1799. Pine; iron. H. 26", W. 52¼", D. 24". (Private collection; photo, Christie's Images/Bridgeman Art Library.)

1767 to 1836. The latter is thought to be the joiner, since the inventory taken of his estate in 1836 includes a lot of boards and woodworking tools such as punches, chisels, cross-cut and hand saws, a small vice, eight planes, and nine augers. This John Flory married Anna Stauffer, whose sister Barbara was likely the owner of the chest illustrated in figure 109 and inscribed with her name, the date 1799, and the initials "JF" on the façade.[53]

Not all of the chests are initialed, however, and construction details indicate that they represent the work of more than one maker. The chest made in 1788 for Abraham Brubacher (1765–1859), which bears the initials "JF," has rather wobbly lettering and a relatively modest amount of decoration (fig. 110). In contrast, the chest made in 1791 for Jacob Dres (fig. 91), which is also initialed "JF," has more accomplished lettering as well as flowers, birds, and two unusual female portrait busts. Another chest, made for Anna Herr in 1792, has female portrait busts similar to those on the Jacob Dres chest but lacks the "JF" initials (figs. 111, 112). The same hand appears to have decorated the chest made in 1794 for Veronica Ober (1784–1856), who married Joseph Shenk, a stepson of Maria Stohler (fig. 35), and thus would have brought this chest to the Shenk farm near Schaefferstown (fig. 113). Another chest, also dated 1794, was made for Veronica's

Figure 110   Chest, probably by John Flory (1767–1836), Rapho Township, Lancaster County, Pennsylvania, 1788. Pine; iron. H. 21½", W. 50", D. 21½". (Private collection; photo, Pook & Pook.)

cousin Jacob Ober (fig. 114). The unicorns on the façade relate closely to those on the chest made for Barbara Stauffer. A different, more elaborate style of lettering appears on the chest made in 1791 for Rahel Friedrich, who came from a well-to-do Moravian family that was also related to the Stohler family by marriage (fig. 115). The Friedrich chest is also unusual in that it is made of walnut, has exceptionally tall ogee bracket feet, and is the only example with drawers. No initials appear on the Friedrich chest, raising the question of whether a hand other than John Flory's might have decorated it. The only known sample of John Flory's writing is his legible but scrawling signature on the inventory of his father-in-law, Jacob Stauffer. It is hard

Figure 111 Chest, probably by John Flory (1767–1836), Rapho Township area, Lancaster County, Pennsylvania, 1792. White pine; iron. H. 24½", W. 50", D. 23". (Private collection; photo, Gavin Ashworth.)

Figure 112 Detail of the chest illustrated in fig. 111. (Photo, Gavin Ashworth.)

Figure 113 Chest, probably by John Flory (1767–1836), Rapho Township, Lancaster County, Pennsylvania, 1794. Pine; iron. H. 26¼", W. 50", D. 23". (Courtesy, American Museum in Britain, Bath, UK.)

Figure 114 Chest, probably by John Flory (1767–1836), Rapho Township, Lancaster County, Pennsylvania, 1794. Pine; iron. H. 22½", W. 51¾", D. 22". (Private collection; photo, courtesy of Christie's Images/Bridgeman Art Library.)

to believe that this is the same hand that executed the accomplished fraktur lettering on some of these chests, particularly the one owned by Rahel Friedrich. The decoration on the façade of that object includes a pair of parrots flanking a crown—typical Otto fraktur motifs (fig. 93) not found on other Flory-type chests. The six geometric compass stars do appear on other Flory-type chests but are also found on the examples made for Barbara Gless and Johannes Miller (figs. 95, 97), now thought to be the work of Henrich

Figure 115   Chest, possibly by Jacob Otto
(ca. 1762–ca. 1825), Rapho Township area,
Lancaster County, Pennsylvania, 1791. Walnut
with pine and walnut; brass, iron. H. 27⅝",
W. 56", D. 26". (Courtesy, G. W. Samaha;
photo, Rob Manko.)

Otto. Given these design similarities, together with the fact that Jacob Otto
is a documented fraktur artist and joiner in Rapho Township, it seems likely
that he had a hand in decorating and/or building some of the chests.[54]

WILLIAM OTTO

Henrich Otto's son William (1761–1841) was baptized at Christ Lutheran
Church near Stouchsburg, where in 1786 he married Agatha Struphauer. By
the early 1800s he had moved to an area of what is now northern Schuylkill
County known as the Hegins Valley, on the south side of Mahantongo
Mountain between Deep and Pine Creeks. After the death of his first wife,
William married Margretta Kessler, daughter of Michael and Magdalena
(Grim) Kessler. According to family and local history, he was a farmer, carpenter, and cabinetmaker who made furniture and coffins. Tradition claims
that William "used to say that when he heard the sound of the saw and the
plane in a dream, that there would be a death in the community within two
weeks." William Otto died intestate in May 1841, leaving a widow and thirteen children. The inventory of his estate included livestock; rye, wheat,
corn, oats, and flax in the ground; household furnishings including a clock,

desk, and kitchen dresser; a weaver's loom and gears; sundry tools and a carpenter bench valued at 25 cents; and "Daufshines & profiles" valued at $2.00 ("Daufshine" being a phonetic spelling of *Taufschein*, or baptismal certificate). A list from the sale of William's estate on July 3, 1841, gives more details about his tools: a smoothing plane; tongue-and-groove plane; two cornice planes; more than twenty unspecified planes; a vice, pincers, chisels, saws, drawing knives, auger, square, several saws and axes, a spoon bit; carpenter's bench; and a "Farb bax" or pigment box. The list also mentions fifty-one "Dauf Schein" and twenty-six pictures. William's sons David and Jonathan bought many of the tools. A second offering, held in November, included the sale of a weaving loom and shafts to David.[55]

At least eight fraktur signed by William are known, along with three pieces of furniture that are attributed to his hand. Most of the fraktur date from the 1830s, when he was in his seventies. Three were made for members

Figure 116 Birth and baptismal certificate for Anna Maria Haberack, by William Otto (1761–1841), Lower Mahantongo Township, Schuylkill County, Pennsylvania, 1834. Watercolor and ink on wove paper. 12" x 15¼". (Private collection; photo, Gavin Ashworth.)

of William's family, including his granddaughters Lidia and Catharine. The birth and baptismal certificate he signed and dated in 1834 for Anna Maria Haberack (fig. 116) is typical of his work, with colorful birds, pinwheels, flowers, and women in striped dresses. The earliest known piece of furniture that can be attributed to William is a chest dated February 11, 1812, and inscribed for "Anamaria Geres" of "Mahantango / taunschip schulkihl / caunty" (fig. 117). Anna Maria Gehres (Kehres) was William Otto's daughter, who was born in 1788 and married George Gehres. Two years later, William made a chest for his wife's nephew John Kessler (fig. 118). Similar to the Gehres chest, the Kessler example is inscribed with the owner's name, location, and a precise date (fig. 119). The third object is a chest of drawers, made for William Otto's son Jonathan (1805–1887), which is embellished with the owner's name, the date April 17, 1824, and location of Mahantongo Township, Schuylkill County (fig. 120). Few examples of Pennsylvania German

Figure 117   Chest, attributed to William Otto (1761–1841), Lower Mahantongo Township, Schuylkill County, Pennsylvania, 1812. Pine; iron, brass. H. 23¼", W. 52¾", D. 18¼". (Courtesy, National Museum of American History, Smithsonian Institution.)

Figure 118   Chest, attributed to William Otto (1761–1841), Lower Mahantongo Township, Schuylkill County, Pennsylvania, 1814. Tulip poplar and white pine; iron. H. 22⅝", W. 51", D. 22½". (Courtesy, Olde Hope Antiques; photo, Gavin Ashworth.)

Figure 119   Detail of the chest illustrated in fig. 118. (Photo, Gavin Ashworth.)

Figure 120   Chest of drawers, attributed to William Otto (1761–1841), Lower Mahantongo Township, Schuylkill County, Pennsylvania, 1824. Pine; brass. H. 44", W. 40", D. 19". (Private collection; photo, Olde Hope Antiques.) The feet are replaced.

furniture have a specific date or location inscribed on them. Perhaps the inclusion of this information on these three pieces is a reflection of William Otto's experience in making fraktur, on which he frequently noted a date and place of birth. The distinctive style of these pieces differs from the furniture more traditionally associated with the Mahantongo Valley, noted for the use of bright green and blue ground colors with contrasting stamped rosettes (figs. 135, 139). Intriguingly, however, a fraktur made for William Otto's grandson William Gehres has several stamped rosettes on it identical to those on this group of furniture—suggesting that there may be some connection after all.[56]

DANIEL OTTO

Of the four Otto sons who became fraktur artists, Daniel Otto was by far the most prolific. Dozens of baptismal certificates drawn or infilled by him are known and feature a bold color palette dominated by red, green, and yellow. The motifs of flowers, birds, lions, and crowns derive from his father's work. More rarely, he drew mermaids and alligators (figs. 121–23). Information about Daniel Otto's personal life is spotty. He was born about

Figure 121 Birth and baptismal certificate for Christian Zimmerman (b. 1799), attributed to Daniel Otto (ca. 1770–ca. 1820), probably Centre County, Pennsylvania, ca. 1815. Watercolor and ink on laid paper 7½" x 12½". (Courtesy, a trustee of the Museum of Fine Arts, Boston and her spouse; photo, Museum of Fine Arts, Boston.)

Figure 122 Drawing, attributed to Daniel Otto (ca. 1770–ca. 1820), probably Centre County, Pennsylvania, ca. 1815. Watercolor, pencil, and ink on laid paper. 8⅛" x 13¼". (Courtesy, Colonial Williamsburg Foundation, 1959.305.2.)

Figure 123 Drawing, attributed to Henrich Otto (1733–ca. 1799), probably Lancaster County, Pennsylvania, ca. 1780. Watercolor and ink on laid paper. 13⅛" x 16½". (Courtesy, Metropolitan Museum of Art, gift of Edgar William and Bernice Chrysler Garbisch, 1966.66.242.1; photo, Gavin Ashworth.)

1770 and died about 1820. He married a woman named Barbara (1769–1857), and they had eight children. Daniel does not appear in the Northumberland County tax records, probably because he was a schoolmaster. The 1800 census lists him as a resident of Mahoney Township, Northumberland County. By 1805 Daniel had moved to Brush Valley in what is now Rebersburg, Miles Township, Centre County, where he and his wife are listed in the records of St. Peter's Lutheran and Reformed Church until 1816. Daniel was likely the schoolmaster at St. Peter's, since he recorded entries in the church register from 1813 to 1816—a task reserved for the schoolmaster or minister in most Pennsylvania German churches. Daniel is listed in the tax records of Miles Township from 1808 to 1817 as a weaver, a trade he probably learned from his father. Circa 1818 he moved to Haines Township, Centre County, where he soon died, since his widow, Barbara, appears in the 1820 census as the head of household. No will or estate papers for Daniel have been found. Unlike his father and brothers, Daniel Otto did not sign his fraktur. For years he was known as the anonymous "Flat Tulip" artist until a comparison of his handwriting in the St. Peter's church register with his signature on an 1812 inventory was found to match that on the fraktur.[57]

In addition to his fraktur art, Daniel Otto has long been associated with a number of painted chests bearing motifs related to those he used on paper. Several examples feature a large central crown flanked by rampant lions and

Figure 124 Chest, painted decoration probably by Daniel Otto (ca. 1770–ca. 1820), probably Centre County, Pennsylvania, ca. 1815. White pine and tulip poplar; iron. H. 27", W. 50", D. 21". (Private collection; photo, Gavin Ashworth.)

birds, but there is a great deal of variety in the execution of the designs, suggesting that they are the work of more than one hand (figs. 124, 125). A rampant lion also appears on one of the end panels of a chest that has been associated with Henrich or Daniel Otto, but it is more likely the product of a decorator mimicking their work (fig. 126). Comparison of the lions (fig. 127) suggests the work of three distinct hands. The lions on the chest in figure 124 and another chest that has lions flanking a large spread-winged eagle (fig. 128) are most similar to Daniel's fraktur and are probably by his hand. Although the chest illustrated in figure 126 has vases with clusters of leaves on the front like those on the chests now attributed to Henrich Otto, it does not appear to have been painted by the same hand. None of the chests associated with Daniel Otto has owner's names or firm provenances, although many have turned up in Centre County, the primary area of his work. The lack of inscriptions on the chests, however, precludes a comparison with Daniel's handwriting and makes it difficult to say with

Figure 125   Chest, probably Centre County, Pennsylvania, ca. 1815. White pine; iron, brass. H. 27½", W. 50¾", D. 21⅞". (Courtesy, Barnes Foundation; photo, Gavin Ashworth.)

certainty that he decorated the chests. It is possible that Daniel had a hand in building chests, as suggested by the fact that both his son Daniel Jr. (ca. 1799–1860) and Daniel Jr.'s son Samuel (1824–1889) were joiners. Following Daniel Sr.'s death, Daniel Jr. is listed in the tax assessments of Miles Township from 1823 to 1829 as a joiner and carpenter. He married Maria Narhood, whose brother Henry Narhood Jr. is listed as a joiner in Miles Township during the 1820s. By 1850 Daniel Otto Jr. and his family moved to Stephenson County, Illinois.[58]

Three generations of the Otto family can be associated with furniture and fraktur, but they were not the only artisans to pursue both lines of work. Mahantongo Valley cabinetmaker Johannes Haas (1814–1856) made a paint-decorated box and fraktur house blessing later owned by his granddaughter Carrie Haas Troutman (1881–1961). Mennonite cabinetmaker Abraham Latschaw (1799–1870) made fraktur in his native Berks County as well as Waterloo County, Ontario, where his family moved in 1822. Joseph Lehn

Figure 126   Chest, probably Lancaster or Centre County, Pennsylvania, 1790–1815. Tulip poplar; iron. H. 23½", W. 48", D. 20¾". (Private collection; photo, Gavin Ashworth.) The feet are replaced.

Figure 127   Details showing the lions on the chests illustrated in figs. 124–26. (Photo, Gavin Ashworth.)

Figure 128   Chest, painted decoration probably by Daniel Otto (ca. 1770–ca. 1820), probably Centre County, Pennsylvania, ca. 1815. Pine; iron. H. 24¾", W. 48", D. 23". (Private collection; photo, Sotheby's.)

Figure 129 Tall-case clock with case by Baltzer Heydrich (1765–1846) and movement by Abraham Swartz, Lower Salford Township, Montgomery County, Pennsylvania, 1823. Cherry with mixed-wood inlays; brass, painted sheet iron, iron, bronze, steel; glass. H. 90½", W. 21⅞", D. 11¼". (Courtesy, Schwenkfelder Library and Heritage Center, Pennsburg, Pa. gift of Mr. and Mrs. Robert Calhoun; photo, Gavin Ashworth.) Inside the pendulum door the date "October 18ᵗʰ 1823" is written in chalk.

(1798–1892) of Elizabeth Township, Lancaster County, who was a cooper by trade, made small woodenwares such as saffron boxes, miniature chests, and seed chests, which he painted with floral decoration and made paper labels on which the recipient's name was rendered in ornate calligraphy. In Montgomery County, Schwenkfelder Baltzer Heydrich (1765–1846) of Lower Salford Township was a carpenter by trade as well as a fraktur artist. A tall-case clock that he made is signed on the inside of the backboard in large, incised *Fraktur* lettering "Baltzer Heydrich / Seinne uher [his clock]

Figure 130 Detail of the inscription inside the clock illustrated in fig. 129. (Photo, Gavin Ashworth.)

Figure 131 Drawing, by Baltzer Heydrich (1765–1846), Lower Salford Township, Montgomery County, Pennsylvania, 1845. Watercolor and ink on wove paper. 12⅞" x 16¾". (Courtesy, Winterthur Museum, 1959.141; photo, Jim Schneck.)

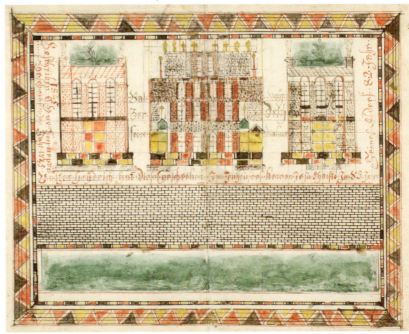

/ 1823" (figs. 129, 130). Some of Heydrich's fraktur feature architectural designs and geometric sawtooth borders reminiscent of the inlaid borders on the clock case (fig. 131). Although it has been speculated that Heydrich also made and decorated painted chests, no documented examples are known.[59]

In addition to furniture with painted decoration done by fraktur artists or built by fraktur artist-joiners such as Baltzer Heydrich, actual fraktur was occasionally used to ornament furniture. The most common method was to

Figure 132   Chest with printed broadside decorated by
Friedrich Speyer (act. ca. 1774–1801), Probably Bern
Township, Berks County, Pennsylvania, ca. 1790. White
pine; iron, brass. H. 28", W. 50⅝", D. 22¾". (Courtesy,
Winterthur Museum, 1955.95.1; photo, Gavin Ashworth.)

paste fraktur to the underside of a chest lid (fig. 132), but more visible displays can also be found. A tall-case clock with movement by Heinrich
Rentzheimer of Salisbury Township, Lehigh County (fig. 133), has a fraktur drawing of a winged angel head and the inscription "Jacob Morry / 1788"
inserted within two openings in the pendulum door (fig. 134). Another tall-
case clock with movement by Daniel Rose of Reading, Berks County, has a
male portrait bust in watercolor inserted at the top of the pendulum door,
and a slant-front desk with a fraktur-like drawing inserted into the prospect
door is also known.[60]
   Fraktur also served as a design source for painted furniture, particularly
in the Mahantongo Valley of Northumberland and Schuylkill Counties,
where furniture was routinely decorated with motifs copied directly from

Figure 133   Tall-case clock with movement by Heinrich Rentzheimer, Salisbury Township, Lehigh County, Pennsylvania, ca. 1788. Walnut with pine; watercolor and ink on laid paper; brass, painted sheet iron, iron, bronze, steel; glass. H. 99", W. 23¾", D. 12½". (Courtesy, James and Nancy Glazer.) The bottom third of the lower section and the feet are rebuilt.

Figure 134   Detail of the fraktur in the waist door of the clock illustrated in fig. 133.

Figure 135 Chest of drawers, Mahantongo Valley, Northumberland County, Pennsylvania, ca. 1835. Tulip poplar and yellow pine; brass. H. 52½", W. 44", D. 20". (Courtesy, Katharine and Robert Booth; photo, Gavin Ashworth.)

Figure 136 Details showing an angel on a fraktur printed by Henrich Ebner, Allentown, Lehigh County, Pennsylvania, ca. 1820 and the chest illustrated in fig. 135. (Courtesy, Katharine and Robert Booth; photo, Gavin Ashworth.)

Figure 137 Kitchen cupboard, Mahantongo Valley, Northumberland County, Pennsylvania, 1830. Tulip poplar and pine; glass; brass. H. 83¼", W. 66", D. 33½". (Courtesy, Philadelphia Museum of Art, Titus C. Geesey Collection, 54-85-32a,b; photo, Gavin Ashworth.)

printed fraktur, such as angels, birds, leaping deer, and praying children. Drawer fronts and kitchen cupboard doors were embellished with angels copied from birth and baptismal certificates made by a number of Pennsylvania German printers, including Gustav S. Peters (fig. 105) and Henrich Ebner of Allentown (figs. 135–38). Leaping deer were taken from fraktur printed by John and Samuel Baumann of Ephrata, while praying children, used on several painted chests, were copied from certificates printed by Jacob and Joseph Schnee of Lebanon (figs. 139, 140). The original source of the praying child image was the painting *The Infant Samuel* by Sir Joshua Reynolds, which he exhibited at the Royal Academy of London in 1776.[61]

A chest made for Michael Braun (b. 1807) and dated 1831 (fig. 141) has pots of flowers on the façade that relate closely to those on fraktur made by Johann Valentin Schuller Jr. (fig. 142). Schuller (1759–ca. 1816) grew up in

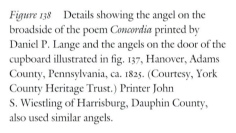

Figure 138 Details showing the angel on the broadside of the poem *Concordia* printed by Daniel P. Lange and the angels on the door of the cupboard illustrated in fig. 137, Hanover, Adams County, Pennsylvania, ca. 1825. (Courtesy, York County Heritage Trust.) Printer John S. Wiestling of Harrisburg, Dauphin County, also used similar angels.

Figure 139 Chest, Mahantongo Valley, Northumberland County, Pennsylvania, ca. 1835. Yellow pine and tulip poplar; iron, brass. H. 28½", W. 49⅞", D. 21". (Courtesy, Katharine and Robert Booth; photo, Gavin Ashworth.) The drawers are false.

Figure 140 Details of a praying child on the chest illustrated in fig. 139 and a praying child from a birth and baptismal certificate with printing attributed to Jacob Schnee, Lebanon, Lebanon County, Pennsylvania, ca. 1815. (Courtesy, Rare Book Department, Free Library of Philadelphia.)

Figure 141 Chest, Mahantongo Valley, Northumberland County, Pennsylvania, 1831. Yellow pine and tulip poplar; iron, brass. H. 29⅞", W. 50", D. 23". (Courtesy, Katharine and Robert Booth; photo, Gavin Ashworth.) The feet are replaced.

Pine Grove Township, Berks (now Schuylkill) County, and moved circa 1800 to Upper Mahoney Township, Northumberland County. In his study of Mahantongo Valley furniture, Henry Reed speculated that Schuller was also a furniture decorator and suggested that he painted a related chest made in 1829 for Andreas Braun, Michael's brother, as well as a chest with a hunt-

Figure 142   Birth and baptismal certificate for Elisabeth Baumgardner (b. 1812), by Johann Valentin Schuller Jr. (1759–ca. 1816), on a form probably printed in Reading, Berks County, Pennsylvania, ca. 1811. Watercolor and ink on laid paper. 7½" x 12⅜". (Courtesy, Philip and Muriel Berman Museum of Art at Ursinus College, Pennsylvania Folklife Society Collection, PAG1998.173.)

Figure 143   Chest, probably Mahantongo Valley, Northumberland County or Centre County, Pennsylvania, 1800–1820. Pine; iron, brass. H. 24¾", W. 50", D. 17¾". (Courtesy, Winterthur Museum, 1957.99.4).

ing scene made in 1834 for a third brother, Peter Braun. Reed also attributed to Schuller the decoration on two paint-decorated kitchen cupboards, one made for Rebecca Braun in 1828 and the other dated 1830 and inscribed "Concortia" (after a broadside poem; fig. 137), on the basis of a fraktur printed by John S. Wiestling and made for Susanna Braun (b. 1814) that was signed by Schuller and includes angels nearly identical to those on the cupboards. Unfortunately, Reed's theory is flawed. He erred in claiming that Wiestling's printing firm was not established until 1827, which led him to assume that Schuller made the Susanna Braun fraktur around that date,

which was close to the dates on the furniture. In fact, John S. Wiestling (1787–1842) began printing in 1811, and the edition of the Braun certificate dates from circa 1813. Furthermore, Schuller is thought to have moved to Ohio circa 1815 and died soon after. This is corroborated by the fact that no fraktur are known by his hand for children born after 1815. Thus, in the case of Johann Valentin Schuller Jr., it appears that his fraktur must have served as the design source for another decorator.[62]

Another example of printed fraktur serving as a design source is an unusual painted chest with Adam and Eve on the façade (fig. 143), copied from popular broadsides that featured a similar rendering (fig. 144). Although this chest has long been attributed to the Mahantongo Valley owing to the stamped rosettes, other details relate more closely to a group of chests from Centre County, such as the hearts straddling the corners, columns, a large central tree, and leaves with a scalloped edge on one side and a smooth edge on the other. The birds sitting atop the flowers on this chest are similar to those on printed fraktur decorated by the Ottos (figs. 107, 108). Although Daniel Otto probably did not paint this chest, it may not be entirely coincidental that he moved from the Mahantongo Valley to Centre County and that this chest bears features found in both regions.[63]

Figure 144   Broadside of Adam and Eve, printed by Heinrich B. Sage, Reading, Berks County, Pennsylvania, ca. 1820. Watercolor and ink on wove paper. 14½" x 12¼". (Private collection; photo, Gavin Ashworth.)

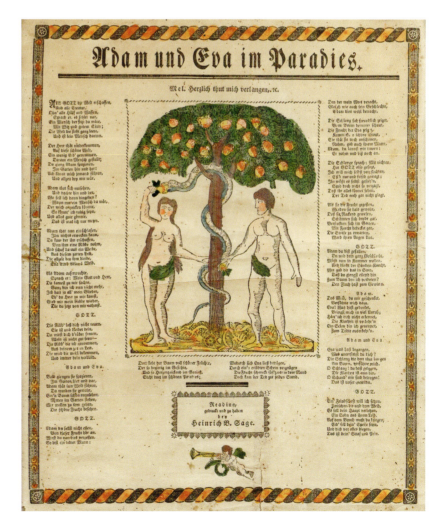

Chests and Pennsylvania German Culture

Chests were important within Pennsylvania German culture both for their decoration and for their function. The chests discussed in this article provide a good opportunity to consider the context in which such objects were made and used. Lift-top chests were probably the single most common storage form in Pennsylvania German households well into the nineteenth century. Clothing, textiles, and all manner of personal belongings were stored inside them in addition to money and other small valuables because of the security provided by their sturdy locks. Many immigrants brought their belongings from Europe in a chest, although few examples survive. Most households had several chests, which were used for storing everything from wood to food to textiles. As one of the most iconic furniture forms associated with southeastern Pennsylvania, painted chests have been the subject of intensive study as well as many misconceptions and mythology. One early writer on the subject claimed that decorated chests were made only as "dower chests" and almost exclusively for young women, who received them between the ages of eight and ten. However, of the chests discussed in this article, seventeen bear the names of male owners and the recipients ranged in age from fifteen to twenty-seven. The dates on chests as well as schranks are often interpreted as marriage dates, but when documented examples are studied it is evident that this was rarely the case. Chests were given to most children during their teenage years and were not necessarily commissioned as "dower chests." Family circumstances, including socioeconomic factors, likely played a large role in determining when and if chests were commissioned. Regardless of when a chest was acquired, it would have been brought along when the owner married and set up housekeeping. In contrast, schranks were typically not acquired until well after marriage, usually by couples in their thirties or forties who had a well-established household and had accumulated or inherited sufficient means to invest in a large, expensive piece of furniture. It is also important to keep in mind that the dates on chests were also sometimes commemorative rather than signaling the time of manufacture.[64]

Countless authors have waxed poetic about the alleged symbolism of the painted decoration on chests, but to date no contemporary documentation has been found to indicate whether the artists or recipients of the chests intended the designs to have religious or gendered meaning. In all likelihood, the designs were not gender specific, since identical decoration is found on chests made for both men and women (as in the Embroidery Artist group). Frances Lichten, one of the first to write about painted chests, claimed that "dowry" furniture was often made by farmers for their own children, although she noted that "it was not necessary to depend entirely on the home workshop for a chest," because "certain village carpenters" also built and decorated chests. However, information gleaned from account books, tax records, probate inventories, and surviving chests indicates that most are the product of professional woodworkers. On decoration, Lichten wrote, "as the farmer-joiner was not apt to be also a decorator, the chest was held for ornamentation until the itinerant decorator made his rounds." This point was likely true in at least some instances, as demonstrated by the chests decorated by Henrich Otto and possibly his sons. It remains unclear, however, whether Otto decorated chests on an itinerant basis or was commissioned to paint them, and it is also possible that he both built and painted chests, given how many of his sons were engaged in woodworking.[65]

Little is known about the nature of how chests were commissioned or how the decoration was determined. Indentured servant agreements suggest that the recipient could say what he or she desired. The document that in 1799 bound eight-year-old Catharina Hiestand of Hereford Township, Berks County, "to learn the art, trade and mystery of House Wifery" for ten years stated that at the end of the term, she was to receive a new suit of clothing, "One Cow, One Bed and Bedstead with Curtains, One Spinning Wheel, And One Chest, either Poplar and painted, or one of Walnut boards." The records of Michael Croll, justice of the peace in Upper Salford Township, Montgomery County, from 1787 to 1794, note freedom dues such as "a chest painted a color she named," while another girl requested a chest worth 25s. The most detailed agreement was in 1795 for Hannah Woodly, who was to receive a "new chest painted blue with lock and hinches" along with a new spinning wheel, cow, and clothing. Another justice of the peace, Peter Rhoads of Allentown, recorded similar terms. Five daughters of Conrad Dock of Salisbury Township were apprenticed as household servants in 1786; the exact terms of their freedom dues varied, but each was to receive a bed and bedstead, chest, spinning wheel, and new suit of clothes.[66]

In addition to the wishes of the client, the skill of the craftsman was a major factor in a chest's decoration. Few woodworkers had the talent and stylistic vocabulary of artists like Henrich Otto, in which case their decoration was limited by their ability and exposure to design sources. It is also difficult to determine the extent to which a decorator's style shaped the look of painted chests from a particular region. The reason black unicorns occur on chests from the Bern Township area of Berks County (fig. 132), for example, might be explained by nothing more than the presence of artists who were familiar with that motif and clients who accepted it. There are numerous instances in which a fraktur artist had a particular style, which was copied by his students. If some of them became fraktur artists, a distinctive local style could develop based on the work of a single individual.

Beginning with the publication of Esther Stevens Fraser's 1925 article on Pennsylvania German chests, in which she attempted to categorize them by county, scholars have tried to localize painted chests by their decoration. The Embroidery Artist chests, with their distinctive ornament, construction features, and hardware, provide an excellent example of the information to be gleaned from such studies—especially when combined with genealogical research documenting objects to specific people and places. Many other local schools of painted furniture decoration existed in southeastern Pennsylvania, which scholars have only begun to explore. Much study also remains to be done of the craftsmen who built and painted this furniture, as well as the design sources that influenced their work. From

Millbach to Mahantongo, Pennsylvania German furniture can be found that bears the unmistakable influence of fraktur artists. It is clear now that some fraktur artists did paint furniture, but in many cases their work on paper was likely copied by other artisans. In an essay on Mahantongo furniture, Don Yoder wrote that "unique in the Dutchland was the transfer by Mahantongo's pioneer craftsmen of the motifs from fraktur documents and printed broadsides to the panels of their painted furniture." Although the decoration on Mahantongo furniture remains one of the best-documented examples of fraktur serving as a design source, it can no longer be regarded as unique.[67]

ACKNOWLEDGMENTS   For assistance with this article, the author thanks Joel Alderfer, Ted and Barbara Alfond, Cory Amsler, Mark Anderson, Gavin Ashworth, David Barquist, Luke Beckerdite, Patrick Bell, Joshua Blay, Laszlo Bodo, David Bohl, Katharine and Robert Booth, Troy Boyer, Philip Bradley, Bart and Margie Braun, Raymond Brunner, Mel Buchanan, Barbara Buckley, Annette Kunselman Burgert, Timothy Burns, Joe Byerly, Jerry Carlson, Stephen and Charlene Catts, Julie Choma, Mike Cooksey, Wendy Cooper, Harte Crow, Dauphin County Courthouse, Dauphin County Historical Society, Peter Deen, Esther, Grace, and Naomi Dierwechter, Nancy Druckman, William K. du Pont, Corinne and Russell Earnest, Mike Emery, Larry and Lori Fink, Liz Flaig, Dan Friestak, Buck Fuller, Nonie Gadsen, Sidney Gecker, Jim and Nancy Glazer, Sara Good, Erik Gronning, Vernon Gunnion, Steve Guttman, Stephanie Hansen, Bill and Connie Hayes, John Hayes, Katherine Hebert, Chip and Vonnie Henderson, Clarke Hess, Ed Hild, Gene Hoffman, Stacy Hollander, David Horst, Charles Hummel, Earl W. Ibach, Char-Ann Ireland, Bonnie Iseminger, Joan and Victor Johnson, Peter Kenny, Katie Kerr, Alan Keyser, Steven Kindig, Kelly Kinzle, Alexandra Kirtley, Robert and Anne Kline, Stacey Kluck, Dennis Kowal, Eric Kramer, Greg Kramer, Paul and Alice Rae Kutisch, Lebanon County Courthouse, Lebanon County Historical Society, Lila Lebo, June Lucas, Rob Manko, Raymond Martinot, Deirdre Pook Magarelli, Jennifer Mass, Catharine Matson, Milly McGehee, Eric Miller, Curt Miner, Kendl Monn, Del-Louise Moyer, Don Moyer, Kenneth Myers, Susan Newton, Thurston Nichols, Candace Perry, Dave Pickel, James Pook, Ron Pook, Janine Pollock, Lois Price, Barry Rauhauser, Nancy Risser, Brett Robbins, Margot Rosenberg, Bill Samaha, Cynthia Schaffner, David Schorsch, John J. Snyder Jr., Gladys Bucher Sowers, Clarence Spohn, Adrienne Stalek, John Steele, Lee Stoltzfus, Peter Tillou, Tulpehocken Settlement Historical Society, Nick Vincent, John Watson, Mary Weigley, Diane Wenger, David Wheatcroft, Chris Wise, Jean Woods, Don Yoder, and York County Heritage Trust. This article is dedicated to the late Pastor Frederick S. Weiser, renowned fraktur scholar, who taught me always to study the handwriting as well as the decoration.

1. *The Accounts of Two Pennsylvania German Furniture Makers: Abraham Overholt, Bucks County, 1790–1833, and Peter Ranck, Lebanon County, 1794–1817*, Sources and Documents of the Pennsylvania Germans, vol. 3, translated and edited by Alan G. Keyser, Larry M. Neff, and Fredrick S. Weiser (Breinigsville, Pa.: Pennsylvania German Society, 1978), pp. 6, 11.

2. *The Journals of Henry Melchior Muhlenberg*, translated and edited by Theodore G. Tappert and John W. Doberstein, 3 vols. (Philadelphia: Muhlenberg Press, 1942; reprint, Rockland, Maine: Picton Press, 1993), 2: 465. For the Miller chest, see Wendy A. Cooper and Lisa Minardi, *Paint, Pattern & People: Furniture of Southeastern Pennsylvania, 1725–1850* (Winterthur, Del.: Henry Francis Dupont Winterthur Museum, 2011), pp. 132–34.

3. The staircase was not likely an original part of the kitchen; rather, a wall would have served as a buffer between the front door and kitchen, thus creating a more formal, enclosed entry containing the staircase and a window. (Charles Bergengren, "Pennsylvania German House Forms," in *Architecture and Landscape of the Pennsylvania Germans, 1720–1920* [Harrisburg, Pa.: Vernacular Architecture Forum, 2004], p. 32.) On the installation at the Philadelphia Museum of Art, see Joseph F. Downs, *The House of the Miller at Millbach: The Architecture, Arts, and Crafts of the Pennsylvania Germans* (Philadelphia: Franklin Printing Co., 1929); and Beatrice B. Garvan, *The Pennsylvania German Collection* (Philadelphia: Philadelphia Museum of Art, 1982), pp. 6–7. Recent dendrochronology testing has dated the construction of the main house and additions to the 1750s, which corresponds to the 1752 date stone and 1757 date on the jamb stove support.

4. The transfer of the Millbach property occurred on September 26, 1753, and is referenced in an indenture between George Miller and Michael Miller dated May 9, 1766, Winterthur Library, Joseph Downs Collection of Manuscripts and Printed Ephemera, Leon E. Lewis Jr. Papers, col. 782, microfilm reel 2662, no. 72. On George Miller in North Carolina, see *Abstracts of the Minutes of the Court of Pleas and Quarter Sessions, Rowan County, North Carolina, 1753–1762* (Salisbury, N.C.: J. W. Linn, 1977), p. 25; James W. Kluttz, *Abstracts of Deed Books 15–19 of Rowan County, North Carolina, 1797–1807* (the author, 1997), book 16, p. 28; *Abstracts of the Deeds of Rowan County, North Carolina, 1753–1785* (Salisbury, N.C.: J. W. Linn, 1983), p. 128; *Abstracts of Wills and Estate Records of Rowan County, North Carolina, 1753–1805 and Tax Lists of 1759 and 1778* (Salisbury, N.C.: J. W. Linn, 1980), p. 34. The author thanks June Lucas for this information. On the Miller tax records, see Gladys Bucher Sowers, *Colonial Taxes, Heidelberg Township, Lancaster County, Pennsylvania, 1751–1783 (now Lebanon County)* (Morgantown, Pa.: Masthoff Press, 2004), pp. 38–46. Gladys Bucher Sowers, *Lebanon County, Pennsylvania, United States Direct Tax of 1798* (Bowie, Md.: Heritage Books, 2004), p. 72; this entry appears under the name Nicholas Miller but is in fact that of Michael Miller. See also Diane Wenger and J. Ritchie Garrison, "Commercial Vernacular Architecture," in *Architecture and Landscape of the Pennsylvania Germans*, p. 100.

5. Inventory of Michael Miller, Heidelberg Township, Lebanon County, December 7, 1815, Lebanon County Register of Wills, inventories M-1, no. 258 (hereafter LebCoROW). According to molinologist Steven Kindig, the half circle with square indentations on the stove support likely a partial representation of the bottom half of the main wooden gear in a grain mill of the period. This gear would have been mounted on the wooden water wheel shaft and been about eight feet in diameter. A carved stone stove support also survives from the Schaefferstown house of Philip Erpf (1724–1801), incised with Erpf's name and the date 1763/1765. For a more complete discussion of the Miller clock, see Lisa Minardi, "A Timely Discovery: The Story of Winterthur's Jacob Graff Clock," *Antiques & Fine Art* 7, no. 5 (Spring 2007): 238–39; also Cooper and Minardi, *Paint, Pattern & People*, pp. 130–34. The Millbach chest was sold at Pook & Pook, *The Pioneer Americana Collection of Dr. and Mrs. Donald A. Shelley*, Downingtown, Pa., April 20–21, 2007, lot 326; the hanging corner cupboard was found in the mill and later sold at Pook & Pook, *The Collection of Richard and Joane Smith*, Downingtown, Pa., October 30, 2010, lot 171 (hereafter Pook & Pook, Smith sale). A door with related paneling from the Miller house is in the collection of the Heritage Center Museum in Lancaster; (Irwin Richman, *Pennsylvania German Arts: More Than Hearts, Parrots, and Tulips* [Atglen, Pa.: Schiffer Publishing, 2001], p. 59). Other furnishings that have been associated with the Miller house include a small sawbuck table with drawer dated 1805 in the collection of the Landis Valley Museum, based on the raised panel of the drawer front (Richman, *Pennsylvania Germans Arts*, p. 71). However, a recent examination of this table determined that it is likely European.

6. The winged angel head was sold at Pook & Pook, *Collection of Richard and Joann Smith*, lot 451; it was excavated on the property by former owners Richard and Joane Smith in the late

twentieth century. The Johannes Miller certificate was illustrated in *Der Reggeboge* 6, no. 4 (December 1972): 9. It was formerly in the collection of Richard and Joane Smith but was sold privately and its present whereabouts are unknown. The maker of this certificate and the New Year's greeting has previously been known only as the "CF Artist" based on the initials on the latter; (Russell D. Earnest and Corinne P. Earnest, *Papers for Birth Dayes: A Guide to the Fraktur Artists and Scriveners*, 2 vols., rev. ed. [1989; East Berlin, Pa.: Russell D. Earnest Associates, 1997], 1: 263). Deed research indicates that the only neighbor of the Millers who fits these initials is Caspar Feeman (Viehmann). Two Caspar Feemans/Viehmanns are known. Caspar Feeman Sr. immigrated in 1730; he made only his mark on the list of passengers and thus is unlikely to have been the fraktur artist (Ralph Beaver Strassberger, *Pennsylvania German Pioneers*, 3 vols., Proceedings of the Pennsylvania German Society, vols. 42–44 [Norristown, Pa.: Pennsylvania German Society, 1934], 1: 31–33, 2: 20–24). This Caspar Feeman was the father of Johann Valentine Feeman (1719–1779) and Caspar Feeman Jr. (ca. 1725–1810), who is most likely the person represented by the "CF" initials. Caspar Jr. married Eve Christina(?) by 1764, when they were the baptismal sponsors of Maria Magdalena Miller, daughter of Frederick and Eva Maria Miller, at St. Luke Church. Caspar Jr. had at least four children: Leonard (b. 1768), Susanna Sophia (b. 1769), George (b. 1771), and Eva Magdalena (b. 1773). A birth and baptismal certificate made for Leonard was sold at Pook & Pook, Downingtown, Pa., April 5, 1996, lot 57. The certificate gives their location as Hanover Township, Lancaster County, which could now be in either Dauphin or Lebanon County. A painted chest made in 1788 for Susanna Feeman, daughter of either Valentine or Caspar Jr., is now in the collection of the Reading Public Museum. It is signed on one of the urns on the front "Michael Stoob" (Stupp) (Monroe H. Fabian, *The Pennsylvania-German Decorated Chest*, rev. ed. [1978; Atglen, Pa.: Schiffer Publishing, 2004], p. 142). Caspar Feeman Jr. died intestate in 1810, residing in Bethel Township, Dauphin (now Lebanon) County. Susanna and Eva Christina Feeman/Viehmann appear several times between 1772 and 1779 in the lists of communicants at St. Luke Church; ("St. Luke Evangelical Lutheran Church, Formerly Known as 'The Heidelberg Congregation,' Schaefferstown, Lebanon County, Pennsylvania, Parish Register [1763]–1834," translated by Frederick S. Weiser, 3 vols., typescript, 1970, pp. 193, 202, 206, Lebanon County Historical Society). On the Feeman/Viehmann genealogy, see Elmer Leonidas Denniston, *Genealogy of the Stukey, Ream, Grove, Clem, and Denniston Families* (Harrisburg, Pa.: by the author, 1939), pp. 476–81. On the Viehmann house, see Lottie M. Bausman, "The Old Feeman Homestead in the Lebanon Valley," *Pennsylvania-German* 11 (1910): 680–84; Eleanor Raymond, *Early Domestic Architecture of Pennsylvania* (1930; reprint, Atglen, Pa.: Schiffer Publishing, 1977), pp. 26–27; Robert C. Bucher, "Grain in the Attic," *Pennsylvania Folklife* 13, no. 2 (Winter 1962–63): 7–11; and Charles Lang Bergengren, "The Cycle of Transformations in the Houses of Schaefferstown, Pennsylvania" (Ph.D. diss., University of Pennsylvania, 1988), pp. 97, 110, 190–93. In the front yard of the house is a large round stone (inscribed "H VALENTIN VEHMAN 1750"), for crushing apples before putting them into a cider press, and a pair of stone gate posts inscribed "ANNO DOM / 1766." The lintels above the front door and kitchen fireplace are also inscribed: "17 VALENDIN VIHMANN 62" and "F 1762 VM" ("F" for Felty, a diminutive form of Valentine), respectively. Circa 1776 Adam Viehmann married Anna Maria Gockley, with whom he had a son, John. After her death, he married Susanna Catharina Wuest in 1779 (Donna R. Irish, *Pennsylvania German Marriages: Marriages and Marriage Evidence in Pennsylvania German Churches* [Baltimore, Md.: Genealogical Publishing Company, 1982], p. 147) and had six children: Susanna, Daniel, Benjamin, Jacob (b. 1783), Valentine (b. 1784), and Joseph (b. 1785).

7. Michael and Maria Elisabeth Miller's ten children are John George (1756–1804), m. Maria Catherine Mayer/Meier (1759–1827); Benjamin (1758–1814), m. Maria Magdalena Pfeffer (1763–1807); Maria Catharine (b. 1761), m. Michael Gunckle; John Michael (b. 1763–d. young); John Frederick (1765–1811), m. Catharina Philippi (1775–1845); John (1766–1848), m. Anna Catharina Lescher (1768–1808); Jonathan (b. 1769); Michael (b. 1772); Philip (b. 1773); and Maria Elisabeth (1775–1843), m. Henry Schultze (1774–1824). The Miller family genealogy is derived from numerous sources, including estate papers; *St. Paul's United Church of Christ, Millbach Cemetery* (Womelsdorf, Pa.: Tulpehocken Settlement Historical Society, 1999); "Church Record of the Millbach Reformed Congregation, Millbach Township, Lebanon County, 1747–1875," typescript, Tulpehocken Settlement Historical Society, Womelsdorf, Pa.; and John T. Humphrey, *Pennsylvania Births, Lebanon County, 1714–1800* (Washington, D.C.: Humphrey Publications, 1996). The financial accounts of the Millbach Reformed Church

show that Michael Miller handled money for the congregation. In 1767 he was reimbursed £4.13.8 for money he spent on renovations to the schoolhouse at the church ("Church Record of the Millbach Reformed Congregation," p. 59). *Records of Pastoral Acts at Christ Lutheran Church, Stouchsburg, Berks County, Pennsylvania*, parts 1 and 2, Sources and Documents of the Pennsylvania Germans, vols. 12–13, translated and edited by Frederick S. Weiser (Birdsboro, Pa.: Pennsylvania German Society, 1989–1990), 12: 43. On the Schultze family, see William Henry Egle, *History of the County of Lebanon in the Commonwealth of Pennsylvania, Biographical and Genealogical* (Philadelphia: Everts and Peck, 1883), pp. 119, 293–95. "Church Record of the Millbach Reformed Congregation," p. 18.

8. Will of Michael Miller, Heidelberg Township, Dauphin (now Lebanon) County, written October 27, 1809, recorded December 9, 1815, LebCoROW, will book A, pp. 92–99.

9. Inventory of Emanuel Schultze, Tulpehocken Township, Berks County, April 11, 1809, Berks County Recorder of Wills (hereafter BerCoROW). Catharine Miller (1797–1820), daughter of Frederick and Catharine (Philippi) Miller, married Daniel Strickler (1792–1863). Jonathan Miller Jr. (d. 1868) married Elisabeth Hiester (1789–1817) in 1812. Catharine Miller married Jacob Hiester (1785–1817), son of Gabriel and Elizabeth Hiester, in 1811. Elisabeth Miller (1783–1867) married Andrew Kapp (1782–1844) in 1805. Catharine Miller (1795–1877) married Jonathan Mohr/Moore (1790–1868) in 1814. (Irish, *Pennsylvania German Marriages*, pp. 87, 153–55). Gladys Bucher Sowers, *Court of Common Pleas Records, 1813–1824, Lebanon County, Pennsylvania* (Morgantown, Pa.: Masthof Press, 2008), p. 22. Records of the Lebanon County Court of Common Pleas, May 1817 term, case no. 6.

10. Records of the Lebanon County Court of Common Pleas, January 1818 term, case no. 61. Sowers, *Court of Common Pleas*, pp. 23, 24, 35. Administrative accounts for the estate of Michael Miller, April 6, 1819, LebCoROW, M-1, pp. 819–21.

11. In 1830 Maria Elisabeth Schultze's household included one female, aged fifteen to twenty, and one female, aged fifty to sixty. In 1840 she is listed as the only occupant, aged sixty to seventy. "Record of the Millbach Reformed Congregation," pp. 38, 43. Inventory of Maria Elisabeth Schultze, Heidelberg Township, Lebanon County, [illegible] 17, 1843, LebCoROW, inventories S, pp. 467–68. Will of Maria Elisabeth Schultze, Heidelberg Township, Lebanon County, written February 27, 1843, recorded May 18, 1843. LebCoROW, will book C, p. 8. Administrative accounts for the estate of Maria Elisabeth Schultze, LebCoROW, accounts, S, no. 1639.

12. Will of John Miller, Millcreek Township, Lebanon County, written May 30, 1848, recorded September 9, 1848, LebCoROW, will book C, pp. 236–37. Inventory of John Miller, taken September 8, 1848, LebCoROW, inventories M-1, pp. 103–4. On the Lesher fraktur, see Frederick S. Weiser, *Fraktur: Pennsylvania German Folk Art* (Ephrata, Pa.: Science Press, 1973), p. 55; and Frederick S. Weiser, "His Deeds Followed Him: The Fraktur of John Conrad Gilbert," *Der Reggeboge* 16, no. 2 (1982): 35–36. On the Weigley genealogy, see Egle, *History of the County of Lebanon*, pp. 353–54, also pp. 201–2, 250, 329. The Weigley house was designed by the Philadelphia architectural firm Isaac Hobbs and Sons; an architectural drawing was sold at Conestoga Auction Co., *Unreserved Antique Auction for Ellwood Miller*, Manheim, Pa., January 31, 2004, lot 104. Will of Westa M. Weigley, Richland Boro, Lebanon County, written November 12, 1929, recorded April 28, 1934, LebCoROW, will book O, p. 402. Inventory of Westa M. Weigley, taken June 11, 1935, LebCoROW inv. book 1, p. 489.

13. The Miller chest was offered at Pennypacker Auction Centre, *Important Americana Antique Sale: The Renowned Collection of Perry Martin*, Reading, Pa., May 26, 1969, lot 306; apparently it did not sell, since it was offered again by Pennypacker Auction Centre, *One-Day Antique Sale . . . the Fine Collections of Mrs. Perry Martin et al.*, Reading, Pa., October 16, 1972, lot 399. According to antiques dealer Vernon Gunnion, Perry Martin bought the Miller chest from Phil Cowan. On line-and-berry inlay, see Cooper and Minardi, *Paint, Pattern & People*, pp. 12, 17–19, 71–78; also Lee Ellen Griffith, "Line and Berry Inlaid Furniture: A Regional Craft Tradition in Pennsylvania" (Ph.D. diss., University of Pennsylvania, 1988); and Lee Ellen Griffith, "The Line-and-Berry Inlaid Furniture of Eighteenth-Century Chester County, Pennsylvania," *Antiques* 135, no. 5 (May 1989): 1202–11. On Quakers in Berks County, see Karen Guenther, *"Rememb'ring Our Time and Work is the Lords": The Experiences of Quakers on the Eighteenth-Century Pennsylvania Frontier* (Selinsgrove, Pa.: Susquehanna University Press, 2005).

14. Egle, *History of the County of Lebanon*, pp. 4, 12, 195–96, 204, 210. The easternmost portion of Heidelberg Township, Lancaster County, joined Berks County, which was established

in 1752. Most of Heidelberg Township then became part of Dauphin County, formed in 1785, with the exception of an area that remained in Lancaster County as Elizabeth Township. When Lebanon County was established in 1813, Heidelberg Township changed counties yet again; it was also subdivided to form Jackson Township and, in 1844, Millcreek Township. The Zeller house, later known as Fort Zeller, has a Germanic floor plan with a central rather than gable-end chimney and direct exterior entry into the kitchen. Surviving details exhibit German baroque features, such as chevron-paneled doors and a carved stone architrave topped by a shield surrounding the front door (Bergengren, "Pennsylvania German House Forms," pp. 26–27). Frank E. Lichtenthaeler, *Storm Blown Seed of Schoharie*, Publications of the Pennsylvania German Folklore Society, vol. 9 (Allentown, Pa.: Pennsylvania German Folklore Society, 1944), pp. 3 105; and Earl W. Ibach, *The Hub of the Tulpehocken* (Womelsdorf, Pa.: the author, 1975).

15. *Johann David Schoepf, Travels in the Confederation [1783–1784]*, translated and edited by Alfred J. Morrison, 2 vols. (Philadelphia: William J. Campbell, 1911), 1: 203. Thomas L. Purvis, "Patterns of Ethnic Settlement in Late Eighteenth-Century Pennsylvania," *Western Pennsylvania Historical Magazine* 70, no. 2 (April 1987): 115. *Cazenove Journal 1794: A Record of the Journey of Theophile Cazenove through New Jersey and Pennsylvania*, edited by Raymond Wickersham Kelsey (Haverford, Pa.: Pennsylvania History Press, 1922), p. 45. John Fanning Watson, "Summer Tour 1829 to Maunk Chunk &c," August 3–15, 1829, Winterthur Library, Joseph Downs Collection of Manuscripts and Printed Ephemera, col. 58x29.6. Egle, *History of the County of Lebanon*, pp. 61–64.

16. On Millbach, see Nancy T. Risser, "An Architectural Overview of Millbach, Pennsylvania" (Ph.D. diss., Pennsylvania State University, 1982). On Weiser, see Paul A. W. Wallace, *Conrad Weiser: Friend of Colonist and Mohawk* (Philadelphia: University of Pennsylvania Press, 1945). *The Account Book of Christ Lutheran Church, Stouchsburg, Berks County, Pennsylvania, 1747–1809*, translated by Frederick S. Weiser (Camden, Maine: Picton Press, 1997), pp. 7, 9, 10. On the Schaeffer genealogy, see Egle, *History of the County of Lebanon*, p. 250. The tavern was known first as the King George Hotel, later the George Washington, and then the Franklin House (*Records of Purchases at the King George Hotel, Schaefferstown, Lebanon County, Pennsylvania, 1762–1773*, Sources and Documents of the Pennsylvania Germans, vol. 10, translated and edited by Frederick S. Weiser and Larry M. Neff [Birdsboro, Pa.: Pennsylvania German Society, 1987]). Sowers, *Colonial Taxes, Heidelberg Township*, pp. 101–8. Wenger and Garrison, "Commercial Vernacular Architecture," p. 91.

17. On the Schaefferstown Lutheran and Reformed churches, see A. S. Brendle, *A Brief History of Schaefferstown* (1901; reprint, Schaefferstown, Pa.: Historic Schaefferstown, 1978), pp. 9–19; also Charles H. Glatfelter, *Pastors and People: German Lutheran and Reformed Churches in the Pennsylvania Field, 1717–1793*, vol. 1, *Pastors and Congregations*, Publications of the Pennsylvania German Society, vol. 13 (Breinigsville, Pa.: Pennsylvania German Society, 1980), p. 332. Similar stonework can be seen on the Heinrich Zeller house (1745); George and Michael Miller house and mill (Millbach, 1752–1784); John George Becker house (near Kleinfeltersville, 1767); Michael Ley house, known as Tulpehocken Manor (near Myerstown, 1769); Valentine Viehmann house (near Millbach, 1762); and Philip Erpf house (Schaefferstown, ca. 1758). The builder of these structures is unknown, but in 1754 there was "a mason living on the Millbach near Tulphocken" (Clarence Spohn and Cynthia Marquet, eds., "Michael Müller/Miller of Cocalico Township, Lancaster County and His 'Debt Book' [1748–1786]," *Journal of the Historical Society of the Cocalico Valley* 20 [1995]: 35). On the angels, see Cooper and Minardi, *Paint, Pattern & People*, p. 57; also Diane Wenger, "The Angels of St. Luke Lutheran," *Historic Schaefferstown Journal* 1 (Spring 2011): 20–41. After they were removed from the church, the angels were sold in 1933 at the estate sale of Frank M. Iba of Schaefferstown, and again at Sotheby's, *Important Americana Including Silver, Folk Art, and Furniture*, New York, October 11, 2001, lot 164. *The Journals of Muhlenberg*, 2: 423. On the Muhlenberg family, see Lisa Minardi, *Pastors & Patriots: The Muhlenberg Family of Pennsylvania* (Collegeville, Pa.: Philip and Muriel Berman Museum of Art, 2011), and Lisa Minardi, "Of Massive Stones and Durable Materials: Architecture and Community in Eighteenth-Century Trappe, Pennsylvania" (master's thesis, University of Delaware, 2006). "Diary of F. A. Muhlenberg from the Day of His Ordination, October 25, 1770, until August, 1774," translated by Rev. J. W. Early and edited by Theodore E. Schmauk, *Lutheran Church Review* 24 (1905): 134. On Stiegel, see George L. Heiges, *Henry William Stiegel and His Associates: A Story of Early American Industry* (1948; reprint, Manheim, Pa.: Arbee Foundation, 1976); also Egle, *History*

of the County of Lebanon, p. 295, and Michael Emery, "Tulpehocken Valley Tour," in *Architecture and Landscape of the Pennsylvania Germans*, p. 56. After Stiegel's glassworks failed, he was forced into debtor's prison for a time and spent his last days working as a schoolmaster.

18. The present owner acquired the Krall chest from Sarah Musselman, of Ephrata, Lancaster County. On Ulrich Krall, see Strassberger, *Pennsylvania German Pioneers*, 1: 23–27, 2: 12–15. Ulrich (1713–1773) and his wife, Magdalena, were the parents of Christian Krall (1741–1802). Christian Krall and his wife, Catharine, had at least seven children: Christian Jr., Jacob, John, Joseph, Magdalena, Elizabeth, and Catherine. After Christian's death, Catharine moved to the town of Manheim, where she died in 1819. Will of Catherine Krall, Manheim, Lancaster County, written August 17, 1819, recorded November 23, 1819, Lancaster County Historical Society (hereafter LanCHS), will book M, pp. 345–46 Lancaster, Pa. Inventory of Christian Krall, Elizabeth Township, Lancaster County, February 17, 1802, LanCHS. The 1794 / M B chest was advertised by antiques dealer Diana H. Bittel in the 1994 Philadelphia Antiques Show catalogue, p. 80. The 1789 clock was sold in the estate sale of Mable A. Youse of Reading, Pa., at Pennypacker Auction Centre, Reading, Pa., October 14, 1961, lot 304. The present owner purchased the Taylor clock from Luther and Pearl Sensenig of Womelsdorf, Berks County, who acquired it from Earl Taylor of Womelsdorf. The clock reputedly descended in the Taylor family. Although the dial is unsigned, the movement is thought to be by a Reading clockmaker. The Illig clock was acquired by the Metropolitan Museum of Art in 1976 from antiques dealers Edgar and Charlotte Sittig, who purchased it from the Illig family sometime before 1964. The Sittigs also purchased the Miller family clock (fig. 10) now at Winterthur.

19. In addition to the inlaid chests made for Maria Elisabeth Miller (1792) and Magdalena Krall (n.d.), twenty-one painted chests associated with the Embroidery Artist are known: Christina Ache (n.d.), Sophia Ache (n.d.), Salome Bahrt (1805), Elisabeth Beinhauer (1797), Catharina Bicer (1790), Dietrich Gackley (1798), Benjamin Hammer (1795), Christina Hoffman (1795), Johannes Lautermilch (1792), Catharina Lebenstein (1789), Catharina Maurer (1795), Eva Catharina Philippi (1792), Peter Rammler (n.d.), Margaretha Stehlts (n.d.), Susanna Schebler (1790), Heinrich Schorck (1793), Maria Stohler (1788), Susanna Zwally (1794), Catharina [illegible] (1793), a chest with no name dated 1796, and a chest façade with neither name nor date. All but two (Heinrich Schorck and Susanna Schebler) were examined for this article. Stepped till lids are found on the following chests: Christina Ache, Sophia Ache, Bahrt, Bicer, Gackley, Hammer, Hoffman, Lautermilch, Lebenstein, Miller, Rammler, Stelts, Stohler, and Zwally. The till lids on the Krall and 1796 no-name chests are missing. Three chests have a flat till lid: Beinhauer, Philippi, and the one dated 1793 for Catharina [illegible]. In addition to the squiggle mark, several chests include other markings: the Miller chest has the letter "H" in *Fraktur* at the inside juncture of the left side board and backboard as well as numerous red squiggles; the Zwally chest has a drawing of a bird on the underside of one of the small drawers in the till (fig. 77); and the Hammer chest has a geometric design drawn in red on the underside of one of the till drawers. Eight chests retain their original straight bracket feet: Sophia Ache, Beinhauer, Gackley, Hammer, Hoffman, Stehlts, Zwally, and a chest dated 1793 with the name Catrina [illegible]; those chests with replaced or missing feet are Christina Ache, Bahrt, Bicer, Krall, Maurer, Lautermilch, Philippi, Schorck, Stohler, and a chest with no name that is dated 1796. The unusual batten feature on the Miller chest also occurs on an example with painted decoration associated with the black unicorn chests from Berks County.

20. These handles are found on the Christina Ache, Sophia Ache, Bicer, Hammer, Krall, Lebenstein, Philippi, Rammler, Stohler, and 1793 Catrina [illegible] chests. Chests that never had carrying handles are Gackley, Hoffman, Lautermilch, Maurer, Miller, Stehlts, Zwally, and 1796 no-name. The Bahrt chest had handles installed at a later date, now removed. Decorated locks appear on the Lebenstein, Miller, Schorck, and Rammler chests as well as the Stelts chest, inscribed "IS"; the Stohler chest, which has wrigglework but no initials or date; the 1796 no-name chest that has the initials "HS"; and another chest of which only the façade survives but retains the lock and has an illegible date. Locks on the Bahrt, Krall, Lautermilch, and Philippi chests are missing; the locks on the Hammer and Bicer chests are plain, though the latter may be a replacement.

21. Family genealogies, county histories, and probate, tax, church, and cemetery records were consulted to help identify the owners of the chests. In a few cases the names on the chests were either illegible or difficult to determine with certainty due to the vagaries of spelling and mixed usage of German and English versions of names.

22. On the Stohler chest, see Virginia Tuttle Clayton et al., *Drawing on America's Past: Folk*

Art, Modernism, and the Index of American Design (Washington, D.C.: National Gallery of Art, 2002), pp. 138–39; also Clarence P. Hornung, *Treasury of American Design: A Pictorial Survey of Popular Folk Arts Based upon Watercolor Renderings in the Index of American Design, at the National Gallery of Art*, 2 vols. (Washington, D.C.: National Gallery of Art, 1950; reprint, New York: Harry N. Abrams, n.d.), 2: 706. The Stohler chest was part of a large collection of Pennsylvania German artifacts given in 1933 to the Metropolitan Museum of Art by Mrs. Robert W. de Forest, who had acquired it from Clarence W. Brazer in 1926; it was deaccessioned in 1969. The history of the chest before Brazer is unknown, but the name "liddea" or Lydia written in German script on the underside of the lid may be that of a later owner. The chest is pictured in Joseph Downs, *Pennsylvania German Arts and Crafts: A Picture Book* (New York: Metropolitan Museum of Art, 1946), pl. 9; Henry J. Kauffman, "Decorated Chests in the Pennsylvania Dutch Country," *Pennsylvania Dutchman* 1, no. 8 (June 23, 1949): 1; Henry J. Kauffman, *Pennsylvania Dutch American Folk Art* (1946; rev. and expanded, New York: Dover Publications, 1964), p. 117; and Fabian, *Pennsylvania-German Decorated Chest*, pp. 151, 199. The Stohler chest was sold at Pook & Pook, *Antique Auction*, Downingtown, Pa., September 20, 2003, lot 290. On Johannes Stohler, see Strassberger, *Pennsylvania German Pioneers*, 1: 392. Stohler named his widow and seven children in his will: George, John, Henry, Ann, Mary (Maria), Elisabeth, and Magdalena. Will of John Stohler, written August 20, 1785, recorded September 16, 1785, Heidelberg Township, Dauphin County, Dauphin County Register of Wills (hereafter DauCoROW), will book A, pp. 20–25, reel S-1. Inventory of John Stohler, taken September 13, 1785, DauCoROW, reel inv S-6. John Shenk was the son of miller Michael Shenk Sr. (d. 1763); his brother Michael Jr. (d. 1790) owned a gristmill and sawmill and was known as "the miller of Lebanon"; Michael Jr.'s son John Shenk (1765–1821) was known as "the miller of Heidelberg." On the Shenk family, see Joanne K. Hoover, "Michael Shenk of Warwick Township, Lancaster County, Pennsylvania: His Descendants and Some of Their Lands," *Pennsylvania Mennonite Heritage* 32, no. 4 (October 2009): 21–27. Will of Johannes Schenck (John Shenk), Heidelberg Township, Lebanon County, written May 6, 1813, recorded April 29, 1814, LebCoROW, will book A, pp. 36–38. Inventory of John Shenk, taken April 27, 1814, LebCoROW inventories, microfiche S 43–45. Sarah Stohler was the daughter of John Stohler and Barbara Krall. The Stohler box was advertised by James and Nancy Glazer in the 1994 Philadelphia Antiques Show catalogue, p. 99. The Kunger box is pictured in Cynthia V. A. Schaffner and Susan Klein, *Folk Hearts: A Celebration of the Heart Motif in American Folk Art* (New York: Alfred A. Knopf, 1984), p. 55.

23. The Lebenstein chest was acquired by the present owner more than forty years ago from Hattie Brunner; she purchased it from Stanley Smith, who bought it at a farm auction near Kleinfeltersville, Lebanon County. When purchased from Brunner, all but the heart was overpainted; this overpaint was removed in 2011 by Peter Deen. On Lebenstein, see Strassberger, *Pennsylvania German Pioneers*, 1: 162–67, 2: 154–61; also Egle, *History of the County of Lebanon*, pp. 196, 210; and Sowers, *Colonial Taxes, Heidelberg Township*, pp. 9, 10, 15, 16, 18, 35, 42, 47, 73, 83, 101, 103, 110, 114. Will of David Lebenstein, Heidelberg Township, Dauphin County, written August 22, 1789, recorded November 17, 1789, DauCoROW, will book A, pp. 180–91, reel L-1. Inventory of David Lebenstein, taken November 14, 1789, DauCoROW, inventories reel L-1. See also Sowers, *Lebanon County, Direct Tax of 1798*, p. 78. Catharina Lebenstein's sister Elisabeth (1769–1792) married Frederick Miller, and sister Anna Maria (1771–1836) married Johann Georg Becker. Two birth and baptismal certificates were made by Friedrich Speyer for the latter's daughters, Elisabeth Becker (b. 1794; now in the collection of the Berman Museum of Art at Ursinus College, Collegeville, Pa.; Alfred L. Shoemaker, *Check List of Pennsylvania Dutch Printed Taufscheins* [Lancaster, Pa.: Pennsylvania Dutch Folklore Center, 1952], p. 47); and Catharina Becker (b. 1796, now in the Dietrich American Foundation collection; Klaus Stopp, *The Printed Birth and Baptismal Certificates of the German-Americans*, 6 vols. [East Berlin, Pa.: Russell D. Earnest Associates, 1997–1998], 2: 190). Millbach Church of the Brethren Cemetery Records, Lebanon County Historical Society. Will of John Royer, Heidelberg Township, Lebanon County, written December 6, 1838, recorded August 18, 1839, LebCoROW, will book B, pp. 523–27. Inventory of John Royer, taken July 17, 1839, LebCoROW, inventory book R, vol. 1, p. 268.

24. The Bicer/Becker chest was acquired by the Detroit Institute of Arts from Israel Sack, Inc. in 1941 and is illustrated in *Antiques* 43, no. 2 (February 1943): 91. The extensive damage and water staining on the underside of the chest suggest that the ball feet, which do not exhibit damage, are replacements. Because the blue paint on the feet appears to match that on the

ground of the chest, the ground may have been repainted when the feet were replaced. The Schorck chest is illustrated in Earl F. Robacker, "The Paint-decorated Furniture of the Pennsylvania Dutch," *Pennsylvania Folklife* 13, no. 1 (Autumn 1962): 2. This chest was sold by T. Glenn Horst & Son Auctioneers, *Pennsylvania German Folk Art and Antiques: The Collections of the Late Dr. Earl F. and Ada F. Robacker*, Farmersville, Pa., session 2, June 23–24, 1989, lot 822. The Schorck name is of Swiss-German origin, and more than forty spelling variations are known (Schürch, Sherg, Shirk, Sherk) (Thomas A. Sherk, *The Sherk Family* [Baltimore, Md.: Gateway Press, 1982], pp. 1–5, 311). Sowers, *Colonial Taxes, Heidelberg Township*, pp. 32, 108. George and Salome Schorck were married on May 26, 1771; (Weiser, "St. Luke Evangelical Lutheran Church," p. 186). Seven of their children were baptized there: Henrich (b. 1772), Catharina (b. 1774), Benjamin (b. 1776), Eva Christina (b. 1778), Elisabeth (b. 1783), Anna Maria (b. 1785), and Johann Georg (b. 1787) (Weiser, "St. Luke Evangelical Lutheran Church" pp. 17, 23, 24, 27, 38, 43, 53). In 1796 they had three children baptized at Christ Lutheran Church: Johannes (b. 1790), Sarah (b. 1793), and Eva Christina (b. [illegible]). (Weiser, *Christ Lutheran Church*, 1: 94, 2: 163). Heinrich Schorck may have moved to Dauphin County as an adult; a Henry Shirk of Lower Paxton Township, Dauphin County, died in 1842, leaving a wife, Elizabeth, and children George, Mary, Nancy, Henry, Elizabeth, Catharine, John, and Samuel (Will of Henry Shirk, Lower Paxton Township, Dauphin County, written March 17, 1842, DauCoROW, will book E, pp. 353–54, reel S-8). Another Henry Shirk, but of Caernarvon Township, Lancaster County, died in 1836 after a long illness, leaving a widow and sons Henry and William. (Administrator's accounts for the estate of Henry Shirk, filed December 22, 1841, LanCHS).

25. For related stove plates, see Henry C. Mercer, *The Bible in Iron: Pictured Stoves and Stoveplates of the Pennsylvania Germans*, 3rd ed. (Doylestown, Pa.: Bucks County Historical Society, 1961), pls. 199, 223–24. Although stove plates with ovolo-end panels were cast at many furnaces, numerous examples with the sawtooth border were made at Elisabeth Furnace. No record of Peter Rammler's baptism has been found, but five of his siblings were baptized at Christ Lutheran Church: Hanna Elisabeth (1761), Magdalena (1763), Catharine (1765), John Leonard (1768), and Johannes (1773). The name "Peter Rammler" appears twice in the confirmation records: once in 1784, "Peter Ramler, of Joh." aged fourteen; and once in 1785 "Peter Ramler, of the late John," aged fifteen. The Peter Rammler who owned the chest is thought to be the Peter confirmed in 1784, whose father did not die until 1788. The reference to the "late John" is likely to John Jacob Rammler, who died in 1784 (Weiser, *Christ Lutheran Church*, 1: 77, 91, 99, 103, 2: 68, 159, 160). On the Rammler genealogy, see also Egle, *County of Lebanon*, p. 346. Peter and Eva Rammler's children baptized at Christ Lutheran Church were Leonard (1795), David (1796), and Catherine (1800); (Weiser, *Christ Lutheran Church*, 1: 91, 95, 103; Peter names three children in his will, Leonard, David, and Peter, and in a codicil he refers to his daughter Catherine, wife of Jacob Zerring (Will of Peter Rammler, East Hanover Township, Dauphin County, written September 4, 1850, recorded October 19, 1850, DauCoROW, will book F, pp. 238–42, reel R-4). Peter's tombstone is inscribed "Johannes P. Rambler" and his dates are given as March 7, 1770–September 25, 1850. (Shell's Church Cemetery Records, Dauphin County Historical Society). On the Ley family, see Egle, *History of the County of Lebanon*, pp. 196–98, 346; Viola Kohl Mohn, "Shadows of the Rhine along the Tulpehocken," *Lebanon County Historical Society* 14, no. 5 (1970): 153–65; also Cooper and Minardi, *Paint, Pattern & People*, pp. 181–83. The pediment is inscribed "GOTT ALLEIN DIE EHR / MICHEAEL LEY UND EFA MAGDALENA LEYIN / CHRISTOPH UHLER 1769 VON LEBANON." In addition to the pediment and schrank inscribed with their names, the Leys also had a pair of personalized date stones set into the house; a pair of sandstone gate posts in the front yard dated 1780; and even the wrought-iron bar used to secure the smokehouse door was inscribed "M 1777 L." Weiser, *The Account Book of Christ Lutheran Church*, pp. 12, 14, 15, 18, 19, 22, 37, 55. Inventory of John Rammler, Heidelberg Township, Dauphin County, taken November 25, 1788, DauCoROW, inventories reel R-2.

26. Joe Kindig advertised the Maurer chest in *Antiques* 45, no. 6 (June 1944): inside front cover. It was later owned by Walter Himmelreich and sold at Pennypacker Auction Centre, *The Renowned Collection of Walter Himmelreich*, Reading, Pa., May 30–31, 1958, lot 370; then acquired by Donald Shelley (Pook & Pook, *Pioneer Americana Collection*, lot 753). Will of Philip Maurer, written February 10, 1776, recorded May 23, 1786, Hanover Township, Lancaster (now Dauphin) County as cited in F. Edward Wright, *Abstracts of Lancaster County, Pennsylvania Wills, 1786–1820* (Westminster, Md.: Willow Bend Books, 2000), p. 137. The will

names his wife, Anna C. Maurer, and children Simon, Eva, Margaret, Catharine, Anna, wife of Christopher Brown, and George. Numerous variations of the Maur/Maurer surname exist, including Mowrer as well as the anglicized Mason. On the Maurer genealogy, see Keith A. Dull, *Early Families of Lancaster, Lebanon, and Dauphin Counties, Pennsylvania* (1997; reprint, Westminster, Md.: Heritage Books, 2006), p. 87. See also Strassberger, *Pennsylvania German Pioneers*, 1: 245–48. Sowers, *Colonial Taxes, Heidelberg Township*, p. 139. Peter Rammler was the nephew of Anna Catharina Rammler, son of her brother Johannes Rammler (b. 1726) and his wife, Anna Barbara Ley. Peter Rammler's brother Philip was named after Philip Maurer Sr., who served as his baptismal sponsor in 1757 (Weiser, *Christ Lutheran Church*, 1: 19). Two of Philip Maurer Sr.'s children were sponsored by Johann Jacob and Eva Margaret Rammler and named after them. Leonard Rammler sponsored another daughter (F. Edward Wright, *Early Church Records of Lebanon County, Pennsylvania* [Westminster, Md.: Willow Bend Books, 2000], p. 325). In 1800 Peter and Eva Rammler's daughter Catharine was baptized at Christ Lutheran Church and sponsored by George and Elisabeth Maurer (Weiser, *Christ Lutheran Church*, 1: 103). He is likely the George Maurer who appears in the 1798 direct tax as occupying a house owned by Michael Rammler in Heidelberg Township (Sowers, *Lebanon County, Direct Tax of 1798*, p. 76).

27. The 1796 chest was sold at Conestoga Auction Company, *The Collection of Mr. Gordon Sleigh*, Manheim, Pa., May 13, 1995, lot 330. The Stehlts chest was sold at Sotheby's, *Important Americana*, New York, January 21–22, 2000, lot 507a; it is also pictured in Fabian, *Pennsylvania-German Decorated Chest*, fig. 223. On the Ache family, see Egle, *History of the County of Lebanon*, pp. 233–35. Henry Ache's first wife was Elisabeth Shuey; after her death he married Maria Catharina Filbert/Philbert, a Berks County native, in 1760. His inventory totaled £141.2.5 and included a weaving loom and equipment along with livestock, farm tools, a still, a house clock valued at £4.10, a "Closset" (likely a schrank) worth £3, and "Kitshen closset" (or cupboard) worth £1.5. (Inventory of Henry Achey, Heidelberg Township, Dauphin County, taken November 9, 1786, DauCoROW, inventories reel 1). On Christina Ache, see Luther R. Kelker, trans. and ed., *Baptismal and Marriage Records by Rev. John Waldschmidt* (1907; reprint, Westminster, Md.: Heritage Books, 2007), p. 9. The sponsors at her baptism may have been Caspar and Eva Christina Feeman/Viehmann, although Kelker transcribed the names as Caspar and Christina Faddeicher. On her marriage, see Irish, *Pennsylvania German Marriages*, p. 70. The Maria Catharina Ache certificate was sold at Sotheby's, *The Fred Wichmann Collection of Pennsylvania-German Fraktur and Related Decorative Arts*, New York, June 9, 1983, lot 38; it was offered again at Sotheby's, *Important Americana: Featuring the Collection of Frank and June Barsalona*, New York, September 30, 2010, lot 13. Johann Henrich Goettel was formerly known as the "Kirchenbuch Artist" (Russell Earnest and Corinne Earnest, "Fraktur-Fest II: A Tribute to Richard S. Machoner," *Der Reggeboge* 41, no. 2 [2002]: 5–7; also Earnest and Earnest, *Papers for Birth Dayes*, 1: 447). The Sophia Ache chest appeared on the *Antiques Roadshow* in 2006 (Tampa, Fla. episode; filmed on June 25, 2005; aired originally on January 23, 2006).

28. The zither descended in the family of Jeanette S. Hamner (1929–2009), who donated it in 2000 to Colonial Williamsburg. Many fraktur contain similar inscriptions, which typically include a reference to Jesus, as in "This heart of mine shall be yours alone, oh Jesus." The second part of the inscription, "sing and play," is a reference to several passages in the New Testament that talk of singing and making music to the Lord. On this zither and others of the form, see Ralph Lee Smith, *Appalachian Dulcimer Traditions*, 2nd ed. (Latham, Md.: Scarecrow Press, 2010), pp. 30, 31, 156, 163–65; and L. Allen Smith, *Catalogue of Pre-revival Appalachian Dulcimers* (Columbia, Mo.: University of Missouri Press, 1983), pp. 15–19. On the Ache family, see Brendle, *A Brief History of Schaefferstown*, pp. 16, 53; also Egle, *History of the County of Lebanon*, pp. 233–35. Inventory of Samuel Ache, Heidelberg Township, Lebanon County, taken January 3, 1833, LebCoROW inventories A-1, pp. 43–44. Inventory of Henry Achey, Heidelberg Township, Dauphin County, taken March 28, 1808, DauCoROW, inventories reel 2. Hermannus Ache, along with Johann Ludwig Ache and Johann Jacob Ache, immigrated in 1752 aboard the *Halifax* (Strassberger, *Pennsylvania German Pioneers*, 1: 483–84, 2: 573). According to family history, Johann Ludwig Ache taught school in Vincent Township, Chester County, then moved to a farm near Linglestown, Dauphin County, where he died in 1792 (Egle, *History of the County of Lebanon*, p. 234). Hermannus Ache lived in Montgomery County and was a schoolmaster and fraktur artist (Mary Jane Lederach Hershey, *This Teaching I Present: Fraktur from the Skippack and Salford Mennonite Meetinghouse Schools, 1747–1836*

[Intercourse, Pa.: Good Books, 2003], pp. 60, 61, 69, 74, 75, 77, 168; see also Earnest and Earnest, *Papers for Birth Dayes*, 1: 44). On Filbert Achey, see ibid., pp. 46–47.

29. The schrank was offered at Pook & Pook, Downingtown, Pa., June 19, 1999, lot 250; and Pook & Pook, April 21–22, 2000, lot 426. Inventory of Michael Miller, Heidelberg Township, Lebanon County, taken December 7, 1815, LebCoROW, inventories M-1, p. 258. Raymond J. Brunner, *That Ingenious Business: Pennsylvania German Organ Builders*, Publications of the Pennsylvania German Society, vol. 24 (Birdsboro, Pa.: Pennsylvania German Society, 1990), pp. 70, 157, 166–67. Inventory of John Sheibly, Earl Township, Lancaster County, taken January 7, 1793, LanCHS.

30. The chest façade was sold by Ronald Gilligan & Son Auctioneering, *Estate Sale of Richard Roy Sleigh and William Gordon Sleigh*, Pennsylvania Furnace, Pa., September 6, 2010. The Bahrt chest was offered at Conestoga Auction Company, *Spring Americana Auction*, Manheim, Pa., February 29–March 1, 2008, lot 705; also at Christie's, *Important American Furniture, Folk Art, Maritime Art, and Prints*, New York, September 25, 2008, lot 27; see also Fabian, *Pennsylvania-German Decorated Chest*, p. 152. According to a receipt from H. R. Sandor dated December 2, 1970, the chest was acquired from Chestertown House, the Southampton, Long Island, home of Henry Francis du Pont. Salome's parents were John Adam Barth and Elisabeth Weisenkind, who were married in 1753 (Wright, *Early Church Records of Lebanon County*, pp. 236, 237, 242). John Adam Barth appears in the tax records of Lebanon Township from 1771 to at least 1783 (Gladys Bucher Sowers, *Colonial Taxes, Lebanon Township, Lancaster County, Pennsylvania, 1750–1783* [Morgantown, Pa.: Masthof Press, 2004]; also Sowers, *Lebanon County, Direct Tax of 1798*, pp. 89, 108; and Egle, *History of the County of Lebanon*, pp. 226, 228, 243). An embroidered hand towel with the name "Salome Bahrtin" is in the collection of the Lebanon County Historical Society and thought to be from Lebanon County (Ellen J. Gehret et al., *This Is the Way I Pass My Time: A Book about Pennsylvania German Decorated Hand Towels*, Publications of the Pennsylvania German Society, vol. 18 [Birdsboro, Pa.: Pennsylvania German Society, 1985], pp. 11–12). The fraktur is illustrated in Weiser, *Fraktur: Pennsylvania German Folk Art*, p. 81, and was sold at Sotheby's, *The Collection of Dr. and Mrs. Henry P. Deyerle*, Charlottesville, Va., May 26–27, 1995, lot 658.

31. The Scheppler chest was offered at Christie's, *Important American Furniture, Folk Art and Prints*, New York, October 8, 2004, lot 38; also Pook & Pook, *Two Day Antique Sale*, Downingtown, Pa., December 1–2, 2000, lot 510. Weiser, *Christ Lutheran Church*, 2: 122. Weiser, *The Account Book of Christ Lutheran Church*, pp. 44, 46. F. J. F. Schantz, trans., *Records of Rev. John Casper Stoever: Baptismal and Marriage, 1730–1779* (Harrisburg, Pa.: Harrisburg Publishing Co., 1896), p. 64. Weiser, *Christ Lutheran Church*, 2: 66. The Minnichs were the children of German immigrant Johann Christopher Michael Minnich (1734–1806), who settled in Bern Township, Berks County. Christopher's will names children George, Philip, Jacob, Benjamin, Jonathan, Adam (1776–1858), Margaretha (m. Philip Lerch), Christina (m. John Schepler), Magdalena (m. George Lesher), Anna Maria (m. Michael Pfiester), and Elisabeth. The Adam Minnich chest was sold at Skinner's, *American Furniture and Decorative Arts*, Boston, November 4, 2006, lot 700; for an illustration, see Cooper and Minardi, *Paint, Pattern & People*, p. 144. On the Bollmans, see "Church Record of the Millbach Reformed Congregation," pp. 17–21.

32. The Lautermilch chest was formerly owned by Emma Nicodemus (Jane E. Myers, *Highlights of the Renfrew Museum* [Waynesboro, Pa.: Renfrew Museum, 1980], p. 19). On the Lautermilch family, see Strassberger, *Pennsylvania German Pioneers*, 1: 48–49, 93, 162–67, 2: 154–61; also Sowers, *Colonial Taxes, Heidelberg Township*, p. 1; Brendle, *A Brief History of Schaefferstown*, pp. 15–16; and Weiser, *Christ Lutheran Church*, 2: 159. Barbara Meyer was the daughter of Catharine Schaeffer and John Meyer (Egle, *History of the County of Lebanon*, p. 250). Weiser, "St. Luke Evangelical Lutheran Church," 1: 85. "Church Record of the Millbach Reformed Congregation," p. 21. Will of John Lautermilch, East Hanover Township, Dauphin County, written March 23, 1850, recorded October 24, 1854, DauCoROW, will book F, pp. 405–8. Inventory of John Lautermilch, October 19, 1854, DauCoROW, inventories reel L-7.

33. The Zwally chest was advertised by Olde Hope Antiques in *Antiques* 177, no. 4 (Summer 2010): 11. Christian Zwally married Sarah Blank in November 1780 (Weiser, *Christ Lutheran Church*, 2: 54). Another Susanna Zwally married Johannes Lengel in 1797 at Christ Lutheran Church (ibid., 2: 70) but is not the Susanna Zwally of this chest based on the genealogical information on the fraktur that descended with the chest. Winterthur Library, Joseph Downs Collection of Manuscripts and Printed Ephemera, Lewis Papers, col. 782, microfilm 2667, L.62. On Susanna Zwally and Frantz Seibert's marriage, see Irish, *Pennsylvania German Marriages*, p.

148. Leonard Holstine gave £5 toward renovations of the church and £3 for building a parsonage in 1747, and £5 for acquiring an organ in 1751 (Weiser, *Christ Lutheran Church*, 1: 36; Weiser, *The Account Book of Christ Lutheran Church*, pp. 1, 3, 7). George Seibert's fraktur was likely made by Andreas Kessler, also known as the "Flat Parrot Artist" (Earnest and Earnest, *Papers for Birth Dayes*, 1: 438–40). Inventory of Frantz (Frances) Seibert, Heidelberg Township, Lebanon County, taken January 1, 1833, LebCoROW, inventories S-1, pp. 350–53. Inventory of Susanna Seibert, Heidelberg Township, Lebanon County, taken January 5, 1861, LebCoROW, inventory book A, pp. 50–51. Egle, *History of the County of Lebanon*, p. 203.

34. The Hoffman chest was advertised by James and Nancy Glazer in *Antiques* 129, no. 1 (January 1986): 98. It was formerly in the collection of George Horace Lorimer, then in that of Kenneth Roberts. On the Hoffman family, see Wright, *Early Church Records of Lebanon County*, pp. 164, 165, 167, 170–72; also Weiser, *Christ Lutheran Church*, 2: 78. John Peter Brossman (1766–1837) was married first in 1791 to Catharine Beier (ibid., 1: 33, 2: 65). The Hammer chest was sold by American Art Association, *Colonial Furniture: The Superb Collection of the Late Howard Reifsnyder*, New York, April 24–27, 1929, lot 492. Milly McGehee Americana advertised the chest in *Antiques* 123, no. 5 (May 1983): 949. Benjamin Hammer was likely the eldest child. Other children were Anna Maria (b. 1774), Johann (b. 1774), Eve Elisabeth (b. 1776), Rosina (b. 1778), Magdalena (b. 1779), Johann Georg (b. 1781), Michael (b. 1782), and Barbara (b. 1783) (Frederick S. Weiser, trans., *Records of Pastoral Acts at Emanuel Lutheran Church, Known in the Eighteenth Century as the Warwick Congregation, near Brickerville, Elizabeth Township, Lancaster County, Pennsylvania, 1743–1799*, Sources and Documents of the Pennsylvania Germans, vol. 8 [Breinigsville, Pa.: Pennsylvania German Society, 1983], pp. 106, 110, 112, 115, 117, 119, 122, 127, 130, also pp. 197, 199, 200, 202). Will of Benjamin Hammer, Mifflin Township, Dauphin County, written May 3, 1844, recorded August 27, 1852, DauCoROW, will book F, pp. 336–41, reel H-5. Inventory of Eve C. Hammer, Washington Township, Dauphin County, taken November 18, 1869, DauCoROW, inventories reel H-13.

35. Sebastian Caquelin/Gackley (1686–1751) immigrated in 1736 with his son John Gackley (1718–1796). This John had a son John Gackley Jr. (1755–1820), who was the father of Dietrich. ("Church Records of the Millbach Reformed Congregation," pp. 29, 31, 35.) Inventory of Dietrich Gackley, taken August 30, 1845, Lower Heidelberg Township, Berks County, BerCoROW.

36. Jacob Philippi (1737–1822) married Anna Christina Trautman (1738–1810). Their children were Christina (1767), Jacob (1774), Christian (1776), Johannes (1779), George (1781), and Eva (1783). Johannes Philippi (1728–1800) married Maria Eva Barbara Eichelberger and had eight children baptized at Emanuel Lutheran Church: Maria Barbara (1758), Johannes (1760), Christoph (1762), Christina Barbara (1763), Anna Elisabeth (1764), Sophia Barbara (1765), Christina Catharina (1767), and Maria Margaretha (1769) (Weiser, *Emanuel Lutheran Church*, pp. 63, 88). A third brother, Johann Adam Philippi (1736–1800), moved to Wythe County, Virginia, circa 1770 and is buried at St. Paul's Lutheran Church in Rural Retreat. Will of Jacob Philippi, Heidelberg Township, Lebanon County, written July 8, 1815, recorded May 20, 1822, LebCoROW, will book A, pp. 334, 335. Catharina's tombstone in the Millbach cemetery gives her dates as 1775–1845. The Catharina(?) chest was purchased by Greg K. Kramer Co. at a Williams-Smith auction in Plainfield, New Hampshire, in 2010. Two labels found inside the till when the author examined the chest at the York Antiques Show on January 28, 2011, read: "Clarence Weimer to Charlotte Meigs Weimer Lebanon, Pa. Circa 1930 to LWB 1952 to Charlotte Bloom" and "Woodbury NJ 1952 Devon Pa 1957 Bellows Falls Vt Charlotte Weimer Sexton 1978." The Weimer family has a long history in Lebanon County. Clarence Weimer (1882–1952) was the son of Lucein Edwin Weimer (1839–1920) and Clara Wallace (1846–1927). Lucein was the son of William Weimer (1796–1862) and Catharine Lutz, who married in 1819. One of Lucein's two grandmothers is the likely original owner of the chest. His paternal grandmother was Catharine(?), wife of Peter Weimer, and his maternal grandmother was Catharine Nagle, wife of John Lutz. The Beinhauer chest sold at Pook & Pook, *Summer Antique Sale*, Downingtown, Pa., June 26–27, 1998, lot 256; according to the catalogue entry, it descended in the Earnest family of Dauphin County. Her full name was Catharina Elisabeth Beinhauer (Weiser, *Emanuel Lutheran Church*, p. 107). Peter Beinhauer (1744–1818) married Christina Weber in 1771 at Trinity Lutheran Church in Lancaster. See ibid., pp. 194, 196, 199, 203. Weiser, *Christ Lutheran Church*, 1: 52. Susanna Beinhauer was baptized in 1781, Johannes in 1782, Johann Peter in 1787, and Magdalena in 1789 (Humphrey, *Pennsylvania Births: Lebanon County*, pp. 12–13). Peter and Christina Beinhauer were baptismal sponsors at Christ Lutheran

Church in 1779 (Weiser, *Christ Lutheran Church*, 1: 52). St. Luke records for 1793–1794 document that Peter Beinhauer provided two days of labor for improvements to the burial ground in 1793 (Winterthur Library, Joseph Downs Collection of Manuscripts and Printed Ephemera, Lewis Papers, col. 782, microfilm 2662, TR 75). Will of Peter Beinhauer, Derry Township, Dauphin County, written May 27, 1818, recorded October 16, 1818, DauCoROW, will book X, pp. 274–78. *Records of Pastoral Acts at Zion Lutheran Church, Harrisburg, Dauphin County, Pennsylvania, 1795–1827*, translated and edited by Frederick S. Weiser, Sources and Documents of the Pennsylvania Germans, vol. 11 (Birdsboro, Pa.: Pennsylvania German Society, 1987), p. 73.

37. Transcribed information from the Rex daybooks was provided by Diane Wenger. On the Rex store, see Diane E. Wenger, *A Country Storekeeper in Pennsylvania: Creating Economic Networks in Early America, 1790–1807* (University Park, Pa.: Pennsylvania State University Press, 2008).

38. Sowers, *Colonial Taxes, Heidelberg Township*, pp. 101–8. Sowers, *Lebanon County, Direct Tax of 1798*, pp. 56, 66. Will of Christian Kastnitz, written August 17, 1808, Bethel Township, Berks County, recorded 1814, BerCoROW. Inventory of Christian Kastnitz, taken 1814, BerkCoROW. Weiser, *Christ Lutheran Church*, 1: 41, 46, 2: 39, 58, 69, 103, 140.

39. The HS lock was sold at Pook & Pook, *American Wrought Iron Utensils, Tools, and Architectural Hardware from the Renowned Collection of James Sorber*, Downingtown, Pa., May 13, 2005, lot 470; the HS 1789 lock was sold at Christie's, *Pennsylvania German Folk Art and Decorative Arts from the Collection of Mr. and Mrs. Richard Flanders Smith*, New York, June 3, 1995, lot 107. On the Seilers, see Strassberger, *Pennsylvania German Pioneers*, 1: 716; also Annette Kunselman Burgert, *Eighteenth Century Emigrants from the Northern Alsace to America* (Camden, Maine: Picton Press, 1992), p. 464. Sowers, *Colonial Taxes, Lebanon Township*, pp. 64, 75, 87, 97, 109, 126, 142, 154, 168, 183, 197, 213, 230, 249, 263, 270, 279, 290, 302, 313. The surname is spelled variously Saylor, Seiler, Seyler, Seylor, and Syler. Weiser, "St. Luke Evangelical Lutheran Church," p. 17; and Weiser, *Christ Lutheran Church*, 2: 70. Inventory of Henry Seiler, June 5, 1785, DauCoROW, inventories reel S-5. Henry Seiler's will of 1785 mentions only one child, Andreas Seiler, who was living in Germany; will of Henry Seiler, Lebanon Township, Dauphin County, written June 14, 1785, DauCoROW, will book A, pp. 14–16, reel S-2. Little is known of the younger Henry Seiler beyond his marriage in 1796 to Elisabeth Neff at Christ Lutheran Church (Weiser, *Christ Lutheran Church*, 2: 70). She may be the Elizabeth Seiler, widow, of Schaefferstown who died in 1845 (Will of Elizabeth Seiler, Heidelberg Township, Lebanon County, written February 11, 1843, recorded December 1, 1845, LebCoROW, will book C, p. 125). Henry Seiler may also be the fraktur artist who signed his work "H. Seiler" and made at least five birth and baptismal certificates for children born between 1794 and 1808 in the Schaefferstown area as well as West Hanover Township, Dauphin County. Interestingly, this H. Seiler copied motifs from the fraktur of Henrich Otto, whose son, Conrad Otto, married a Barbara Seiler (Earnest and Earnest, *Papers for Birth Dayes*, 2: 696). On Christopher Seiler, see Sowers, *Colonial Taxes, Heidelberg Township*, p. 89; Sowers, *Lebanon County, Direct Tax of 1798*, p. 79; Winterthur Library, Joseph Downs Collection of Manuscripts and Printed Ephemera, Lewis Papers, col. 782, microfilm 2662, TR 75, microfilm 2667, M2, M5; and Egle, *History of the County of Lebanon*, p. 59. Inventory of Christopher Seiler, Swatara Township, Lebanon County, taken November 29, 1822, LebCoROW, inventories reel S-1, pp. 180–82. Christopher Seiler died intestate, and no mention of his son Henry is made in the administrative accounts of Christopher's estate (Administrative accounts of Christopher Seiler, recorded June 28, 1824, LebCoROW, inventories reel S-1, p. 709).

40. Esther Stevens Fraser, "Pennsylvania Bride Boxes and Dower Chests, Part II: County Types of Chests," *Antiques* 8, no. 2 (August 1925): 82. The drawing is now in the collection of the Philadelphia Museum of Art (acc. no. 25-95-2; see Garvan, *Pennsylvania German Collection*, p. 333). John Joseph Stoudt, *Consider the Lilies How They Grow: An Interpretation of the Symbolism of Pennsylvania German Art*, Publications of the Pennsylvania German Folklore Society, vol. 2 (Allentown, Pa.: Schlechter's for the Pennsylvania German Folklore Society, 1937), pp. 291, 293, 295, 296. The Margaret Kern chest is now in the collection of the Winterthur Museum (acc. no. 1959.2804; see Catherine E. Hutchins, ed., *Arts of the Pennsylvania Germans* [Winterthur, Del.: Winterthur Museum, 1983], pl. 13; Fabian, *Pennsylvania-German Decorated Chest*, pp. 157, 196); the Rickert chest is in the collection of the Philadelphia Museum of Art (acc. no. 25-95-1; see Garvan, *Pennsylvania German Collection*, p. 20; Fabian, *Decorated Chest*, p. 194); the 1804 chest was in the collection of Asher J. Odenwelder of Easton, Pa., then in

that of Mr. and Mrs. Donald Wendling; see Fabian, *Pennsylvania-German Decorated Chest*, fig. 236. *Antiques* 45, no. 6 (June 1944): inside front cover. Frances Lichten, *Folk Art of Rural Pennsylvania* (New York: Charles Scribner's Sons, 1946), p. 107, also pp. 95, 216–17.

41. Hornung, *Treasury of American Design*, 2: 703, 719. The description of Otto as a printer is erroneous and stems from confusion of his name on broadsides and blank fraktur certificates now known to have been printed by the Ephrata Cloister for him to infill and decorate. For more on the Ephrata press and printed fraktur, see Stopp, *Printed Birth and Baptismal Certificates*, 2: 98–104. *Pennsylvania Dutch Folk Arts from the Geesey Collection and Others* (Philadelphia: Philadelphia Museum of Art, 1956), p. 12; the Dres chest is in the collection of the Philadelphia Museum of Art (acc. no. 58-110-1; see Garvan, *Pennsylvania German Collection*, p. 23). Shelley, *Fraktur-Writings*, pls. 289–92. Donald L. Shelly, *The Fraktur-Writings or Illuminated Manuscripts of the Pennsylvania Germans*, Publications of the Pennsylvania German Folklore Society, vol. 23 (Allentown, Pa.; Schlecter's, 1961). Fabian, *Pennsylvania-German Decorated Chest*, pp. 157, 196. Fabian also illustrated another painted chest with decoration "based upon Otto" p. 197, fig. 219. The Kern chest was first published by Fraser, "Pennsylvania Bride Boxes and Dower Chests," p. 81; at that time it was owned by collector T. van C. Phillips of Westtown, Chester County, Pa. The feet and base molding were missing when the chest was published and were subsequently replaced. Fabian attributed the Kern chest to Lancaster County, likely because of the applied architectural façade, which is often associated with that county, but genealogical research indicates that Margaret Kern probably lived in Berks County. She may be the Margaret Kern born in 1771 in Alsace Township, Berks County, to Matthias Kern. Another chest with closely related painted decoration bears the name Jacob Hill; he is believed to be the Jacob Hill born in 1752 to Johann Daniel Hill and Anna Catherine Seibert of Windsor Township, Berks County, who married Christina Gortner in 1783 and died in 1823 in Lycoming County, Pa.; the Hill chest sold at Conestoga Auction Company, *Folk Art, Ceramics and Antique Furniture*, Manheim, Pa., June 4–5, 2004, lot 1104. Fabian, *Pennsylvania-German Decorated Chest*, pp. 151, 199. Lita Solis-Cohen, "The Philadelphia Antiques Show," *Maine Antique Digest* (June 2001): D-12.

42. Frederick S. Weiser and Howell J. Heaney, *The Pennsylvania German Fraktur of the Free Library of Philadelphia: An Illustrated Catalogue*, 2 vols., Publications of the Pennsylvania German Society (Breinigsville, Pa.: Pennsylvania German Society, 1976), 1: xxii–xxiii. Strassberger, *Pennsylvania German Pioneers*, 1: 576–81, 2: 673–76. Henrich Otto's father-in-law may be the Jacob Dautrich of Heidelberg Township, Berks County, who died in 1804, leaving a widow, Magdalena, and sons John and Jacob Jr. In 1805 a Jacob and Eva Dauterich had a son Jacob, baptized at Christ Lutheran Church (Weiser, *Christ Lutheran Church*, 1: 112). The Ottos' eldest child, George, was born September 25, 1757, and died March 5, 1813; he married Christina Krebs (1772–1844) and is listed in the 1790 census as a resident of Mahoney Township, Northumberland County. Shortly after 1800 George Otto moved to Butler County, where he died and was buried at St. John's Lutheran Church in Cranberry Township. A David Otto, possibly another son, died in 1803 in Butler County. In 1758 a daughter (probably Margaret) was baptized at the Muddy Creek Reformed Church near Ephrata. In 1759 daughter Anna Maria was baptized at the Bethany (Little Cocalico) Reformed Church near Ephrata. Son William (1761–1841) was baptized at Christ Lutheran Church in Stouchsburg. In 1766 twins Johann Heinrich and Anna Barbara were baptized at the Cocalico Reformed Church; a printed certificate decorated by Henrich Otto for Anna Barbara's baptism survives (for an illustration, see Shelley, *Fraktur-Writings*, pl. 238). Other children include Jacob (ca. 1762–ca. 1825), Conrad (ca. 1770–1857), Johann C. Otto (1770–1854), and Daniel (ca. 1770–ca. 1820). On the Otto genealogy, see Earnest and Earnest, *Papers for Birth Dayes*, 2: 594–95; and Trudy E. Gilgenast, *Pennsylvania German Broadsides: A Reflection of Daily Life, 1741–1890* (Wilmington, Del.: Cedar Tree Books, 2009), p. xix. The two latest examples of fraktur that have been attributed to Henrich Otto are a birth and baptismal certificate for Barbara Schuder, born November 5, 1797, in Mahoney Township, Northumberland County (*Made in Pennsylvania: A Folk Art Tradition* [Greensburg, Pa.: Westmoreland Museum of American Art, 2007], p. 27), and a bookplate for Johannes Latscha dated April 7, 1799. These are very similar to one another and may be his work but differ somewhat from signed examples, for example, in the style of the pomegranate motif and the parrots, which are much more slender than his typical birds. No Ottos are listed in the Northumberland County probate records for the period 1772–1813 (Charles A. Fisher, *Wills and Administrations of Northumberland County, Pennsylvania* [Baltimore, Pa.: Genealogical Publishing Co., 1974]).

43. The Merkie certificate is in the collection of the Free Library of Philadelphia (Weiser and Heaney, *The Pennsylvania German Fraktur of the Free Library*, 2: fig. 214). The comet broadside was sold at Pook & Pook, *Fraktur and Related Works on Paper: The Pioneer Collection of Dr. and Mrs. Donald A. Shelley*, Downingtown, Pa., October 8, 2004, lot 23; see also Shelley, *Fraktur-Writings*, pl. 65. The Beck bookplate is in the collection of the Schwenkfelder Library and Heritage Center, Pennsburg, Pa., and is pictured in John Joseph Stoudt, *Early Pennsylvania Arts and Crafts* (New York: A. S. Barnes and Company, 1964), p. 340, fig. 336. Other certificates signed by Otto include ones made for Johannes Fastnacht, born June 26, 1775, in Earl Township, Lancaster County (Annette Kunselman Burgert, *Eighteenth Century Emigrants from German-Speaking Lands to North America* [Birdsboro, Pa.: Pennsylvania German Society, 1985], frontispiece); Eva Maria Kapp, born in 1777 to Michael and Maria Kapp of Heidelberg Township (Sotheby's, *Important Frakturs, Embroidered Pictures, Theorem Paintings, and Cutwork Pictures from the Collection of Edgar William and Bernice Chrysler Garbisch*, New York, January 23–24, 1974, lot 29); Anna Margretha Huwer (Huber), born in 1715 in Germany, immigrated to Lancaster County, and married Thomas Schirz in 1740 (Pook & Pook, *Fraktur and Related Works on Paper*, lot 63); Magdalena Nasz (b. 1751) of Cocalico Township, Lancaster County; and Michael Senger (b. 1788), son of Michael and Johanna Senger (Shelley, *Fraktur-Writings*, pls. 186, 187).

44. The church records give Barbara's date of birth as March 30, 1759, but her tombstone says 1758. *Records of Pastoral Acts at Trinity Evangelical Lutheran Church, New Holland, Lancaster County, Pennsylvania, 1730–1799*, Sources and Documents of the Pennsylvania Germans, vol. 2, translated and edited by Glenn P. Schwalm and Frederick S. Weiser (Breinigsville, Pa.: Pennsylvania German Society, 1977), p. 59. Frederick Gless died intestate in 1789.

45. The camel motif is unknown on any other Pennsylvania German furniture but does appear on at least one fraktur (Frederick S. Weiser, *The Gift Is Small, the Love Is Great* [York, Pa.: York Graphic Services, 1994], p. 69).

46. The Schorck chest was sold at Horst Auction Center, Ephrata, Pa., May 25–26, 2001, lot 1036. A possible fourth related chest was sold at Pennypacker Auction Centre, Reading, Pa., October 21, 1968, lot 511. The photograph of this chest in the auction catalogue is dark, but a central wreath (similar to that on the Miller chest) encircling a pair of crowns, resembling those on Henrich Otto's fraktur, is visible. On Schorck's marriage, see Irish, *Pennsylvania German Marriages*, p. 60. George David Schorck and Susanna Sheaffer (daughter of Philip Sheaffer) had three children: Johannes (b. 1775), Susanna (b. 1776), and David (1781–1861) (Sherk, *The Sherk Family*, pp. 306–7). Inventory of George David Schorck ("David Shirk"), Lebanon, Lancaster (now Lebanon) County, taken September 15, 1783, LanCHS. The painted schrank was advertised by Joe Kindig Jr. & Son in *Antiques*, 58, no. 5 (November 1950): inside front cover.

47. Capital Roman letters also appear on a birth and baptismal certificate made and signed by Otto for Magdalena Nasz, born in 1751 in Cocalico Township, in the words ANNO, AMERICA, and PENSILVANIA. For an illustration, see Shelley, *Fraktur-Writings*, pl. 186.

48. Karl Münch (1769–1833) emigrated from Germany in 1798. He served briefly as schoolmaster in Schaefferstown, then moved to Rehrersburg, Berks County, before relocating to the Lykens Valley of Northumberland County in 1804. While in Schaefferstown he executed an elaborate religious text with household interior scene for Elisabeth Huston in 1799 (for an illustration, see Cooper and Minardi, *Paint, Pattern & People*, p. 62; on Münch, see Earnest and Earnest, *Papers for Birth Dayes*, 2: 566–68). Georg Friedrich Rick made and signed a birth and baptismal certificate in 1771 for Maria Catharina Mayer (b. 1759) of Heidelberg Township, on which he identified himself as schoolmaster of Millbach (Earnest and Earnest, *Papers for Birth Dayes*, 2: 644). On Friedrich Speyer, see ibid., 2: 722–25. Dulheurer's move to Baltimore is discussed in his autobiography. He established a German-language newspaper there, but this venture appears to have been unsuccessful. Dulheurer was also a religious zealot and itinerant preacher (Earnest and Earnest, *Papers for Birth Dayes*, 1: 201–4). Although Dulheuer's handwriting was sophisticated, a comparison of his letters and numerals shows little relation to those on the chests. On Schmidt, see Weiser, *The Account Book of Christ Lutheran Church*, pp. 64–65; and Strassberger, *Pennsylvania German Pioneers*, 1: 690, 2: 783.

49. On Eichholtz, see Thomas R. Ryan, ed., *The Worlds of Jacob Eichholtz: Portrait Painter of the Early Republic* (Lancaster, Pa.: Lancaster County Historical Society, 2003), pp. 39–40. On Bachman, see Benno M. Forman, "German Influences in Pennsylvania Furniture," in Hutchins, ed., *Arts of the Pennsylvania Germans*, p. 134. On Overholt, see Keyser, Neff, and Weiser, *The Accounts of Two Pennsylvania German Furniture Makers*, pp. 5, 10, 150. Monroe

Fabian erroneously stated that "Peter Rank of Lebanon County, who signed chests he had painted with floral decorations, also mentions in his account book that he painted such a chest" (Fabian, *Pennsylvania-German Decorated Chest*, p. 57). No signed chests by Peter Ranck's hand are known, nor does any reference to floral decoration appear in his account book. Chests with floral decoration by his relative Johannes Ranck are known.

50. Conrad Otto's son Peter is also thought to have made fraktur (Earnest and Earnest, *Papers for Birth Dayes*, 2: 587, 594–95, 601–2; also *Genealogical and Biographical Annals of Northumberland County, Pennsylvania* [Chicago: J. L. Floyd, 1911], pp. 537–40, 894).

51. Irish, *Pennsylvania German Marriages*, p. 222. On Jacob Otto, see Earnest and Earnest, *Papers for Birth Dayes*, 2: 593. The Maria Breneise certificate is in the collection of the Philadelphia Museum of Art (acc. no. 28-10-91; see Garvan, *Pennsylvania German Collection*, p. 298). The Danner certificate was sold at Sotheby's, *Important Americana from the Collection of Mr. and Mrs. James O. Keene*, New York, January 16, 1997, lot 119; it is illustrated in *American Folk Arts from the Collection of Ruth and James O. Keene* (Detroit: Detroit Institute of Arts, 1960), p. 38.

52. Commissioners Orders, LanCHS, 1822. Inventory of John Otto, West Hempfield Township, Lancaster County, taken January 13, 1824, LanCHS. The Johannes Flori chest was sold at Ziegler Auction Company, Hummelstown, Pa., February 26, 2011; the inscription is similar to that on other chests, but the design of three arched-head panels on the front and a grain-painted ground are unlike elements of any of the other chests and are thought to have been heavily restored. The Rahel Hummer chest is illustrated in Fabian, *Decorated Chest*, fig. 136; she is likely the daughter of John Hummer (d. 1810) of Rapho Township, a Dunkard. The Abraham Brubacher chest was sold at Pook & Pook, *The Americana Collection of Richard and Rosemarie Machmer*, Downingtown, Pa., October 24–25, 2008, lot 119; see also Fabian, *Pennsylvania-German Decorated Chest*, fig. 135. He is likely the Abraham Brubacher (1765–1859), son of Peter Brubacher (1725–1811), a Mennonite farmer and close neighbor of John Flory. The Jacob Dres chest is in the collection of the Philadelphia Museum of Art (acc. no. 58-110-1; see Garvan, *Pennsylvania German Collection*, p. 23; also Fabian, *Pennsylvania-German Decorated Chest*, fig. 225). He is likely the Jacob Dres/Trace, born in the late 1760s, who lived in Mount Joy Township; his family is said to have come from Berks County. Rahel Friedrich (1776–1804) was the daughter of John Friedrich and Juliana Bühler, who were members of the Donegal Moravian congregation in Mount Joy Township; she married Michael Schetterle, a millwright, in 1800 at Trinity Lutheran Church, Lancaster, and died in 1804 after the birth of their second child. Daniel Rickert (1776–1834) was born in Manor Township, Lancaster County; his father, Leonard Rickert, moved to Rapho Township in the late 1780s. Daniel married Magdalena Göpfert in 1802, and in 1809 they joined the Lititz Moravian congregation. The Pedrus Schneider chest is illustrated in *American Folk Arts from the Collection of Ruth and James O. Keene*, p. 38; he is likely Peter Snyder (1765–1823), son of Mennonite farmer and miller Jacob Snyder (1727–1794) and Maria Hershey (1730–1798), who lived in Rapho Township and were close neighbors of John Flory. Peter married Mary Longenecker (1778–1824). Abraham Gisch (ca. 1775–1855) married Franey Eshleman; he was a blacksmith, followed the Dunkard faith, and lived in Rapho Township. Anna Herr's identity is uncertain, as there were several Herr families in Rapho and Mount Joy Townships in the late 1700s. Susanna Badrof is likely Susanna Barbara Batruff (1772–ca. 1860), daughter of Johann Andreas Batruff/Bartruff (1724–1795), who immigrated in 1752, and Christina Sophia Klein (1738–1778). Susanna was baptized in 1772 at Zion Lutheran Church, Manheim; in 1793 she married Heinrich Sarber (1769–1842) and lived in Manheim, where her father operated a store and tavern. The Susanna Badrof chest is owned by the Reading Public Museum. The Bastian Keller chest was sold at Pennypacker Auction Centre, Reading, Pa., May 13, 1975, lot 279; he was the son of Sebastian Keller Sr. (1729–1808) and his first wife, Rosina, who were householders at Ephrata Cloister. Sebastian Sr. married Catherine Hummer by 1790 and moved to Rapho Township, where Sebastian Jr. owned a one-hundred-acre farm and two-storey log house. Christian Lang is likely the son of Christian Lang Sr. who appears in the 1790 census in Rapho Township as a neighbor of Leonard Rickert and was likely Mennonite. Jacob Ober was likely Jacob Ober III (ca. 1780–ca. 1824), son of Jacob Ober Jr. (1729–1804) and Elisabeth Stauffer of Rapho Township. The Jacob Ober chest was sold at Christie's, *American Furniture, Silver, Prints, Scrimshaw, and Folk Art*, New York, January 16–17, 2003, lot 289. Veronica Ober (1784–1856) was the daughter of Henry Ober (1740–1822) and Veronica Stauffer (b. 1742); her father was a Mennonite farmer in Rapho Township. She married Joseph Shenk (1779–1857) of Heidelberg Township, son of John Shenk and his first wife, Barbara Hershey (his second wife, Maria Stohler, owned the chest illustrated

in fig. 35). The Barbara Stauffer chest was offered at Christie's, *Important American Furniture, Folk Art, Silver and Prints*, New York, January 20–21, 2005, lot 514; Barbara was the daughter of Jacob Stauffer (1745–1798) and a first cousin of Veronica Ober. The author thanks Clarke Hess and Jean Woods for their help with this genealogical information. Two miniature chests with related decoration, one with a pair of white horses, are also known.

53. The initials "JF" appear on chests made for Abraham Brubacher, Jacob Dres, Pedrus Schneider, and Barbara Stauffer, while the initials "Jo Fl" are found on the chest made for Rahel Hummer. (Fabian, *Pennsylvania-German Decorated Chest*, pp. 64, 154–56, 225). Both John Florys are descended from the same man, Joseph Flory (1682–1741), a French Huguenot who emigrated from Germany in 1733. Joseph's son John (1718–1781) was the father of the elder cousin John Flory (1754–1831), who married Susanna Baumann (as documented by a birth and baptismal certificate made for their daughter Hannah [b. 1800] that was sold at Pook & Pook, *Fraktur and Related Works on Papers*, lot 81). The younger cousin John Flory (1767–1836) descended from Joseph's son Joseph Jr. (1714–1781), who had a son David (1742–1795), who in turn had a son John (1767–1836) (Walter Q. Bunderman, comp., *Flory, Flora, Fleury Family History* [Myerstown, Pa.: Lebanon County Flory Reunion Organization, 1948], pp. 93, 137–38). Inventory of John Flory Sr., Rapho Township, Lancaster County, taken April 12, 1836, LanCHS.

54. Rahel Friedrich's aunt, who was also named Rahel Friedrich (1750–1792), married Frederick Stohler (1725–1815). He was the brother of Maria Stohler's father, Johannes Stohler (1714–1785). With thanks to Clarke Hess for this information. The Rahel Friedrich chest was formerly owned by Art Feeman, an antiques dealer who lived in Jonestown, Lebanon County (Fabian, *Pennsylvania-German Decorated Chest*, fig. 137). F. Edward Wright, *Abstracts of Lancaster County Pennsylvania Wills, 1786–1820* (Westminster, Md.: Family Line Publications, 1995), p. 213. Inventory of Jacob Stauffer, Rapho Township, Lancaster County, taken January 14, 1800, LanCHS.

55. On William Otto, see Earnest and Earnest, *Papers for Birth Dayes*, 2: 603–4; Weiser, *Christ Lutheran Church*, 2: 60; Robert M. Kline and Frederick S. Weiser, "Fraktur-Fest," *Der Reggeboge* 4, nos. 3–4 (September–December 1970): 12; and Henry M. Reed, *Decorated Furniture of the Mahantongo Valley* (Lewisburg, Pa.: Center Gallery of Bucknell University, 1987), pp. 55–63, 40. The dream tradition was noted in a letter from a descendant of William Otto to Frederick S. Weiser (Winterthur Library, Joseph Downs Collection of Manuscripts and Printed Ephemera, Frederick S. Weiser Papers, col. 876, box 18, folder 2). It was also recounted in the 1940s to Don Yoder by James M. Schrope (1863–1957) of Hegins; (Reed, *Decorated Furniture*, p. 73). Inventory of William Otto, Lower Mahantongo Township, Schuylkill County, filed June 14, 1841; vendue lists of William Otto, dated July 3, 1841, and November 6, 1841; photocopies are in the Winterthur Library, Joseph Downs Collection of Manuscripts and Printed Ephemera, Frederick S. Weiser Papers, col. 876, box 18, folder 2.

56. For other examples of William Otto's fraktur, see John Joseph Stoudt, *Sunbonnets and Shoofly Pies: A Pennsylvania Dutch Cultural History* (New York: A. S. Barnes, 1973), pp. 128–29; this fraktur sold at Pennypacker Auction Centre, Reading, Pa., May 23, 1977, lot 321; also a fraktur in the collection of the Reading Public Museum, dated 1837, for Mary Otto, daughter of Peter Otto, illustrated in *The Reading Public Museum and Art Gallery: Selections from the Permanent Collection* (Reading, Pa.: Reading Public Museum and Art Gallery, 1986), p. 123; one for Lidia Otto, daughter of David Otto, dated 1838, sold at Sotheby's, *The Collection of Dr. and Mrs. Henry P. Deyerle*, lot 359, and one for Sarah Kunzleman dated 1840, Sotheby's, *The American Heritage Auction of Americana*, New York, January 27–30, 1982, lot 896. Although Anna Maria Gehres has been identified in other sources as Otto's niece or great-niece, the more likely case is that she was his daughter and he made the chest shortly after her marriage to George Gehres. (Reed, *Decorated Furniture*, pp. 25–27, 40; also Fabian, *Pennsylvania-German Decorated Chest*, pp. 172–73). The Gehres chest is in the collection of the National Museum of American History, Smithsonian Institution; see also Fabian, *Decorated Chest*, p. 173. The Kessler chest is illustrated in ibid., p. 172; it was sold at Pook & Pook, *Fine Art and Period Antiques*, Downingtown, Pa., April 23–24, 2010, lot 322. It was formerly in the collection of George Horace Lorimer (Parke-Bernet Galleries, *Fine American and English Furniture Collected by the Late George Horace Lorimer*, New York, part 2, October 24–28, 1944, lot 758). The Jonathan Otto chest of drawers was formerly in the collection of Adele Earnest; (Reed, *Decorated Furniture*, p. 25). Few other groups of painted chests have inscriptions with a location; one with black unicorns and lions is from Bern Township, Berks County (Patricia J. Keller, "Black-Uni-

corn Chests of Berks County, Pennsylvania," *Antiques* 140, no. 4 [October 1991]: 592–603). Another group is from the vicinity of Franklin Township, Adams County; for an example, see Pook & Pook, *Period Furniture, Fine Art and Accessories*, Downingtown, Pa., January 15, 2011, lot 47. William Gehres was the son of Anna Maria Otto and George Gehres; his fraktur certificate is illustrated in Peter H. Tillou, *Nineteenth-Century Folk Paintings: Our Spirited National Heritage; Works of Art from the Collection of Mr. and Mrs. Peter Tillou* (Storrs, Conn.: University of Connecticut, 1973), pl. 26; it was sold at Sotheby's, *American Folk Art from the Collection of Peter Tillou*, New York, October 26, 1985, lot 17. The maker is unknown (Earnest and Earnest, *Papers for Birth Dayes*, 1: 50).

57. On Daniel Otto, see Frederick S. Weiser and Bryding Adams Henley, "Daniel Otto: the 'Flat Tulip' Artist," *Antiques* 130, no. 3 (September 1986): 504–9; Earnest and Earnest, *Papers for Birth Dayes*, 2: 588–92.

58. A related chest with a crown, formerly in the Earl and Ada Robacker collection, is illustrated in Fabian, *Pennsylvania-German Decorated Chest*, fig. 166. A chest nearly identical to the one at the Barnes Foundation was sold at Christie's, *The John Gordon Collection of Folk Americana*, New York, January 15 and 19, 1999, lot 237. The chest with lions and eagle was sold at Sotheby's, *The American Folk Art Collection of Don and Faye Walters*, New York, October 25, 1986, lot 101. The chest with lion on the end panel is pictured in Fabian, *Pennsylvania-German Decorated Chest*, pp. 158–59; and *The Olde Hope Collection: A Catalogue of American Antiques* 6 (Summer 2008): 24–25. Another chest likely painted by the same hand with unicorns on the front has a lion on one end; it was sold at Conestoga Auction Company, *The Personal Collection of Selma and Ray Mead Formerly of York, Pa.*, Manheim, Pa., October 4, 2003, lot 343. On Daniel Otto's children, see Winterthur Library, Joseph Downs Collection of Manuscripts and Printed Ephemera, Frederick S. Weiser Papers, col. 876, box 22, folder 6, "Daniel Otto"; extracts from Tilden, *History of Stephenson County* (1880) and *Portrait and Biography Album of Stephenson County* (1888), p. 314.

59. On Johannes Haas, see Reed, *Decorated Furniture*, p. 72. On Abraham Latschaw and Joseph Lehn, see Clarke Hess, *Mennonite Arts* (Atglen, Pa.: Schiffer Publishing, 2002), pp. 59–61, 69–72. On Heydrich, see Dennis K. Moyer, *Fraktur Writings and Folk Art Drawings of the Schwenkfelder Library Collection*, Publications of the Pennsylvania German Society, vol. 31 (Kutztown, Pa.: Pennsylvania German Society, 1997), pp. 142–47. A small painted box has been attributed to Mennonite fraktur artist David Kulp (1777–1834) of Bucks County, based on the close relationship of the decoration to his fraktur, but there are doubts about its authenticity (Cory M. Amsler, *Bucks County Fraktur*, Publications of the Pennsylvania German Society, vol. 33 [Kutztown, Pa.: Pennsylvania German Society, 1999], pp. 151–65, 270–74).

60. Jacob Morry/Mori (1727–1793) lived in Upper Saucon Township, Lehigh County. A schrank with brass-inlaid decoration was made for his son Peter Mori (d. 1828) in 1791; for an illustration, see Cooper and Minardi, *Paint, Pattern & People*, p. 52. The maker of the fraktur in the clock door is unknown, but the designs show the influence of Mennonite schoolmaster Andreas Kolb (1749–1811), who taught school in southern Lehigh County from the late 1780s to 1804 (Mary Jane Lederach Hershey, "Andreas Kolb, 1749–1811," *Mennonite Quarterly Review* 61 [April 1987]: 121–201). The Rose clock was exhibited by antiques dealer Kelly Kinzle at the 2009 Philadelphia Antiques Show; Philip H. Bradley Co. sold the desk.

61. Frances Lichten was the first scholar to compare Mahantongo furniture and fraktur (Lichten, *Folk Art of Rural Pennsylvania*, p. 107; also Shelley, *Fraktur-Writings*, figs. 291, 292). On Mahantongo furniture, see Philip D. Zimmerman, "Mahantongo Blanket Chests," *Antiques* 162, no. 4 (October 2002): 160–69; Reed, *Decorated Furniture*, pp. 55–63; Frederick S. Weiser and Mary Hammond Sullivan, "Decorated Furniture of the Schwaben Creek Valley," in *Ebbes fer Alle-Ebber, Ebbes fer Dich; Something for Everyone, Something for You*, Publications of the Pennsylvania German Society, vol. 14 (Breinigsville, Pa.: Pennsylvania German Society, 1980), pp. 354–56, 384–90; also Frederick S. Weiser and Mary Hammond Sullivan, "Decorated Furniture of the Mahantango Valley," *Antiques* 103, no. 5 (May 1973): 932–39. For an illustration of the Reynolds painting, see Weiser and Sullivan, " Decorated Furniture of the Schwaben Creek Valley," pp. 386–87.

62. When the Michael Braun chest was published in Reed, *Decorated Furniture*, p. 58, its whereabouts were unknown and its date read as "1801," a source of puzzlement since Michael Braun was not born until 1807. Recent examination determined that the original date was 1831, and the unusual melon-shape ball feet were replacements. On Schuller, see Reed, *Decorated Furniture*, pp. 29, 34–35, 45, 49, 58–61; Lisa M. Minardi, "Fraktur: Art and Artifact; A Study

of the Fraktur Collection of the Berman Museum of Art at Ursinus College" (Distinguished honors thesis, Ursinus College, 2004), p. 78; also Shoemaker, *Check List of Pennsylvania Dutch Printed Taufscheins*, p. 48; and Earnest and Earnest, *Papers for Birth Dayes*, 2: 682–84. The Andreas Braun chest is privately owned; the Peter Braun chest is in the collection of the Dietrich American Foundation; the Rebecca Braun kitchen cupboard is at the Barnes Foundation; the 1830 Concortia cupboard is at the Philadelphia Museum of Art (acc. no. 54-85-32a, b; see Garvan, *Pennsylvania German Collection*, p. 31). On Wiestling, see Stopp, *Printed Birth and Baptismal Certificates*, 3: 10, 24.

63. This chest, described as "Chest with Birds, Tulips and Adam and Eve," was advertised by A. H. Rice in 1926, along with other Mahantongo furniture, in *Antiques* 10, no. 5 (November 1926): 426. The chest is inscribed on the underside of the lid: "Reuben J. Carter," who was likely a later owner. Only one other paint-decorated chest with an image of Adam and Eve is known. On Adam and Eve broadsides, see Don Yoder, *The Pennsylvania German Broadside: A History and Guide* (University Park, Pa.: Pennsylvania State University Press, 2005), p. 294; Gilgenast, *Pennsylvania German Broadsides: A Reflection of Daily Life*, pp. 217–24; and Russell Earnest and Corinne Earnest, *Flying Leaves and One-Sheets: Pennsylvania German Broadsides, Fraktur, and Their Printers* (New Castle, Del.: Oak Knoll Books, 2005), pp. 200–203.

64. On immigrant chests, see Cooper and Minardi, *Paint, Pattern & People*, p. 29. On the acquisition of chests, see Jeanette Lasansky, *A Good Start: The Aussteier or Dowry* (Lewisburg, Pa.: Oral Traditions Project of the Union County Historical Society, 1990). A chest dated 1789 and inscribed with the name Maria Eitenyer was actually made in 1835; the date 1789 was the year of her birth (Cooper and Minardi, *Paint, Pattern & People*, pp. 146–47).

65. Stoudt, *Consider the Lilies How They Grow*, p. 31. Two identical chests, both dated 1796 and painted with black unicorns and lions, were made for Adam Minnich and Maria Grim of Bern Township, Berks County (Cooper and Minardi, *Paint, Pattern & People*, pp. 144–46; and Garvan, *Pennsylvania German Collection*, 23). Lichten, *Folk Art of Rural Pennsylvania*, pp. 84–85.

66. William T. Parsons, "Schwenkfelder Indentures, 1754–1846," in *Schwenkfelders in America: Papers Presented at the Colloquium on Schwenkfeld and the Schwenkfelders*, edited by Peter C. Erb (Pennsburg, Pa.: Schwenkfelder Library, 1987), p. 51. Henry S. Dotterer, "The Docket of Michael Croll, Justice of the Peace," in *The Perkiomen Region, Past and Present* (Philadelphia: Perkiomen Publishing Co., 1895), 1: 39–45, cited in Martha B. Kriebel, "Women Servants and Family Life in Early America," *Pennsylvania Folklife* 28, no. 1 (Autumn 1978): 4. William T. Parsons and Phyllis Vibbard Parsons, "'Be it Remembered that These Indentured Servants and Apprentices,'" *Pennsylvania Folklife* 28, no. 1 (Autumn 1978): 14, 15, 22, 23.

67. Fraser, "Pennsylvania Bride Boxes and Dower Chests," pp. 79–84. Examples of localized chest studies include Charles Hummel and Helen Cain, "The Carnation Chests: New Discoveries in Pennsylvania-German Art," *Antiques* 122, no. 3 (September 1982): 552–57; Keller, "Black-Unicorn Chests"; and Wendy A. Cooper, Patricia Edmonson, and Lisa M. Minardi, "The Compass Artist of Lancaster County," in *American Furniture*, edited by Luke Beckerdite (Lebanon, N.H.: University Press of New England for the Chipstone Foundation, 2009), pp. 62–87. Don Yoder, in Reed, *Decorated Furniture*, p. 71.

Figure 1   Map of Southeastern Pennsylvania,
showing bounderies of Maryland, Delaware, and
New Jersey. (Artwork, Nichole Drgan.)

Wendy A. Cooper and Mark Anderson

The Nottingham School of Furniture

▼ F O R D E C A D E S furniture collectors and dealers have used the word "Octoraro" to describe several distinctive groups of furniture made in southern Chester County, Pennsylvania, and northern Cecil County, Maryland, in the vicinity of the Octoraro Creek. The broad eastern branch of this creek forms the boundary between southern Chester County and Lancaster County, Pennsylvania, continuing south into Maryland (fig. 1). One group, comprising various case forms, is distinguished by the use of ogee feet with bracket cusps that scroll around to form a circle or stop just short of a circle. Another group, largely consisting of high chests, has short cabriole legs dovetailed to battens that attach to the case bottom with large wooden screws. However, to date this latter group cannot be firmly associated with the Nottingham area through any well-documented examples. Research by the authors has identified many additional structural and stylistic features used by cabinetmakers and house joiners working in this area, which was settled primarily by English Quakers and Scots-Irish Presbyterians.[1]

Early Settlement

Part of William Penn's original land grant, the southernmost portion of Chester County was noted by the late seventeenth century for its valuable natural resources. Soils were fertile, timber of all sorts was abundant, and numerous rivers and creeks provided transportation and power for saw mills, gristmills, and other industrial enterprises. However, in 1680 Charles Calvert, the third Lord Baltimore, gave his nephew George Talbot "Susquehanna Manor," a thirty-two-thousand-acre tract that extended from the Susquehanna River to the Delaware River and included a portion of southern Chester County, which gave rise to disputes that continued for the next eighty years.

In early 1701 a small group of Quakers from the settlement of New Castle on the Delaware River (then part of Penn's lands) moved to the rich watershed of the Octoraro Creek and the North East River. At a meeting of the Commissioners of Property in Philadelphia, Cornelius Emerson represented "twenty families, chiefly of the county of Chester" in requesting twenty thousand acres "to make a Settlmt. on a tract of land about half-way between Delaware and Susquehannough, . . . on Otteraroe river." The following year the commissioners granted the families an eighteen-thousand-acre tract "between the main branch of the North East river and Octorara creek." The tract was quickly surveyed and divided into thirty-seven parcels, each containing a little less than five hundred acres. Those desiring to

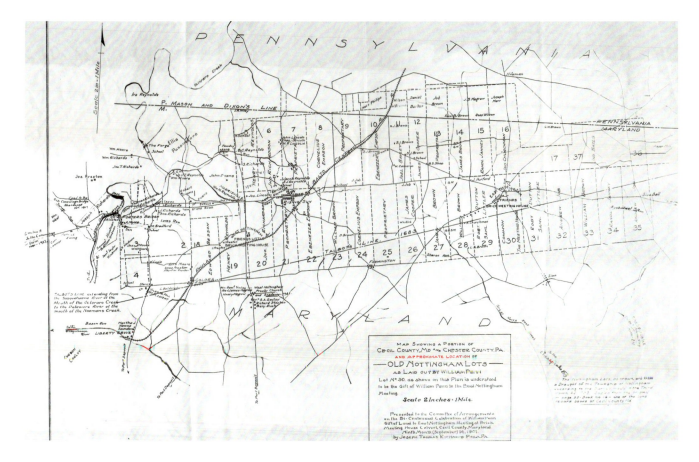

Figure 2 1901 reproduction of "A Draught of the Township of Nottingham according to a Survey made thereof in the third Month AD 1702." (Courtesy, Chester County Historical Society.)

purchase land drew lots, which resulted in the entire area being called Nottingham Lots (after Penn's birthplace) (fig. 2). This grant was a clever move on the part of the commissioners, for it secured the southern boundary of Pennsylvania for more than sixty years. Both Quakers and Scots-Irish Presbyterians were encouraged to settle there. By 1709 the Quakers built their first meetinghouse, presumably of logs. In 1724 that structure was replaced with a brick meetinghouse that became known as the Brick Meeting in East Nottingham Township. The same year the New Castle Presbytery directed two pastors to serve the Nottingham community, thus accommodating the Scots-Irish settlers. Among the first families who settled there were Browns, Englands, Chandlees, Churchmans, Haineses, Gatchels, and Kirks.[2]

Between 1701 and the early 1760s the boundary between Pennsylvania and Maryland was constantly in dispute, which resulted in angry battles and occasional bloodshed among the inhabitants. It was not until 1763 that the proprietors of both colonies petitioned the Royal Astronomer at Greenwich, England, for help with a new survey. Anglican Charles Mason (1738–1786) and Quaker Jeremiah Dixon (1733–1779) arrived in America on November of that year and spent fifty-eight months establishing boundaries between Pennsylvania, Delaware, Maryland, and Virginia. Although the line they drew determined that approximately 16,700 acres of the Nottingham Lots were in northern Maryland, the inhabitants were culturally and religiously more closely linked to Philadelphia than to any other commercial or style center. Some of the objects discussed in this article were undoubtedly made in Cecil County, Maryland, but most craftsmen from the Nottingham area drew their inspiration from Philadelphia styles during the eighteenth and early nineteenth centuries.[3]

Seminal Clockmaking and Cabinetmaking Traditions

The sophistication of furniture made in the Nottingham area in the second half of the eighteenth century is best understood against the backdrop of earlier craftsmanship. Members of the Chandlee family of clockmakers were among the earliest artisans to settle on the Nottingham Lots. Benjamin Chandlee (1685–1745) emigrated from County Kildare, Ireland, in 1702, apprenticed with Philadelphia watchmaker Abel Cottey, and married his master's daughter Sarah in 1710. Following Abel's death in 1712, Benjamin, Sarah, and her mother, Mary, moved to Nottingham Lot number fifteen, which Cottey had purchased in 1706. Chandlee trained his fifth child, Benjamin Jr. (1723–1791), in the clock and instrument making trade, and Benjamin Jr. worked with his father until 1741, when Benjamin Sr. and his wife sold their property and moved to Wilmington, Delaware. At that date Benjamin Jr. and his brothers, Cottey and William, moved to Nottingham Lot number thirty, which their grandfather had purchased in 1703.[4]

Although none of the artisans who made cases for Chandlee movements before the late 1780s has been identified, several pieces of furniture can be attributed to early Nottingham makers. A spice box with line-and-berry inlay and distinctive herringbone banding is attributed to the shop of Thomas Coulson (1703–1763), who emigrated from Derbyshire, England, probably before his marriage to Mary Wiley in 1725 (fig. 3). The box

Figure 3   Spice box, attributed to the shop of Thomas Coulson (1703–1763) and possibly to John Coulson (1737–1812), Nottingham area, Chester County, Pennsylvania, 1740–1750. Walnut and red cedar, sumac, and holly inlay with white oak. H. 19¾", W. 16¼", D. 11". (Private collection; photo, Laszlo Bodo.)

descended in the Hartshorn (Hartshorne) family of West Nottingham and bears the partial signature of Coulson's son John (1737–1812). When Thomas died in 1763, he left John all his "Utensils of Husbandry," two horses, two cows, and half of his joiner's tools.[5]

Two desks attributed to Scots-Irish cabinetmaker Hugh Alexander

Figure 4 Desk attributed to Hugh Alexander
(1724–1777), Nottingham area, Chester County,
Pennsylvania, or Cecil County, Maryland,
1745–1760. Walnut and red cedar, maple, holly
and sumac inlay, with chestnut, tulip poplar,
white cedar. H. 45¾", W. 39⅛", D. 22⅛". (Courtesy, Winterthur Museum; photo, Laszlo Bodo.)
The sides of the case extend down to form supports for the foot faces. This feature occurs on
later desks from the Nottingham area (see figs. 36
and 37).

(1724–1777) also attest to the high level of workmanship available in the Nottingham area (fig. 4). These pieces have complex interiors with numerous
secret drawers and line-and-berry inlay and herringbone banding on the exterior drawers. In October 1757 a man named James Brown bound his son
William to Alexander for eighteen months "to learn the Arts, Trades or Mys-
teries of a Carpenter & Wheel Wright." Since Brown was one of the most
common names in Nottingham, it is difficult to determine exactly who these
men were. A plain walnut desk with an interior similar to the two attributed
to Alexander is inscribed "James Brown" in chalk on the bottom of a valance
drawer, but it is unknown whether this James was a maker or an owner, or
possibly the father of Alexander's apprentice William Brown (fig. 5). The
cleverly concealed drawer in the medial molding of this desk is consistent
with Nottingham makers' penchant for hidden and unusual drawers.[6]

Figure 5 Desk, probably Nottingham area, Chester County, Pennsylvania, or Cecil County, Maryland, 1740–1760. Walnut with tulip poplar. H. 41⅜", W. 40", D. 20⅜". (Private collection; photo, Gavin Ashworth.) A unique feature of this desk is the shallow secret drawer concealed by the medial molding above the small upper drawers.

Architectural Contexts and Connections

Architecture in the Nottingham area was strongly influenced by Philadelphia styles. By the second quarter of the eighteenth century, stone and brick had replaced logs as the preferred building materials. Architectural features like glazed brick dates, date stones, pent roofs, and second-storey doors and balconies became hallmarks of sophistication. Among the most aspiring examples of extant early Nottingham architecture are houses built by Quakers William Knight (1745), Mercer Brown (1746), Jeremiah Brown (1757), and John (1745) and George Churchman (1785) (fig. 6). The interior woodwork and built-in furniture in all these houses has precedent in classical architecture, but local characteristics are apparent in the form and detail of paneled doors, stair brackets, keystones, and moldings.[7]

The three-bay stone house of Isaac and Mary Haines is distinguished by

Figure 6   Exterior of the John and George Churchman House, Rising Sun, Cecil County, Maryland, 1745 and 1785. (Photo, Laszlo Bodo.) The three-bay stone addition was added to the west side in 1785.

its deep, pent eaves and a 1774 date stone with two intertwined hearts and the initials "I H M" (fig. 7). The built-in cupboard in the main parlor has a distinctive keystone-shaped upper panel, a local variant on an arch-headed tombstone panel (fig. 8). The proportions of the cupboard are also unusual, owing to the upper section being almost twice as high as the lower—a proportional arrangement similar to that on certain freestanding furniture

Figure 7   Detail of the date stone on the Isaac and Mary Haines House, Rising Sun, Cecil County, Maryland, 1774. (Photo, Laszlo Bodo.)

Figure 8   Detail of a built-in cupboard in the Isaac and Mary Haines House, Rising Sun, Cecil County, Maryland, 1774. (Photo, Laszlo Bodo.)

Figure 9 Corner cupboard, Nottingham area, Chester County, Pennsylvania, or Cecil County, Maryland, 1770–1800. (Courtesy, Chester County Historical Society; photo, Gavin Ashworth.)

forms from the region. Another built-in cupboard, likely by the same maker, was removed from an unidentified house in the Nottingham area during the 1970s (fig. 9). The paint on that object is modern, although based on remnants of the original blue. The keystone device in these cupboard panels may have classical precedents, as seen in the arched cornice above a door in the Haines House and a number of other buildings in the Nottingham area (fig. 10).[8]

Figure 10 Detail of an interior doorway in the Isaac and Mary Haines House, Rising Sun, Cecil County, Maryland, 1774. (Photo, Laszlo Bodo.)

Figure 11 Corner cupboard, Nottingham area, Chester County, Pennsylvania, or Cecil County, Maryland, ca. 1770–1800. Walnut and lightwood inlay. H. 77¾", W. 43½", D. 25½". (Courtesy, Baltimore Museum of Art.) Since no early history of ownership survives for this cupboard, the possibility of extrapolating a name from the "IMW" initials on the upper door panel is remote.

Figure 12   Detail of the cornice of the cupboard illustrated in fig. 11.

Figure 13   Detail of the right front foot of the cupboard illustrated in fig. 11. With its tall shallow cove and underscale ovolo, the base molding conforms to a common local pattern.

As was the case in many rural areas, house joiners occasionally made free-standing furniture, and cabinetmakers periodically received commissions for architectural work. The corner cupboard illustrated in figure 11 has an upper keystone panel almost identical to those on the preceding examples (figs. 8, 9), suggesting that the same person may have made them all, whether he was a cabinetmaker, a house joiner, or both. Additionally, the cupboard has an elaborate cornice featuring Greek key and drilled dentil moldings and a guilloche fret (fig. 12)—details that occur on other locally made case pieces and architectural components. The lower part of the feet on the cupboard are restored, but the bracket cusps survive and are articulated with a shallow drilled hole (fig. 13). On other Nottingham-area case pieces, like the massive clothespress illustrated in figure 14, the cusps were either drilled all the way through or the cusps were sawn and finished with gouges and files (fig. 15).[9]

Figure 14 Clothespress, Nottingham area,
Chester County, Pennsylvania, or Cecil County,
Maryland, 1780–1800. Walnut with tulip poplar
and maple. H. 85⅝", W. 71¼", D. 25". (Private
collection; photo, Gavin Ashworth.) The cornice
of this press has Greek key and drilled dentil elements similar to those on the cupboard illustrated
in figs. 11 and 12.

Figure 15 Detail of the right front foot of the clothespress illustrated in fig. 14. (Photo, Gavin Ashworth.)

Figure 16 Tall-case clock with movement by Benjamin Chandlee Jr., Nottingham area, Chester County, Pennsylvania, or Cecil County, Maryland, 1760–1775. Walnut with tulip poplar. H. 107", W. 22½", D. 11½". (Courtesy, Winterthur Museum; photo, Laszlo Bodo.) The carved appliqués on the plinth are rabbeted to overlap the square corners of the base panel, presumably to allow for seasonal shrinkage and expansion. The feet and base molding are restored.

Figure 17 Tall-case clock with movement by Benjamin Chandlee Jr., Nottingham area, Chester County, Pennsylvania, or Cecil County, Maryland, 1760–1775. Walnut with tulip poplar. H. 99", W. 21¾", D. 12¼". (Courtesy, Chester County Historical Society; photo, Laszlo Bodo.) The clock was photographed in the house of Susanna Brinton of Gap, Lancaster County, Pennsylvania, before 1924. By that date the upper portion of the sarcophagus top had been removed. The short cabriole legs are visible in that image.

The Nottingham School and Philadelphia Influence

Furniture made in the Nottingham area was strongly influenced by contemporaneous Philadelphia work. The career of Quaker "shop joyner" John Mears (1737–1819) offers one possible path of stylistic transfer. The son of William Mears "late of Georgia, deceased," John may have served his apprenticeship in Philadelphia before 1760, when he married Susanna Townsend. Among the Quakers who witnessed their marriage were cabinetmakers Solomon Fussell, William Savery, Jacob Shoemaker, Samuel Mickle, and Thomas Sugars, suggesting that Mears had apprenticed with one of these men or was working with them. Susanna's parents, Charles and Abigail, moved to Nottingham in 1766, and she and John received their transfer to the Nottingham Monthly Meeting the following year. Mears's name appears on the Nottingham tax list in 1768, and in 1767–1768 and 1773 he made furniture for noted Lancaster lawyer Jasper Yeates. In 1767 Yeates paid Mears £8 for a walnut bookcase and walnut "Dressing Drawers." The following year Mears supplied Yeates with a walnut dining table, a small walnut corner(?) table, a plain card table, and an "Elbow Chair." He later worked in Reading, Berks County, and eventually was among the first settlers in Catawissa, Columbia County. Mears was no doubt familiar with Philadelphia stylistic details and may have introduced them to the Nottingham area.[10]

One group of closely related Nottingham furniture has distinctive Philadelphia-inspired features and consists of two tall-case clocks, two high chests of drawers, a matching dressing table, and a desk-and-bookcase (figs. 16, 17, 24, 25, 29, 33). Both clocks have movements by Benjamin Chandlee Jr. and histories of ownership confirming that their cases were made locally. The original owners' ages and marriage dates suggest that the clocks date between 1760 and 1775.

According to family history, Rowland (Roland) Rogers (1717–1787) of West Nottingham commissioned the clock illustrated in figure 16. He married Rachel Oldham circa 1760. Judging from Rogers's will, he owned a considerable amount of land. When he died in 1787, much of his estate—presumably including his clock—passed to his eldest son, Elisha, who received "all that Part of my Plantation I now live upon." Moses Brinton (1725–1789), born in Thornbury Township, Chester County, was the original owner of the other clock (fig. 17). In 1747 he married Elinor Varman

(Varmon) (1724–1788) at Leacock Meeting in Lancaster County, and in 1748 his father gave him two hundred acres in Leacock Township. In 1761 the couple built presumably their second house on land given them by Elinor's father (fig. 18). Although the precise date when they purchased the clock is unknown, it is mentioned in Moses's will. He left his son Joseph (1754–1809) the plantation on which he lived along with his "Eight Day Clock, Desk, & the Sum of twenty five Pounds together with one . . . third Part of my Mechanical or Carpenter Tools."[11]

Moses Brinton was connected to Nottingham through several marriages. His mother was a Pierce, and his maternal grandmother was a Gainer, both

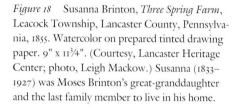

Figure 18 Susanna Brinton, *Three Spring Farm*, Leacock Township, Lancaster County, Pennsylvania, 1855. Watercolor on prepared tinted drawing paper. 9" x 11¾". (Courtesy, Lancaster Heritage Center; photo, Leigh Mackow.) Susanna (1833–1927) was Moses Brinton's great-granddaughter and the last family member to live in his home.

Figure 19 Detail of the left front foot of the clock illustrated in fig. 17. (Photo, Laszlo Bodo.)

surnames common in that area. The most direct link was through Moses's father, Joseph, whose second marriage was to Mary Elgar, widow of Joseph Elgar, at the East Nottingham Meeting in 1748. Witnesses at this marriage included members of the Churchman, Chandlee, Pierce, and Brown families. An important additional bond to the Nottingham area was through Mary's daughter, who also in 1748 married William Chandlee, brother of clockmaker Benjamin Jr.[12]

The Rogers and Brinton clock cases share numerous structural and stylistic details (figs. 16, 17). Both have similar cornice, arch, and waist moldings, engaged quarter-columns that are not fluted, and a medial groove on the face of the hood door. The Brinton example retains its original cabriole legs and claw-and-ball feet (fig. 19), a detail rarely encountered on colonial American clock cases. A square tenon is integral with the head of the cabriole foot. On the front feet this tenon simply fits into the square pocket left behind the base molding when the quarter-column plinth stock stops short. On the rear feet the tenon fits into a pocket created by notching the side board behind the base molding. Although the feet of the Rogers clock are replaced, there is no reason to doubt that the originals differed from those on the Brinton case.[13]

Figure 20   Detail of the hood of the tall-case
clock illustrated in fig. 16. (Photo, Laszlo Bodo.)

Figure 21   Detail of a chalk sketch inside the
clock illustrated in fig. 16. (Photo, Laszlo Bodo.)

Other clock cases from the Nottingham area survive, but none is as elaborate as the Rogers and Brinton examples. The Rogers case has carved appliqués on the tympanum and hood spandrels (fig. 20), above the waist door, and at the corners of the base panel (fig. 16). On the Brinton clock, the maker used fretwork in place of the tympanum and spandrel appliqués and omitted the ornament above the waist door (fig. 17). The carving on these cases is distinctive in that it has leaves with raised outer edges and broad, concave depressions in the center (fig. 20). To produce this effect, the carver used gouges to make deep, hollowing cuts—an idiosyncratic technique not usually associated with urban work. In addition to foliate motifs, this artisan's vocabulary included scrolls, fluted corbels, flower heads, shells, and fanlike devices. Chalk sketches inside the hood of the Rogers clock indicate that the carver worked out some of his designs freehand rather than transferring them with patterns (fig. 21).[14]

Another case with a movement by Benjamin Chandlee Jr. has a closed ogee cornice that is stylistically earlier than the broken-scroll variants on the Rogers and Brinton clocks (fig. 22). The hood of this case is further distinguished by having a corbel-shaped keystone, a central fluted pilaster interrupted by a large ovolo-shaped element and capped with a standard plinth and ball-and-spire finials. The colonnettes are not fluted, but they display slight entasis and have small rings below the capital molding. Similar rings also occur on the waist and plinth columns. The most noteworthy feature of this case is its deeply fielded and carved plinth panel (fig. 23). As the cupboards illustrated in figures 8, 9, and 11 suggest, unconventional panel designs are common on furniture and interior architecture details from the Nottingham area.

Figure 22 Tall-case clock with movement by Benjamin Chandlee Jr., Nottingham area, Chester County, Pennsylvania, or Cecil County, Maryland, 1750–1775. Walnut with white pine. H. 103¼", W. 20⅞", D. 11⅛". (Courtesy, Chester County Historical Society; photo, Gavin Ashworth.)

Figure 23 Detail of the plinth panel of the tall-case clock illustrated in fig. 22. (Photo, Gavin Ashworth.)

Two high chests of drawers and a dressing table have carving closely related to and possibly by the same hand as that on the Rogers and Brinton clocks. The high chest illustrated in figure 24 descended in the family of Wilmington, Delaware, physician Dr. James Avery Draper (1835–1907). When his daughter Cornelia died in 1942, her inventory listed "1 Highboy in walnut, Chippendale" valued at $100.00 and "1 Walnut Low Boy, Chippendale" valued at $75.00. There is no evidence that the Drapers were connected to Nottingham, but it is possible that they may have acquired the high chest and dressing table from Wilmington friends or neighbors. For instance, Margaret Churchman Painter Pyle (1828–1885), mother of illustrator Howard Pyle, was a neighbor and patient of Dr. Draper and a descendant of John and George Churchman of Nottingham. The other high chest has no family history but was in Port Deposit, Cecil County, Maryland, in the late nineteenth century (fig. 25).[15]

Figure 24 High chest of drawers, Nottingham area, Chester County, Pennsylvania, or Cecil County, Maryland, 1760–1780. Walnut with tulip poplar, hard pine, white cedar. H. 92¾", W. 43½", D. 25". (Private collection; photo, Laszlo Bodo.) The pediment scrolls on this chest have a more exaggerated S-curve than those on the example illustrated in fig. 25, but both sets of moldings have oversize volutes with identical appliqués. Similar volutes occur on other furniture from the Nottingham area.

Both high chests have extremely tall upper cases with bold broken scroll pediments and a shallow drawer in the tympanum (figs. 24–26). The pronounced cusps on the skirt of the high chest and dressing table (figs. 24, 29)—missing on the high chest illustrated in figure 25—are similar to those on the stair brackets of the Haines House (fig. 27). On the Draper example, the pediment is detachable, but on the other high chest it is integral. Despite these differences, it is obvious that the two high chests are from the same shop. Their cabriole legs were laid out with the same patterns, and their two-part waist moldings (small molding, deep cove, ovolo, and cyma attached to the upper case, and shallow cove and small molding attached to the lower case) are identical. The Draper high chest retains its original cartouche, which was likely inspired by Philadelphia examples (figs. 26, 28). The cartouche is not laminated for thickness, like many of its urban counterparts, but does have leaf clusters nailed into notches at either side. This

Figure 25 High chest of drawers, Nottingham area, Chester County, Pennsylvania, or Cecil County, Maryland, 1760–1780. Walnut with tulip poplar and oak. H. 95⅜", W. 43¾", D. 25½". (Courtesy, Jeffrey Tillou.) The center ornament is not original.

Figure 26 Detail of the pediment of the high chest of drawers illustrated in fig. 24. (Photo, Laszlo Bodo.)

Figure 27 Detail of a stair bracket in the Isaac and Mary Haines House, Rising Sun, Cecil County, Maryland, 1774. (Photo, Laszlo Bodo.)

Figure 28 Cartouche attributed to the Garvan high chest carver, Philadelphia, Pennsylvania, ca. 1765. Mahogany. (Courtesy, Philadelphia Museum of Art.)

allowed the maker to cut his cartouche from a narrower board, a material- and labor-saving technique duplicated on the skirt appliqués of both high chests and the dressing table (figs. 24, 25, 29) and related to the fabrication and carving of the plinth panels on the Rogers and Brinton clock cases (fig. 30). As on the Rogers clock, the carver of the Draper chest sketched designs on interior surfaces of that object. There is a rudimentary drawing of a cartouche on the rear top board of the lower case (fig. 31).[16]

Figure 29 Dressing table, Nottingham area, Chester County, Pennsylvania, or Cecil County, Maryland, 1760–1780. Woods and dimensions not recorded, location unknown. (Courtesy, Philip Bradley Antiques, Inc.)

Figure 30 Detail of the plinth of the tall-case clock illustrated in fig. 16. (Photo, Laszlo Bodo.)

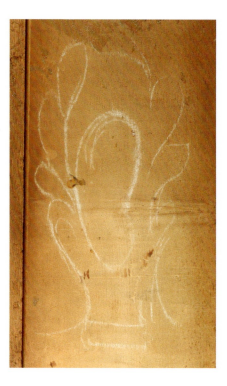

Figure 31 Detail of a chalk sketch in the high chest of drawers illustrated in fig. 24. (Photo, Laszlo Bodo.)

Figure 32   Detail of the leg carving on the high chest of drawers illustrated in fig. 24. (Photo, Laszlo Bodo.)

Figure 33   Desk-and-bookcase, Nottingham area, Chester County, Pennsylvania, or Cecil County, Maryland, 1760–1780. Walnut with tulip poplar, white oak, white cedar. H. 96½", W. 42½", D. 24". (Private collection; photo, Gavin Ashworth.)

Figure 34   Detail of the pediment of the desk-and-bookcase illustrated in fig. 33. (Photo, Gavin Ashworth.) This rosette pattern occurs on one other case piece from the Nottingham area (see figs. 53, 54).

The design of the high chests and dressing table is primarily frontal, as indicated by the exposed framing of the pediments and orientation of the carving. On all three pieces, the rear legs and sides of the front legs are unadorned (fig. 32). Contemporaneous Philadelphia case pieces occasionally have rear legs that are plain or carved only on the sides, but there is no urban precedent for the treatment of the front legs in this Nottingham group.

A desk-and-bookcase likely commissioned by educator and Anglican clergyman Joseph Coudon (Cowden) (1742–1792) represents a different stylistic interpretation for furniture from the Nottingham area (fig. 33). Although the design of its cartouche is unique (fig. 34), the scroll volutes extending horizontally from the shoulders are applied in a manner similar to the leaf clusters on the aforementioned skirt appliqués (figs. 24, 25, 29) and cartouche of the Draper high chest (fig. 26). The stylized leaves on the tympanum of the desk-and-bookcase also relate to other Nottingham work in having deeply fluted lobes with thin, high ridges (fig. 20). However, the carving on the Coudon example lacks the foliate gouge carving seen on the previously discussed group of clock cases, high chests, and dressing table.[17]

Of all the case pieces from the Nottingham area, the Coudon desk-and-bookcase is the most architectural. Monuments and overmantels with similarly shaped tops and bold applied moldings appear in numerous eighteenth-century design books, including Batty Langley's *The City and Country Builder's and Workman's Treasury of Designs* (1st ed., 1740). At least nine copies of that book were in Philadelphia during the eighteenth century. Similarly, plate 3 in Abraham Swan's *The British Architect* (1st ed., 1745) illustrates a Greek key as the lowest element in a cornice molding. This detail occurs on a number of case pieces from the Nottingham area but is relatively rare in furniture made elsewhere.[18]

The Coudon desk-and-bookcase rests on ogee feet with the standard profiles seen on other Nottingham-area pieces. The outer edge is a conventional ogee, but the inner face has an exaggerated drilled cusp that nearly

Figure 35 Detail of the right front foot of the desk-and-bookcase illustrated in fig. 33. (Photo, Gavin Ashworth.) The maker drilled out the circular piercing in the feet. Marks from the wing cutter of the bit are visible on the inner edge.

Figure 36 Desk, Nottingham area, Chester County, Pennsylvania, or Cecil County, Maryland, 1770–1800. Walnut with oak, chestnut, and tulip poplar. H. 47", W. 43", D. 22⅞". (Courtesy, Chester County Historical Society; photo, Laszlo Bodo.) The drawers that support the fallboard have appliqués with convex spiraling like that on the rosettes of the high chests illustrated in figs. 24 and 25 and chest-on-chests shown in figs. 42 and 43.

Figure 37 Desk, Nottingham area, Chester County, Pennsylvania, or Cecil County, Maryland, 1770–1800. Walnut with oak, chestnut, and tulip poplar. H. 45½", W. 42", D. 22½". (Private collection; photo, Gavin Ashworth.)

Figure 38 Detail of the right front foot of the desk illustrated in fig. 36. (Photo, Gavin Ashworth.)

touches the other side and points toward a small fillet above (fig. 35). A small fillet appears in almost the same position on the stair brackets from the Haines House (fig. 27). On most objects with this foot design, the sides of the case extend to the floor and act as supports, and the desks illustrated in figures 36 and 37 share that detail. The latter desk has a history of descent in the Reynolds and Barclay families of Rising Sun in Cecil County, Maryland. As was the case with the feet on the Coudon desk-and-bookcase, the maker of the desk illustrated in figure 36 used a drill to define the inner edge of the cusps (fig. 38). On the desk feet, the tips of the cusps are integral with a cyma-shaped element of the bracket rather than being separate and more fully defined (fig. 35). The desk illustrated in figure 37 has another foot variant typical of the Nottingham region.[19]

All these desks have a central prospect door with flanking letter drawers and tiers of drawers surmounted by pigeonholes with valances on either side, but no interiors from this region are identical. The Coudon interior is the most elaborate and individualistic, featuring a well, serpentine blocked drawers in the outer tiers, concave blocked drawers in the inner tiers, and four document drawers (one stacked over the other at each side) with moldings and reeded fluting simulating pilasters (fig. 39). The prospect door of the desk illustrated in figure 37 is unique in having a reeded, serpentine sec-

Figure 39   Detail of the interior of the desk-and-bookcase illustrated in fig. 33. (Photo, Gavin Ashworth.)

Figure 40   Detail of the prospect door and document drawers in the writing compartment of the desk illustrated in fig. 37. (Photo, Gavin Ashworth.) The carving on the prospect door is stylistically related to that on the ornament of the Coudon desk (fig. 33). Most desks from the Nottingham area have document drawers with fluted faces.

Figure 41 Desk-and-bookcase, Lancaster, Pennsylvania, 1770–1790. Walnut with tulip poplar and white pine. H. 102 ¾", W. 37", D. 24". (Courtesy, Sumpter Priddy Antiques.)

Figure 42 Chest-on-chest, Nottingham area, Chester County, Pennsylvania, or Cecil County, Maryland, 1760–1780. (*Antiques* 41, no. 1 [January 1942]: 8.) The cartouche on this example is similar to that on the Coudon desk-and-bookcase, with the exception of having gouge work on the flat surfaces around the cabachon.

tion surmounted by a lobed shell; additionally, the document drawers depart from local convention in having applied, reeded columns that are rounded at the top (fig. 40). The presence of similar columns on the document drawers of a Lancaster County desk-and-bookcase suggests that craftsmen or furniture from that town may have influenced production in the Nottingham area, or perhaps John Mears took this creative approach to Lancaster from Nottingham (fig. 41).[20]

Other structural and stylistic details typical of Nottingham-area furniture can be observed on four chest-on-chests. All have upper cases that are unusually tall in relation to their lower sections, and the one in figure 42 has an ornament likely carved by the hand responsible for the Coudon example (figs. 33, 34). This chest-on-chest also has a broken-scroll pediment with spiral-carved rosettes like those on other pieces from the region (figs. 24, 25) and a narrow drawer in the tympanum similar to the one in the high chest illustrated in figure 25. Unfortunately, the location of this piece is unknown, and the only existing image of it was so poorly silhouetted that it is impossible to determine if the feet are original and represent a common local pattern.

Another chest-on-chest has similar proportions, moldings, and pinwheel rosettes but different drawer organization (fig. 43). With three carved shells and two sets of idiosyncratic foliate appliqués, this object is one of the more highly embellished case pieces from the Nottingham area (fig. 44). Although no other example has comparable appliqués, the stippled grounds of the drawer shells and placement of the examples in the upper case have

Figure 43 Chest-on-chest, Nottingham area, Chester County, Pennsylvania, or Cecil County, Maryland, 1760–1790. Walnut with white oak and tulip poplar. H. 90½", W. 43", D. 22¾". (Courtesy, Yale University Art Gallery.) The feet and base moldings are integral.

Figure 44 Detail of the upper carved drawer of the chest-on-chest illustrated in fig. 43. No other work by this carver has been identified.

Figure 45 Chest-on-chest with carving attributed to Nicholas Bernard, Philadelphia, Pennsylvania, 1770–1800. Mahogany with tulip poplar, yellow pine, and white cedar. H. 97", W. 42½", D. 24". (Courtesy, Historical Society of Dauphin County, Harrisburg, Pa.; photo, Gavin Ashworth.)

Figure 46 Detail of a Dutchman on the chest-on-chest illustrated in fig. 43. Dovetail layout lines scribed across the Dutchman prove those components were part the original construction.

precedents in Philadelphia and Lancaster work (fig. 45). Several construction details on this chest-on-chest also occur on other locally made case pieces. The waist molding is virtually identical to that on the cabriole leg high chests illustrated in figures 24 and 25, and the feet are supported by extensions of the case sides. The case sides and top are joined with dovetail splines, or Dutchmen (fig. 46). Although normally used for repairs or later reinforcements, Dutchmen are original features on many examples of Nottingham-area furniture.[21]

A chest-on-chest and related tall chest of drawers have additional features associated with Nottingham-area work (figs. 47, 48), the most distinctive

Figure 47   Chest-on-chest, Nottingham area, Chester County, Pennsylvania, or Cecil County, Maryland, 1770–1800. Walnut with oak and tulip poplar. H. 87¾", W. 46⅛", D. 24¾". (Private collection; photo, Gavin Ashworth.) This chest-on-chest and the chest illustrated in fig. 48 are made of water mill–sawn boards just over one inch in thickness. The oak backboards of the chest-on-chest are original, but extraneous nail holes and remnants of plaster suggest they are reused architectural components. The sides of the chest-on-chest are paneled, a feature occurring on other case pieces from the Nottingham area. The molding on the face of the thin upper drawer differs from that of the example illustrated in fig. 48. Chests with an upper row of three arches are relatively common in Chester County, particularly the areas around New Garden, London Grove, West Fallowfield, and West Marlborough Township.

Figure 48   Tall chest of drawers, Nottingham area, Chester County, Pennsylvania, or Cecil County, Maryland, 1770–1800. Walnut with tulip poplar. H. 69¼", W. 44", D. 23". (Private collection; photo, Gavin Ashworth.) The cornice fret is similar to those on tall-clock cases from the Nottingham area.

being long, thin drawers below the cornice. Like the preceding chest-on-chest, this example (fig. 47) has a tall upper case and lower section that is proportionally fairly short. The cornice features a Greek key molding like those seen on the corner cupboard and clothespress illustrated in figures 11 and 14, as well as the upper case of a related chest-on-chest (not illustrated). The feet of the chest-on-chest and tall chest of drawers represent other

Figure 49   Detail of the left front foot and base molding of the chest-on-chest illustrated in fig. 47. (Photo, Gavin Ashworth.) The feet and base moldings are integral.

Figure 50   Detail of the right front foot and base molding of the tall chest of drawers illustrated in fig. 48. (Photo, Gavin Ashworth.) The feet and base moldings are integral.

Nottingham-area variants. They are relatively tall, but the feet of the chest-on-chest have brackets that are drilled through, whereas those on the tall chest of drawers are not, similar instead to those on the desk illustrated in figure 37 (figs. 49, 50). As is expected of furniture from this region, the case and feet are supported by extensions of the sides. Another chest-on-chest combines details found on the preceding pieces, including fretwork and a shallow molded drawer (fig. 51). The applied molding outlining the tympanum and stop fluting of the keystone are unusual features (fig. 52), although keystones with different decorative treatments are common on clock cases and interior details from the region.[22]

A keystone with interrupted fluting graces the tympanum of a tall-case clock with movement by Benjamin Chandlee Jr. (figs. 53, 54). This detail relates stylistically to the reeded fluting on the document drawers of the Hugh Alexander desk (fig. 4) and Coudon desk-and-bookcase (fig. 39). Other features linking the clock case and Coudon desk-and-bookcase are the boldly reeded edges of their scroll volutes and applied rosettes.

Several design elements on the chest-on-chest and the tall clock case have parallels in clock cases attributed to the shop of Quaker Jacob Brown (1746–1802), a West Nottingham joiner. Almost all of the movements found in Brown's cases are by Benjamin Chandlee Jr. or his sons, Ellis (1755–1816) and Isaac (1760–1813). One case, likely also from the Brown shop, has a movement by Duncan Beard of Appoquinimink, Delaware.[23]

Figure 51   Chest-on-chest, Nottingham area, Chester County, Pennsylvania, or Cecil County, Maryland, 1780–1800. Walnut with tulip poplar and white oak. H. 100½", W. 43½", D. 23¼". (Private collection; photo, Gavin Ashworth.) The backboards of the pediment are joined with Dutchmen like the side and top boards of the chest-on-chest illustrated in figs. 43, 44, and 46.

Figure 52 Detail of the pediment of the chest-on-chest illustrated in fig. 51. (Photo, Gavin Ashworth.)

Figure 53　Tall-case clock with movement by Benjamin Chandlee Jr., Nottingham area, Chester County, Pennsylvania, or Cecil County, Maryland, 1765–1790. Walnut with tulip poplar and yellow pine. H. 96⅛", W. 21½", D. 10¾". (Private collection; photo, Gavin Ashworth.)

Figure 54　Detail of the hood of the tall-case clock illustrated in fig. 53. (Photo, Gavin Ashworth.)

Figure 55 Tall-case clock with movement by Benjamin Chandlee Jr., and case by Jacob Brown, Nottingham area, Cecil County, Maryland, 1788. Walnut with tulip poplar and hard pine. H. 107½", W. 25½", D. 14½". (Private collection; photo, Laszlo Bodo.) The sides of the plinth extend to the floor to support the case and feet, which are integral with the base molding.

Figure 56 Detail of the hood and movement of the tall-case clock illustrated in fig. 55. (Photo, Laszlo Bodo.) The rosettes, which are similar to those on other locally made pieces, have stippling in the concave areas. The latter technique is repeated on the drawer shells of the chest-on-chest illustrated in figs. 43 and 44. Although the fabric behind the spandrel fret is replaced, evidence of the original textile survives.

154   COOPER AND ANDERSON

The Shop Tradition of Jacob Brown

Jacob Brown's trade has been known for approximately twenty-five years, owing to the publication of a tall-clock case he made in 1788 for James McDowell (1742–1815) of Lower Oxford Township in southern Chester County (figs. 55, 56). Exactly when McDowell commissioned the clock movement and case is unknown, but on August 11, 1788, Chandlee had completed his part and wrote to McDowell:

> I should take it very kind, if thee would please to send me the price of the Clock, by Stephen Yarnall, as I have some money to make up this week, & that makes me stand in Very great need of it, I am Sorry I have to trouble thee so soon for it, but it is not in my pwer to make out without it., please to inform me when thee expects the case home, & I will Come up & sett up the Clock.

Two months later McDowell received a letter from Brown apologizing for his delay in completing the case:

> Friend James Mc Dowel I am Sorry That I have Disapointed you So much About your Clock Case if I had thought I Could knot Served you Beter I would knot under took for to have Done it I am Sorry for to inform you that 3 of my Boys have all got the feaver and cant Work one Stroke for me and 3 of my own Chil Dren is onwell Likewise But we will Lay all those maters aside If I keep my own health you Shall Have your Clock Case Some Day Next Week from your Disapointed friend to Serve[24]

Scholars originally believed that Jacob Brown the joiner was born in 1724, but that would have made him sixty-eight and the father of three young children when he wrote McDowell in 1788. A more likely candidate is the Jacob Brown who was born in 1746 and died in Cecil County, Maryland, in 1802 and whose estate inventory identified him as a joiner and listed unfinished furniture, woodworking tools, "291 feet of cherrytree plank," "931 feet of walnut plank," and "375 feet of ½ inch walnut."[25]

Less than three weeks after Brown's death, his widow Elizabeth and son William sold all Jacob's personal property to "pay off the before mentioned Legacies" (see appendix). Among the "goods and chattels" were unfinished furniture and piecework, including several sets of table legs, a walnut chest, a cherry corner cupboard, two heads for bookcases, two table frames, and three clock cases. Samuel Cother, John Porter, and William Graham bought woodworking tools, cherry and walnut lumber, and unfinished furniture, which suggests they were either journeymen in Brown's shop or established local joiners. Family members also bought much of the stock-in-trade, indicating that they intended continuing Jacob's business, which apparently also included undertaking. Elizabeth purchased her husband's hearse, along with the unfinished table frames and clock cases. Presumably she acquired the furniture for one of her sons to complete. As Jacob's executor, William was undoubtedly old enough to take over his father's business. Probably the younger Brown trained with his father along with other siblings and apprentices.[26]

The design and construction of the clock case that Jacob Brown made for McDowell indicate that he was one of the Nottingham area's most creative and capable joiners. The hood is capped with a graceful, broken-scroll ped-

Figure 57   Detail of the plinth of the tall-case
clock illustrated in fig. 55. (Photo, Laszlo Bodo.)

iment with drilled dentil moldings; a carved, keystone-shaped appliqué on
the tympanum; spiral rosettes with a pronounced central button; and a center plinth with an applied, reeded corbel surmounted by a Greek key. The
turned and uniquely carved finials (two of which are original) represent a
creative alternative to the standard ball and sphere form. Parallels with other
Nottingham pieces can be seen in the fret under the hood (fig. 56), which is
similar to that on the tall chest and chest-on-chest illustrated in figures 48
and 51, and the design of the base plinth (fig. 57), which has clear antecedents
in the Rogers and Brinton clock cases (figs. 16, 17, 30). Another closely
related clock case with a movement by Benjamin Chandlee Jr. has a similar
plinth, frieze fret, keystone surmounted by a reeded corbel, and spiral

Figure 58   Tall-case clock with movement by
Benjamin Chandlee Jr., case attributed to Jacob
Brown, Nottingham area, Cecil County, Maryland, 1780–1802. Walnut with tulip poplar.
H. 99⅜", W. 22¼", D. 12⅜". (Private collection;
photo, Gavin Ashworth.) Details shared by this
clock case and the McDowell example (figs. 55
and 56) include spiral rosettes, a corbel on the
plinth of the tympanum, drilled dentil molding,
and gouge-carved plaques above the colonnettes.

Figure 59 Detail of the hood, movement, and secret drawer of the tall-case clock illustrated in fig. 58. (Private collection; photo, Gavin Ashworth.) No other American clock with a secret drawer is known.

rosettes but differs from the McDowell example in having a hood that is more typical of those with arched dials and broken-scroll pediments (fig. 58). A unique feature in the hood is the reeded corbel that is the face of a diminutive drawer, exactly large enough to conceal the key to the case (fig. 59).[27]

Jacob Brown, his son William (d. 1826), or other craftsmen trained in his shop were probably responsible for numerous tall clock cases that housed movements not only by Benjamin Chandlee Jr. but also by his sons Ellis and Isaac, all working in Nottingham. Many of these cases are simpler in design but continue to employ a central fluted keystone and spiral-carved rosettes. The top edge of their plinths echoes the shape of the door, and many have white-dial movements. A particularly refined example from this group has a movement by Ellis Chandlee (figs. 60, 61).[28]

Figure 60 Tall-case clock with movement by Ellis Chandlee (1755–1816), case attributed Jacob Brown (d. 1802) or William Brown (d. 182?), Cecil County, Maryland, 1800–1815. Walnut with tulip poplar. H. 94", W. 21", D. 11". (Private collection; photo, Philip Bradley Antiques.)

Figure 61 Detail of the hood and movement of the tall-case clock illustrated in fig. 60.

Conclusion

Closely reliant on architectural traditions, Nottingham-area joiners and cabinetmakers creatively employed a variety of stylistic motifs influenced by Philadelphia design. This is most evident in a small pre-Revolutionary group of clocks and high chests with monumental proportions and distinctive carving. A group of desks, tall chests of drawers, chest-on-chests, and clock cases share similar construction techniques (full-height sides and the use of Dutchmen) while using various ornamental details such as fretwork, Greek key moldings, drilled dentil moldings, spiral-carved rosettes, and central keystone motifs. Secret and unusual drawers are also a mark of the creativity in this artisanal community. Almost all the casework features extra thick boards, often highly figured walnut, resulting in massively built pieces. The variety of ogee bracket feet with pronounced cusps—sometimes closed and occasionally blind—is a prominent feature of this regional group. The most characteristic hallmark of this work is the originality with which makers mixed and matched ornament, never exactly repeating a form or combination of details. The shop of Jacob Brown (1746–1802) and his followers was likely responsible for many of the later clock cases and possibly some of the other casework.

ACKNOWLEDGMENTS   The authors thank the following colleagues and friends for their invaluable assistance with this article: Mr. and Mrs. Steve Adams, Alan Andersen, Gavin Ashworth, Joseph Bearden, Luke Beckerdite, Laszlo Bodo, Philip Bradley, Skip Chalfant, Edward Coudon, Sarah Coulson, Heather Coyle, Ellen Endslow, Richard Englander, Thére Fiechter, Jim Gergat, Lee Ellen Griffith, Jim Guthrie, Lowell Haines, Erin Harrington, Ed Hinton, Leigh Keno, Jennifer Kindig, Mary Kirk, Sasha Lourie, John and Marjorie McGraw, Leigh Mackow, Lisa Minardi, Richard Mones, Scott Moran, Susan Newton, Patricia O'Donnell, Edward Plumstead, Barry Rauhauser, Margaret Schiffer, Katharine Schutt, Roy Smith, John J. Snyder Jr., Peggy Sprout, Susan Stautberg, Jeffrey Tillou, Floyd Warrington, Fran Wilkins, Wendell Zercher.

1. "Octoraro," occasionally spelled "Otteraroe" on early maps, is derived from the Native American word *Ottohohaho*. According to nineteenth-century Lancaster County historian Jacob Mombert, it translates: "Where money and presents are distributed" (Jacob Isidor Mombert, *An Authentic History of Lancaster County in the State of Pennsylvania* [Lancaster, Pa.: J. E. Bakk & Co., 1869], p. 386). For further discussion of the Nottingham school, see Wendy A. Cooper and Lisa Minardi, *Paint, Pattern & People: Furniture of Southeastern Pennsylvania, 1725–1850* (Winterthur, Del.: Winterthur Museum, 2011), pp. 108–13. For an extensive survey of tall chests with feet attached with wooden screws, see Laura Keim Stutman, "'Screwy Feet': Removable Feet Chests of Drawers from Chester County, Pennsylvania, and Frederick County, Maryland" (master's thesis, University of Delaware, 1999). The furniture discussed in this article will more correctly be referred to as from the Nottingham area, not "Octoraro" furniture.

2. George Johnson, *History of Cecil County, Maryland* (Elkton, Md., 1881; reprint, Baltimore, Md.: Genealogical Publishing Company, 1989), p. 147. For more on the settlement of the Nottingham Lots and East and West Nottingham Townships, see J. Smith Futhey and Gilbert Cope, *History of Chester County* (Philadelphia: Louis H. Everts, 1881), pp. 195–98. Also Pamela James Blumgart, ed., *At the Head of the Bay: A Cultural and Architectural History of Cecil County, Maryland* (Crownsville, Md.: Maryland Historical Trust Press, 1996), pp. 31–35; and East Nottingham Trustees, *The Nottingham Lots: A Tercentenary Celebration, 2001* (Xlibris Corporation, 2006).

3. A. Hughlett Mason, *The Journal of Charles Mason and Jeremiah Dixon* (Philadelphia: American Philosophical Society, 1969), pp. 4–8. See also Edward E. Chandlee, *Six Quaker Clockmakers* (Philadelphia: Historical Society of Pennsylvania, 1943), pp. 21–30. Today the geographic area under discussion extends south from the borough of Oxford, Chester County, Pennsylvania, through East and West Nottingham Townships (Pa.) and into northern Cecil County, including the areas in and around Calvert and Rising Sun, Maryland. The Brick Meeting is in Calvert, and a number of the earliest surviving dwellings are near Calvert and Rising Sun. Early maps of southeastern Pennsylvania often denote the post road southward as the Nottingham Road, further supporting the strong relation between Philadelphia and the Nottingham Lots.

4. For more on the Chandlee family and their work, see Chandlee, *Six Quaker Clockmakers*; and Frank Hohmann, *Timeless: Masterpiece American Brass Dial Clocks* (New York: Hohmann Holding, 2009), pp. 198–99, 325–26. It is important to note that throughout his entire career, Benjamin Chandlee Jr. (as well as his sons Ellis and Isaac) inscribed "Nottingham" on both their brass dials and white-painted dials. This suggests that even after the Mason-Dixon Line was drawn, by 1768 Chandlee still considered his home to be Nottingham.

5. For more on Nottingham-area line-and-berry furniture, see Cooper and Minardi, *Paint, Pattern & People*, pp. 70–78. For the 1763 will and inventory of Thomas Coulson, see Chester County Archives, West Chester, Pa., no. 2087. Also see Lee Ellen Griffith, "Line-and-Berry Inlaid Furniture: A Regional Craft Tradition in Pennsylvania, 1682–1790" (Ph.D. diss., University of Pennsylvania, 1988); and Lee Ellen Griffith, "The Line-and-Berry Inlaid Furniture of Eighteenth-Century Chester County, Pennsylvania," *Antiques* 135, no. 5 (May 1989): 1202–11. The distinctive light and dark herringbone inlay appears to be a hallmark of Nottingham work and sometimes is seen on drawer fronts without any line-and-berry inlay;

for an example, see Margaret Berwind Schiffer, *Furniture and Its Makers of Chester County, Pennsylvania* (Philadelphia: University of Pennsylvania Press, 1966), figs. 136, 137. Recently Dr. Harry Alden identified by microanalysis the light yellowish wood in this banding as sumac.

6. The attribution of the two desks to Hugh Alexander is based on the fact that one of them is said to have been made by him for his brother James and is still in the possession of descendants of James Alexander. The straight bracket feet on the Winterthur desk (fig. 4) are replacements copied directly from the original ones on the James Alexander desk. A related desk with herringbone inlay surrounding the drawers is illustrated in an ad for the House with the Brick Wall, *Antiques* 15, no. 1 (January 1929): 11. The interior is almost identical to that of the Alexander desk. For more on the Alexander family, see Rev. E. John Alexander, *A Record of the Descendants of John Alexander, of Lanarkshire, Scotland, and His Wife, Margaret Glasson, Who Emigrated from County Armagh, Ireland, to Chester County, Pennsylvania, A.D. 1736* (Philadelphia: Alfred Martien, 1878), pp. 16–26. The light yellow wood on five interior drawer fronts and framing the prospect door of the attributed Alexander desk are sumac.

7. The Churchman House was built on lot 16 of the Nottingham tract by the son of John Churchman, one of the original settlers and first owner of that lot. John Churchman (1705–1775) was a prominent Quaker minister who traveled widely in the colonies and abroad. A built-in corner cupboard in the 1745 part of the Churchman House exhibits the same characteristic as later cupboards, with the upper section being extremely large in comparison to the lower portion. For more on John and his son George, see Futhey and Cope, *History of Chester County, Pennsylvania*, pp. 497–88; and *The Nottingham Lots*, pp. 28–33. For more on the Churchman, Knight, and Brown Houses, see Blumgart, *At the Head of the Bay*, pp. 187, 214–15, 464–67. In most instances the craftsmen who built these houses are not known, but in the case of the Mercer Brown House a number of initials are incised in the bricks identifying local artisans like William White, who sold Brown five hundred bricks, and Samuel England, who also supplied bricks. The initials of Hezekiah Rowls (1729–1802), a local joiner, are incised into bricks in both the Mercer Brown House and the Churchman House. When Rowls died in 1802, his inventory listed "To all the carpenter tools of all kinds . . . $53.33" and "To sundries of Boards in shop and out of Doors . . . $10." See Cecil County Register of Wills (Inventories), Annapolis, Md., vol. 13, pp. 398–402, MSA C 620-17. In his will, which was finally probated in 1807, all of his carpenter's tools were given to his son Elihu; see Cecil County Register of Wills (Wills), vol. 6, pp. 252–55, MAS 646-5. We thank Sasha Lourie for providing this information on Rowls. For more on the Knight House, see Elizabeth B. Reynolds, "'The Planters Wisdom': Four Eighteenth-Century Houses in Maryland's Nottingham Lots Region" (master's thesis, University of Delaware, 2002), pp. 20–22. Additional information and images of these houses can be accessed through the Maryland Historical Trust's Inventory of Historic Properties in Cecil County: www.mdihp.net/dsp_county.cfm?criteria2=CE.

8. For a detailed examination of the Haines House, see Reynolds, "'The Planters Wisdom,'" pp. 22–27, 39–41, 144–47. Isaac Haines's affluence is demonstrated in his 1805 inventory, in which the most costly item was his eight-day clock valued at $32.00.

9. The corner cupboard in figure 11 was given to the Baltimore Museum of Art in 1970 by J. Gilman D'Arcy Paul, who had a house in Harford County and a great interest in northern Maryland architecture and furniture. Where he acquired the cupboard is unknown, but it is reasonable to question the originality of the inlaid initials, since a female first name beginning with "W" is almost unheard of in eighteenth-century Nottingham. Perhaps it was inlaid later and meant to be "WMI," in which case there would be a wide possibility of original owners. The cornice molding over a corner fireplace on the second floor of the Haines House is deeply molded with a drilled dentil lower portion; see www.mdihp.net/dsp_county.cfm?search=county&criteria1=W&criteria2=CE&criteria3=&id=6557&viewer=true. The Cross Keys Tavern in Chrome, Pennsylvania, has keystone motifs over the doorway of the central room similar to the molding in the Haines House. For images, see http://lcweb2.loc.gov/ammem/collections/habs_haer/. Another Nottingham-area freestanding painted cupboard in a private collection has an upper paneled door of a related but simpler design, lacking the keystone shaping beneath the circular top portion.

10. In John G. Freeze, *History of Columbia County, Pennsylvania, from the Earliest Times* (Bloomsburg, Pa.: Elwell & Bittenbender, Publishers, 1883), p. 104, Mears is described as "born in Georgia about 1737 and came to Philadelphia with his mother, then the wife of John Lyndall, about 1754. He followed the business of ship-joining and cabinet-making. . . . He was the virtual founder and patriarch of the town of Catawissa. . . . Through the difficult country . . . he laid out and built the first carriage road, connecting the valleys of the Susquehannah and

the Schuylkill, a great and laudable achievement in those times . . . . he was a Quaker preacher and physician, and though his methods were vigorous and rude, his manly presence, his patriotic services and sufferings, his integrity and enterprise won him universal respect, and embalmed his memory in the community. He died in the year 1819. . . ." There are no probate records for Mears in the Columbia County Court House, Bloomsburg, Pa., simply a record of his death. Marriage certificate (recorder's copy), John Mears and Susannah Townsend, "5 mo 8 1760," in Philadelphia Monthly Meeting Marriages, 1759–1814, MR-Ph359, Friends Historical Library, Swarthmore, Pa. For Mears's and Townsend's transfer to the Nottingham Meeting, see William Wade Hinshaw, *Encyclopedia of American Quaker Genealogy* (Ann Arbor, Mich.: Edwards Brothers, 1938), 2:595, 669. For additional references to Mears, see John J. Snyder Jr., "Carved Chippendale Case Furniture from Lancaster, Pennsylvania," *Antiques* 107, no. 5 (May 1975): 964, 973; also Richard S. Machmer et al., *Berks County Tall-Case Clocks, 1750 to 1850* (Reading, Pa.: Historical Society Press of Berks County, 1995), pp. 16, 29. See Jasper Yeates's Account Book, p. 34, Lancaster Historical Society, Lancaster, Pa., and Historical Society of Pennsylvania, Yeates Papers, Business Papers, Bills, Receipts, 1740–1768, Box 1, Collection #740. We thank Jim Gergat for calling the latter reference to our attention.

11. In 1793 Elisha Rogers sold John Price "that part or parcel of land and premises bequeathed by Rowland Rogers to the said Elisha Rogers." Presumably that tract included his father's house and contents, including the clock illustrated in figure 16. When Price died in 1815, he left to his grandsons Hiland and Jacob "all the personal property . . . except the Clock which I desire to Stand in the Rum She is now in" (Will of John Price, May 8, 1816, Cecil County Register of Wills, vol. 7, p. 160). The clock then descended from Hiland to Millicent (Melicent) R. Price, who married Judge James McCauley in 1849. It remained in the McCauley family until acquired by Winterthur Museum in 2003. Moses's parents were Joseph Brinton (1692–1751) and Mary Peirce (b. 1690). In 1748 Moses moved to Lancaster County after his father gave him two hundred acres in Leacock Township. Brinton was an educated, wealthy, well-respected Quaker. From 1773 to 1777 he served as one of five trustees of the General Loan Office of Pennsylvania, frequently going to the printing office to have paper currency printed for loans. See Moses Brinton Account Book, 1774–1798, no. 250, Chester County Historical Society, West Chester, Pa.

12. For references to the Brinton and Elgar marriages and who witnessed them, see Alice L. Beard, *Births, Deaths and Marriages of the Nottingham Quakers, 1680–1889* (Westminster, Md.: Heritage Books, 2006), p. 147.

13. To ascertain that the feet on the Brinton clock were original, they were carefully removed and extensively examined. For an illustration of the Brinton tall clock before 1924 (retaining its feet but having lost the sarcophagus top) pictured in the home of Susanna Brinton (1833–1927), see Gilbert Cope, comp., and Janetta Wright Schoonover, ed., *The Brinton Genealogy* (Trenton, N.J.: Press of MacCrellish & Quigley Company, 1924), opp. p. 161. The presence of the ball-and-claw feet on the clock in this photo gives further credibility to their originality. A typed note inside the door of the case states that Susanna "willed it to her nephew Moses Robert Brinton, of Drexel Hill, Pa., who after having the clock completely overhauled set it up in his home. . . ." For an illustration of the Rogers clock when it had been dropped through the floor of the Macauley homestead, see Chandlee, *Six Quaker Clockmakers*, p. 78.

14. Another Nottingham-area sarcophagus tall-case clock in a private collection with an early Benjamin Chandlee Jr. movement also has chalk drawings on the inner topmost surface of the backboard that echo rococo design motifs.

15. We thank Philip Bradley Jr. for calling our attention to the dressing table, which appears to have brasses identical to those on the Draper high chest and may have been made as a companion piece. Joana S. Donovan, *Alexander Draper (1630–1691) Early Settler of Delmarva & His Descendants* (Baltimore, Md.: Gateway Press, 2002), p. 82. When Margaret Churchman Painter Pyle died in 1885, it was reported in *Every Evening* the following day that Dr. James Avery Draper said the cause of death was "cancer of the stomach"; http://howardpyle .blogspot.com/2010/11/howard-pyles-mother-died-125-years-ago.html. Possibly artist Howard Pyle (1853–1911) inherited family furniture, as well as collecting some, for when his estate was sold at auction, it contained numerous pieces of antique furniture. See Philadelphia Art Galleries, *Estate Sale of Howard Pyle, 1912*. For the "Inventory and Appraisement of Cornelia Draper late of 1303 Rodney Street, Wilmington, Delaware . . . ," see Delaware Public Archives, Dover, Probate 22523. We thank Jennifer Kindig for supplying the history of this high chest.

16. Chalk drawings and indecipherable script appear several places on the interior surfaces of the Draper high chest. The most fascinating yet puzzling inscriptions are on the inner surface

face of the backboard of the removable pediment; it appears to have the word/name "gatchel" (a Nottingham surname) but, in addition, a large cojoined script that appears to be the initials "B C." Other script on the top of the upper case appears to be the name "Lydia."

17. The Coudon desk-and-bookcase sold at Sotheby's, *Important American Folk Art, Furniture and Silver*, May 19, 2005, lot 256. According to family history, Coudon was born in southern Chester County or northern Cecil County, and by 1765 he was a schoolmaster in the Cecil County Free School. We thank Edward Coudon for sharing information on his ancestor with us. For more on Coudon and his desk-and-bookcase, see Cooper and Minardi, *Paint, Pattern & People*, p. 112.

18. Morrison H. Heckscher, "English Furniture Pattern Books in Eighteenth-Century America," in *American Furniture*, edited by Luke Beckerdite (Hanover, N.H.: University Press of New England for the Chipstone Foundation, 1994), pp. 180–83.

19. The desk illustrated in figure 37 sold at William H. Bunch Auctions, Chadds Ford, Pa., February 26, 2008. Inscribed on one of the document drawers are the names Barclay Reynolds, Amanda Reynolds, Eugene Reynolds, and Sophie C. Reynolds, with Rising Sun written below each name. Cite Keno desk sold to Nusrala – coming.

20. For the Lancaster desk-and-bookcase, see Christie's, *Important American Furniture, Silver, Prints, Folk Art and Decorative Arts*, New York, January 18–19, 2001, lot 75.

21. For a complete discussion of this chest-on-chest, see Gerald W. R. Ward, *American Case Furniture in the Mabel Brady Garvan and Other Collections at Yale University* (New Haven, Conn.: Yale University Press, 1988), pp. 189–91. For a Lancaster example of carved shells with stippled grounds, see Winterthur's desk-and-bookcase originally purchased by wealthy iron-forge owner Michael Withers; see Cooper and Minardi, *Paint, Pattern & People*, pp. 103–5. Like the shells on the Withers desk-and-bookcase valance drawers, the shells on the prospect doors of figures 36 and 37, as well as several tall chests with "bonnet" drawers with carved shell fronts, have stippling between the lobes. For a tall chest with this feature, see Schiffer, *Furniture and Its Makers of Chester County, Pennsylvania*, nos. 149, 150.

22. For another tall chest of drawers with a Greek key motif and signed by Hiett Hutton (1756–1833), see Cooper and Minardi, *Paint, Pattern & People*, pp. 13–14, 232. Hutton was born in Nottingham and married Sara Pugh in East Nottingham Meeting in 1792. He died in New Garden Township (see Schiffer, *Furniture and Its Makers of Chester County, Pennsylvania*, p. 124); to date it is not known where or with whom he apprenticed, but there is no question that his work exhibits characteristics of Nottingham-area furniture. For another tall chest with a Greek key design likely from the Nottingham area, see Schiffer, *Furniture and Its Makers*, figs. 149, 150. The surviving upper portion of a chest-on-chest (now on a separate frame) has a Greek key beneath the cornice molding and a narrow drawer with molded face at the top identical to the one on the tall chest illustrated in figure 48. Another group of tall chests with characteristics related to the Nottingham furniture, though with a different ogee foot profile but having drilled cusps, can be attributed to Adam Glendenning on the basis of a high chest signed by Glendenning (private collection) of West Fallowfield Township north of Oxford and bordering Lancaster County. For the signed Glendenning example, see Philip H. Bradley Co. ad, *Maine Antiques Digest* (June 1993): 50. This tall chest has drilled dentils in the cornice, and, though the feet are replacements, they were based on a related example in the Chester County Historical Society (1997.42). For another tall chest from the same group, see Pook & Pook Auction, Downington, Pa., April 25, 2009, lot 464.

23. The clock with Duncan Beard movement is privately owned but presently on loan to the Biggs Museum, Dover, Delaware.

24. Quoted in Cooper and Minardi, *Paint, Pattern & People*, p. 109.

25. For the first reference to Brown, see Schiffer, *Furniture and Its Makers of Chester County, Pennsylvania*, p. 40. For the inventory and vendue of Jacob Brown, see Cecil County Register of Wills (Inventories), vol. 12, pp. 481–86, Maryland State Archives, Annapolis. Jacob Brown had a wife named Elizabeth, four daughters (two married), and seven sons (at least two under twenty-one). His inventory lists a "Mullato Girl now in our Possession . . . [to] be . . . manumitted . . . and set free at the age of twenty-one Years." While Brown may have been born in what was then Chester County, Pa., when he died he was living in Cecil County, Md. The failure over time of scholars to look in Maryland probate records for Brown is responsible for perpetuating the belief that he had to be the Jacob Brown born in 1724. For a clock and case closely related to the Jacob Brown example illustrated in figure 55 but having a Greek key at the top of the waist instead of a fret and an applied central ornament on the plinth panel, see Chandlee, *Six Quaker Clockmakers*, p. 90.

26. Chandlee, *Six Quaker Clockmakers*, p. 90. Some of the boards listed among Jacob's "goods and chattels" were one-inch thick, a dimension often encountered in furniture from the Nottingham region. No workbenches were listed among the effects sold. If Jacob intended for his family to continue his business, the benches may have passed directly to William or one of his other sons.

27. The timber used in this clock is very heavy, often measuring $1\frac{1}{8}''$ thick. For whatever reason, Brown used $\frac{1}{8}''$-thick plating on the tympanum, a feature that has been observed on another tall-case clock with movement by Benjamin Chandlee Jr. that is probably from Brown's shop. A clock case closely related to the one in figures 58 and 59 was shown by Philip Bradley Antiques at the 2011 Philadelphia Antiques Show, though the plinth panel was of the simpler variety seen on the clock case illustrated in figure 60, and the movement was by Ellis and Isaac Chandlee with a white dial as shown in Chandlee, *Six Quaker Clockmakers*, pp. 198–99.

28. For additional cases with movements by Benjamin Chandlee Jr., Ellis Chandlee, Ellis and Isaac Chandlee, and Isaac Chandlee related to the one in figures 60 and 61, see Chandlee, *Six Quaker Clockmakers*, pp. 84–88, 92, 100, 102, 154–58, 160, 164, 172, 174, 214–19. The Chester County Historical Society has an Ellis Chandlee clock and an Isaac Chandlee clock with Brown-type cases; the Isaac Chandlee is illustrated in Chandlee, *Six Quaker Clockmakers*, pp. 218–19. While many of these later clocks do not have histories of ownership, a white-dial Isaac Chandlee example recently given to the Lancaster Historical Society does have a history of descent through a branch of the Brown family.

Appendix

No. 47   *Jacob Brown*   June 9th 1802
481

A list and Inventory of all and singular the goods and chattles of Jacob Brown late of West Nottingham Cecil County sold at public Vendue the 21st day of April 1802 by Elizabeth Brown and William Brown Executors

ARTICLES SOLD	PURCHASERS NAMES	PRICE
2 Sider barrels	Eliz^th Brown	-.3.9
2 d^o	to do	-.3.-
1 Tierce	to do	-.2.6
1 open ended hogshead	Philip Ward	-.2.-
2 Barrels	d^o	-.1.-
2 ditto	Wm Brown	-.1.1
1 barrel & 1 Keg paid	Daniel Job	-.1.1
2 Barrels	Asahel Churchman	-.1.1
2 d^o	Wm Brown	-.-.6
2 d^o	D^o	-.-.6
2 d^o	D^o	-.-.8
3 Vessels paid	Daniel Job	-.1.6
1 Keg	Wm Brown	-.-.7
1 Iron pot	Philip Ward	-.1.8
1 d^o	Wm Brown	-.1.3
1 large iron pot	Abner Kirk	-.11.3
1 dutch oven	Wm Brown	-.-.7
1 Barrel	Eliz^th Brown	-.-.6
1 d^o	D^o	-.-.4
Wearing apparel	D^o	2.5.0
Bed & furniture	D^o	5.-.-
Childrens bed & furniture	D^o	1.17.6
one desk	D^o	-.15.-
1 Bottle case with 4 Bottles	Hannah Cother	-.5.-
1 bottle case full of bottles	to d^o	-.16.-
1 Hechle	Eliz^th Brown	-.8.-
flax at 9.00 per lb	D^o	-.15.-
1 Tea table paid	Joseph Cummings	-.18.-
1 pair of hand bellows pd	Timothy Currans	-.1.-
1 looking glass	Abner Kirk	-.15.-
one arm chair	Elizabeth Brown	-.5.-
1 high chair for children	Abner Kirk	-.3.9
1 Slate	Asahel Churchman	-.3.-
1 pair of sheepsheers	Wm Brown	-.2.4
2 Chairs	Samuel Cowdess	
2 d^o	Eliz^th Brown	-.5.-
2 d^o	D^o D^o	-.3.1
2 d^o	Eliz^th Brown	-.1.1
2 d^o	D^o	-.5.1

ARTICLES SOLD	PURCHASERS NAMES	PRICE
1 Big wheel	D^o	-.6.1
1 wine seive paid	Saml Brown Wheelright	-.5.6
reel & spools	Elizabeth Brown	-.2.6

2 Bags	D^o	-.-.8
1 Small table	Abner Kirk	-.2.7
1 Iron candle stand	Samuel Cother	-.4.6
1 Spinning wheel	Elizth Brown	-.2.6
1 d^o pd	Wm Kinly	-.2.-
1 feather bed at 2/2 per lb	Timothy Currans Jr	4.12.1
1 do at 2/7 per lbs wt 34 lbs	James Morten	4.7.10
1 Table	Elizth Brown	-.-.8
1 Saddle & saddle bags		
1 bridle	Elizabeth Brown	1.2.6
Old saddle w saddle bags & bridle	Saml Brown wheelright	-.2.6
11 geese first choice at 3/0	Elijah Rogers	1.13.-
11 d^o second choice 3/1	John Brown Junr	1.13.11
11 d^o at 3/1	Wm Winchester	1.13.11
a lot of Walnut stuff	John Porter	-.9.4/0
a lot of table legs	Saml Cother	-.18.6
a stack of cherry tree boards at		
1£10S4dper Hund 125feet	Wm Graham	1.17.11
a stack of walnut boards at		
at 1£3"0 per Hund 273 feet	Saml Cother	3.2.6
A stack of narrow walnut boards at		
11/4 per Hund 54 feet	John Porter-	-.9.6
a stack of walnut boards at		
11/3/3 Meas_d 120 feet	Eliz Brown	-.13.6
half inch walnut 1 at 7/6	D^o	
per hundred 33 feet		
a stack of cherry tree at 1£ 2-6 per		
Hund 104 feet	Saml Cother	1.3.2
2 small stacks cherry tree	Eliz Brown 62 feet	0.4.8
one stack of walnut at 15 per		
Hun^d 88 feet	D^o	0.13.½
one stack of walnut boards at 1.4.1 per		
Hun^d 86 feet	Saml Cother	1.-.8
a stack of half inch walnut boards		
[ill] pr hund 132 feet	D^o	-.17.1
one stack of wide walnut boards at		
1.6.0 pr H 168 feet	Wm Brown	2.3.6

(page) 482

ARTICLES SOLD	PURCHASERS NAMES	PRICE
A stack of walnut boards at		
12/1 per h.d 52 feet	Wm Brown	-.6.3/3
3 Walnut plank at the rate of		
7/6 per hund 60 feet	John Porter	-.4.8
A stack of ½ Inch walnut boards		
at 10/2 per hund 188 feet	Wm Graham	-.19.-
A lot of walnut boards	D^o	-.11.1
A stack of ½ Inch walnut boards at		
5 S pr H. 22 feet	John Porter	-.1.1
A lot of walnut boards	D^o	-.11.3
4 Gouges	Asahel Churchman	-.2.7
4 Chisels	D^o	-.2.9
2 Chisels & 2 Gouges pd	Joshua Brown	-.1.7
3 Chisels & 1 Gouge	Wm Cook	-.5.1
4 Chisels pd	Thos Job	-.11.3
Chisels & some gouges	Abner Kirk	-.10.½
2 round shaves	Wm Cook	-.1.6
1 d^o	Roger Kirk	-.1.10/2
2 planes	Sam_l Cother	1.17.6
2 d^o for making cornish	to Do	2.4.6
2 Cornish plancs	Thomas Patten	-.16.6
2 bench planes pd	Thos Job	-.3.8
2 d^o	D^o	-.4.6
2 d^o small ones pd	Joshua Brown	-.1.7

2 d^o pd	John Knight	-.3.2
2 Wooden squares	Roger Kirk	-.-.6
a square & level	Edward Mitchell	-.1.-
3 Gauges	Nathaniel Oldham	-.-.6
2 planes	Thomas Job	-.-.11
2 pannel planes	Wm Rogers	-.3.-
2 planes	James Lewis	-.1.-
3 D^o	Asahel Churchman	-.1.7
4 D^o	to Do	-.1.-
3 D^o	to James Cooper	-.1.4
3 D^o	Wm Graham	-.1.3
1 Hand saw	Joshua George	-.7.7
1 sash saw	Saml Cother	-.6.7
handsaw	Wm Cook	-.7.6
1 old tennant saw pd	Joshua Brown	-.7.7
1 D^o pd	Saml Brown W.right	-.1.3
1 hand saw	Bartholomy Owen	-.11.6
a Crank & gudgen	Edward Mitchell	-.1.6
a paif of pinces & driver	to do	-.1.7
a hold fast	Thos Job	-.1.7
1 Hammer pd	Doc^t William Miller	-.2.-
2 Augers	Edwd Mitchell	-.1.6
2 drawknives	Wm Mitchell	-.3.4
an Auger & spike gimblet	Andrew M^{c}vey	-.1.1
2 Screw Augers	John Porter	-.2.6
1 D^o	Asahel Churchman	-.4.-
1 D^o pd	James Harlan	-.6.0
one drawing knife	Wm Cook	-.7.6
1 Iron square	Isabel Churchman	-.11.11
1 falling ax paid	James Allen	-.4.6
1 D^o	Wm Allen	-.1.3
1 post ax	Ruben Hains	-.3.6
1 falling ax	James Wade	-.5.7
1 broad ax	Edwd Mitchell	-.10.4
1 broad ax	Ja^s Wade	-.7.-
1 foot adz	Samuel Cother	-.6.7
1 Cooper adz	Roger Kirk	-.4.2
1 broad ax	Saml Cother	-.9.6/2
1 brace stock of bits	John Porter	1.0.-
1 head of a book case	David Cummings	-.2.-
1 D^o paid	James Rutherford	-.3.-
1 Table frame	Elizabeth Brown	-.10.9
1 D^o	D^o	-.3.9
1 Table	Wm Brown	-.8.-
1 table frame	Wm Graham	-.13.6
1 case of drawers unfinished	Jonathan White	3.3.6
1 book case	Reuben Haines	1.13.6
1 Walnut chest	Andrew Egan	-.18.2
1 Cherry tree cupboard	Benjamin Hudson	2.5.-
a set of table legs	Robert Ramsey pd	-.4.-
one set d^o	Wm Brown	-.2.-
a lot of lumber cupboard shelves &	Wm Graham	-.16.8

(page) 483

ARTICLES SOLD	PURCHASERS NAMES	PRICE
2 Clock cases not finished	Elizabeth Brown	1.-.-
1 do	to D^o	-.15.-
1 desk	to d^o	1.-.-
1 stove	to d^o	-.7.6
1 pair of wheels	Wm Brown	1.10.-
1 harrow an ax chain	Elizth Brown	-.4/5.2
1 plow	Ezekiel Cook	1.10.6
1 D^o	Elizth Brown	-.15.-

1 plow	Wm Brown	-.7.6
1 pair timber wheels	Ezekiel Cook	7.3.6
1 Carriage bed	D^o	-.3.9
1 hoe	Philip Ward	-.3.3
1 pair bedsteads	Hannah Cother	-.11.6
1 pair D^o	John Reynolds	-.9.-
1 Do pd	Elizth England	-.8.-
2 pigs the first choice	Asahel Churchman	1.10.-
2 second choice	Philip Ward	1.11.7
2 pigs third choice	Wm Brown	1.5.6
1 boar pig	Abner Kirk	-.10.-
4 pigs the first choice in the smaller pen	Elizth Brown	1.10.-
2 pigs the residue	David Cummins	1.15.-
1 colt	Asahel Churchman	8.-.-
1 bay horse	Abner Kirk	15.-.-
1 sorrel horse	Elizth Brown	10.-.-
1 draw knife	Wm Graham	-.4.-
1 wheel barrow	Edwd Michell	1.6.-

Sales Continued the 23rd of the 4th month april

A box of chissels & gouges	Elizabeth	-.5.?
a lot of Joiners planes	D^o	-.12.-
1 Iron square	D^o	-.4.-
1 Tennant saw	D^o	-.4.1
1 hand saw	D^o	-.8.-
2 draw knives	D^o	-.8.-
2 Augers	D^o	-.3.4
1 small tennant saw	D^o	-.2.7
1 screw nut	James Wade	-.5.-
1 falling ax	Elizth Brown	-.3.9
1 broad ax	D^o	-.6.1

ARTICLES SOLD	PURCHASERS NAMES	PRICE
1 falling ax	D^o	-.4.2
2 bench planes	D^o	-.4.1
1 small plane	D^o	-.-.11
Bedstead stuff	D^o	-.4.9
1 scythe & hangings	Roger Kirk	-.4.-
1 old scythe & D^o	Elizabeth Brown	-.3.5
1 screw clamp	Sam$_l$ Cother	-.5.1
1 Wheel laithe	D^o	-.7.7
1 smaller wheel laithe pd	Isaac Allen	-.15.6
1 smiths bellows	Joshua Brown	1.-.2
1 Grindstone	Elizth Brown	-.6.-
1 Sled	D^o	-.3.5
1 hoe	Enoch Bennett	-.-.5/2
2 D^o	Eliz. Brown	-.2.4
1 D^o	Eli Kirk	-.1.3
1 D^o	Eliz. Brown	-.1.7
1 Dung fork	Hannah Cother	-.2.3
1 Hay fork	Eliz. Brown	-.1.3
1 Mattock	D^o	-.3.10
1 D^o	Roger Kirk	-.5.1
1 spade	Hannah Cother	-.1.3
1 Shovel	Roger Kirk	-.2.7
1 D^o	Eliz. Brown	-.2.2
1 Spade	D^o	-.5.1
1 bill hook	Roger Kirk	-.4.11
1 Mall and 1 Wedge	James Wade	-.2.6
2 smith hammers	Wm Graham	-.3.9
2 D^o	D^o	-.2.-
1 nailers stake & hammer	D^o	-.10.8
1 old broad ax	Wm Cook	-.1.3

1 D°	Eli Kirk	-.1.10/2
1 smiths vise	Roger Kirk	1.10.-
1 bech(?) iron	Wm Graham	-.10.2
1 pair smiths shears	Saml Cother	-.2.7
1 cross cut saw	James Wade	-.7.6
1 D°	Roger Kirk	-.1.6
1 shoeing box & sundries	Wm Brown	-.5.1
a Quantity of old Iron	Joshua Brown	-.11.5
chest of old iron	John Reynolds	-.10.-
Anvil	D°	1.5.-

(page) 484

ARTICLES SOLD	PURCHASERS NAMES	PRICE
1 Hearse	Eliz^th Brown	1.6.3
2 pigs the first choice	Hannah Cother	1.14.-
1 colt	Wm Brown	6.11.-
2 Spring calves	Eliz^th Brown	-.18.9
1 yoke of oxen	D°	18.15.-
1 Cow	D°	5.12.6
a small yoke oxen	D°	6.15.-
1 red and white - -	D°	4.10.-
1 Brindle cow	Hannah Cother	8.2.-
a cutting box	Eliz^th Brown	-.3.9
a set of plow Geirs	D°	-.6.1
a pair of sleigh runners	Roger Kirk	-.7.6
corn at 3/1 per Bush	Eliz^th Brown	
flax from the brake	D°	-.15.-
2 Brick bands for sleigh	Roger Kirk	-.9.4½
2 Chisels and a gouge	D°	-.2.-
the like quantity	Saml Cother	-.3.1
1 Auger	Edward Loney ?	-.4.-
1 Iron square	D°	-.12.2
two planes	Wm Brown	-.1.½
2 d°	Roger Kirk	-.1.6
2 d°	Wm Cook	-.-.10
1 square	Joshua Brown	-.-.2½
1 small table	Wm Cook	-.1.6
1 rifle gun	Wm Graham	1.1.-
1 other gun	Eliz. Brown	-.11.3
fire shovel & tongs	John Reynolds	-.9.2
1 branding iron	Joshua Brown	-.1.3
1 pair of steel yards	Eliz. Brown	-.3.9
1 warming pan	D°	-.1.1½
2 books perrygrine pickle	Johnathan White	-.8.1
2 other books	John Porter	-.4.-
6 plates	Wm Cook	-.5.-

484

ARTICLES SOLD	PURCHASERS NAMES	PRICE
1 Slate	Eliz^th Brown	-.3.1
A lot of earthen ware	Enoch Bennett	-.-.9
1 grid iron & griddle	Eliz^th Brown	-.8.-
1 pan and mug	Enoch Bennett	-.-.10
a tea kettle & frying pan	Eliz^th Brown	-.3.9
1 Iron pot	D°	-.3.9
1 dutch oven without lid	D°	-.2.6
1 large iron pot	D°	-.10.4
1 Churn	D°	-.7.6
3 old pails and a tub	D°	-.2.5
a box of knives & forks	Eliz^th Brown	-.1.6
a lot of old pewter ware	D°	-.5.6
a pair of smoothing irons	D°	-.6.-
1 Case of draws	Margaret Brown	2.-.6

1 Chaff bed & furniture	Eliz_{th} Brown	1.2.8
1 D^o not quite so good	D^o	-.15.2
1 Dough trough	D^o	-.7.6
a side of harness leather at		
1/7 per lb//W 9 3/4	Roger Kirk	-.13.5
1 tar can	W_m Cook	-.2.-
a lot of earthenware	Eliz. Brown	-.1.3
2 Jugs	Philip Ward	-.-.8
a lot bottles of jugs	Enoch Bennett	-.-.9
2 bottles	Margaret Brown	-.1.-
tee ware	Elizabeth Brown	-.1.6
fire shovel & tongs	D^o	-.3.9
the cradle	D^o	-.-.9
a set of stock bands at 10 d per pound	Joshua Brown	-.15.-
grain in the ground & Mulatt girl	Eliz. Brown	08.12.6
		211.15.11

?? Examined by D. Smith Reg
May 10th 1803

Figure 1   Detail of Amos Doolittle, *Connecticut From the best Authorities*, first printed by Matthew Carey, Philadelphia, Pennsylvania, 1795. (Courtesy, Connecticut Historical Society.)

Thomas P. Kugelman

Felix Huntington and the Furniture of Norwich, Connecticut, 1770–1800

▼ LOCATED AT THE navigational head of the (New) Thames River (fig. 1), Norwich was the primary commercial center for the eastern half of Connecticut during the eighteenth century. The town's merchants and seamen were heavily involved in the coastal, West Indian, and European trades, and imported goods "in the latest fashion" were widely available, both before and after the Revolution. With 7,325 inhabitants, Norwich's population was second only to New Haven's by 1782. Although Bozrah, Franklin, and Lisbon had been entirely within Norwich's boundaries, they became independent towns in 1786; nonetheless, because of their proximity to Norwich, furniture produced in those towns is included in this study.

Eastern Connecticut furniture attracted little attention among early scholars. The Hudson-Fulton exhibition of 1909 included, without attribution, a shell-carved, blockfront desk formerly owned by Ebenezer Huntington (1754–1834) (figs. 2, 3). Four years later, Luke Vincent Lockwood's *Colonial Furniture in America* (2nd ed.) mentioned but did not illustrate a high chest bearing the inscription "made by Joshua Read of Norwich in the

Figure 2   Desk, attributed to Felix Huntington, Norwich, Connecticut, 1775–1790. Mahogany and zebrawood with white pine. H. 43¼", W. 44¼", D. 22". (Courtesy, Art Institute of Chicago, gift of the Antiquarian Society through the Jessie Spalding Landon Fund, 1948.122.)

Figure 3   Desk illustrated in fig. 2 with the fall-board open.

year 1752." Between 1936 and 1965, Ada Chase published a series of articles on Norwich-area craftsmen. Although she singled out Ebenezer Tracy (1744–1803) and Felix Huntington (1749–1823) as probable makers of case furniture, Chase did not identify any examples of their work. Houghton Bulkeley, Connecticut's premier furniture scholar of the 1950s and 1960s, published a list of Norwich cabinetmakers in 1964 but, with the exception of the Joshua Read high chest, was unable to link other makers with specific objects.[1]

The first attempt to assemble and exhibit a group of historic artifacts from Norwich occurred in 1965, when The Society of the Founders of Norwich and Friends of the Slater Museum mounted "Craftsmen & Artists of Norwich." The exhibition featured a range of paintings and decorative arts, including forty-four pieces of furniture. A chest-on-chest (fig. 4) was tentatively attributed to J. Backus, presumably Norwich joiner and wheelwright John Backus (1740–1814). Of the eleven other objects illustrated in the exhibition catalogue, none would be considered of Norwich origin today.[2]

In the 1974 exhibition "New London County Furniture, 1640–1840," Minor Myers and Edgar Mayhew attributed sixteen pieces of case furniture

Figure 4 Chest-on-chest, attributed to Ebenezer Tracy, Lisbon, Connecticut, 1796. Cherry with white pine, tulip poplar, birch, and chestnut. H. 81¼", W. 40¼", D. 20½". (Courtesy, Connecticut Historical Society, gift of Frederick K. and Margaret R. Barbour in memory of Newton C. Brainard, 1965.53.0; photo, Gavin Ashworth.) This object is inscribed "Lisbon / 1796." The feet and base molding are restored.

and half a dozen chairs to Norwich and/or Colchester but, in every case, without an attribution to a maker. The authors did, however, note that the inscription "Lisbon/1796" on the chest-on-chest previously attributed to Backus was similar to writing by Ebenezer Tracy, best known as a Windsor chairmaker. Since Ebenezer and his son are the only cabinetmakers listed among Lisbon taxables in that year, the piece is almost certainly from the elder Tracy's shop. The first publication to attribute seating other than branded Windsors to specific New London County shops was Robert Trent and Nancy Nelson's "New London County Joined Chairs, 1720–1790" (1985). Their exhibition and catalogue identified two groups of chairs associated with the William Lathrop and Felix Huntington shops. These sources were the primary references for furniture made in eastern Connecticut until 2005, when Thomas and Alice Kugelman and Robert Lionetti's *Connecticut Valley Furniture: Eliphalet Chapin and His Contemporaries, 1750–1800* identified the work of major Colchester shop traditions and established a base line for differentiating furniture produced in Norwich and other regional towns and communities.[3]

Late Eighteenth-Century Norwich Cabinetmakers
In addition to Felix Huntington, whose work is the principal focus of this essay, the checklist, compiled from various sources, lists approximately two dozen woodworkers active in the Norwich area during the last quarter of the eighteenth century. Evidence suggests, however, that only a few of these tradesmen produced formal case furniture. Ebenezer Carew (1745–1801), Huntington's cousin by marriage, had a shop with five joiners' workbenches on the Norwichtown Green, virtually next door to Felix. Given their close proximity, they may well have been frequent collaborators. Ebenezer Tracy had unfinished case furniture and a large inventory of cabinet woods, including mahogany and cherry, in his probate inventory (see fig. 4). Jesse Birchard (1736–1809) of Bozrah, to whom two high chests are tentatively attributed, is another likely candidate (fig. 5). Both Tracy and Birchard appear to have produced stylish, distinctive furniture of high quality that can be differentiated from the output of Huntington's shop. As yet unidentified is the Lebanon or Norwich craftsman responsible for creating a group of highly distinctive furniture for the Trumbull family (fig. 6).[4]

A dozen related case pieces with ownership histories in and around Norwich can now be attributed to the shop of Felix Huntington. These include four chests of drawers, two blockfront desks with shell-carved fallboards, two chest-on-chests, a desk-and-bookcase, and a clock case. Many of these objects have a documented connection to the Huntington family. A group of chairs with similar associations is also discussed here.[5]

Felix Huntington was uniquely fortunate to have been born into one of the colony's most powerful, affluent, and influential families. His relatives included three Revolutionary War generals, a president of the Continental Congress who later became the state's governor, several ministers, judges, merchants, and an array of skilled tradesmen. He spent his entire life in a town where he had easy access to goods from Europe and the West Indies,

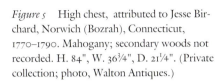

Figure 5 High chest, attributed to Jesse Birchard, Norwich (Bozrah), Connecticut, 1770–1790. Mahogany; secondary woods not recorded. H. 84", W. 36¾", D. 21¼". (Private collection; photo, Walton Antiques.)

Figure 6 Chest-on-chest, probably Lebanon or Norwich, Connecticut, 1770–1790. Cherry with white pine. H. 86½", W. 42", D. 23½". (Courtesy, Baltimore Museum of Art.)

including high-quality mahogany, exotic woods, imported leather, and other luxury items.

Born in Norwich on November 28, 1749, Felix was the fourth of five children and third son of Daniel (1711–1753) and Rebecca Huntington (1726–1798). The younger Huntington's maternal grandmother, Rebecca Lathrop (1695–1774), was the sister of Norwich joiner William Lathrop (1688–1778), in whose shop Felix probably trained. There is no evidence that Daniel Huntington was a joiner, and he died when Felix was three years of age. In 1773 Felix married Anna Perkins (1756–1806), whose maternal grandfather, James Brown (ca. 1700–1765), came from Newport; however, no family connection to a major cabinet shop there has been established. None of the couple's three sons was trained in their father's craft, perhaps a result of the financial difficulties he encountered when they were still young.[6]

Felix lived and worked in the "old" part of town, now known as Norwichtown. When he completed his apprenticeship in 1771, he purchased the land for his first shop from his great-uncle Ebenezer Lathrop, brother of William. In 1791 Huntington was forced to sell his home and shop to settle his debts. Four years later, he built a new shop nearby, next door to pewterer Samuel Danforth (1770–1827). In 1800 Felix bought a house across the street, owned by his cousin Ebenezer Carew, in whose joiner's shop he probably worked during the years he did not have a business of his own.[7]

In a number of primary and early secondary sources, Huntington is variously identified as a cabinetmaker, joiner, and carpenter. His only trade advertisement, placed in 1778, requested "A QUANTITY of Hogs Bristles," presumably for use in brushes. The most enlightening document pertaining to his career is an October 1792 petition from Huntington to the State General Assembly:

> Shewing to this Assembly that for some Years before the late War [Felix Huntington] . . . carried on the Business of Cabinet making in said Norwich until the Commencement of the War when the Custom of said Huntington failing in Order to vend more of his Work he build a Vessell and fitted her for Sea and likewise purchased several Shares in sundry other Vessels and that by sundry heavy losses by Sea in the Course of the War at the Time when Peace took Place he was indebted to sundry Persons about fifteen Hundred Pounds in the whole that for the Term of nine Years he hath strove to the utmost of his Power to struggle through his embarrassment and extricate himself from Debt, and that there still remains due from him about One thousand Pounds lawful Money, that he finds himself in the decline of Life hath a large Family of small Children to support by his Labour and that he is unable to pay all his Just Debts Praying for an Act of Insolvency in his favour as per Petition on file, and no one of the said Creditors appearing to object they having been duely Notified.

His petition was granted with the provisions that he deliver "all his Estate and Effects for the Use of his Creditors in proportion to their respective Debts and demands excepting only one Cow, and such necessary wearing Apparel for himself and Family, and such Household furniture and Tools of his Trade as are exempted by Law."[8]

In July 1792 tax collector Ebenezer Bushnell placed an ad for the sale of Felix's real estate to pay back taxes for 1790 and 1791. In May 1794, presumably fulfilling his role as one of the bankruptcy commissioners, merchant Andrew Huntington advertised for sale at his store: "For the benefit of the Creditors of Felix Huntington . . . An Easy Chair, a large Table, Mahogany Clock Case, a dozen silver handle Knives and Forks, a Shagreen Case, a pair brass Candlesticks, a parcel of Ivory, and sundry other Articles." In addition to selling some of his own possessions, Felix attempted to satisfy some of his creditors with cabinetwork. A surviving promissory note reads: "In Value Rec[d] I promise to pay Gurdon Bill Twelve dollars & twenty eight Cents on demand to be taken in Cabinet work if deli[d] when called for in a reasonable time if not Cash with Interest untill paid. Norwich December 6, 1798 Felix Huntington."[9]

Census records also provide a glimpse into Huntington's troubled finances and their impact on his productivity. In 1790 his household included four males over the age of sixteen (presumably apprentices and/or journeymen) in addition to his family, but in 1800 and 1810 there were none. Also noteworthy is his omission from town tax assessments by trade in 1797

Figure 7   Desk, attributed to Felix Huntington, Norwich, Connecticut, 1775–1790. Mahogany with white pine and tulip poplar. H. 43½", W. 44", D. 22½". (Private collection; photo, Gavin Ashworth.)

and 1798. These documents, covering the years 1795 to 1798, identify individuals by name and occupation for each town in the state. The lists are incomplete, and identification of trades varies. Of the two surviving Norwich lists, the one for 1797 identifies all craftsmen as "mechanics."[10]

In 1815, at age sixty-five, Huntington advertised his house and shop for sale. Five years later the census recorded him living with his son Felix Augustus. Although the elder Huntington's headstone in the Norwichtown Burying Ground and most subsequent publications record his death as having taken place in September 1822, the *Norwich Courier* and other newspapers reported it as September 3, 1823.[11]

Furniture from the Shop of Felix Huntington
Like most eighteenth-century Connecticut craftsmen, Felix Huntington did not sign or label his work. All attributions to his shop are based on circumstantial evidence, which includes histories of ownership, account book entries, correspondence, probate inventories, shipping records, and simi-

Figure 8   Detail of the desk illustrated in fig. 7 showing the fallboard open. (Photo, Gavin Ashworth.)

larity to documented objects. Also assumed is that Huntington family members and business associates would have given more patronage to him than to other local cabinetmakers. This theory is supported by a letter, dated July 4, 1782, from John Chester of Wethersfield to his brother-in-law Joshua Huntington (a second cousin of Felix) in which he orders seating furniture but takes issue with the cost of case furniture: "The Chairs we will have . . . [but Felix] Huntington has rather raised the price of Bureaus. I understood [from] you he asked £7 for one swell'd and trimmed. £6 is certainly higher for a plain one without trimmings. You shall hear more from me soon on this business." A second letter written eight months later included Felix's bill, presumably with payment for the chairs, but, regrettably, the invoice has not survived.[12]

Huntington's furniture production can be divided into two periods, separated by his bankruptcy and the sale of his shop in 1791. Compared with the work of some contemporaries, the number of case pieces associated with his shop is relatively small. Huntington's most productive years, and those

Figure 9 Detail of the left shell on the fallboard of the desk illustrated in fig. 7. (Photo, Gavin Ashworth.)

Figure 10 Detail of the center shell on the fallboard of the desk illustrated in fig. 7. (Photo, Gavin Ashworth.)

Figure 11 Detail of the left front foot of the desk illustrated in fig. 7. (Photo, Gavin Ashworth.)

yielding the majority of his best work, are the 1770s and 1780s, a prosperous time for Norwich as well as for members of his extended family. Evidence confirms that Huntington continued making furniture during the federal period, but the quality and quantity of his work appear to have declined. Although he maintained a shop until at least 1815, little documented furniture made after 1800 is known.[13]

Several design and construction features differentiate the products of Huntington's shop from furniture made by other makers. His work reflects a strong Rhode Island influence and encompasses a variety of sophisticated case and seating forms with a preference for certain details including enclosed ogee heads without rosettes; four-drawer lower cases; serpentine façades; canted corners with stop-fluting and lamb's-tongue terminals (figs. 20, 24); proficiently carved shells; cock-beaded drawer fonts; ogee and straight bracket feet with paired horizontal cusps (figs. 11, 18); and, on later work, straight bracket feet with canted corners and a conventional vertical cusp (figs. 13, 14). His chair designs feature interlacing splats, most often of the so-called "owl's-eye" variety, prominent crest ears, and over-the-rail upholstered frames (figs. 25–27). Much of Huntington's formal furniture is made of mahogany and mahogany veneer; cherry is more common in his later work. Secondary woods used in his shop include white pine, tulip poplar, maple, chestnut, and, occasionally, butternut. As was the case in most cabinet shops, Huntington and his workmen used patterns, design formulas, and standardized construction and assembly techniques. In Huntington's case, construction and assembly practices appear to have been enforced less rigorously than in shops managed by some of his contemporaries. Although this makes some attributions problematic (figs. 12–14), several structural details recur in furniture associated with him: backboards are oriented horizontally and nailed into rabbets; drawer dividers are blind-dovetailed at the sides and covered with facing strips at the front; drawer runners are set in dadoes in case sides in earlier case pieces and nailed in later work; wooden pins are often used as fasteners (fig. 21); feet are reinforced with small triangular blocks (fig. 16); the bottoms of drawers are dadoed to the sides and front; drawer sides are rounded at the top in early work but not on later case works; and cutouts for hardware are rounded and chamfered on serpentine and blocked drawer fronts (fig. 19). Variations in the construction of Huntington's furniture probably reflect shortcuts owing to economic shifts and the individual work habits of journeymen and/or collaborators. It is also possible that he subcontracted specialized work like carving, since the shells on his furniture differ significantly from piece to piece. With the exceptions of Ebenezer Carew and a possible apprentice named Nathan Clark (1766–1839), Huntington's workmen remain unidentified.[14]

The most elaborate and securely documented object attributed to Huntington's shop is a mahogany blockfront desk originally owned by his second cousin, Revolutionary War hero Major General Ebenezer Huntington (figs. 2, 3). The desk remained in Ebenezer's family home for more than a century until the death of the last of three unmarried daughters in 1885. New London collector George Smith Palmer (1855–1934) bought the desk

Figure 12   Desk-and-bookcase, attributed to Felix Huntington, Norwich, Connecticut, 1785–1800. Mahogany and cherry with white pine and tulip poplar. H. 83", W. 43½", D. 20¼". (Courtesy, Scotland Historical Society; photo, Gavin Ashworth.)

from Huntington heirs and subsequently sold it, along with other objects, to the Metropolitan Museum of Art in 1918. Thirty years later the museum transferred the desk to the Art Institute of Chicago.[15]

Although the Ebenezer Huntington desk has Rhode Island–inspired details like a shell-carved fallboard, its double-cusped ogee feet set it apart from Rhode Island work. Elaborately scrolled feet and aprons have long been associated with southeastern Connecticut furniture, but the design of Huntington's foot is so idiosyncratic that it can be considered diagnostic of his shop's work. As the feet on the desk reveal, his ogee model is distinguished by having rounded blocking that conforms both to the façade and the outer edge of the foot, paired cusps oriented horizontally and scrolled upward at the inner edge, and a prominent bead at the inner edge with a wider bead, or astragal, at the base (see fig. 11).

Huntington's desk is unique in its use of zebrawood (*Goncalo alves*)—a dark-figured exotic probably imported from Brazil—for the interior drawer fronts (fig. 3). Although there is no reason to assume that this was not intentional, exotics occasionally entered the mahogany trade inadvertently, as evidenced by the occasional use of corbaril (an extremely hard wood that is very difficult to cut) in early Boston furniture. Unlike corbaril, zebrawood would have provided a contrast in color and figure to the mahogany used elsewhere as primary wood on the desk.[16]

A nearly identical desk also has strong family connections to Norwich, but the identity of its first owner is uncertain (figs. 7–11). Its principal difference lies in the simpler interior, which is flat rather than serpentine in configuration; the shell on its prospect door likewise has straight rather than serpentine lobes (fig. 8). Compared with the flamboyant amphitheater-style interiors of contemporary desks attributed to nearby Colchester shops, both Huntington interiors are surprisingly restrained.[17]

A desk-and-bookcase originally owned by Windham merchant Judge Ebenezer Devotion Jr. (1740–1829), another of Felix Huntington's second cousins, is relatively austere when compared with the preceding desks (fig. 12). The former object is identified in Devotion's will as "My Mahogany Desk & Bookcase [with] all my Library of Books and Manuscripts." His account book records numerous transactions with Felix Huntington over a twenty-year period beginning in 1779 that included purchases of a mahogany bureau, a half dozen chairs, a "large" table, a cherry "Pembroke"

Figure 13 Chest of drawers, attributed to Felix Huntington, Norwich, Connecticut, 1785–1795. Cherry with white pine and chestnut. H. 34½", W. 38½", D. 19½". (Courtesy, Hartford Steam Boiler Inspection and Insurance Company; photo, Gavin Ashworth.)

table, a pair of "backgamd" (backgammon) tables, and two sideboards, one cherry, the other mahogany. Huntington also settled a large account balance of £15.4 in 1798, presumably with furniture.[18]

The construction of the lower section of the Devotion desk-and-bookcase matches that of the blockfront desks, but the former object displays a number of cost-cutting features. The feet are simplified versions of those on the block-front desks (figs. 2, 7), and the writing compartment has a single row of drawers surmounted by pigeonholes with simple ogee-shaped valences. With a central vertical divider cut to allow access to a latch for the doors and two rows of fixed shelves, the interior of the bookcase section is also quite plain.

Judging from surviving examples, chests of drawers, or bureaus, appear to have been a mainstay of the Huntington shop. The most common model features a serpentine façade, canted corners and either cusped ogee or plain bracket feet (figs. 13–16). A cherry bureau that descended in the same line as the Devotion desk-and-bookcase displays the neat, precise construction associated with Huntington's earlier work, although the feet and nailed drawer runners suggest that the piece was made after 1785. Most of the bracket foot examples probably postdate Felix's bankruptcy in 1792. The chest illustrated in figure 14 supports that theory, having stamped federal brasses and a number of cost-saving structural shortcuts: the edge of the top

Figure 14   Chest of drawers, attributed to the shop of Felix Huntington, Norwich, Connecticut, 1795–1805. Cherry with white pine and chestnut. H. 35½", W. 38½", D. 19". (Private collection; photo, Sotheby's.)

Figure 15 Chest of drawers, attributed to Felix Huntington, Norwich, Connecticut, 1775–1790. Mahogany with white pine and chestnut. H. 32", W. 37½", D. 21½". (Private collection; photo, Sotheby's.) The design of this chest is essentially the same as that of the lower section of the chest-on-chests illustrated in figs. 17 and 22. The faces of the front feet differ from those of the chest-on-chests in having a quirk bead rather than rounded beading. The chest is unusually small with a 33-inch case width and an elegant molded top with generous overhang and rounded corners.

Figure 16 Detail of the foot blocking on the chest illustrated in fig. 15. (Photo, Sotheby's.) The triangular blocking of the right front foot is original. The square blocking elsewhere is replaced.

Figure 17 Chest-on-chest, attributed to Felix Huntington, Norwich, Connecticut, 1775–1790. Mahogany with white pine and tulip poplar. H. 81¼", W. 40¾", D. 20". (Courtesy, Connecticut Historical Society, gift of Frederick K. and Margaret R. Barbour, 1960.7.12; photo, Gavin Ashworth.)

is beaded rather than molded; the rear foot bracket is angled rather than being ogee-shaped; and the base molding is a simple cove without a fillet at the top and bottom. This chest could represent the work of an apprentice or journeyman from Huntington's shop.[19]

The mahogany chest-on-chest illustrated in figures 17–21 has a relatively low arching pediment with no scroll terminations, a design likely influenced by Newport furniture. The roof boards are lined on the interior with pages from the June 10, 1784, issue of the *Norwich Packet*. More unusual is the pitched pediment of the chest-on-chest illustrated in figure 22. The some-

Figure 18   Detail of the right front foot of the chest-on-chest illustrated in fig. 17. (Photo, Gavin Ashworth.)

Figure 19   Detail of a serpentine drawer from the lower case of the chest-on-chest illustrated in fig. 17, showing the rounded and chamfered cutout for the lock. (Photo, Gavin Ashworth.)

Figure 20   Detail of the left chamfered corner of the chest-on-chest illustrated in fig. 17. (Photo, Gavin Ashworth.)

Figure 21   Detail of the bottom rail of the lower case of the chest-on-chest illustrated in fig. 17, showing wooden pins used as fasteners. (Photo, Gavin Ashworth.)

Figure 22 Chest-on-chest, attributed to Felix Huntington, Norwich, Connecticut, 1785–1800. Mahogany with white pine, tulip poplar, and chestnut. H. 90½", W. 41¼", D. 20½". (Private collection; photo, Christie's.) Pitched pediments are rare in Connecticut case furniture. Although different in design, the construction of this chest-on-chest is similar to the example illustrated in fig. 17. The finial, side plinths, and brasses are replaced.

Figure 23 Tall clock case, attributed to Felix Huntington, Norwich, Connecticut, 1785–1800. Mahogany with white pine and chestnut. H. 88¾", W. 20", D. 9¾". (Private collection; photo, David Stansbury.) The movement is by Nathaniel Shipman. The feet, fretwork, and finials are restored.

Figure 24 Detail of the right front corner of the clock case illustrated in fig. 23, showing chamfering and a lamb's-tongue terminal similar to that on the chest-on-chest illustrated in figs. 17 and 20. (Photo, David Stansbury.)

what awkwardly conceived upper case suggests that Huntington's shop was unaccustomed to producing this particular form. The center plinth, with its virtually straight sides, and the unusual wide-lobed shell differ significantly from those on the bonnet-top example. The pitch-pediment chest-on-chest also has a curious labor-saving feature; the lower case drawer locks are attached above the right brasses, where the drawer front is thinner than in the middle. This eliminated the need for a deep lock mortise, which would have been required for the more conventional placement of locks at the top center of each drawer.[20]

The account books of Norwich clockmakers Joseph Carpenter (1747–1804) and Nathaniel Shipman (1764–1853) record several transactions with Felix Huntington, including the purchase of at least five clock cases each between 1787 and 1790. In 1789 Huntington's cases in mahogany sold for £5 and cases in cherry, £3. The clock illustrated in figure 23 descended in the family of Felix's older brother, Levi (1747–1802), a Norwich merchant and frequent collaborator in the cabinetmaker's business ventures. It was listed in Levi's probate inventory as "1 Brass Clock 200 / [£10]." The silvered brass dial is inscribed "Shipman / Norwich" and elaborately engraved in the manner of Norwich's senior clockmaker, Thomas Harland (ca. 1735–1807), Shipman's presumed master. The arched door at the waist has a complex applied molding and is flanked by chamfered stop-fluted corners with lamb's-tongue ends, comparable to those of the chest-on-chest (figs. 20, 24).[21]

Several sets of side chairs have been attributed to the Huntington shop based on family ownership (figs. 25, 26). As with his case furniture, the formal chairs are made of either mahogany or cherry. Distinguishing characteristics include knee brackets attached to the front seat rail and legs, and crests with prominent ears, some having spiral carving (fig. 28). Furniture scholar Robert F. Trent has suggested that much of the upholstery was the work of Felix's cousin Jonathan Huntington Jr. (1751–after 1792).[22]

Partial provenances for the two sets of mahogany side chairs mentioned above and an easy chair (fig. 29) are recorded on early twentieth-century copper plaques: "This chair was in the Jabez Huntington House, 16 Huntington Lane, Norwich Town, Conn. Bought by Edith Huntington Wilson in 1922. This chair left to her cousin Sydney (Stevens) Williston in 1939." Major General Jabez Huntington (1719–1786), patriarch of the Revolutionary War–era Huntington clan, owned the house now known as the Bradford-Huntington House. His life and marriage dates suggest that the chairs were commissioned by one of his children, most likely his son,

Figure 25 Side chair, attributed to Felix Huntington, Norwich, Connecticut, 1775–1795. Mahogany with maple. H. 37½". W. 21¼", D. 17". (Private collection; photo, Nathan Liverant & Son Antiques.) The front knee brackets are missing, and the legs are pieced out at the bottom.

Figure 26 Side chair, attributed to Felix Huntington, Norwich, Connecticut, 1775–1795. Mahogany with maple. H. 37¼", W. 20¼", D. 16½". (Courtesy, Leffingwell Inn, The Society of the Founders of Norwich, Connecticut, Inc., gift of Henry La Fontaine, #193; photo, Connecticut Historical Society.)

Major General Zachariah Huntington (1764–1850), another of Felix's second cousins. The house was purchased from his descendants in 1922 by antiquarian Edith St. George (Huntington) Wilson (1866–1939), a distant relative.[23]

One of the aforementioned sets has over-the-rail upholstery and distinctive owl's-eye splats—a design long associated with the Norwich area (fig. 25). These splats differ from those on similar chairs produced in Massachusetts in that their large circular piercings ("eyes") are positioned much higher. Nail holes on the underside of the front seat rail and inner edges of the front legs indicate that these chairs originally had knee brackets. The other set has slip seats, uncarved ears, and more complex strapwork (fig. 26).[24]

Many other side chairs have been attributed to the Huntington shop based on their similarity to the examples with commemorative plaques. One mahogany chair with a slip seat and uncarved ears reputedly descended in the family of an unidentified Huntington descendant. Another pair from a cherry set, possibly dating from 1782, descended in the Devotion family with the chest of drawers and desk-and-bookcase illustrated in figure 12 and 14.[25]

The most elaborate set of side chairs attributed to Huntington's shop

Figure 27   Side chair, attributed to Felix Huntington, Norwich, Connecticut, 1775–1790. Mahogany with maple and white pine. H. 38¼", W. 21", D. 17". (Courtesy, Lyman Allyn Museum, 1999.16.) Two chairs from the set represented by this example retain their original gilt leather upholstery and oval brass nails. A third chair was reupholstered between 1958 and 1990.

Figure 28   Detail of the spiral carving on the right crest ear of the side chair illustrated in fig. 27.

have embossed, gilt "Spanish" leather upholstery attached over the rail with oval brass nails (fig. 27). Identical leather was used to cover walls in an unidentified Norwich house and a trunk lined with an 1805 Norwich newspaper. Advertisements listing imported nests of gilt leather trunks, presumably of different sizes, appeared in New London County by 1763. Decorated leather and leather goods of this type were popular in Europe in the mid-eighteenth century. Much of this leather was produced in the Netherlands and imported to the colonies from England.[26]

Robert Trent has attributed simpler joined chairs with upholstered seats, such as those with cross slats, to the Huntington shop. Although these objects have ears, crest rails, and knee brackets similar to those on the chairs illustrated in figures 25 and 26, they lack secure documentation and have details that differ from seating in the Huntington group. Many of these divergent chairs were likely produced in other shops, especially that of Ebenezer Tracy, the region's most prolific chairmaker.[27]

Huntington's shop did, however, produce a range of less expensive turned and painted chairs. In 1789 he delivered "writing chairs" valued at 20s. each, three dozen green Windsors, and an easy chair to the brig *Polly*,

Figure 29   Easy chair, attributed to Felix Huntington, Norwich, Connecticut, 1775–1795. Mahogany with maple and white pine. H. 57", W. not recorded, D. 21". (Private collection; photo, Nadeau Auctions.) This chair has stop-fluted front legs with unusual chamfering at the corners. As with the blockfront desks (figs. 2, 7), the chair reflects strong Newport influence.

scheduled to debark for the West Indies. Governor Samuel Huntington (1731–1796) of Windham, another of Felix's second cousins, owned "7 Green Armed chairs" valued at £2.6 and "5 High top'd green Chairs" (probably Windsors) valued at 10s.[28]

Ledgers and account books, including those of merchant Andrew Huntington, clockmaker Nathaniel Shipman, and Judge Ebenezer Devotion, confirm that Huntington's shop produced an array of household furnishings. Among the objects listed are various types of tables and stands, looking glasses, sideboards, firescreens, and pitchpipes. Future research will undoubtedly identify some of the objects and possibly other work associated with Huntington.[29]

Some of the apprentices and journeyman who worked in Huntington's shop may have established cabinetmaking businesses of their own (see checklist). A desk with structural and stylistic features associated with his work has a plaque inscribed with the following provenance: "From the Maker Nathan Clark To Ruth Parker Married Dec. 10th 1793 To Olive Clark Durkee March 25th 1822 To Eliza Durkee Gifford May 13th 1840 To Herbert Morton Gifford Oct. 17th 1877 To Paul Morton Gifford Sept. 13th 1911." Nathan Clark (1766–1839) of Mansfield, the presumed maker of the desk, apparently presented it as a wedding gift to his wife, Ruth Parker (1765–after 1850). The dates on the plaque suggest that it passed from generation to generation at the date of the recipient offspring's marriage.[30]

The Clark desk exhibits most of the index characteristics of the Huntington shop's case furniture (use of mahogany and mahogany veneer, dadoed drawer supports, cock-beading on exterior drawers, double-cusp feet with small triangular blocks, strips covering drawer blade dovetails), but its execution is less refined. The use of maple for the drawer dividers and vertically laminated feet (mahogany on pine) are also atypical of Huntington's work. Variations of this type are common in the work of apprentices and journeymen who developed work habits in one shop and subsequently modified or augmented them to expedite production, take advantage of locally available materials, or accommodate consumer expectations.

Little is known about Clark other than his Revolutionary War pension file, which states that he spent his adult life in Mansfield, about twenty miles northwest of Norwich in Windham County. There is no record of him as a cabinetmaker, nor does he appear as a woodworker in the surviving Mansfield tax assessments for 1795 and 1797. Although there is no reason to doubt the plaque's assertion that Clark made the desk, one must acknowledge the possibility that he either bought or inherited the piece and that subsequent family tradition was in error. The latter seems unlikely, however, since a desk of this caliber would have been an unlikely purchase for a young man who, at the very least, subsidized his income by farming.[31]

The objects described above constitute the largest and most cohesive group of furniture attributable to a single shop in southeastern Connecticut. Their association with Norwich and the Huntington family combined with the documentary evidence surrounding the life and career of Felix Huntington are persuasive in identifying him as the shop master. The per-

Figure 30 Desk, attributed to Nathan Clark, Norwich or Mansfield, Connecticut, 1785–1793. Mahogany and cherry with maple and white pine. H. 43", W. 42", D. 20". (Courtesy, Connecticut Historical Society, museum purchase in memory of Newton Case Brainard, 1966.85.0; photo, Gavin Ashworth.)

vasive influence of Newport design, especially in the blockfront examples, is readily apparent, as are regional idiosyncrasies evident in the bold ogee feet, embellished canted case corners, and elaborate strapwork chair backs. These designs, for the most part, lack the imaginative flair of Samuel Loomis III (1748–1814) and other nearby Colchester contemporaries but remain in keeping with the fashion of the day. Nevertheless, Huntington's craftsmanship is meticulous and his decorative vocabulary impressive for the context in which he worked. He deserves to be included in the first rank of Connecticut's eighteenth-century cabinetmakers.[32]

Checklist

Furniture Craftsmen Working in Norwich, 1770–1800[33]

ALLYN, STEPHEN BILLINGS (1774–1822), advertised with DANIEL HUNTINGTON 3D from the Chelsea section of Norwich in 1797, that they "carry on the Cabinet and Chair making business . . . [and] doubt not but that they shall be able to exhibit as good work, and as cheap as can be had from New-York or elsewhere." The partnership dissolved by 1802, when Huntington advertised alone. In 1807 Allyn advertised that he had moved his shop to his dwelling house. In 1810 he advertised with JOEL HYDE (1764–1853) of Preston "FOR SALE, A FEW THOUSAND FEET CHERRY BOARDS." In 1821 Allyn announced his departure for the West Indies; he died in Demerara, British Guiana, the following year. His probate inventory included five workbenches, a lathe, many tools, and a considerable quantity of lumber, including cherry and mahogany boards. The implication is strong that he was a major furniture producer during the federal period.[34]

AVERY, JABEZ (1733–1779), his son RICHARD (1764–1824), and his father, JOHN (1706–1766), all owned joiners' tools. Jabez's inventory indicates he was also a turner, and an Avery genealogy describes him as a coach maker. Jabez was the uncle of joiners AMOS and JOHN GAGER.[35]

AVERY, OLIVER (1757–1842), a first cousin of clockmaker John Avery, was born across the Thames River in Preston. He was living in Norwich at the time of the Revolution. In 1781 he advertised as a "CABINET AND CHAIR MAKER, Near the Court House, Norwich . . . [where] he carries on said business in all its various branches." Shortly thereafter he moved to Stockbridge, Massachusetts, where he appeared in the 1790 census. In 1799 he moved to (North) Stonington, Connecticut, where his house still stands. Oliver's account books (1788–1831) and other papers are at the Winterthur Museum. These papers document his production of several furniture forms, including clock cases.[36]

AYER, JOSEPH (1733–1793), lived in Franklin. His probate inventory includes a shop, bench, lathe, and a large assortment of woodworking tools.

BACKUS, JOHN (1740–1814), was a lifelong resident of Norwich. His probate inventory lists "Joiner's & Turner's Tools @ $120" and "Lumber & Stock in the Shop, Barn &c, unfinished @ $20." Also listed are a number of finished and unfinished wheels of various sizes and reels, implying that he made spinning wheels. John had tools bequeathed to him by his brother SIMON (1729–1764), whose inventory indicates that he also had a brief career as a Norwich joiner.

BIRCHARD, JESSE (1736–1809), lived in Bozrah and married the widow of Norwich chairmaker OZIAS BACKUS (1739–1764). A few weeks before his death Birchard advertised "FOR SALE . . . a small BARN and SHOP for the Cabinet and Chair Making business." The 1790 census lists four adult males and one under sixteen in his household, implying that he may have had one or more apprentices and/or journeymen. Birchard's inventory lists a bench, lathe, and woodworking tools. Two similar mahogany scroll-top high chests have been attributed to him, based on ownership by descendants and attachment of his Revolutionary War pass to the side of a drawer (fig. 5).[37]

BRANCH, STEPHEN (1744–1828), was in born in Preston. Circa 1790 he moved eight miles north to Lisbon, where he built a house that stands today. Branch's inventory lists a large assortment of joiner's tools and a lathe. His father was Preston joiner THOMAS BRANCH (1698–1778).

BRIGDEN, TIMOTHY (1749–1813), was born in Wethersfield into a family of chairmakers that included his father, THOMAS (1703–1781), and brother MICHAEL (1743–1828). He moved to Norwich shortly after completing his training, circa 1770. In addition to the customary assortment of tools, his inventory lists a separate "Bench Shop" and "Turning Shop" as well as a "Man'd" and "Water Lathe." His lumber supply included planks of butternut.

CAREW, EBENEZER (1745–1801), a lifelong resident of Norwich, was closely related through his mother and by marriage to numerous HUNTINGTON and LATHROP craftsmen. He sold the house he had built on the Norwichtown green to FELIX HUNTINGTON in 1800. In 1778 he advertised for an apprentice in "the joiner's business," and for a runaway apprentice in 1791, at which time he described himself as a "House Carpenter & Joiner." The 1790 census lists seven males over the age of sixteen in his household, all but two of whom may have been apprentices and/or journeymen. Town tax assessments for 1797 describe him as a "mechanic" with a relatively high assessment of $25. His probate inventory is extensive and includes "5 Joiners Work benches . . . 1 Turning Lathe . . . 1 Duff Tail [Saw] . . . etc." The tools and lumber make it clear that he was both a house and a shop joiner, and, perhaps, the busiest joiner in town.[38]

CASE, SAMUEL (1762–1791) and his brother ASAHEL (1769–1828) both owned joiner's tools. Samuel owned a lathe and unfinished table legs, window frames, and clapboards, indicating he was both a house and a shop joiner. Asahel owned a box of rush, suggesting he may have made chairs.

DOWNER, JABEZ (1749–1791), was a resident of Franklin. His inventory includes tools and a lathe, as well as unfinished chair, table, and bedstead parts, and wheel spokes for carts. He also owned a large quantity of cherry, maple, pine, oak, and ash lumber. No case furniture is mentioned, even among his limited personal belongings.

FARGO, JASON (1735–1782), owned, in addition to the customary tools and a lathe, "1 Set for a Stand Leg" and "Part of a Set furniture for draws."

GAGER, AMOS (1772–1809), and his older brother JOHN (1764–1817) worked in Franklin. Amos had the more comprehensive inventory with unfinished bedstead, table, chair, and wagon parts as well as large quantities of chestnut, oak, and ash. He had two benches and a lathe. A flat-top maple high chest that descended in the family is privately owned, but its maker is unidentified.[39]

GRIST(E), JOHN (1734–1832), a cousin of JESSE BIRCHARD and nephew by marriage of WILLIAM LATHROP, is said to have sold his joiner's shop in 1783 before moving to Pennsylvania five years later. The Griste genealogy reports that he apprenticed as a cabinetmaker at age fourteen.[40]

HUNTINGTON, DANIEL, 3D (1776–1805), a cousin once removed and likely apprentice of FELIX HUNTINGTON and brother of Norwich silversmith Philip Huntington, advertised when he completed his apprenticeship in 1797 with STEPHEN BILLINGS ALLYN as quoted above. In 1802 he advertised alone for "A JOURNEYMAN Cabinet Maker." There is no probate inventory on file.[41]

HUNTINGTON, FELIX (1749–1823): See article.

KELLEY, HEZEKIAH (1761–1822), advertised in 1793 the dissolution of a cabinetmaker partnership with DAVID HAMILTON (1766–1798) who is otherwise unknown as a woodworker. The same year Kelley made seven clock cases for Daniel Burnap of East Windsor. The four adult males in his 1790 household could have included as many as three apprentices or journeymen. By 1795 he had become a merchant, identified as such in 1797 town tax assessments and confirmed with an ad. He invested heavily in the West Indies trade with disastrous results, filing for bankruptcy in 1801. He was still in Norwich in 1813 but died in Illinois. JOHN BACKUS was his wife's uncle and a likely master.[42]

LATHROP, WILLIAM (1688–1778), was one of a dynasty of Norwich woodworkers that includes his cousin once removed ZEBEDIAH LATHROP (1743–1783) and great-nephew ISAAC LATHROP (1765–1826). He was a likely master to another great-nephew, FELIX HUNTINGTON. An exceptional set of early maple Queen Anne chairs, inscribed in 1756 with the name of his niece Elizabeth Lathrop, has been attributed to him. The account book of Isaac Huntington (1688–1764) records a chest and cradle made by Lathrop in 1720. His probate inventory (at age ninety) lists only a few household tools. Zebediah's inventory contains a full complement of joiner's tools and barrel parts. Isaac advertised as a shop joiner in 1788 but was living in Rome, New York, by 1798.[43]

LESTER, TIMOTHY (ca. 1769–1810), advertised first in 1791 in a partnership with ELEAZER HAZEN (1772–1849) as "Lester & Hazen, CABINET & CHAIR-MAKERS . . . [who] supplied every kind of FURNITURE that can be comprehended in their line of business . . . by practicing with some of the best workmen on the Continent." The partnership was dissolved a year later, and Lester continued to advertise alone intermittently until 1799, including requests for apprentices. The 1800 census suggests he may have had an apprentice at the time. In 1802–1803 he was engaged as a "machinist" to assist in the building of a hemp-spinning mill. His inventory, in addition to three benches and mahogany, maple, and cherry boards, has unfinished furniture that includes a stand and washstand. Among his tools is a "vaniering saw." Clapboards, window frames, and other materials for house joinery are present as well.[44]

TIFFANY, ISAIAH, JR. (ca. 1723–1806), was born in Woodstock and moved with his family to Lebanon in 1743. Ten years later he moved to Norwich, where he remained for about twenty years before returning to Lebanon. His account book, covering the years 1746–1772, demonstrates the versatility of his talents and occupations. Early in his career he produced a substantial quantity of seating and case furniture, including nine high chests, three desks, and three clock cases, as well as many chairs and tables. Many of these date before his move to Norwich, where he advertised as a merchant of imported goods in 1768. None of his cabinetwork has been identified with certainty.[45]

TRACY, EBENEZER (1744–1803), known primarily for his Windsor chairs, also produced a full range of other furniture. Working in Lisbon, Ebenezer and his son ELIJAH (1766–1807) are the only two woodworkers in this checklist specifically identified as cabinetmakers in town tax assessments. In 1796 Ebenezer received the unusually high assessment of $80, the highest of anyone in town; his son was assessed the more customary $17. Elijah advertised in 1796 for an apprentice "to the Cabinet and Windsor Chair making business." A Newport-influenced cherry bonnet-top chest-on-chest, inscribed "Lisbon / 1796," is almost certainly from Ebenezer's shop (fig. 4). The 1800 census indicates that he had seven males under the age of twenty-five in his household at the time, four of whom were family members. Preston clockmaker JOHN AVERY (1755–1815) made seven lathes for the shop between 1792 and 1800, along with brass furniture escutcheons, brands, and other items. The number of tools, unfinished chairs and case furniture (including a sideboard and large stock of brasses and locks), board feet of mahogany, cherry, birch, beech, mangrove, chestnut, and other lumber dwarf comparable amounts in other probate inventories. The 2,148 board feet of cherry suggest that the shop produced a significant amount of case furniture in addition to chairs. The presence of mangrove, a tropical wood most often used in ship building, may be unique in a Connecticut cabinet-maker inventory. The shop was sold by family members in 1810 to Preston joiner JOEL HYDE (1764–1853). Furniture scholar Nancy Evans has reviewed his life, work, extended family of craftsmen, and influence in great detail.[46]

WILLIAMS, MOSES (1724–1803), spent most of his working life in Norwich; he moved to Preston after 1788. Even as he approached eighty,

Williams appears to have been a busy chairmaker; his probate inventory included "400 chair rounds, 4 Great Chairs finished, 3 do. Unfinished, 440 feet Maple Boards [and] 1 Joyners Shop with all the Tools & Stuff Contained therein." The shop and tools were valued separately from his house and land at $200.00 — more than all of his personal belongings put together.

ACKNOWLEDGMENTS   The author thanks furniture scholar and conservator Robert Lionetti for his long-standing collaboration and support and for corroborating much of the technical detail in this article.

1. Henry W. Kent and Florence N. Levy, *The Hudson-Fulton Celebration*, 2 vols. (New York: Metropolitan Museum of Art, 1909), 1: 68, no. 169. Luke Vincent Lockwood, *Colonial Furniture in America*, 2 vols., 2nd ed. (New York: Charles Scribner's Sons, 1913), 1: 92. Joshua Read (1725–1795) left Norwich for Windsor, Massachusetts, where his son Simon was born in 1763. There is no other record of him as a cabinetmaker. The Read high chest is illustrated in Houghton Bulkeley, "The Norwich Cabinetmakers," *Connecticut Historical Society Bulletin* 29, no. 3 (July 1964): fig. 1. It is highly unusual in having a mirror, reportedly original, between pairs of upper-case small drawers. Ada R. Chase, "Ebenezer Tracy, Connecticut Chairmaker," *Antiques* 30, no. 6 (December 1936): 166–69; Chase, "Amos D. Allen, Connecticut Cabinetmaker," *Antiques* 69, no. 2 (August 1956): 146–47; Chase, "Two 18th-Century Craftsmen of Norwich," *Connecticut Historical Society Bulletin* 25, no. 3 (July 1960): 84–88; Chase, "Joseph A. Carpenter, Jr., Silversmith and Clockmaker," *Antiques* 85, no. 6 (June 1964): 695–97; and Chase, "Thomas Harland's Clock—Whose Case," *Antiques* 87, no. 6 (June 1965): 700–701. Bulkeley, "The Norwich Cabinetmakers," pp. 76–85.

2. *Craftsmen & Artists of Norwich*, edited by Jo Darmstadt (Stonington, Conn.: Pequot Press, 1965), pp. 50–60 with addenda. The catalogue includes an expanded list of Norwich cabinetmakers by Houghton Bulkeley (pp. 1–11). The chest-on-chest illustrated in fig. 4 (cat. 29) is inscribed as made in Lisbon; John Backus was a lifelong resident of Norwich. His probate inventory indicates that he was a wheelmaker (see checklist).

3. Minor Myers Jr. and Edgar deN. Mayhew, *New London County Furniture, 1640–1840* (New London, Conn.: Lyman Allyn Museum, 1974). The chest-on-chest inscribed "Lisbon / 1796" on the inside of the backboard is no. 70. Town tax assessments by trade for the years 1795–1798 for each town in Connecticut are in the William L. Warren Collection, Connecticut Historical Society, Hartford, Conn. (hereafter CHS). Ebenezer Tracy and his son Elijah are the only cabinetmakers listed in Lisbon's 1796 assessments (see checklist). Ebenezer's assessment was by far the highest of anyone in town. Robert F. Trent and Nancy L. Nelson, "New London County Joined Chairs," *Connecticut Historical Society Bulletin* 50, no. 4 (Fall 1985): 1–200. Thomas P. Kugelman and Alice K. Kugelman with Robert Lionetti, *Connecticut Valley Furniture: Eliphalet Chapin and His Contemporaries, 1750–1800* (Hartford: Connecticut Historical Society, 2005), pp. 201–83. For much of the eighteenth century Colchester was part of Hartford County, with economic and social ties to Hartford, Middletown, and other valley towns.

4. Ebenezer Carew's mother and wife were both Huntingtons. His brother-in-law Jonathan Huntington Jr. (1751–after 1792) is believed by Robert Trent ("New London County Joined Chairs," p. 23 and n22) to have been Felix's principal upholsterer. Carew's ads and probate inventory indicate he was both a house and a shop joiner (see checklist). For details of Ebenezer Tracy's probate inventory, see checklist. For illustrations of the Birchard high chests, see *Antiques* 131, no. 1 (January 1987): 4; and Wallace Nutting, *Furniture Treasury*, 3 vols. (New York: Macmillan Co., 1928), 1: fig. 375. Birchard's Revolutionary War pass is glued to a drawer side of the high chest that descended in a branch of his family (fig. 5). The Nutting example, formerly in the George S. Palmer Collection, has full twisted columns at the upper case corners similar to those associated with high chests attributed to the neighboring town of Preston. The attribution to Birchard's shop was part of a presentation by the author at the Winterthur Furniture Forum in 2009. The Trumbull family furniture included a shell-carved, blockfront chest-on-chest with unusual oblong claw-and-ball feet and Corinthian capitals (fig. 6), a marble-top table, and an elaborately carved candlestand. For details, see Nancy E. Richards and Nancy Goyne Evans, *New England Furniture at Winterthur: Queen Anne and Chippendale Periods* (Winterthur, Del.: Winterthur Museum, 1997), pp. 248–49, 285–86, and

William V. Elder and Jayne E. Stokes, *American Furniture, 1680–1880, from the Collection of the Baltimore Museum of Art* (Baltimore, Md.: Baltimore Museum of Art, 1987), pp. 80–81. The chest-on-chest was last owned by Jonathan George Washington Trumbull (1787–1853), grandson of Jonathan Trumbull Sr. He was related through both his mother and wife to joiners in the Lathrop and Backus families (see checklist).

5. Nine pieces were examined in the course of this study. Two of the chest of drawers are mahogany, a primary wood rarely used in furniture from this area.

6. William Lathrop is credited with making a chest and cradle in 1720 in the Isaac Huntington account book, CHS. A set of formal Queen Anne chairs inscribed with the date 1756, by Lathrop's niece Elizabeth, are attributed to him as well. See also Trent and Nelson, "New London County Joined Chairs," p. 79 and no. 21; and checklist. William B. Brown, "Chad Browne of Providence, R.I.," *New England Historical and Genealogical Society Register* 80, no. 2 (April 1926): 176.

7. Mary E. Perkins, *Old Houses of the Ancient Town of Norwich* (Norwich, Conn.: Bulletin Co., 1895), pp. 191–92, 213–14.

8. *Norwich Packet*, November 23, 1778. *Public Records of the State of Connecticut*, edited by Leonard W. Labaree (Hartford: State of Connecticut, 1948), 7: 539–41. *Public Records of the State of Connecticut*, edited by Leonard W. Labaree (Hartford: State of Connecticut, 1951), 8: 62–63.

9. *Weekly Register* (Norwich, Conn.), July 17, 1792; *Norwich Packet*, May 22, 1794. Felix Huntington promissory note, MS file no. 72896, CHS. Gurdon Bill (1757–1815) was a Norwich sea captain and another of Felix's second cousins. His brother-in-law Daniel Lathrop Coit (1754–1833) was one of Felix's two bankruptcy commissioners.

10. Town Tax Assessments, 1795–1798, Warren Collection, CHS. Ebenezer Carew is listed in 1797 but not in 1798 (see checklist).

11. *Norwich Courier*, July 5, 1815. The property apparently did not sell. A follow-up advertisement placed by his son Felix Augustus in 1821 offers the house, shop, and land once again. Hale Cemetery Inscriptions, Connecticut State Library, Hartford (hereafter CSL). *Norwich Courier*, September 10, 1823. This is confirmed in both the *American Mercury* and the *Connecticut Courant* of September 16, 1823, among others. His headstone has either been misread or was carved sometime after his death when memories were faulty. His death is not recorded in town vital records or family genealogies. No probate records survive.

12. "Huntington Papers: Correspondence of the Brothers Joshua and Jedediah Huntington during the Period of the American Revolution," in *Collections of the Connecticut Historical Society, Vol. 20* (Hartford, 1923), pp. 159–60, 171.

13. Kugelman, Kugelman, and Lionetti, *Connecticut Valley Furniture*, p. 133. The authors have identified at least eight high chests from the Eliphalet Chapin shop in East Windsor, a dozen high chests from the Wethersfield Willard group, and eight Higgins group block-and-shell chests from Chatham. The shop master for the last two groups has not been conclusively identified. The account book of Judge Ebenezer Devotion Jr. records the purchase of a mahogany sideboard from Huntington in 1799. Lance Mayer and Gay Myers, *The Devotion Family* (New London, Conn.: Lyman Allyn Museum, 1993), p. 53.

14. In general, shops in the Connecticut River valley appear to have enforced standardized work practices more rigorously than in other regions, perhaps because craft traditions were more tightly controlled and based on family ties.

15. Kent and Levy, *The Hudson-Fulton Celebration*, 1: 68, no. 69; and Nutting, *Furniture Treasury*, 1: fig. 629. See also Judith A. Barter, Kimberly Rhodes, and Seth A. Thayer, *American Arts at the Art Institute of Chicago* (New York: Hudson Hills Press, 1998), p. 104 (acc. no. 1948.122).

16. Zebrawood identified by J. T. Quirk, Center for Wood Anatomy Research, U.S. Forest Products Laboratory, Madison, Wis., March 1, 1976 (Art Institute of Chicago, acc. no. file 1948.122). Also known as tigerwood, zebrawood belongs to the species *Astronium* and was most often imported from eastern Brazil. Norwich merchants like Ebenezer Huntington were heavily involved in the West Indian trade. The authenticity of the pigeonhole valances of the desk could not be established.

17. Christie's, *Important American Furniture, Prints, Folk Art, and Decorative Arts*, New York, October 12, 2001, lot 134. Possible first owners, based on descent, include John Chester (1749–1809) of Wethersfield, Thomas Coit (1752–1832) of Norwich, or Gustavus Wallbridge (1738–1819) of Norwich and Bennington, Vermont. For the Colchester desks, see Kugelman, Kugelman, and Lionetti, *Connecticut Valley Furniture*, pp. 209, 222, nos. 93, 99.

18. Mayer and Myers, *The Devotion Family*, pp. 52–53. Ebenezer Devotion probate file, CSL. The desk-and-bookcase was bequeathed to an unmarried son and daughter who shared the judge's personal estate. It descended in the family of their sister, Eunice (Devotion) Waldo (1770–1854), and is still in the Edward Waldo homestead, now owned by the Scotland Historical Society, Scotland, Conn.

19. Only two of the chests were available for complete inspection (figs. 13, 14). Information on the others is based on photographs and communication with Connecticut antiques dealer and furniture scholar Arthur Liverant. A virtually identical mahogany chest, also examined, was owned by Nathan Liverant and Son and is illustrated in their brochure, Spring 2002. That firm's files include a number of similar bureaus with both straight and serpentine façades, indicating that the Huntington shop, and probably others in the region, produced comparable examples. Sotheby's, *Important Americana*, New York, October 11, 2001, lot 262; Edwin Nadeau Auction, Windsor, Conn., October 20, 2007, lot 75 (fig. 14). Sotheby's, *Important Americana*, New York, January 19, 2008, lot 295 (fig. 15). The chest has an unsubstantiated history of ownership in the Hyde family of Norwich. A virtually identical example is illustrated in *Antiques* 141, no. 2 (February 1992): 269.

20. The bonnet-top chest-on-chest was purchased from Joe Kindig & Son in 1959. For the pitch-pediment example, see Christie's, *Important American Furniture, Folk Art, Silver, Prints, and Decoys*, New York, January 18–19, 2007, lot 620. It has a twentieth-century brass plaque inscribed "Madeleine P. Nichols from Sara J. Pattison / Com. Isaac Hull," implying ownership by Commodore Isaac Hull (1773–1843), naval hero of the War of 1812 as commander of the *USS Constitution*. Before his service in the newly formed U.S. Navy, Hull was active in the West Indian trade from Norwich and New London as master and part owner of several ships. The Connecticut Ship Database (Mystic Seaport) lists him as master of the Norwich ship *Minerva* and schooners *Beaver* and *Olive* from 1795 to 1798. Sara J. Pattison has been identified as Sarah Jarvis Dennis (1828–after 1920) who married Elias Pattison of New York. Their granddaughter, Madeleine P. Nichols (b. ca. 1911) of Boston, was the recipient on the plaque. She had no documented connection with the Hull family. However, both the Pattisons and Hull heirs (two nieces) were living in New York City in the latter part of the nineteenth century, and the chest-on-chest could have changed hands at that time. It next appeared in the shop of Ansonia, Connecticut, dealer Harry Arons in 1963 and was subsequently exhibited in the Diplomatic Reception Rooms in Washington, D.C. Historic Deerfield owns a cherry desk-and-bookcase (acc. no. 54.208) with a pitch pediment that has New London County features, including double-scrolled returns on the ogee feet. The combination of chestnut, butternut, tulip poplar, and pine as secondary woods is also associated with that region. The pediment does not extend the full depth of the upper case, and the joinery is unlike that from the Huntington shop.

21. Chase, "Two 18th-Century Craftsmen," p. 85; and Chase, "Joseph A. Carpenter, Jr., Silversmith and Clockmaker," pp. 695–97. The Carpenter account book (private collection) covers the years 1787–1803; Shipman's account book (Society of the Founders of Norwich) covers the years 1785–1812. Carpenter, a cousin of Felix Huntington by marriage, also supplied Huntington with eight-day brass movements on three other occasions, one as late as 1795, for which the latter presumably made cases. The Shipman clock is in a private collection. It was purchased from a seventh-generation descendant in 1988 (Betty [Huntington] Culhane to owner, January 15, 1988). The first four generations lived in Norwich, ending with Levi's great-grandson Jedediah Huntington (1837–1885).

22. Trent and Nelson, "New London County Joined Chairs," p. 23. Jonathan's occupation is documented by a bill for upholstering a set of chairs in the account book of the Preston blacksmith Calvin Barstow (1750–1826). Trent hypothesized that Jonathan might have trained in the Boston area, accounting for the fact that some chairs have over-the-rail upholstery, which is rare in New London County seating.

23. According to Chase, "Two 18th-Century Craftsmen," p. 85, Zachariah was one of Felix Huntington's creditors in 1792. Edith Wilson was only distantly related to previous owners of the Bradford-Huntington House; her eighteenth-century Huntington ancestors had moved to Vermont, and she was born in Spencerport, New York. Her cousin Sydney (Stevens) Williston (1880–1944), to whom the chairs were bequeathed, resided in Northampton and Marblehead, Massachusetts. The earliest reference to the chairs outside the family is Israel Sack, Inc., *Antiques from Israel Sack Collection* 15 (February 1967): no. 946.

24. For information on the chair illustrated in figure 25, the author thanks Kevin Tulimieri

of Nathan Liverant and Son. For antecedents of this splat design, see John T. Kirk, *Connecti-cut Furniture: Seventeenth and Eighteenth Centuries* (Hartford, Conn.: Wadsworth Atheneum, 1967), no. 233; and Richards and Evans, *New England Furniture at Winterthur*, p. 59, no. 33. The three surviving examples all descended in branches of the East Hartford family of Gover-nor William Pitkin (1694–1769). Early generations of the Pitkin family were all from the Hart-ford area. The Hartford-area origin is further supported by a privately owned corner chair of similar design with history of descent in the Talcott family. Whether these earlier chairs were made in Hartford or Norwich remains unknown. The set of chairs represented by figure 26 is illustrated in *American Antiques from Israel Sack Collection*, 10 vols. (Alexandria, Va.: Highland House, 1970), 2: 375, no. 946. An image was unavailable. One chair from this set is also shown in Kirk, *Connecticut Furniture: Seventeenth and Eighteenth Centuries*, no. 246. The seat frame is branded "J.A. BELL" (Winterthur Museum, Winterthur, Del., Decorative Arts Photographic Collection [hereafter DAPC], acc. no. 67.490.68.3060). A likely candidate is James Andrews Bell (1816–after 1863), an upholsterer who was born in New Haven and moved with his fam-ily to Pittsfield, Massachusetts, before 1825. Local newspapers and census records list him there from 1850 until his enlistment in the Civil War. He could have worked in the Norwich area during the 1830s or 1840s and reupholstered the chairs at that time. An apparently identical chair (fig. 26) with no family history is in the Leffingwell Inn, Norwich (no. 193, gift of Henry LaFontaine). A similar pair made of cherry with over-the-rail upholstery is in the collection of Historic Deerfield (acc. nos. 2039 a, b; Trent and Nelson, "New London County Joined Chairs," nos. 54, 55). For the wing chair, see Edwin Nadeau Auction, Windsor, Conn., Octo-ber 11, 2008, lot 50. Lot 60 in the same sale was an upholstered mahogany lolling chair with square back, said also to be from the Jabez Huntington House. The spiral carving at the end of the arms is similar to that on the ears of Huntington shop side chairs.

25. Christie's, *Property of Marguerite and Arthur Riordan*, New York, January 18, 2008, lot 588. For the Devotion chairs, see Mayer and Myers, *The Devotion Family*, p. 20, fig. 7; these chairs are at the Brookline (Mass.) Historical Society.

26. An assembled set of seven chairs, two of which retained their original gilt leather uphol-stery, were owned by Norwalk dealer John Kenneth Byard in 1958 (DAPC 71.70, microfilm roll no. 1652-9A). He sold one of the chairs with original leather to Mystic Seaport, where it was exhibited in the Buckingham House until 1989. It sold at Skinner, *Americana Auction*, Bolton, Mass., March 31, 1990, lot 205, and was privately owned until acquired by the Lyman Allyn Museum in 1999. Byard's remaining six chairs were on view at the Cincinnati Art Museum until offered for sale at Northeast Auctions, *Americana Auction*, Manchester, N.H., August 6, 2006, lot 1738. The one chair in that group with original leather, differing in details of splat design from the others, had been reupholstered (Brock Jobe to Thomas Kugelman, March 2, 1991; and personal inspection, March 13, 2010). Another chair, apparently from the same set, still retaining its original leather and oval tacks, allegedly descended in the family of Ebenezer Hough (1767–1846) of Bozrah until acquired by the Museum of Art, Rhode Island School of Design in 1999 (acc. no. 1999.67). Hough was a farmer; his will directed that his personal estate be sold and the proceeds divided among his children. A search of Norwich probate invento-ries conducted in 1991 by James Sexton, covering the years 1769–1826, failed to identify any likely owners of gilt leather objects (CHS acc. file 1999.61.0). The wall covering is illustrated in Catherine Lynn, *Wallpaper in America* (New York: W. W. Norton, 1980), p. 15. The frag-ment, said to be from the Stephen Gifford House, is owned by the Society of the Founders of Norwich. A number of individuals by that name resided in Norwich; none of them is associ-ated with a historic building. The gilt leather trunk, owned by the Connecticut Historical Society (acc. no. 1999.61.0), has no ownership history; the newspaper lining it, *The* (Norwich) *Courier*, dated April 17, 1805, is most likely at least a generation later than the leather covering. On April 6, 1763, *The New-London Summary, or, The Weekly Advertiser* reported: "Thomas & Benjamin Forsey, HAVE just Imported . . . at their Store in New London, VIZ . . . Nests of hair and gilt leather Trunks." Embossed leather wall covering was also used in the Branford home of Connecticut Governor Gurdon Saltonstall (1666–1724). For information on the European origin of gilt leather, see John W. Waterer, *Spanish Leather* (London: Faber & Faber, 1971); this pattern is illustrated on p. 119, pl. 66.

27. Trent and Nelson, "New London County Joined Chairs," nos. 57–59.

28. Nancy Goyne Evans, *American Windsor Chairs* (New York: Hudson Hills Press, 1996), pp. 289, 291, figs. 6–97. The shipment included some case furniture as well. The invoice for the brig *Polly* is in the Joseph Williams Papers at Mystic Seaport, Mystic, Conn. A Windham

native, Samuel Huntington married Martha Devotion (1739–1794), sister of Judge Ebenezer Devotion Jr. The Winterthur chairs are noteworthy in having seats made of butternut, a wood occasionally used by Huntington in case furniture. Evans points out that since the chairs are unmarked they could also be the work of Ebenezer Tracy or another contemporary chair-maker. Samuel Huntington's probate inventory contains much formal cherry and mahogany furniture, very likely from Huntington's shop.

29. Chase, "Two 18th-Century Craftsmen," p. 85. The ledger of Andrew Huntington (Society of the Founders of Norwich) is quoted but could not be located during a recent inquiry. Chase mistakenly identifies Andrew as Felix's father. See also Mayer and Myers, *The Devotion Family*, p. 53.

30. Dates all refer to weddings. Inheritance was by direct descent to a daughter or son. Paul Morton Gifford died in 1961 in the nearby town of Woodstock. The desk apparently never left eastern Connecticut, probably accounting for its good condition and original hardware.

31. Tax assessments, Warren Collection, CHS. Simeon Allen (b. ca. 1758) is the only Mansfield cabinetmaker listed (in 1797).

32. Kugelman, Kugelman, and Lionetti, *Connecticut Valley Furniture*, pp. 201–55, nos. 104, 105, for the work of Samuel Loomis. Of particular interest is a mahogany blockfront desk with shell-carved lid that relates to the two Huntington desks (see figs. 104B and 104C). In addition to its distinctively carved shells, it has full spiral columns at the corners that swell in the middle.

33. Earlier compilations include checklists in Myers and Mayhew, *New London County Furniture*, pp. 106–32; and Houghton Bulkeley, "The Cabinetmakers," in Darmstadt, ed. *Craftsmen & Artists of Norwich*, pp. 1–12. Craftsmen working in Bozrah, Franklin, and Lisbon, which were within the boundaries of Norwich until incorporated as separate towns in 1786, are included. Those identified as house joiners exclusively and transients who died young or moved away are omitted. Probate inventories are on file alphabetically at the CSL. Most are in the Norwich Probate District.

34. *Courier* (Norwich, Conn.), May 31, 1797; April 29, 1807; July 25, 1810; January 10, 1821. Joel Hyde worked as a cabinetmaker in Lisbon after 1810.

35. Elroy M. Avery and Catherine Avery, 2 vols. *The Groton Avery Clan* (Cleveland, 1912), 1: 326.

36. Ibid., 1: 283. *Norwich Packet*, January 23, 1781. Winterthur acc. no. 55x26 (Mic.102).

37. *Courier*, June 14, 1809. For illustrations of the two high chests, see *Antiques* nt. 4 above.

38. *Norwich Packet*, July 20, 1778; December 1, 1791. Tax assessments by trade for the years 1795–1798 are in the Warren Collection, CHS. Not all towns are represented for each year, and the trade designations vary from town to town. Many towns simply refer to manual tradesmen as mechanics. Norwich, Bozrah, Franklin, and Lisbon are all represented by at least one such list. Carew and the Tracys are the only individuals in this checklist identified in the assessments.

39. The high chest, examined by the author, is similar to one illustrated in Myers and Mayhew, *New London County Furniture*, p. 19, no. 10. The shaping of the front apron and absence of knee returns are distinctive.

40. Perkins, *Old Houses of the Ancient Town of Norwich*, p. 217; and J. C. Griste, *History of the Griste Family in America* (Morris, Ill., 1901), p. 1 (online transcription).

41. *Courier*, May 31, 1797; September 29, 1802.

42. *Norwich Packet*, February 7, 1792; *Courier*, March 1, 1798; March 4, 1801. In 1795 and 1796 a David Hamilton was master of the schooner *Anna*, a ship of which Kelley was part owner. In 1797 Hamilton took over the helm of the schooner *Lucy*; he died in Newburgh, New York, the following year. Presumably, Hamilton the mariner and cabinetmaker are one and the same. Penrose R. Hoopes, *Shop Records of Daniel Burnap* (Hartford: Connecticut Historical Society, 1958), p. 55. Hoopes mistakenly records Kelley as being in Norwich, Vermont; however, the original manuscript (CHS) makes no such designation. Burnap would have known him from his apprenticeship days in Norwich. The Connecticut Ship Database (Mystic Seaport) records ten ships in which Kelley invested between 1795 and 1813. Four additional ships in which he had ownership interest were seized by French privateers between 1797 and 1800 and the cargo confiscated. Kelley received insurance settlements as partial recovery for his losses in two instances (Greg H. Williams, *The French Assault on American Shipping, 1793–1813* [Jefferson, N.C.: McFarland, 2009], pp. 104, 248, 271, 303).

43. Isaac Lathrop ad in the *Norwich Packet*, October 2, 1788. The chairs are illustrated in Trent and Nelson, "New London County Joined Chairs," pp. 79, 93, figs. 20, 21. Isaac Huntington account book, p. 24, CHS.

44. *Norwich Packet*, May 5, 1791; January 15, 1795; June 2, 1796; June 20, 1799. *Weekly Register* (Norwich, Conn.), August 28, 1792; September 10, 1793. Eleazer Hazen's identity, uncertain in earlier publications, is based on the description of him as a cabinetmaker in Tracy E. Hazen, *The Hazen Family in America* (New Haven, Conn.: Tuttle, Morehouse & Taylor Co., 1947), p. 144. He married in Worthington, Massachusetts, in 1798 and later moved to Waterville, New York, and Ravenna, Ohio.

45. Isaiah Tiffany account book, CHS. For a summary, see Newton C. Brainard, "Isaiah Tiffany's Ledger," *Connecticut Historical Society Bulletin* 17, no. 4 (October 1952): 30–32. *New London Gazette*, July 22, 1768. A cherry chest-on-chest at Yale, illustrated in Gerald W. R. Ward, *American Case Furniture in the Mabel Brady Garvan and Other Collections at Yale* (New Haven, Conn.: Yale University Press, 1988), p. 182 (acc. no. 1984.32.40), is inscribed on the underside of the upper case with initials that have been interpreted as "IT." A mahogany blockfront bureau with similar feet and a history of ownership in the Jonathan Trumbull family of Lebanon is illustrated in *Antiques* 147, no. 3 (March 1995): 345 (C. L. Prickett ad). Trumbull purchased a "Case of Draws without trimming . . . 32.0.0 [and] Dressing Table without trimming . . . 8.0.0" from Tiffany in 1749/50. Whether the illustrated pieces are Tiffany's work is uncertain; they appear to postdate the ledger entries by at least two decades.

46. Tax assessments, Warren Collection, CHS. Elijah Tracy ad in the *Norwich Packet*, April 7, 1796. The chest-on-chest is owned by CHS (acc. no. 1965.53.0) and illustrated in Myers and Mayhew, *New London County Furniture*, no. 70. In the catalogue description the authors note the similarity of the writing on the case to that of Tracy. The chest has chamfered corners similar to those of the Huntington shop. A one-drawer blanket chest, branded "EB Tracy," is illustrated in *Antiques* 99, no. 2 (February 1971): 268. Two bureaus, branded by family members, demonstrate additional evidence of this shop tradition's output of case furniture. A straight-front Chippendale bureau with shaped top and chamfered corners, branded "A. D. Allen" by Tracy's son-in-law, probably working in Windham, is illustrated in Kirk, *Connecticut Furniture*, no. 70. A federal bureau, branded "S. Tracy" by Ebenezer's nephew Stephen, may predate the latter's move to Cornish, New Hampshire, in 1810 (Historic Deerfield, acc. no. 91.262, illustrated in database). For Tracy's dealings with John Avery, see Amos G. Avery, *Clockmakers and Craftsmen of the Avery Family* (Hartford: Connecticut Historical Society, 1987), p. 71. Mangrove is known for its resistance to water. Several species are known, all of which grow in tropical and subtropical tidal areas of the West Indies. The white mangrove is also known as buttonwood. Its value in the Tracy inventory is low, about one-tenth that of mahogany. See Evans, *American Windsor Chairs*, pp. 285–302.

Nancy Goyne Evans

Documentary Evidence of Painted Seating Furniture: Late Colonial and Federal Periods

▼ ALMOST EVERY SHOP that produced furniture in the late colonial and federal periods finished the surfaces of its products with some type of protective coating—wax, oil, varnish, color in varnish or size, stain, or paint. Color, stain, and paint also masked the natural color of the wood. The application of ornament further enhanced the aesthetic experience.

The material presented in this study is drawn from a large body of documents, consisting of craftsmen's account books and sheets, clients' business records, court and shipping records, probate records for general households and those of craftsmen, a manuscript price book, newspapers, technical books and articles published in the period under study, and selected primary references from recent publications. The geographic coverage is broad: New England, the Middle Atlantic region, the South from Maryland to Georgia, and Kentucky and Ohio in the "West." Within these political boundaries, the culture varied from rural to urban economies. Material originating in Massachusetts, Connecticut, New York, and Pennsylvania is the most plentiful.

The most popular furniture form in the late colonial and federal periods was the chair, beginning with common woven-bottom utilitarian styles constructed with slats, splats, or banisters, followed by the Windsor chair, and culminating in the fancy chair. Some material used for this study contains information pertaining to the purchase and cost of raw materials, tools, and accessories used in painting and other surface coatings. Recipes for paint colors provide further insight on period practice.

References in late colonial and federal period records to surface coatings on furniture, especially paint, are relatively frequent; actual color identification is unusual. Jacob Bigelow in his two-volume *The Useful Arts* noted that the object of "common painting" is "to produce a uniform and permanent coating upon surfaces, by applying to them a compound, which is more or less opaque." He further noted that "in many cases painting is applied only for ornament, but it is more frequently employed to protect perishable substances from the changes to which they are liable when exposed to the atmosphere, and other decomposing agents." Bigelow concluded by stating, "The effect and durability of different coverings employed in this way, depends upon the kind of pigment used, and still more upon the vehicle, or uniting medium, by . . . which it is applied."[1]

SIDE CHAIRS AND ARMCHAIRS
GENERAL COMMENTS ON SURFACE EMBELLISHMENT

General references to paint and other surface coatings on chairs describe a substantial body of data that includes all constructions and styles. A few references note the number of finish coats applied to surfaces, new or refurbished. That number varies from one to four, one coat likely identifying the inexpensive utilitarian chair, higher numbers pointing to more sophisticated seating enhanced with ornament. For instance, work done by Silas E. Cheney at Litchfield, Connecticut, in 1821 for Orin Judd involved "Painting 9 Chairs 4 Coats." The first coat was a primer. The three remaining coats may have included the pigment of choice, although since these chairs also were ornamented, the fourth coat likely was a varnish finish designed to protect the embellished surfaces.[2]

"Old Chairs" are among the large group of refurbished seating itemized in craftsmen's accounts. Artisans in urban centers regularly solicited this type of work in local newspapers as a complement to new production and structural repairs. Early-nineteenth-century craftsmen who advertised this service include Joseph Very of Portland, Maine; George Dame of Portsmouth, New Hampshire; and Reuben Sanborn of Boston. Another Boston craftsman described the expectations of consumers: "Chairs repaired and repainted to look as good as new." James Always of New York perhaps offered the ultimate service: "He has good accommodations for drying old chairs when re-painted, and he will take them from any part of the town, and return them in good order."[3]

The basic utilitarian chair ubiquitous to households had several names, one being "Common chair." After leaving Massachusetts in 1809, Allen Holcomb worked as a journeyman in the shop of Simon Smith at Troy, New York, where he recorded "painting 6 Common chairs 2 C[oa]ts." By 1813 Holcomb had resettled in Otsego County. Just as familiar to householders was the term "kitchen chair," describing the chair's principal place of use. True Currier of Deerfield, New Hampshire, recorded selling "seven kitchen chair frames painted" in 1828 at a charge of 50¢ apiece. Emphasis on the term "frame," one with cross slats in the back, suggests that the seats were open, or without woven "straw" or "flag" (rush) to provide a solid bottom for sitting. An earlier account from the Amherst, Massachusetts, shop of Nathaniel Bangs addresses that feature in charging Captain Oliver Allen 60¢ apiece for "five Chair fraims and for painting and bottoming."[4]

Two alternative surface coatings for the common slat-back, or kitchen, chair were color in size (a gluelike material) and stain, both priced about the same for similar construction. From the early eighteenth century these finishes were in use on chairs constructed with three to five slats, often identified as three-, four-, and five-back chairs. Two New England shop accounts highlight the variable terminology: Joseph Brown of Newbury, Massachusetts, sold "4 Culler'd Chairs 4 backt" in 1741, followed by Isaiah Tiffany's sale of "6 Chairs 4 Slats Colour'd" in 1756 at Norwich, Connecticut. Solomon Fussell of Philadelphia sold both colored and stained ("dyed") chairs during the late 1730s and 1740s, the slats numbering from three to five. Fussell's basic price for his three-slat side chair was 4 shillings. Each additional slat added a price increment: four-slat chairs cost 4s. 6d. to 5s.; five-slat chairs fetched 5s. 6d.; and Fussell's "best" five-slat chairs cost 6s. or 6s. 6d. In the prevailing barter economy, several individuals found Fussell's products useful for settling debts. In 1741 Joseph Marshall ordered "½ Duz best 5 Slat Chairs Dyed dd [delivered to] walter Coal [Cole]" and "½ Duz: three Slat Coular'd Chairs dd to ye plasterer." Whereas delivery of finished chairs to a customer or his creditor may have been routine for Fussell, the practice had changed by the end of the century, and it was the customer's responsibility to fetch furniture from the woodworker's shop. Unusual events elicited comment, as noted in 1797 by Jacob Merrill Jr. of Plymouth, New Hampshire, in a client account: "going to your house & Colouring Six frames."[5]

The Windsor chair became an important market commodity in the post-Revolutionary period, catapulted to the forefront in the mid-1780s by the introduction of the bow-back side chair, also known as a "dining Windsor chair." With its oval back, the bow-back Windsor required little space at the dining table, a boon in the large families typical of the period. Consumers had been aware of the basic benefits of Windsor seating since its introduction to American vernacular furniture in the mid-1740s: Windsor chairs were economical, the price somewhat more than slat-back seating but within range of middle-class pocketbooks; the construction was durable and practical; wooden seats were not subject to constant repair and replacement as were woven bottoms of straw, rush, or cane; and scuffed surfaces could be refreshed with a coat of paint. Bright-colored paint on furniture and walls had the power to bring life to dark and drab interiors. By 1800 Lawrence Allwine of Philadelphia offered "the best windsor chairs . . . painted with his own patent colours," cited for their "brilliancy and durability." A varnish finish protected painted surfaces, whether plain or ornamented. In April 1801 Oliver Goodwin, a Charleston, South Carolina, merchant, announced his receipt from New York of "300 Fancy Windsor Chairs . . . executed . . . with permanent and lasting varnishes to exceed anything . . . ever introduced in the southern States."[6]

Windsor chairs sent to the local woodworker for a fresh coat of paint might also need repair. Silas E. Cheney recorded a job at Litchfield, Connecticut, in 1820 that required "giting out nails out of 8 . . . Chair Seat[s] & Smothing Out Seats" before he could paint. Many chairmakers did their own painting; others, particularly proprietors of large shops, employed painting specialists as needed. Edward Jenner Carpenter, apprentice to Miles and Lyons at Greenfield, Massachusetts, noted in his journal on May 16, 1844, the shop visit of Mr. Wilson "to paint chair[s]." Wilson departed eight days later for his home in Colrain, a rural village nine miles northwest of Greenfield. Nelson Talcott of Portage County, Ohio, recorded similar activity in that decade, although his interaction with journeymen painters often was formalized with a contract. Typical, perhaps, was Talcott's arrangement with William B. Payne, who began working on contract in

February 1841 "at painting chairs": "He [Payne] is to paint the Grountt work . . . of comon [Windsor] Chairs at three cents pr chair and be Bourded, or at three and three fourths cents each and Bourd himself—if he Bourds himself and Bourds with the said Talcott he is to have his Bourd for one dollar thirty seven ½ cents per Week." Whichever boarding plan Payne chose, his piecework arrangement required that he paint approximately 167 chairs during a six-day work week to earn an average journeyman wage of 83.3¢ per day (5s.), or 200 chairs during the same period to earn a high wage of $1.00 per day (6s.). His profit depended on his skill and proficiency at the job.[7]

Records indicate that journeymen led itinerant lives on occasion, picking up work where they could. Of relevance is an itinerancy recorded by Jacob S. Van Tyne, a sign and ornamental painter who left Cayuga County, New York, in January 1836 for a sojourn of more than three years, which took him as far afield as Virginia, Kentucky, and Ohio. The itinerant life bred uncertainty and anxiety, as Van Tyne noted in his journal in May 1838: "Arrived at Union Town, Pa, With my spirits very much cast down being out of money and in a strange place among total strangers." He related how, while walking in town, "I happened to cast my eye up and saw a sign of a House, sign, and Ornamental Painter by the name of W. Maquilken. I immediately went in and applied for work and was successful. O! How thankful aught I to be for this interposition of Gods providence in thus snatching me from the immediate jaws of want and poverty and placing me out of the reach of either." Van Tyne's work pleased his employer, who within eleven days raised the painter's wages to $16 per month, which, as Van Tyne noted, "Encouraged me very much and put me more in mind of the goodness of God in thus turning the scale of fortune in my favour."[8]

Fancy chairs represented a step up from Windsor seating in cost and sophistication, especially those with seats of woven cane rather than rush. Many shops that made Windsor chairs also framed fancy chairs, and the same specialists painted either type of seating. Among those painters were men who worked at times in Portage County, Ohio, for Nelson Talcott, who probably supplied the painting materials used by his workmen. A charge against Sylvester Tyler Jr. in 1840 for "Paint for 1 2/6 Set Fancy chairs," or eight chairs, suggests that Taylor occasionally took on outside jobs on his own time while working in Talcott's shop. A similar circumstance is suggested in the accounts of James Gere of Groton, Connecticut, who often employed area workmen to paint chairs. In 1824 John Ashley Willet, who resided independently at Norwich, was credited with painting and ornamenting fancy and Windsor chairs. On two occasions he was debited for "paint & Varnish &c. for Chairs," the charges appearing to have occurred at a time when he was boarding with Gere.[9]

Unlike the surface coatings on Windsor chairs, those on fancy chairs also employed materials other than paint. An early record of "12 Chairs Making & Japanning" dates to 1794, when William Lycett of New York produced seating for Chancellor Robert R. Livingston. In japanning, paint pigment was mixed with varnish and applied in layers over a special ground coat. The object of the process, which was imported from Europe, was to imitate

Figure 1 Advertisement of Samuel M. Dockum and Edmund M. Brown. (*New-Hampshire Gazette* [Portsmouth], December 11, 1827.)

oriental lacquer. Somewhat cheaper was the practice of staining fancy chairs. In 1819 at the death of Benjamin Bass, a cabinetmaker and chairmaker of Boston, appraisers itemized three groups of stained fancy seating in the shop: thirty-six chairs were "partly stain'd," twelve more frames were fully stained, and a third group consisted of "12 Stain'd Chairs Flagg'd," that is, coated frames with rush seats in place.[10]

Fancy chairs and, in particular, Windsor chairs became important products of commerce in the post-Revolutionary period. Many chair shops, large and small, marketed seating furniture to customers beyond the local area in overland, coastal, and overseas locations. Because chairs were vulnerable to surface damage in transit, some craftsmen took steps to turn this situation to their advantage. The Wilmington, North Carolina, firm of Vosburgh and Childs whose business, like that of most Southern craftsmen, was compromised by Northern imports, advertised: "How far preferable chairs must be manufactured in the state, warranted to be both well made and painted with the best materials, to those that are imported, which are always unavoidably rubbed and bruised." Thomas Henning Sr. of Lewisburg, West Virginia, addressed the hazard of overland transport, stating, "He would like to deliver chairs unpainted, and paint them where they are to be used, as hauling always injures the appearance of chairs that are painted." Still other strategies were employed. Silas Cooper of Savannah, Georgia, traveled to "the north" to purchase "fashionable CHAIRS," which on his return he "finished on the spot," ensuring the paint was "not injured by transportation." When Dockum and Brown, chair retailers at Portsmouth, New Hampshire, "received ONE THOUSAND CHAIRS, of various kinds and colors," from Boston in 1827, they engaged "first rate workmen from Boston" to paint and gild the chairs at Portsmouth (fig. 1).[11]

COLOR REFERENCES TO PAINTED SURFACES:
COMMON-CHAIR PRODUCTION

References to surface color are relatively common for chairs, unlike other furniture forms, a situation that permits an investigation of some depth by actual color group. First to be considered are "common" chairs with woven bottoms. In the seating hierarchy, they were first in the market and lowest priced. Among consumers, the most popular color choice in woven-bottom common seating probably was black, with white chairs and red chairs coming in second and third. White chairs were the cheapest, however, and this is where the discussion begins. The term "white" in this instance did not identify a paint color but instead denoted the absence of color, or chairs left "in the wood" without a surface coating. Later in the century the term came to identify a surface actually painted white.

The accounts of two craftsmen, Solomon Fussell of Philadelphia and John Durand of Milford, Connecticut, best amplify this point. Fussell produced "white" chairs between 1738 and 1748. Durand's construction of unpainted chairs, which he referred to as "plain" chairs rather than white chairs, extends from 1763 to 1776 in this study. Together the accounts exhibit price variations for this basic chair from 1s. 4d. to 3s. 8d., an indication

Figure 2 Slat-back side chair attributed to John Durand (1735–1780) or Samuel Durand I (1738–1829), Milford, Connecticut, 1760–1770. Maple, ash, and poplar; rush. H. 37⅝", W. 18⅞", D. 13½". (Courtesy, Stratford Historical Society, Stratford, Connecticut, gift of Miss Martha Miles.) Surface finish not original.

that customer options existed. When supplied, woven rush was the common seating material of both craftsmen's chairs.[12]

Durand's product probably took the form of an open-frame chair with plain cylindrical front legs, back posts with minimal turned ornament, and two cross slats uniting the posts. Chairs of this type have family or other histories in Milford. Durand's sale to Deacon Joseph Treat of "half a Dozen plain Chair[s]" in 1776 priced at 1s. 4d. each describes side chair frames without "bottoms," or woven seats, and little turned work other than back-post finials (fig. 2). Plain chairs priced by Durand between 3s. and 3s. 8d. likely included one or more structural options beyond a basic frame: woven rush seats, turned work in the legs and posts, and possibly a third cross slat in the back.[13]

Fussell's "white" chair production at Philadelphia may have paralleled Durand's work. His cheapest "white" frame, as sold to Abraham Linkcorn in 1743 for 2s. 3d., is described as "one white Chair w[ith] out armes." This chair and Fussell's white chairs priced at 3s. possibly had only two back slats, and both probably lacked rush seats. The difference between the two likely was in turned work. Fussell's accounts further suggest that by increasing the white-chair price by 3d., the customer could acquire chairs with woven bottoms, as recorded for Richard Tyson, who bought "6 white Chairs & Mating" for 3s. 3d. apiece. Again, these chairs may have had only two cross slats in the backs because three-slat chairs sold to William Moss cost 3s. 6d. the chair, an indication that a third slat raised the price by at least 3 pence. Moss's further purchases of "4 Reed [red] 3 Slat Chairs" and "4 Black 3 Slat Chairs" priced individually at 4s. and 4s. 6d., respectively, reinforces this reasoning. The greater pricing of the three-slat red and black chairs reflects the addition of paint to the wooden surfaces and possibly the introduction of more turned ornament.[14]

Several decades later, in 1770, Fussell's former apprentice William Savery sold "Eight white Rush bottom Chairs" priced individually at 4s. to the prominent Philadelphian General John Cadwalader, whose residence stood in Second Street between Spruce and Pine. The unit price of the chairs and their placement in a richly appointed town house, albeit in a service area, suggests the frames were painted white rather than left "in the wood." Cadwalader's purchase suggests that a new era sometimes requires a new interpretation of terminology.[15]

Entries in the accounts of other craftsmen confirm the information gleaned from the records examined above: white chairs priced under 3s. usually had two back slats, and those priced at about 3s. to less than 4s. probably had three back slats. Supporting this conclusion are the early-eighteenth-century records of Miles Ward of Salem, Massachusetts, and John II and Thomas Gaines of Ipswich. Isaiah Tiffany penned similar midcentury records in eastern Connecticut, followed by accounts kept by David Haven at Framingham, Massachusetts. Two items from a list of "goods and things" given by John Baker of Rehoboth, Massachusetts, to his daughters Rebecca and Bathsheba in the 1760s serve to sum up: each received "six three-backs Black chairs" valued at 3s. apiece and "2 two-backs white chairs," probably unpainted, that cost 2s. apiece.[16]

Figure 3 Banister-back side chair, Portsmouth, New Hampshire, area 1760–1800. Maple and ash; rush. H. 40¾", W. 19", D. 13¼". (Courtesy, Historic New England, Boston, Massachusetts, gift of Joseph W. Hobbs; photo, David Bohl.) Surface paint not original.

Date and price are the criteria in interpreting common "black" chairs listed in craftsmen's eighteenth-century accounts. If the date is early and the price low, slat-back chairs seem indicated. That style constituted Solomon Fussell's entire black-chair production at Philadelphia during the late 1730s and 1740s. The chairmaker's records describe his price structure for the slat-back models in black offered at his shop: a three-slat chair varied from 4s. to 4s. 6d.; the four-slat chair was 4s. 6d. or 5s.; and the five-slat model stood at 5s. to 5s. 6d. Thus, with the addition of each slat, the basic chair price increased by 6 pence. The cost of wood was negligible. The real expense of adding a slat was the labor: sawing the back piece to shape, shaving it to thickness and bending it to a lateral form, then cutting two mortise holes in the back posts, fitting the slat into the mortises, and pinning it in place. Special requests added an increment to chair cost. A customer who ordered a four-slat armchair paid about 6d. for the elbow pieces. Another customer who bought six new five-slat chairs substituted a "turn'd frunt" with thick double-vase turnings separated by a central disk (see fig. 6) for the basic cylindrical stretcher at an extra cost of 4d. or 5d.[17]

Several New England craftsmen recorded the production of black slat-back chairs. In the 1720s and 1730s Miles Ward of Salem, Massachusetts, charged 4s. 6d. to 5s. for black "4 back" (slat) chairs. Elisha Hawley still made black chairs late in the century at Ridgefield, Connecticut, the price ranging from 2s. 8d. to 4s., suggesting that he sold two-, three-, and possibly four-back common chairs in the local market. Ward also recorded a somewhat more expensive set of black chairs purchased in 1737 by John Low at 6s. apiece. These may have been banister-back chairs with relatively plain crests and somewhat more ornate turnings than those usual on the slat-back chair. A "Great black Chair" priced at 8s. by Jacob Hinsdale, a contemporary of Ward at Harwinton, Connecticut, likely describes a banister-back armchair (fig. 3). At Milford John Durand possibly identified banister-back seating in 1774 in the sale of "half a Dozen black Chairs" priced individually at 6s. The banister-back style was especially popular along the Connecticut coast.[18]

Some significance may be associated with the absence of a red chair from the production of three craftsmen who framed both black and white chairs before 1740. The records of Miles Ward and the Gaines family of Massachusetts and Jacob Hinsdale of Connecticut are silent on the subject. In contrast, the records of Solomon Fussell, who framed common chairs at Philadelphia from 1738 to 1748, indicate that he constructed "red" chairs with three to five back slats in addition to his white ("in the wood") and black slat-back production. Fussell priced red and black chairs the same, although his red chairs appear to have been less in demand than his black or white chairs. As usual, payment was flexible; Isaac Knight Sr. paid for his "6 Reed 5 Slat Chairs" with "a Hog."[19]

What was the red paint used on chairs made by Fussell and other craftsmen at various locations, including New Hampshire, upstate New York, Nantucket Island, and Connecticut? Two nineteenth-century authors, Hezekiah Reynolds in *Directions for House and Ship Painting* (1812) and Nathaniel Whittock in *The Decorative Painters' and Glaziers' Guide* (1827), identified the principal pigments available for making red paint: vermilion, red lead, Venetian red, Spanish brown, and red ochre. A review of several dozen records dating between the mid-eighteenth and early nineteenth centuries indicates that craftsmen, based on their possession of these pigments, overwhelmingly favored Spanish brown and red lead as ingredients for red paint. Taking the analysis a step further, Spanish brown likely was the popular choice for painting "red" chairs in the eighteenth century because it is mentioned more frequently in records and because some red lead in the possession of craftsmen was destined for use as a drier in the preparation of linseed oil and varnish rather than as a pigment for exterior, interior, or furniture paint. Spanish brown, as known in the eighteenth century, was a reddish brown earth containing iron oxides that was processed for use as a pigment. The color probably was akin to the barn red known today.[20]

As early as 1750 James Claypoole, a painter and glazier of Philadelphia, listed Spanish brown among a selection of imported pigments and related material offered for sale at his shop. The trade in this commodity expanded, and when Kenneth McKenzie, a fellow artisan in the craft at New York City, died in 1804, appraisers itemized among the painting materials on the premises forty "Kegs Spanish brown g[roun]d in oil 900 lb" valued at 4d. per pound. Already by 1800 it was not uncommon for purveyors of painting materials to stock products of demand, including Spanish brown, in quantities of one ton or more, as advertised by John McElwee at Philadelphia.[21]

Beyond the Philadelphia shop of Solomon Fussell, red chairs were made in more northerly locations. John Durand of Milford, Connecticut, who constructed white ("plain") chairs and some black chairs, had a substantial production of red chairs in the 1760s and 1770s. Unit costs of 4s. 6d. to 8s. suggest that several styles were represented, a circumstance supported by known production in coastal Connecticut. Durand's "red" chairs priced in the lower range probably included banister-back and splat-back ("york") chairs of basic turned side-chair form. The price increased with the selection of special options: arms, an ornamental crest, or embellished turnings. A red chair produced by Durand in the mid-price range of 6s. or 7s. had a splat back and distinctive turned front supports with trumpet-shaped legs and pad feet, a seating type probably referred to locally as a "fiddle-back" chair (fig. 4). Supporting this reasoning are the accounts of Titus Preston of the inland town of Wallingford. For a customer whose daughter was setting up housekeeping in 1804, Preston supplied a quantity of furniture, including Windsor chairs for the dining parlor (7s. 8d. each) and "6 red fiddle back chairs" for other household use (6s. apiece).[22]

The slat-back style was part of red-chair production in other areas. For Ezekiel Robinson of Rockingham County, New Hampshire, Moody Carr made "a red Chaire for your Pew" in 1800, identified as a slat-back chair by its 3s. price. Three-back and four-back chairs painted red were popular on Nantucket Island in the late eighteenth century, judging by the numbers listed in inventories, which well exceed those painted black. Another back style may be represented by the "8 Red Common Chairs" purchased for 5s. each in 1793 from James Chestney of Albany, New York, by Madame

Figure 4   Fiddle-back side chair possibly made by John Durand or Samuel Durand I, probably Milford, Connecticut, 1760–1800. Maple; rush. H. 40³⁄₁₆", W. 18¹⁄₈", D. 15¹⁄₄". (Courtesy, Winterthur Museum, Winterthur, Delaware.) Black surface paint over a red primer; possibly original.

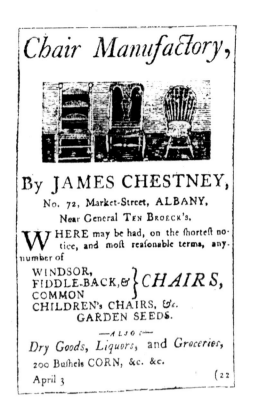

Figure 5 Advertisement of James Chestney.
(*Albany Chronicle* [New York], April 10, 1797.)

Schuyler. Chestney's advertisement for his "Chair Manufactory," published in a local newspaper in 1797, illustrates the three chair styles he framed (fig. 5). The 5s. price best describes Chestney's "fiddle-back" chair with a back splat and trumpet-style legs.[23]

Craftsmen's accounts identify several other paint colors used for common-chair surfaces, although their occurrence is infrequent. Most references focus on the color brown. The Gaines family of Ipswich, Massachusetts, produced at least one set of brown four-slat chairs. Between 1738 and 1748 their contemporary at Philadelphia, Solomon Fussell, sold brown chairs with three, four, and five slats priced from 4s. to 5s. Fussell's customers may have favored brown chairs over red seating, although the numbers do not equal those of the shop's black or "white" slat-back production. Other evidence of slat-back seating occurs in a list of furniture in the home of merchant Benjamin H. Hathorne at Boston, where "3 Brown Kitchen [Chairs]" valued at 5s. 3d. apiece probably were new and likely had arms. "5 new Brown Chairs" each valued at 4s. in 1793 also stood in the Nantucket home of widow Mary Pease, a trader. It is not known whether the "6 Chocolate coloured rush bottom'd Chairs" in the Chester County, Pennsylvania, household of William Jones in 1789 duplicated the brown color of other rush-bottom chairs.[24]

The more expensive fiddle-back chair also figures in a discussion of brown seating. At his death in 1794, John Avery Sr., a Preston, Connecticut, silversmith and clockmaker, possessed "Six brown Fiddle back [Chairs]" still valued at 5s. each. These and the red fiddle-back chairs described above are complemented in records analyzed for this study by two additional color choices for similar seating. At least one set of green chairs, among several sets listed in the late-eighteenth-century accounts of Elisha Hawley of Ridgefield, Connecticut, was constructed in the fiddle-back style. The 7s. unit price is comparable to that of two unidentified sets of green chairs produced in the shop. "Seven blew fiddle back chairs," possibly with arms, constructed in 1781 by James Wheeler Geer for a customer at Preston were more expensive at 8s. 8d. the chair.[25]

The remaining common-chair production identified by color in craftsmen's accounts appears to describe chairs with slat backs. Oliver Moore, a craftsman of rural East Granby, Connecticut, constructed "six citching chairs painted green and varnished @ 6s.," or $1.00 apiece, in 1820 for Erastus Holcomb. The unit price seems high until one takes into account the fact that the surfaces received paint and varnish, two separate tasks, and the chairs may have had arms. Several inventories describe "rush bottom chairs painted blue" with low evaluations, including two estates probated at Baltimore in the 1770s. Among several inventories from Chester County, Pennsylvania, that list blue rush-bottom chairs, two name locations. In the home of Thomas Pim, who died in 1786, the chairs stood in a back room over the parlor. In 1823 appraisers located blue chairs in the south room of the upper storey at the home of Elijah Funk. Other records describe yellow chairs. In 1824 Captain Nathaniel Kinsman bought "4 yallau Chairs" with rush seats from Samuel Beal of Boston for 4s. 6d. apiece. At the death of James Chapman of Ellington, Connecticut, appraisers identified an alternative seating material: "6 yellow split [splint] bottom chairs." Splints for weaving chair seats (or baskets) were harvested from the inner bark of selected trees, frequently the hickory tree.[26]

An unusual color reference to common seating in early records is "orange," a word that may identify paint, stain, or pigment in varnish or size. If the coating was paint, a recipe in the accounts of William Fifield of Lyme, New Hampshire, may apply. The basic pigment was stone yellow, a mixture of white lead and yellow ochre proportioned at fourteen parts to five, with a tiny amount of ivory black, followed by the addition of red lead to increase the mixture by half. In 1789 William Jones of Chester County, Pennsylvania, owned "3 Rush bottom Chairs Orange color" in a home filled with rush seating in black and chocolate color, probably all with slat backs. Another record describes "6 Orange Coular chairs" purchased at Philadelphia in 1747 from Solomon Fussell at 6s. 6d. apiece. The pricing was unusual for common chairs made by Fussell, although two other sets of similar price shed further light on the appearance of these orange chairs. One set is identified as "6 Best Dyd [stained] 5 Slat Chairs." The description of the second set appears to define the word "best": "6 turned frunts archback Dyd Chairs." These are the iconic Delaware Valley chairs with bold double-baluster front stretchers and back slats arched along both edges, as further confirmed at the death in 1766 of Daniel Jones, another Philadelphia chairmaker (fig. 6). Whereas appraisers itemized a varied stock of slat-back seating, of relevance here are chairs described as "6 five Slats arch'd & turn'd fronts, Blue." Other shop stock had "plain Backs & turn'd fronts." Of further interest is the inventory item "About half a pound of Prusia Blew at ⅓ an Oance."[27]

Figure 6   Slat-back armchair, Delaware Valley, 1750–1775. Maple and hickory; rush. H. 43", W. 24⅞", D. 20½". (Courtesy, Winterthur Museum.) Surface paint not original.

COLOR REFERENCES TO PAINTED SURFACES: WINDSOR-CHAIR AND FANCY-CHAIR PRODUCTION

In terms of mainstream production and price structuring, Windsor seating and fancy-chair work followed common-chair production as the popular focus in household seating. Of the many Windsor and fancy chairs listed in documents of the late colonial and federal periods, only a fraction is identified by color and/or decoration. Nonetheless, this small body of material is sufficiently sizable to allow a discussion of the various color choices individually, although the line between the two construction forms often is blurred in records. The discussion proceeds from the most to least common consumer options in surface color, as indicated by the material gathered for this study. Green heads the list of solid color grounds; blue was the least favorite choice. An investigation of grained surfaces, principally those in imitation of wood, forms a separate topic at the end of this section, followed by a discussion of ornament, the focus principally on post-1800 production, when chair styles offered broad, flat surfaces for decoration.

Green Chairs

Green was a color choice for Windsor-chair surfaces from the time this construction form was introduced until well into the nineteenth century. In

1730, little more than a decade after Windsor seating was made in England, John Brown, a chairmaker of London, offered for sale "ALL SORTS OF WINDSOR GARDEN CHAIRS, of all Sizes, painted green or in the Wood." As most early Windsor production was destined for garden use, green paint was an obvious choice. This was the color introduced to America through early imports of Windsor furniture, and it was the color adopted by American craftsmen when domestic production began in the 1740s at Philadelphia. John Fanning Watson, a chronicler of early life in that city, stated in the early nineteenth century, "When the first windsor chairs were introduced, they were universally green."[28]

Because green was the single color choice for Windsor seating through the Revolution, most documents relative to early production are silent on the subject of color. Shipping records are the first sources to identify green surfaces. In 1775 James Bentham of Charleston, South Carolina, announced the arrival of a vessel carrying "Green Windsor chairs" from Philadelphia, the principal center of Windsor chairmaking in America. Several references originating at Newport, Rhode Island, a community whose initial Windsor production followed that of Philadelphia, date earlier. Aaron Lopez, a merchant with international shipping interests, ventured Newport-constructed "round back wooden bottom Green Chairs" (low-back Windsors) in 1767 and 1768 to several markets in his business sphere: Savannah, Georgia; coastal Maryland; the Bay of Honduras; and Surinam. The American ports also received green chairs "with high backs." In the postwar years Stephen Girard, a rising Philadelphia merchant, launched his shipping enterprise. "Green windsor Chairs," including dozens of fan backs with scroll-carved crests and bow-back side and armchairs, were marketed in the late 1780s at Charleston, South Carolina, and Cape Français, Haiti.[29]

Knowledge, production, and use of Windsor seating spread rapidly in the post-Revolutionary years. In 1779 Samuel Barrett of Boston requested his brother-in-law at Worcester, Massachusetts, to purchase at auction "6 Green Chairs (if made at Philadelphia)." Philadelphia Windsors were the standard by which similar seating was measured, although Boston craftsmen had yet to develop a local industry. The situation changed quickly, as indicated in April 1786 by Ebenezer Stone, who solicited custom at his shop on Moore's Wharf, where he sold "WARRANTED Green Windsor Chairs . . . painted equally as well as those made at Philadelphia." Three years later David Haven of Framingham sold "6 Dining Chairs Partly Painted," or with a priming coat only. Haven also supplied "¼ lb of Verdegrees & 2 oz of Wt [white] Lead" to make green paint, enabling his client to finish the chairs himself and reduce the cost. As indicated by Haven, verdigris, a copper acetate, was the pigment that produced the light green or light bluish green paint of early Windsor production (fig. 7). James Claypoole, a painter of Philadelphia, imported verdigris along with a variety of painting materials by 1750. Verdigris was still current for compounding green paint at the end of the century, as indicated in the records of Samuel Wing, a furniture craftsman of Sandwich, Massachusetts, whose papers contain a recipe for green paint signed by Obed Faye, a Windsor chairmaker of

Figure 7 Detail, left arm post of sack-back Windsor armchair, Rhode Island, 1780–1800. White pine (seat) with maple, oak, hickory, and ash. H. 39⁹/₁₆", W. 23", D. 16¼". (Courtesy, Winterthur Museum.) An alligatored surface comprising multiple chipped layers of paint and resin. The "Windsor" green visible in chipped areas is the second coat of paint and probably predates 1815. This is the ubiquitous green made from the pigment verdigris, the color dulled owing to deterioration and yellowing of the protective resin coat.

Nantucket. This recipe, like others, directed the preparer to begin with linseed oil boiled with a drying agent, such as rosin, litharge, or red lead, which was added to measured amounts of verdigris, finely ground in a drying oil, and white lead to achieve the desired intensity of color. Wing may have used Faye's recipe to fill an order for chairs received in 1799 from Ebenezer Swift of Barnstable, who requested the craftsman to "give them chairs a good Green coler as you can."[30]

By 1800 New York had been a center of Windsor chairmaking for at least three decades. As early as 1772 Elizabeth Rutgers's household contained a green low-back Windsor chair, although whether a New York product or a Philadelphia import is uncertain. Like Philadelphia, New York developed a significant export trade in Windsor seating, which began to flourish in the 1790s. The "8 dozen green WINDSOR CHAIRS" from New York received in 1797 by merchant John Curry at Charleston, South Carolina, were a mere prelude to the explosion of activity that followed in that city. By the late 1790s Windsor furniture had long furnished East Coast homes, and some householders already engaged local craftsmen to repair or refurbish their seating. Stephen Girard of Philadelphia employed William Cox in 1787 for "Mendding and Painting 3 Old Windsor Chairs." Shortly thereafter, Joseph Stone completed a repair for William Arnold at East Greenwich, Rhode Island, by putting "one post in a green Chair." Business was brisk at the shop of Daniel Rea Jr., a painting specialist of Boston, who charged 2s. or 3s. for repainting a Windsor chair green.[31]

Green Windsors were prominent in the chair production of two generations of the Tracy family of eastern Connecticut from the late 1780s into the nineteenth century. Records identify a range of chair styles and describe several special customer options. Ebenezer Tracy Sr., the family head, trained three young men of the second generation who followed in his footsteps— a son, a nephew, and a son-in-law. The "Green Arm'd Chair" that Tracy exchanged for goods in 1788 with Andrew Huntington, a merchant of Norwich, is the earlier of two armchair styles listed in family records. A price range of 8s. to 12s. for this sack-back chair describes structural options beyond the basic frame. These included stretchers with embellished tips, three-dimensional knuckle arm terminals, and an extension headpiece above the back bow. More popular when introduced from New York after 1790 was the smaller, continuous-bow armchair, described by Amos D. Allen, Tracy's son-in-law, as a "fancy" chair. Prices from 8s. to 15s. 6d. again dictated customer options: bracing spindles to strengthen the chair back; a fixed "cushion," or stuffed seat, to cover the chair bottom; "edging," or narrow painted lines, to accent and define structural features.[32]

The Tracy family produced two side chairs often finished in green paint, fan-backs and bow-backs. The bow-back Windsor often served as seating around a dining table, its compact design maximizing seating space. Appropriately, Amos D. Allen identified his bow-back Windsors as "dining chairs," pricing them from 6s. 6d. to 14s., depending on customer selection of special features, as described above. Allen's comprehensive order book also identifies another option in his side-chair production. Seat tops could be painted to contrast with the green or other principal color. The accounts identify "bottoms" of black and "mahog[an]y colour" contrasted with green. Ebenezer Tracy's eldest son, Elijah, and his nephew Stephen also produced dining chairs, called simply "green chairs." Elijah, like his father, did business with John Avery Jr., a clockmaker and metalworker, acquiring in 1799 and 1800 metalwork for turning lathes. Avery received a bed press (bedstead storage case) and two sets of "12 green Chairs," at a unit price of 6s. 6d. Avery passed along eighteen of the chairs in sets of six to three customers at the same price.[33]

Information from household inventories provides another perspective on the green Windsor chair by identifying its geographic spread, the social level of its owners, and its disposition in the home. Inventories originating from New Hampshire to Georgia and westward to Kentucky describe the broad acceptance of Windsor furniture in early American life. As to who used this type of seating, the social spectrum is broad. Individuals with basic occupations included farmers and storekeepers. Artisan trades are described, in part, by furniture makers, metalworkers, millers, a shoemaker, and a butcher. Doctors and lawyers represented men of the professions. Records provide particular insight into the ownership and use of green Windsor chairs in the closely knit society on Nantucket Island during the three decades from the Revolution to the War of 1812, when forty-three inventories list chairs of this construction and color. Occupations relating to seafaring are prominent. Twelve decedents were "mariners." Five individuals were merchants, and five more were "traders" engaged in the coasting trade. Several coopers, a ship's carpenter, and a block maker also owned green Windsor chairs. Several owners were termed "gentlemen" at their deaths.[34]

Many green chairs listed in Nantucket households appear to have been used on the first floor—a few in parlors but many in a room reserved for dining. "Table chair," an alternative term for "dining chair," appears in some records. When Oliver Spencer, a "trader" of Nantucket, died in 1794, appraisers listed "6 Green Table Chairs" among his furnishings. Several records describe a distinctive Windsor chair with a tall, reclining braced back that originated on the island or nearby (fig. 8). Henry Clark, a mariner, owned a "Great Green Chair & Cushion [Green]" in 1801, the cushion suggesting that his chair was designed for taking his ease. Two other chairs, one belonging to Jonathan Burnell, a merchant, and one to Peter Coffin, a yeoman, are each described as a "Mans Green Chair," suggesting the chairs had distinct, identifiable features linking them with the head of a household. Tall chairs of this type appear to have been located on the first floor, placing them near the principal hearth to which they could be drawn for warmth in cold weather. A few Nantucket inventories locate smaller green Windsors in upstairs chambers.[35]

Bedchambers also were the choice of off-islanders for the placement of green Windsor chairs. Elias Hasket Derby, a wealthy merchant of Salem, Massachusetts, furnished his southwest and southeast chambers in this manner. Another group of "6 Green Chairs" was located in his counting room "on the wharf." Upper and lower hallways, or passages, were

Figure 8 Tall, braced fan-back Windsor armchair branded by Charles Chase (1731–1815), Nantucket, Massachusetts, 1790–1805. White pine (seat) with ash, birch, and oak. H. 42¾", W. 27⅜", D. 20". (Courtesy, Winterthur Museum.) Present surface black; original surface verdigris green.

depositories for a total of fourteen green Windsors in the New York home of Johannah Beekman before 1821. The "large entry" in the Newburyport, Massachusetts, home of Captain Jonathan Dalton was the site of a "high green [arm] Chair" two decades earlier. Windsors placed in entrance halls served as repositories for outer clothing when individuals entered the house. The chairs also provided supplemental seating for the adjacent dining room and parlor. The garret in many homes, including that of Beekman, served as storage for surplus seating and "old" chairs. Some New England inventories list a "keeping room," a family sitting room, or parlor, whose function at times was expanded to include dining. In the home of Daniel Danforth, a shopkeeper of Hartford, Connecticut, "6 Green dining chairs" stood in the "Lower Keeping Room" in company with a "Breakfast Table."[36]

Other inventories describe special options in green Windsor seating. William Chappel, a farmer of Lyme, Connecticut, owned "½ Doz Green Chocolate bottom windsor Chairs." Rufus Porter in "The Art of Painting" described chocolate as a mixture of lampblack with Venetian red. At New Haven Eneas Munson, a physician, who like Chappel died in 1826, owned "10 Green & Black Chairs." Whether black described the seat color or the ornament is unclear. Seven years later at Shippensburg, Pennsylvania, the inventory of chairmaker Thomas Devor itemized "2 Green Strip[e] chairs." That the chairs were ornamented is clear, but was green the color of the chairs or the decoration? Other inventory data suggest green was the ground color. Stuffed seats were a more expensive option. To the construction and painting costs of the wood-seat chair was added a charge for stuffing materials, a finish cover (leather or cloth), and labor. Stuffing a seat, on average, almost tripled the price of a Windsor. An inventory drawn about 1816 for the estate of Gerrit Wessel Van Schaick, a resident of Albany, New York, describes an unusually large set of stuffed Windsor chairs as "1 3/12 Dozen Green Chairs with Stuffed bottoms." Insight on suitable cloth covers for Windsor chairs can be found in the estate records of General George Mason of Rockland County, Virginia: "Eighteen Windsor chairs with green Moreen bottoms" and "Two armed ditto covered with ditto." Moreen, a worsted woolen, was popular for upholstery in the period of this study.[37]

Chairmakers' inventories from the second quarter of the nineteenth century illuminate new options available in green Windsor seating late in the period under study. Ebenezer P. Rose, a craftsman of Trenton, New Jersey, had a dining room furnished with "10 Sage Col[or] Chares" still valued at $1.00 apiece in 1836 at his death. Sage color is defined as a gray-green, although records are silent on how to compound paint of this hue. Thomas Sheraton offered a clue in his *Dictionary*, when identifying green pigments suitable for use in oil. One choice besides the ubiquitous verdigris was "terra verte," a green earth that was refined to produce a soft grayish green pigment.[38]

When Charles Riley of Philadelphia died in 1842, appraisers itemized an estate with a shop in full production. Olive green, an important color, covered fifteen six-chair sets in two styles—"ball backs" and "Baltimore backs."

Figure 9 Shaped-tablet-top Windsor side chair with splat, branded by John Swint (act. ca. 1847 and later; chair one of four), Lancaster, Pennsylvania, 1847–1855. Yellow poplar (seat). H. 33", W. 18⅜", D. 14⅝". (Courtesy, Lancaster.History .org, Lancaster, Pennsylvania; photo, Winterthur Museum.) Original decoration and surface paint approximating the olive green current by the second quarter of the nineteenth century.

The ball-back chairs had bent backs with short ball-centered spindles at the lower back. The Baltimore-style chairs had large tablet tops set on turned posts or rabbeted to sawed Grecian posts (fig. 9; see fig. 29). Rufus Porter provided two recipes in his *Scientific American* article for duplicating this dull yellowish green color. One is a mixture of blue, red, and yellow, the other a combination of lampblack and chrome yellow. The forty-three pounds of chrome yellow in Riley's shop suggests his choice of recipe. Also in the shop was "1 Sett Pea Green [Chairs]." Each of two recipes indicates this color was little different from the light green that had been used on Windsor chairs for almost a century. Each recipe calls for white lead with the addition of verdigris or Paris (French) green. Of the two pigments, verdigris is more common in records.[39]

Painted fancy chairs with woven seats of rush or cane were introduced in America before 1800 through English imports and immigrant craftsmen. Two London chairmakers, Samuel Claphamson and William Challen, settled at Philadelphia and New York, respectively. Claphamson advertised "fancy" and "bamboo chairs" in January 1785. When changing addresses in 1797, Challen assured his New York customers he was prepared to supply "every article in the fancy chair line, executed in the neatest manner, and after the newest and most approved London patterns."[40]

Like other vernacular seating, fancy-chair construction frequently is unidentified in records. Unit price, pattern, and decorative treatment, if indicated, can provide insights. Cane seats were less common than rush seats and also more expensive. The green of the fancy chairs discussed here is without further description except for "3 Pea green cane seat chairs" in the household of Lambert Hitchcock in 1852 at Unionville, Connecticut. As stated, pea green could have been prepared using the pigment verdigris, although, according to Sheraton, green paint made with verdigris might be manipulated to vary the color: "In painting chairs with a green ground, common verdigrise may be used. . . . The green may be compounded to any shade by means of white lead, and king's yellow, both of which must first be ground in turpentine out of the dry colours."[41]

In general, fancy chairs were priced higher than Windsors. Thomas Howard, a Providence, Rhode Island, craftsman, noted the price range in 1822, when advertising a new shipment of seating furniture from the New York City area: "4000 Fancy and Windsor Chairs, of a superior quality, new and handsome patterns, from 50 cents to five dollars." Windsor chairs priced at $2.00 or more and fancy chairs from $3.00 usually represented high-end seating, often distinguished by special structural features, elaborate decoration, and/or extensive gilding. Fancy green chairs made in 1816 at Newark, New Jersey, by David Alling had cross backs (see fig. 19), slat backs, or ball backs, the last-named pattern notable for a horizontal ball-accented fret across the back (see fig. 26). Earlier, in 1810, Nolen and Gridley, warehousemen of Boston, advertised imported New York chairs of green and gold with "double Cross Backs." Top-of-the-line fancy seating might exhibit extensive hand-painted ornament or complex bronzework (stenciling), either accented with gilding.[42]

Yellow Chairs

Yellow was a new color available for the surfaces of Windsor seating at Philadelphia in the post-Revolutionary period. Its appearance in the market in the 1780s coincided with the introduction of a new side chair having a back bow anchored in the seat, a pattern also described at Philadelphia as an oval-back Windsor, and turned work simulating the jointed character of bamboo. Providing inspiration for the new chair back was formal seating furniture constructed locally after neoclassical oval-back designs current in England. Six new bow-back chairs painted yellow and valued at 9s. ($1.50) each stood in the shop of John Lambert at his death in 1793 during a yellow fever epidemic that raged in Philadelphia. The bow-back Windsor quickly became the popular chair for dining.[43]

The common yellow pigment of the period was patent yellow, a bright chloride of lead (fig. 10). Formula improvements about 1800 using additives such as antimony and bismuth enhanced the color's "brilliancy and

Figure 10   Detail, slat-back Windsor side chair, southeastern central Pennsylvania, 1820–1830. Yellow poplar (seat) with maple. H. 35", W. 17½", D. 15⅝". (Courtesy, Winterthur Museum.) Original decoration and surface paint in bright yellow, the formula either the patent yellow or chrome yellow current in the early nineteenth century.

durability." This likely was the "new discovery in the preparation of Paints" advertised by chairmaker Lawrence Allwine in 1800 at his Philadelphia "Patent Paint Ware House." By 1804 Harmon Vosburgh retailed "Patent Mineral Yellow" of his "own manufacture . . . warranted equal to any ever imported, and 50 per cent cheaper" at his New York varnish and patent yellow manufactory. Patent yellow remained the standard for a decade or more, until the bright new chrome yellow, a lead chromate, seized the market. By 1818 William Palmer, a fancy chairmaker of New York, "succeeded in making this new and beautiful PAINT a permanent color."[44]

The fashion for yellow dining chairs was disseminated from Philadelphia. James Chase of Gilmanton, New Hampshire, sold "Six Dining Chars painted yallow" in 1804 to Reuben Morgan of Meredith for 7s. 6d. ($1.25) the chair. Earlier, Amos D. Allen had sold six yellow chairs to Dr. Samuel Lee, a neighbor at Windham, Connecticut. When Lee died in 1815, the dining chairs were still in his home. Yellow dining chairs trimmed in blue were perhaps more popular than plain ones at Solomon Cole's Glastonbury shop near Hartford, where the chairmaker priced his ornamented seating about

25 percent higher than plain chairs. New York estates of the late 1790s and early 1800s that describe yellow Windsors, some trimmed in green or white, provide information on the broad socioeconomic background of the owners of yellow Windsor seating: two decedents were "gentlemen"; other owners included a merchant, lawyer, silversmith, shipmaster, and blacksmith. At Boston Daniel Rea Jr. used more descriptive language when recording two groups of chairs painted "Patent yellow": one group was "Creas'd in Green," highlighting the "bamboo" grooves, while the other was "Strip'd." Providing additional insight into the range of decorative options is a notice by Ephraim Evans at Alexandria, Virginia, in 1802 following the theft of a set of chairs from his shop: "STOLEN . . . Six round back Chairs, painted yellow, tip'd with black, the seats painted mahogany colour." At Saybrook, Connecticut, the estate of cabinetmaker Samuel Loomis contained yellow Windsor chairs with painted "black bottoms." Another option, available at the shop of Amos D. Allen, was stuffed seats, or "green cushions," probably covered in moreen.[45]

Yellow paint on Windsor chairs was not limited to the bow-back style. Captain John Derby of Salem, Massachusetts, purchased yellow fan-back chairs in 1802 for $1.39 apiece. Solomon Cole's chair production at Glastonbury, Connecticut, included yellow fan-backs embellished with green ornament. The order book of Amos D. Allen of Windham describes another chair style in 1799: "6 Fancy [continuous-bow] Ch[air]s without braces, Edged [pinstriped] . . . Yellow." Cargo lists of the early nineteenth century provide insights on yellow chairs in the new square-back patterns and the scope of the export trade in seating furniture. Itemized in a mixed cargo shipped in 1801 to Havana, Cuba, by Philadelphia chairmaker Anthony Steel are "One Dozen yellow Double back Square tops," a pattern with curved double rods, or "short bows," forming the crest. When the ship *George and Mary* left Providence, Rhode Island, in 1810 with a cargo from New York for sale at Buenos Aires, Argentina, the invoice of furniture included "12 [Bent Back] Yellow [Winsor Chairs]" valued at $1.25 apiece. New York patterns also were part of a chair consignment containing yellow Windsors shipped to Nathan Bolles of New Orleans in 1819 by David Alling, proprietor of a chair manufactory at Newark, New Jersey. Itemized are Windsors with slat backs and plain spindles or organ spindles, the last-named feature a distinctive New York pattern (see fig. 26).[46]

Supplementing bright yellow seating in the market were Windsor chairs painted in paler tones of yellow (fig. 11). "Straw" and "cane" were terms in use, although both probably identified the same color, the terminology a matter of individual shop practice or preference. Sheraton, who provided a recipe for straw-colored paint in his *Cabinet Dictionary* (1803) but none for cane color, intimated the yellows were the same, when describing the canes used in fancy-chair seats as "of a fine light straw colour." The base for formulating straw color was white lead, the pigment varying, depending on recipe date. Sheraton recommended king's yellow, a yellow orpiment. In *Directions for House and Ship Painting* of 1812, Hezekiah Reynolds named spruce yellow, whereas Rufus Porter, writing in 1845, preferred chrome yel-

Figure 11 Slat-back (or triple-back) Windsor side chair branded by Silas Buss (chair one of four), Sterling, Massachusetts, 1820–1830. White pine (seat). H. 34⅞", W. 16½", D. 15¾". (Courtesy, Marblehead Museum and Historical Society, Marblehead, Massachusetts; photo, Winterthur Museum.) Original decoration and surface paint in pale yellow termed either "straw" or "cane" color in the early nineteenth century.

low. Chrome yellow is bright, whereas the other recipes produced a light brownish yellow. Reynolds's spruce yellow is an ochre, or earth, and Sheraton recommended as an additive to his formula "a little Oxford ochre."[47]

References to straw- and cane-colored paint occur in documents originating in both New England and Philadelphia, although use of one or the other term appears to have been shop specific, based on limited evidence. Straw color in reference to paint was a viable term from the 1790s, whereas the first use of cane color dates after 1800. Both terms were current until almost 1850. The popularity of straw- and cane-colored paint is explained indirectly by Sheraton in defining the word "BAMBOO": "A kind of Indian reed, which in the east is used for chairs. These are, in some degree, imitated in England, by turning beech into the same form, and making chairs of this fashion, painting them to match the colour of the reeds or cane." Simulated bamboowork appeared in America in the mid-1780s with the introduction of the bow-back Windsor at Philadelphia. Yellow paint helped to promote the exotic background of the new turned style, although craftsmen soon offered a broad palette of color choices for "bamboo" seating.[48]

An early reference to straw-colored chairs can be found in the shipping records of Stephen Girard of Philadelphia, who in 1791 purchased two dozen Windsors of this color from William Cox at $1.67 each, probably for shipment to Haiti in the Caribbean. Later, between 1818 and 1832, Luke Houghton of rural Barre, Massachusetts, framed five sets, comprising six or twelve straw-colored chairs, each chair priced from 83¢ to $1.50, suggesting there were options in structural pattern and decoration. Philemon Robbins of Hartford, Connecticut, noted the sale of six straw-colored chairs in 1836, although his customers appear to have favored bright yellow seating.[49]

In the 1810s Stephen Girard, formerly a customer of William Cox (d. 1811) for straw-colored chairs, patronized the shop of Joseph Burden, who on one occasion supplied him with "4 Dozen Cane couloured Chairs" at $17.00 the dozen and four matching settees, each priced at $10.00. The furniture was placed on board the ship *Rousseau* bound for China via South America, where it was sold. The firm of Verree and Blair of Charleston, South Carolina, identified a less successful waterborne venture in announcing the sale of cane-colored Windsors in 1807 from the ship *Thomas Chalkley*, which "put into . . . port in distress, on her passage from Philadelphia to St. Thomas." Chair manufacturer David Alling of Newark, New Jersey, also identified cane-colored chairs as a popular commodity during the 1810s, when Moses Lyon was his painter and ornamenter. Itemized in Lyon's work are cane-colored Windsors of three spindle types: "plain" (cylindrical), "organ," and "flat." Organ spindles, located in the lower backs of chairs, are cylindrical with thick rounded tops and slim lower tips like organ pipes (see fig. 26). The common flat spindle is of so-called arrow shape. Lyon also "tipped," or pinstriped, several sets of cane-colored Windsors.[50]

Cream color, a pale yellow tint that equaled the popularity of straw- and cane-colored paint, was selected occasionally for Windsor seating in the early nineteenth century (fig. 12). The closeness of cream color to the yellow palette is demonstrated in the accounts of Philemon Robbins of Hartford,

Figure 12   Tablet-top Windsor side chair with stenciled identification of Cornelius E. R. Davis (one of six with a settee), Carlisle, Pennsylvania, ca. 1831–1835. Yellow poplar (seat). H. 32⅞", W. 19¼", D. 15⅛". (Courtesy, Cumberland County Historical Society, Carlisle, Pennsylvania; photo, Winterthur Museum.) Original decoration and surface paint in cream yellow.

Connecticut, who in 1834 sold Thomas C. Perkins "3 yellow Chairs plain colour to border on a cream colour." In his recipe for cream-colored paint, Hezekiah Reynolds combined spruce yellow (an ochre) with white lead in the proportion of one part to thirty to achieve a "yellow tinge." Reynolds used the same ingredients in straw-colored paint, altering the proportions to one part to ten. Elijah Eldredge recommended the addition of stone yellow, an ochre, to white lead in compounding cream-colored paint, resulting in a tint similar to that achieved by Reynolds.[51]

Six "Cream Color'd Chairs" stood in the Danbury, Connecticut, home of furniture maker Ebenezer Booth White in 1817. Sales of similarly painted Windsors at the Connecticut shops of Thomas Safford and Silas E. Cheney further describe a modest interest in this light color. Titus Preston of Wallingford provided more detail in 1801, when Polly Scovel acquired two six-chair sets of cream-colored Windsors. Both groups had striped decoration, and one set had painted "green bottoms" that likely reflected the color of the striped ornament. Preston's price of $1.17 a chair was the same as that recorded by Safford and Cheney. Within two years, David Russell recorded the sale of cream-colored chairs with mahogany-colored seats at Winchester, Virginia. Later, in 1842, Charles Riley's probate record describes an extensive shop inventory at Philadelphia that lists "1 Sett Cream Col'd Ball Back [Chairs]." The pattern probably identifies Windsors with tablet tops (crests) in the Baltimore style and short ball-centered spindles in the lower back below a cross rail.[52]

Supplementing Windsor seating, many chairmakers framed fancy chairs to satisfy a market that preferred higher-end painted and decorated furniture. Records collected for this study include references to yellow, cane-colored, and cream-colored fancy seating, colors available at one time or another at David Alling's New Jersey chair manufactory. During the late 1810s, when Alling made yellow and cane-colored seating, he also produced fancy chairs and a few Windsors in a painted finish he called "Nankeen." The term possibly can be equated with Alling's later use of "cream color" in the 1830s. Nankeen was a popular cotton cloth of pale, light brownish yellow produced originally at Nanking, China, and exported through the port of Canton, where after the Revolution American merchants purchased the textile directly. Although Alling is the only person in this study to identify Nankeen-colored paint, the term also may have had currency at New York, where Alling had frequent contact by water with suppliers and craftsmen. Nankeen-colored seating available at Alling's shop included slat-back and ball-back fancy chairs; the Windsors had organ spindles.[53]

When Elizur Barnes of Middletown, Connecticut, charged Arthur W. Magill 67¢ in 1822 for "Painting 8 Seats yellow," he identified rush-bottom fancy chairs. Sheraton advocated painting rush seats because, as he explained, it "preserves the rushes and hardens them." Sheraton commented, alternatively, on the use of canework in furniture, noting that it introduced "lightness, elasticity, cleanness, and durability." The light straw color of cane further interested him because it provided "the most agreeable contrast to almost every colour it is joined with."[54]

Fancy chairs painted yellow, among other colors, were available in the mid-1830s at the Hartford, Connecticut, manufactory of Philemon Robbins and partners, whose accounts describe an active business association with suppliers of seating furniture, among them Lambert Hitchcock. Hitchcock shipped hundreds of chairs to Robbins from his factory in Hitchcocksville (Riverton), and other stock was available in the mid-1830s at Hitchcock's chair store in Hartford. In September 1835 a Mr. Churchill purchased "2 cane seat yellow Hitchcock ch[airs]" from Robbins for $3.00. A previous order for another customer had required that Robbins "send to M[essrs] Hitchcock for 18 cream color Roll top cane seat chair[s] . . . with out gilt but d[ou]ble . . . bl[ack] stripe."[55]

Like Windsor furniture, fancy seating was a commodity of waterborne commerce, albeit a more modest one. Yellow-painted chairs are named in several records dating to the 1810s. On June 1, 1814, the New York shop of Alexander Patterson prepared "12 Yellow & gilt chairs" priced at $5.25 the chair for shipment up the Hudson River on the sloop *Columbia* to Gerrit Wessel Van Schaick, a resident of Albany. Packing the chairs for shipment cost an additional $1.50, although no further detail is provided. With woven seats already in place (as per chair cost), the chairs probably were nested in bundles of two, the seats in contact, vulnerable surfaces wrapped with sheeting or haybands, and the exterior wrapped with straw matting tied in place.[56]

David Alling, a manufacturer of Newark, New Jersey, from about 1800 until 1855, derived considerable income from his export business in seating furniture. In 1819 and 1820 he sent four large consignments of fancy chairs of mixed pattern, color, and ornament to his agent in New Orleans. Among the shipments were three sets of handsome yellow fancy chairs, each one-dozen set priced at $50.00. Gilt decoration enriched all three sets, and one set also had "bronsed" ornament. Alling's records also describe the structural features of the chairs: one set had "dimond front rounds," or front stretchers centered by a small, diamond-shaped tablet (fig. 13); another set had slat-style front stretchers (see fig. 23) and legs flaring outward at the base; the third set had distinctive New York ball backs, with narrow cross rods anchoring two rows of small beads (see fig. 31). Stephen Girard's maritime pursuits carried his vessels well beyond North America, and his Philadelphia suppliers provided a variety of seating furniture to meet the tastes of his markets. In July 1816 the ship *North America* left the city carrying 128 fancy chairs, including twenty-two side chairs and six armchairs described as "[Fancy chairs] bent [back] Cane colour." A principal destination was Port Louis on the Isle de France (Mauritius), east of Madagascar, where the entire cargo of chairs was landed. The vessel then proceeded to India and the East Indies.[57]

White Chairs

White, along with black, green, red, and blue, was a paint color identified as suitable for Windsor chairs in an invoice book kept by Joseph Walker, supercargo on the sloop *Friendship* in 1784 on a voyage to Savannah, Georgia. Aside from green, all the colors were newly fashionable. The principal

Figure 13 Slat-back (or fret-back) fancy side chair, New York City or possibly central Connecticut, 1810–1820. Woods unknown; rush. Dimensions unknown. (Present location unknown; formerly in an institutional collection; photo, Winterthur Museum.) Original decoration and surface paint in white yellowed by a resin finish. A side chair of identical structure but different decoration has a nineteenth-century history in the Day family of Hartford, Connecticut.

ingredient in white paint was white lead, a lead carbonate, known in its pristine and brightest form as flake white. Spanish white, or whiting, an alternative pigment made from clay, was sold as a finely powdered chalk. Painters sometimes used Spanish white as an adulterant in lead paint, if, indeed, they did not employ a more common chalk.[58]

Other references to white paint followed. In the mid-1780s Benjamin Franklin furnished his home in Philadelphia with two dozen white Windsor chairs. The purchase likely occurred in 1785, on his return from national service in France, or in 1786, when he enlarged his residence on Market Street. The chairs were inventoried at his death in 1790. Other records from the 1790s describe increasing local interest in white Windsor seating. General Henry Knox, secretary of war in the new federal government located at Philadelphia during the 1790s, patronized William Cox in 1794 for twelve white bow-back, or oval-back, side chairs at $1.87 apiece and "12 Oval back'd white color'd Arm chairs with Mahogany Arms," the $3.12 unit price a reflection of the use of mahogany in the construction. Knox's purchase of similar seating from Cox the following year for triple the number of side chairs and armchairs was made at price increases of 11¼ and 6¾ percent, respectively. Six settees accompanied the seating; two were priced at $7.50 apiece, the remaining four at $15.00 apiece. The dual pricing suggests the long seats accommodated two and four people, respectively.[59]

By 1796 the price of Windsor chairs at Philadelphia had increased again by 16¾ percent for side chairs and 11¾ percent for armchairs. William Meredith, a lawyer and banker of the city, purchased white oval-back Windsors from John Letchworth that year at $2.50 and $3.75 apiece, probably to furnish a dining parlor. Something beyond plain white seating is suggested in the prices of all these groups of Philadelphia chairs. Although the dates are too early for gilt ornament, the "creases" of the bamboowork and the grooves of the seats and bows probably were "picked out" in a contrasting dark color using a slim brush called a pencil.[60]

Records indicate that Windsor prices began to normalize by 1800, the year the federal government moved to the new federal city at Washington. William Dutilh and Samuel Coates Jr., Philadelphia merchants, purchased white oval-back Windsors that year for their export ventures. John B. Ackley supplied Coates's chairs. The previous year Taylor and King sold Stephen Girard "Wite Dining Chairs" described as "New fashion'd," a term that marks the early stage of a shift from round- to square-back seating, the common Windsor profile until about 1850. The cross rod at the tops of Girard's chairs was either of serpentine or simulated bamboo form.[61]

Some hint of ornament on white and other chairs occurs in several records. When working for Amos Bradley at East Haven, Connecticut, in 1808, Charles Stow received credit for "penciling 6 white Chairs." Two years later Tapping Reeve, proprietor of a law school at Litchfield, patronized Silas E. Cheney for six white "Doining" chairs with "striped" (penciled) decoration. "6 white gilt Table Chairs," their high valuation in 1810 suggesting they were almost new, stood in the home of Lydia Pinkham, widow of Captain Bethuel Pinkham of Nantucket. Several other individuals owned white fan-back Windsors, a pattern still current in New England in 1804, when James Chase sold white fan-backs to a customer at Gilmanton, New Hampshire. Two craftsmen identified the color of the decoration on white fan-back chairs sold at their shops: John Doggett of Roxbury, Massachusetts, named green; Stephen Tracy in Connecticut ornamented white chairs in yellow. Aside from use in the dining parlor, white Windsor chairs served as furnishings for bedchambers.[62]

Prices for white fancy chairs in the early nineteenth century varied widely—from $1.75 to $8.00 the chair, indicating customers could choose from a broad range of structural and ornamental options (fig. 13). Supplementary information is sparse, with few patterns identified. David Alling produced single cross-back chairs at Newark, New Jersey (see figs. 19, 34), and Nolen and Gridley of Boston imported double cross-back chairs from New York. Alling also framed slat-back fancy chairs, a crest type identified with various mid-back features—spindles, graduated cross slats, three-stick cross rods, pierced frets, and ball frets formed of cross sticks and beads (see fig. 26).[63]

Decoration was the second component that determined the pricing of the fancy chair, although descriptions are rare. Basic striping and a simple ornament in the crest probably sufficed in the lowest-priced seating. William Palmer, a fancy chairmaker of New York, supplied a client in 1803 with white chairs ornamented in yellow. Perhaps he also retailed the "14 White & Green fancy chairs" itemized in the 1819 estate of Whitehead Fish, cashier of the local Merchants' Bank. Of particular note in records is gilded decoration, some described as "Elegant." Chairs purchased from Palmer for $8.00 apiece in 1804 by Nicholas Low, a New York merchant and landholder, probably fit this description, although the account merely describes "6 Drawing room chairs white & Gold." Undoubtedly, these high-priced chairs were of handsome pattern and ornament. As noted by Sheraton, drawing-room chairs "should always be the produce of studied elegance."[64]

Sheraton also commented on the process of gilding, described as "the art of spreading or covering thin gold over any substance." Some of his remarks center on "Gilding chairs." Because of the small areas of chair gilding compared with other types of surface gilding and the rapid drying quality of japanners' gold size, the ornamenter had to work quickly and with expertise. Any irregularities in the edges of gilded ornament could be "trimmed up by japanning the uneven edges with a colour suitable to the ground," using a slim brush. In preparing the colorless size to produce the tacky surface that secures the gold leaf, the gilder colored the material to distinguish the sized areas from the ground color. Red lead, vermilion, and ochre were recommended for a light ground and white lead for a dark ground. To protect the gold work when completed, Sheraton advised a coating of copal varnish diluted with turpentine "that it may dry quick, and be more transparent over the gold." Surfaces of expensive seating were safeguarded for delivery, as noted by Samuel Gridley of Boston, who in 1810 shipped to Joshua Ward of Salem "12 white fancy Chairs" priced at $4.50 apiece, each wrapped in matting at an additional cost of 25¢ the chair.[65]

"Bronzing," a painted or stenciled technique, which began to influence the vernacular chair market during the 1810s, was another method of decorating surfaces on fancy and related seating. Bronzing, gilding, and freehand ornamental painting were skills practiced by Moses Lyon in this period, when employed by David Alling at Newark, New Jersey. An item of particular note is the stock of "white and gold double cross [back]" chairs with "Bronzed Tops" imported from New York in 1810 by Nolen and Gridley of Boston. Other stock offered by the firm included white-and-gold fancy chairs with "green tops" ornamented with "double shells," a motif reflecting a popular collecting pastime (see fig. 15). Most fancy-chair purchases could be supplemented with "Settees to match," as advertised by William Challen in 1809 after migrating from New York to Lexington, Kentucky. Consumers also could choose to protect the rush seats of their fancy chairs with a coat of paint. Charles Dyer, a customer of Elizur Barnes at Middletown, Connecticut, paid the craftsman 25¢ for "white Paint for Cheir Seets" in 1824, which he appears to have applied himself.[66]

Black Chairs

Although Joseph Walker of Philadelphia named black in an invoice book of 1784 as one of several colors suitable for painting Windsor furniture, currency of the color is better associated with the start of the nineteenth century. Amos D. Allen of Windham, Connecticut, supplied several customers in 1801 and 1802 with black "Dineing" chairs, probably in the bow-back style. One set had "edged," or penciled, ornament, and one customer, Patty Parrish, paid for her four chairs "in cloth," likely woven herself. Another probable customer was Allen's neighbor Captain Stephen Payne of Lebanon, whose probate records list black dining chairs. Payne purchased furniture from Allen, including dining chairs of unspecified color. His property along the Lebanon-Windsor town line adjoined that of Allen's, and Allen was both an appraiser and a creditor of Payne's estate in 1815.[67]

Titus Preston's work for customers at Wallingford likely included more than one style of black dining chair. Bow-backs seem indicated in Polly Scovel's purchase in 1801 of twelve chairs with "striped" decoration priced at $1.25 apiece. Several years later Cornelius Cook took seven chairs to the shop to be painted black and striped, the cost at 29¢ apiece suggesting that painting and ornamenting Scovel's new chairs represented about 23 percent of the cost. When Amos Bristol acquired "black dining chairs" from Preston in 1814, styles had shifted from round to square backs. New square-back Windsors with penciled grooves, described as "42 Black and Yellow Bamboo Chairs," stood in the Boston shop of Ebenezer Knowlton in 1811, the year Stephen Girard's ship *Montesque* left Philadelphia for a voyage to China via South America, where the vessel deposited a cargo of "6 Dozen black Chairs" priced at $1.42 each and six matching settees at $10 each.[68]

Black Windsor seating continued as a choice through the 1850s. Lewis Bancel, proprietor of a day and boarding school in lower Manhattan, furnished the premises in the 1820s with more than 350 vernacular seats, including black "wooden chairs." Windsor seating still was integral to home furnishing several decades later on the western frontier. Basic appointments in the parlor of an Ohio home in the country are perhaps typical. The walls were whitewashed and the floor covered with homemade striped carpet. Black Windsors stood in a straight line against one wall.[69]

Complementing bow- and square-back Windsor seating painted black were chairs of fan-back pattern. Early-nineteenth-century records suggest a pricing structure. Stephen Tracy, who occupied the shop of his late uncle and master, Ebenezer Tracy Sr., near Norwich, Connecticut, in 1803, sold "6 Fanback Chairs black and yallow" in 1805 and 1806 for $1.17 apiece. At East Haven, Amos Bradley charged $1.33 for black fan backs, which in 1802 may have had simulated bamboo turnings with creases accented in light-colored penciling. More extensive decoration is implied in the unit charge of $1.42 for "6 fanback Chairs black, ornamented" sold in 1807 by Solomon Cole of Glastonbury. The decoration may have included short, vertical grasslike sprigs adjoining penciled creases (see fig. 26). When Samuel Barrett, a Concord, Massachusetts, gristmill and sawmill owner, died in 1825, his black fan-back Windsors were of an age to be worth only 33¢ apiece.[70]

Lampblack was the principal ingredient in black paint. A carbonaceous substance, or soot, it was formed by burning tar, pitch, or resin. Sheraton described the pigment as having "a greasy or oily quality," and therefore it was "a bad drier." After grinding lampblack very fine in turpentine, painters mixed it with linseed oil boiled with the drying agents litharge and red lead. Rufus Porter, writing in his serial publication, *Scientific American*, stated that "the best black is composed of lampblack and Prussian blue." For oil painting Sheraton recommended using black over a light red ground, although the prevalence of that ground in American work is yet to be assessed (see fig. 4).[71]

Gray of a medium to medium-light shade could serve as an alternative to black (fig. 14). Again the pigment was lampblack. In mixing gray paint, the proportion of lampblack to white lead determined the exact shade. Other

Figure 14 Detail, slat-back (or ball-back) Windsor side chair, Hudson River valley, ca. 1820–1828. Yellow poplar (seat). H. 33⁹⁄₁₆", W. 16¼", D. 15". (Courtesy, Fenimore Art Museum, Cooperstown, New York; photo, Winterthur Museum.) Original decoration and surface paint in medium gray.

grays could be produced by admixing Prussian blue and verdigris, or stone yellow (an ochre) and verdigris, with white lead. Most references to gray-painted seating date to the second quarter of the nineteenth century. An exception is the set of "4 lead coloured wooden chairs" that stood in the bedroom over the "yellow Hall" in 1806 in the household of Samuel Broome, owner of a marble quarry at Whitemarsh, Montgomery County, Pennsylvania. Twelve more "Lead"-colored chairs, probably new, stood in John Oldham's chair shop at Baltimore in 1835 at his estate appraisal. Gray chairs sold the previous year to various customers by Philemon Robbins at Hartford, Connecticut, were described as "quaker color wood seat chairs." Two sets had a rocking chair en suite. "Slate" was the term for gray chairs in the 1840s at the Philadelphia chair shop of Charles Riley.[72]

Catharine Gansevoort (widow of Peter Jr.) of Albany, New York, deposited a dozen fancy chairs in the shop of James Chestney in 1815 for repair and refurbishing. One chair was mended, three bottomed, and all refreshed by "Painting bl[ac]k & penciling with yellow." Fancy chairs thus finished were popular in the early 1800s, although it is unlikely that Mrs. Gansevoort knew of Sheraton's comment on the subject: "Black chairs look well when ornamented with yellow lines." Sheraton described the composition of yellow paint for lines as a mixture of "King's yellow [yellow orpiment] and white flake [lead], with a trifle of orange lead, ground finely up in spirits of turpentine very thick." The lines were applied with a pencil "of camels hair, very long," the length ranging from half an inch to an inch, "according to the thickness of the line to be drawn."[73]

Equally popular among prosperous householders were black fancy chairs ornamented in gold (fig. 15; see also fig. 34). William Palmer of New York sold "highly finished black and gold . . . Fancy Chairs, with cane and rush bottoms" along with his fancy white seating. Black chairs bought in 1799 by Stephen Arnold of East Greenwich, Rhode Island, for $3.25 apiece had gold ornament on a japanned ground simulating lacquer. In japanning Sheraton recommended starting with a ground of white lead. Lampblack applied over this base was "ground up in turpentine, very fine, . . . then laid on in white hard varnish, very thin, and repeated." On completion, Arnold's chairs were packed for shipping at a charge of 12½¢ apiece. In 1814 Palmer did business with Andrew Bell of Perth Amboy, New Jersey, whose black-and-gold chairs cost $3.50 each.[74]

Public interest in black-and-gold fancy seating was broad. In 1807 Samuel Gridley offered "Black and Gilt" fancy chairs at Boston, although the seating probably was imported from New York. Four years later Thomas Boynton, a young Boston chairmaker, framed "6 broad top black gilt [chairs]" for a local customer, the crest either a deep slat or a wide tablet framed on the post tops. Meanwhile, Stephen Girard of Philadelphia bought a set of black-and-gold side chairs and armchairs from John Mitchell, probably for his export trade. Girard had considerable business in South America, whereas other merchants favored the coastal South. Notices at Charleston, South Carolina, in 1807 and 1808 offered black-and-gold chairs and settees with cane or rush seats from Philadelphia and New

Figure 15   Slat-back fancy side chair with "Cumberland spindles," New York City or environs, 1810–1820. Maple, birch, and yellow poplar; rush. H. 35", W. 19", D. 15¾". (Courtesy, Winterthur Museum.) Original decoration and surface paint in black.

York. By 1816 the firm of Stibbs and Stout at Cincinnati, Ohio, made fancy flag bottom and Windsor chairs in colors including "Black . . . handsomely gilt and ornamented."[75]

Several accounts illuminate the structural features of fancy seating finished in black and gilt. James J. Skerrett of Philadelphia patronized the shop of Haydon and Stewart in 1818, purchasing "Six Urn spindle Black & Gold Chairs" for the large sum of $4.50 apiece. The urn-spindle design may describe a Baltimore style with rich surface decoration. Later, in 1833, David Alling of Newark, New Jersey, made fancy-chair shipments to two firms in Columbus, Georgia. Smith and Morgan received twenty-four fancy chairs in two lots described as "cane seat, black gilt panel, scroll top chairs" priced at $2.50 and $2.25 the chair. One group had "grecian front posts," the other, "round front posts." What was the appearance of these chairs? The panel likely was a slat-type crest; the "scrolls" formed the rear tips of the back posts. The "front posts" were legs. "Grecian front posts" were sawed to "sabre," or hollow, form; "round" posts were turned to a fancy cylindrical style. Alling's shipment to T. and M. Evans contained a dozen "black paw'd gilt grecian f[oo]t" fancy chairs priced at $2.50 each. The back pattern is unknown; the legs were of saber form ending abruptly at the base in short "paw'd" animal feet. Alling's delivery of chairs to Columbus is of interest, since the community lies inland about two hundred miles from the coast. The site was the head of navigation by steam vessel on the Chattahoochee River, which flows south along the eastern boundary of Alabama to Lake Seminole to join the Flint River. The confluence of the rivers forms the Apalachicola River, which continues a southerly course to the Gulf of Mexico.[76]

Brown Chairs

Brown represents a greater diversity of hue, shade, and nomenclature than other surface colors used for seating furniture. Most terms are time-specific. For example, "mahogany" color and "chocolate" are descriptive words associated almost exclusively with late-eighteenth-century work. Nineteenth-century terms represent a broader range of hue: "brown," "tea color," "drab," "stone color," "dark color," "light color," "rust," and "cinnamon."

Mahogany was the popular brown of Windsor seating from the late 1780s until after 1800 (fig. 16). Chairs of this color were acquired new or by repainting older seating. An early import notice for mahogany-colored chairs appeared in 1789 at Charleston, South Carolina, where John Minnick sold Windsors of this color. Most references to mahogany-colored Windsors center on Philadelphia or describe its influence. A local request for mahogany-colored chairs originated with Solomon Maxwell at Christiana, Delaware, a small community south of Philadelphia on the wagon road between the Delaware River and the head of Chesapeake Bay. Maxwell wrote in 1794 to Lawrence Allwine, chairmaker of Philadelphia: "Mr Alwine, I wish you to send me half a dozen good round back windsor Chairs painted mehogany colour." When completed, Allwine shipped the bow-back Windsors to Maxwell through the merchant house of Levi Hollingsworth and Son.[77]

Figure 16 Detail, Philadelphia fan-back Windsor side chair painted mahogany color, from John Lewis Krimmel, *Quilting Frolic*, Philadelphia, Pennsylvania, 1813. Oil on canvas. 16⅞" x 22⅜". (Courtesy, Winterthur Museum.)

Other merchants were prominent in the Windsor trade out of Philadelphia. Stephen Girard's purchase of "6 Mahogney Dining Chairs" from Taylor and King in 1799 was part of a larger order. An extensive cargo of twenty-five dozen Windsor chairs shipped the next year by William Dutilh contained four dozen mahogany-colored bow-back chairs comparable to Girard's "dining chairs." At times Philadelphia chairmakers acted as their own middlemen in the export trade, as recorded in 1801, when Anthony Steel shipped two dozen mahogany-colored Windsors in a cargo totaling sixteen dozen side chairs, three dozen armchairs, and five settees. Steel placed the lot on the ship *Hope* bound for Havana, where the captain delivered the furniture to John Dutilh. A sophisticated group of mahogany-colored Windsors was purchased in 1800 by merchant Samuel Coates Jr. from John B. Ackley, likely for a customer along Chesapeake Bay. Priced at $3.50 apiece were "6 Oval back Chairs Painted Mohagny Colour, stuff seats, hair Cloth Cover, one row brass Nails." Accompanying these bow-back side chairs were two stuffed-seat armchairs priced at $4.50 apiece.[78]

Other evidence of mahogany-colored Windsors originated in Virginia, where in 1803 David Russell of Winchester sold six chairs of this description. In 1815 eighteen mahogany-colored Windsors furnished the home of Sarah B. Mason, widow of George Mason of Gunston Hall near Mount Vernon. Craftsmen and families in New England were acquainted with mahogany-colored seating owing to the coastal trade in Philadelphia Windsors. At Boston, ornamental painters Daniel Rea Jr. and George Davidson repainted chairs in mahogany color for clients in 1795 and 1796, respectively. Rea further provided ornament, likely pinstriping, and completed his work with a coat of varnish. After repairing a set of chairs at Windham, Connecticut, in 1800, Amos D. Allen repainted the surfaces, reserving "Mahogy colour" for the seats. Elsewhere, mahogany-colored Windsors were popular on Nantucket Island, where nine inventories dating between 1803 and 1810 list sixty-three chairs of that color used principally for dining or use in bedchambers. Most owners had been mariners, traders, or merchants and may have participated in the island's extensive trade with Philadelphia. Philadelphia Windsors with local histories remain on the island today.[79]

What prompted the popularity of mahogany color for Windsor seating? When it was introduced, householders realized that inexpensive seating painted mahogany color made excellent companion or supplemental seating to formal furniture of mahogany and other woods. How mahogany-colored paint was formulated is less clear. Although recipes abound for mahogany stain, sources are silent on ingredients used in mahogany-colored paint. An answer appears to emerge from recipes for graining wood in imitation of mahogany. The pigment in mahogany-colored paint likely was an ochre, or earth, with terra di sienna and stone yellow prominent candidates. Yellow in their natural states, both earths often were "burnt," or roasted, to create a "rich reddish brown," the same hue noted by the *Oxford English Dictionary* in describing the color of mahogany wood.[80]

Recipes for chocolate-colored paint, an alternative hue for Windsor chairs although less popular than mahogany, advised mixing lampblack with Spanish brown, a reddish brown earth containing iron oxides, or Venetian red, an artificially prepared ferric oxide of a brown, red-yellow hue. Both produced a deep dark brown of low brilliance. Several authors recommended mixing red lead and litharge in the compound to give the paint a "drying quality."[81]

In 1798 Hopkins and Charles, a Charleston, South Carolina, firm, noted the arrival from Philadelphia of "An excellent Assortment of Yellow, Green, Mahogany, and Chocolate Colored CHAIRS and SETTEES." The notice describes the currency of chocolate color at that date and confirms that chocolate and mahogany were distinguishable colors. Further evidence of chocolate brown paint on Windsor chairs comes from probate records. The high value of a dozen Windsors of that color in the home of merchant Isaac A. Kip of New York in 1805 indicates they were relatively new. The date suggests either the bow-back pattern or an early square-back design. Chocolate-colored Windsors, likely with square backs, were identified in 1819 in the Concord, Massachusetts, home of Francis Barrett, a painter who may have applied the color himself.[82]

References to the color "brown" without particular description of the hue were current for vernacular seating principally in the 1810s and later. Few records date earlier, although in 1795 General Henry Knox, member of the new federal government at Philadelphia, purchased "24 fann'd back'd Brown Color'd Chairs" from chairmaker William Cox as well as a large order of Windsor seating painted white. Although brown paint for vernacular seating gained favor in the early nineteenth century, information in contemporary records regarding its composition is rare. Only Sheraton provided insight in a short discourse on "brown" in various media from watercolor to "common oil painting" on wood. In the latter, he named the ingredients as lampblack, Spanish brown, and Venetian red, with the addition of a small amount of red lead "for . . . binding the Spanish brown more effectually." The *Oxford English Dictionary* reinforces Sheraton's insights by defining "brown" as "a composite colour produced by a mixture of red, yellow, and black." The resulting color actually was the "chocolate" brown current in the late eighteenth century.[83]

Several nineteenth-century records that identify brown chairs describe structural features. Thomas Boynton made brown bent-back chairs in 1811 at Boston and continued to produce chairs of this profile after his relocation to Vermont. During the same decade David Alling produced brown chairs at Newark, New Jersey, in at least three spindle patterns: plain, organ, and flat. After painting, many chairs were "ornamented." At this date Windsors sold for more than $1.00 the chair. Luke Houghton of Barre, Massachusetts, retailed sets of brown Windsors in 1817 and 1818, at unit prices of $1.16½ and $1.25. Jacob Roll and Isaac Deeds of Cincinnati, Ohio, filled an order for brown Windsors at $1.50 apiece in 1818 for B. V. Hunt. By the 1830s the market had changed. Cheaper production methods emphasizing quantity over quality drove the unit price below $1.00. Philemon Robbins of Hartford, Connecticut, sold brown Windsor chairs for 67¢ and 75¢ apiece. At John Oldham's death in 1835, appraisers of his Baltimore, Maryland, shop valued each chair in a set of brown Windsors at 58¢.[84]

Figure 17   Tablet-top (or fret-back) fancy side chair, southeastern Pennsylvania or Maryland, 1825–1835. Woods unknown; rush. Dimensions unknown. (Present location unknown; formerly in an institutional collection; photo, Winterthur Museum.) Original decoration and surface paint in light stone color (drab).

The terms "stone," "drab," "light color," and "dark color" used by painters and chairmakers to describe painted surfaces identify subtle variations of the same color—a brownish yellow ranging from light to medium dark. The critical terms in this interpretation include "drab stone Colour"; "drab, or light stone colour"; "stone brown"; and general references to light and dark stone color. Seven artisan recipes provide specific insights. The medium in all but one recipe is white lead. The principal pigment in all recipes is yellow ochre, described by the *Oxford English Dictionary* as an "earthy pigment . . . varying in colour from yellow to deep orange-red or brown, . . . *esp.* a light brownish yellow." The addition of Prussian blue, lampblack, or ivory black mentioned in four recipes dulled and appreciably darkened the color. The pigments umber, burnt umber, or Venetian red present in four recipes introduced a reddish or reddish brown character to the color. As summed up in *Smith's Art of House Painting* (1821), the painter mixed his ingredients "by degree to the colour required." Thus, stone color was variable in hue and brilliance (fig. 17; see also fig. 35).[85]

Although paint recipes (also known as receipts) make specific reference to stone color, whether of light or dark hue, chairmakers preferred to use the basic terms "light color" and "dark color." "Drab" was an alternative term in moderate use among craftsmen to identify light stone color. An early, and therefore unusual, reference to stone-colored seating occurs in the 1793 inventory of the estate of John Lambert, a Philadelphia chairmaker whose premises contained "8 . . . Fan backs Stone Colour" priced individually at 6s. 3d., which in the new decimal-based currency of the 1790s was equivalent to about $1.04 the chair. Half a century later, Joseph Jones, a chairmaker of neighboring Chester County, demonstrated the close link of the words "stone" and "drab" when itemizing a bill to a local customer: "6 S[traight B[ack] drab stone Colour [Chairs]."[86]

Two chairmakers with substantial businesses, David Alling of Newark, New Jersey, and Philemon Robbins of Hartford, Connecticut, found good markets in drab, or light stone–colored, Windsor chairs. In 1815 and 1816 Moses Lyon's work for Alling included "ornamenting" and/or "tipping" drab-colored chairs. Alling further described drab Windsors of three spindle types: plain (cylindrical), organ (simulated organ pipes), and flat (arrow, urn, or other flat profile). The unit cost of ornamenting these chairs was 12½¢ for plain-spindle Windsors and 19¢ for the other patterns. Alling's retail prices for Windsor chairs during the 1810s ranged from a low of $1.75 the chair to a high of about $2.90. By the 1830s his prices had moderated considerably. The highest prices now were the previous lowest figures. Philemon Robbins's accounts for the 1830s describe the rising impact of warehouse merchandising and the demand for cheap goods by a burgeoning population. Robbins sold his lowest-priced Windsors, some painted "drab" color, for 50¢ to 75¢. Whereas "common" was a word applied to inexpensive rush-bottom slat-back seating in the eighteenth century, the term now identified cheap Windsor seating. Even recycled chairs found a market, as when Robbins recorded the sale of "8 drab wood seat chairs second hand" priced at 58¢ apiece.[87]

The terms "light color" and "dark color" describing light stone (drab) and dark stone paint probably had their genesis in the 1820s. When Peter Peirce, a Templeton, Massachusetts, craftsman, died in 1829, appraisers itemized the contents of a shop in full production. Among the completed furniture were "12 lite col[ore]d comon [chairs]" valued at 42¢ apiece and "38 Dark col'd [common chairs]" estimated at 40¢ each wholesale. Contemporary production at Luke Houghton's shop ten miles distant at Barre also included light- and dark-colored Windsors, the retail prices varying from below to just above $1.00 a chair. Priced at $1.12½ apiece were "1 doz of best light Chair[s] dubl [double] Back," that is, chairs with two cross slats in the back. Two other records shed further light on patterns available in light or dark stone color. Dark "wood-seat" chairs sold in the mid-1830s by Philemon Robbins at Hartford, Connecticut, had "five rods," or spindles. An 1842 appraisal of Charles Riley's premises at Philadelphia itemized six completed "Setts Light Ball Back" chairs, that is, a pattern with a tablet top, a mid-back cross slat, and short spindles at the lower back with a ball turning at the center. Nelson Talcott, who worked in Portage County, Ohio, in the 1840s described sets of light-colored chairs by their function, that of dining, rather than by pattern.[88]

Chairs of tea color were prominent in the 1830s at Philemon Robbins's shop at Hartford. Otherwise, mention of this color is uncommon. Because Robbins also made Windsors painted drab color (light stone), dark color (dark stone), and brown (dark reddish brown), the obvious question is how tea color differed. Confirming that tea color identified paint rather than colored varnish is the account entry "to pntng [painting] R[ocking] Chair first dark then Tea." The item also suggests that tea color was of medium hue, perhaps between a light and a dark stone color. Tea color was more prominent in the shop's fancy-chair stock than in its Windsor line, and pricing indicates the former was more highly ornamented. Square-back Windsors with "five rods," or spindles, were part of the pattern selection. Since Robbins was a cabinetmaker, it is of note that several patrons chose tea color for forms other than chairs: a double dressing table, a bureau and dressing glass, a washstand.[89]

Rust- and cinnamon-colored chairs identified in two Delaware Valley documents dating to the 1830s and 1840s may have been close in hue. Appraisers, who in 1836 inventoried the estate of Ebenezer P. Rose, a chairmaker of Trenton, New Jersey, found "2 Rust [Chares]" in his home. A few years later "1 Sett Cinomen Col'd [Chairs]" made up part of the shop stock in Charles Riley's facility at Philadelphia. Neither color is identified in early-nineteenth-century paint recipes, although the "fawn"-colored paint listed by A. Otis in his "Collection of Receipts" of 1836 appears to describe the reddish brown color. Otis directed the painter to grind "burnt," or roasted, terra di sienna in linseed oil. The sienna was then mixed with white lead to the depth of color desired.[90]

Fancy seating furniture was available in brown hues similar to those current in Windsor seating, although at higher prices (see fig. 34). When David Alling of Newark, New Jersey, employed Moses Lyon as a decorator in the

1810s, his fancy seating was relatively sophisticated. Whereas Alling's prices for Windsors ranged from $1.75 to $2.90 the chair, the cost of fancy seating was higher by about 58 percent or more. The prices reflect Alling's location near the commercial center at New York and his broad clientele base in the South, where local craftsmen offered little competition. Few Northern chairmakers enjoyed these commercial advantages.[91]

References to mahogany- and chocolate-colored fancy chairs are rare because those terms had largely passed from use by the 1810s, when fancy seating became a viable market product. Mahogany color was no longer in vogue, and chocolate was the new "brown." When the merchant houses of Brown and Ives at Providence, Rhode Island, and Stephen Girard at Philadelphia undertook voyages to South America in 1810, brown fancy seating was part of their furniture cargoes. The Providence firm acquired its venture furniture at New York, including a dozen "Brown and Gold chairs," before the *George and Mary* sailed for Buenos Aires, Argentina, in April. Girard's ship *Montesque* left Philadelphia in December bound ultimately for China. A year later, the vessel's captain recorded furniture sales at Valparaiso, Chile, that included a dozen "Brown Gilt [side] chairs" and an eight-piece set of side chairs and armchairs of similar surface valued at $32.00, which sold at Valparaiso for $50.00. Furniture speculations were not always as profitable, however.[92]

Early-nineteenth-century accounts occasionally reference light stone–colored (drab) fancy chairs (see fig. 17) by pattern. A Norwich, Connecticut, notice of 1830 for Congdon and Tracy describes light-colored chairs with "double backs," or two cross slats. A bill to Benjamin Sharpless in 1842 from Joseph Jones of West Chester, Pennsylvania, lists "Ball B[ack] Chairs Drab, bronz bands," the backs an open-ball fret, the price over $2.00 apiece. Drab-colored chairs, sold in the mid-1830s at Hartford, Connecticut, by Philemon Robbins, had turned roll tops. Priced at $1.50 each, the chairs had rush or cane seats. A shop supplier of drab fancy seating was Lambert Hitchcock, who opened a chair store at Hartford in the mid-1830s to complement his factory at Hitchcocksville. Isaac Wright was another Hartford artisan-patron of Hitchcock's for drab chairs.[93]

Several chairmakers of the many who produced "dark-colored," or dark stone, fancy chairs worked from the 1820s to midcentury. Probate records indicate that at least one patron of the shop of Benjamin Branson at New York owed the estate $6.00 in 1831 for "painting One Dozen fancy Chairs Dark." Appraisers of Charles Riley's estate at Philadelphia assigned a price of $1.35 to each of six dark-colored, cane-seat fancy chairs forming a set in his shop, the unit price sufficient to account for modest decoration. Like Riley, Philemon Robbins of Hartford, Connecticut, had a large business. His production of dark stone–colored fancy chairs with roll tops and cane or rush seats paralleled his output of light-colored (drab) and tea-colored fancy seating, some of it acquired from Lambert Hitchcock. Prices stood above $1.00 apiece. A "plain" chair retailed for $1.06; one with "gilt" could command as much as $1.56.[94]

Red Chairs

The red paint employed on Windsor and fancy seating furniture until the early 1800s likely was the reddish brown surface coating made with the pigment Spanish brown used on common rush-bottom chairs during the eighteenth century. Given the dominance of green for Windsor chairs until after the Revolution, red paint probably was a viable option for Windsor seating only with the introduction of the bow-back pattern in the mid-1780s. At his death in 1796, Robert Casey, a resident of Baltimore County, Maryland, owned "6 green Chairs," probably Windsors, valued at 3s. (50¢) apiece and a "½ Dozen Windsor Chairs (red)" estimated at 7s. 6d. ($1.25) apiece. The number of chairs in each group is a reasonable indication that all were side chairs. The modest valuation of the green chairs suggests they were older fan-back Windsors, whereas the high valuation of the red chairs suggests they were relatively new and in the current bow-back style.[95]

Once introduced to bow-back seating, red paint was a choice for other Windsor patterns. Probate records indicate that painted Windsor armchairs were popular on Nantucket Island, where many householders had an armchair to supplement their side chairs, and a few residents owned several armchairs, even sets of half a dozen. The "6 Round back Red Chairs" owned by Jonathan Burnell in 1799 and appraised at $1.67 apiece were armchairs. They may have been new bow-back Windsors, although the high valuation suggests a more complex pattern, such as a sack-back chair. Amos D. Allen of Connecticut noted another style of Windsor armchair painted red in his order book: "9 Fancy Ch[air]s red, cushions green, edged white @ 15/6," or $2.57 apiece. "Fancy" was the term for the continuous-bow Windsor used by the Tracy family of chairmakers, of which Allen was a member. "Cushions" were stuffed work nailed in place; edging was painted pinstriping.[96]

The use of "red" paint on Windsor seating continued into the early nineteenth century, when James Chase of Gilmanton, New Hampshire, sold sets of bamboo-turned square-back chairs to several customers, including one order supplemented by "one Great [arm] Char painted Read." In 1817 at the death of William Hemphill, an attorney of West Chester, Pennsylvania, "6 Red Windsor Chairs" were part of the furnishings of his "office." Other red "Wooden" chairs furnished the extensive boarding and day school run by Lewis Bancel during the 1820s in lower Manhattan, still the center of city business at that date.[97]

In March 1820 David Alling, an entrepreneur chairmaker of Newark, New Jersey, shipped two dozen each of bent-back Windsors and rush-bottom fancy chairs painted "read" and gilded to Nathan Bolles, a New Orleans retailer. Given the date, Alling's proximity to the furniture style center at New York, and the pricing, $2.92 apiece for the Windsors and $4.58 each for the fancy chairs, the red of these chairs probably was the bright hue called "coquelicot," introduced to the market sometime before 1807, probably at Baltimore, New York, or Philadelphia (see fig. 34). The French word identifies the European corn poppy of bright orange-red color. Although coquelicot had currency in Windsor work (fig. 18), it was more common as a surface finish for fancy seating. The bent-back Windsors

Figure 18 Detail, slat-back Windsor rocking armchair with "flat sticks" (spindles), southern New Hampshire, 1820–1830. Maple and unidentified woods. H. 31", W. 19⅜", D. 16⅝" (seat). (Present location unknown; formerly in a private collection; photo, Winterthur Museum.) Original decoration and surface paint in coquelicot red.

from Alling's shop were matched in general pattern by the "60 Bent Back Coquilicot Winsor Chairs" acquired in New York in 1810 by Brown and Ives, merchants of Providence, Rhode Island, for exportation to Buenos Aires on the *George and Mary*. These chairs were accompanied by "72 Bamboo Coquilicot [Chairs]" with straight backs. Bent-back seating has rear posts shaved on the faces to permit their being bent with steam. Bamboo posts are solid and straight (although canted in their sockets) and marked with "creases" to simulate the grooves of the plant. Use of coquelicot color moved quickly from the East Coast to the Midwest. Stibbs and Stout were new to business at Cincinnati, Ohio, when they announced their partnership in 1816 to pursue fancy flag-bottom and Windsor chairmaking in fashionable colors that included coquelicot.[98]

A paint recipe to produce the brilliant orange-red color of coquelicot has yet to be located. Only red and scarlet are identified. In 1812, when Hezekiah Reynolds proposed a red coating for "painting inside work," he named five pigments identified in craftsmen's records: Venetian red, vermilion, red lead, Spanish brown, and red ochre. Each produced a different hue. Spanish brown and red ochre are earth derivatives and heavily tinged with brown. Venetian red also has a strong brown character. Red lead, roasted, produced a bright orange-red, although it had a tendency to turn black, making it unsuitable for special work. Only vermilion, described variously as bright scarlet, yellowish red, or red tinged with orange, appears to have produced a suitable imitation of the red poppy. In his *Decorative Painters' and Glaziers' Guide* (1827) Nathaniel Whittock stated that vermilion could be "depended on for durability." It was expensive to produce, as indicated in craftsmen's accounts, where the cost of vermilion is higher than that of other red pigments and its occurrence less frequent. When painting with vermilion, Elijah Eldredge recommended grinding the pigment in oil, then brushing the work "twice over." An anonymous collection of recipes for surface coating dating to about 1800 advises painting "Scarlet Red" using vermilion with a primer of red lead. Following a move from Boston to

Vermont in 1811–12, Thomas Boynton continued to order supplies from Boston for his chairmaking business, including "orange red" paint.[99]

Early-nineteenth-century fancy chairs painted red were mainly of coquelicot color (fig. 19). Samuel Gridley of Boston, who imported seating furniture from New York, advertised in April 1807 that he stocked coquelicot and gilt fancy chairs with cane or rush seats. Several years later, the partnership of Nolen and Gridley offered coquelicot chairs ornamented with a "gold Grecian Border" and double-cross-back chairs decorated with an "Eagle." Meanwhile, Patterson and Dennis of New York introduced a cutting-edge style in coquelicot and gilt with "cane bottoms and cane backs, an entire new pattern." By 1809 William Challen of New York had relocated to Lexington, Kentucky, to make fancy chairs in a range of colors, including coquelicot trimmed in gold, with settees to match. The same year Stephen Girard, a Philadelphia merchant, outfitted the *Voltaire* for a voyage to China with stops in South America, a good market for painted seating furniture. On board were "One Dozen Cocolico Chairs" priced at $4.17 apiece and a settee valued at $20.00.[100]

Several uncommon terms for Windsor and fancy seating colors, namely "blossom," "pink," and "rose," appear closely related, if not the same pink of bluish purple hue. "Flesh color," another pink surface, probably exhibited a yellow or orange tinge. A dozen "blossom Couler" chairs with "organ Spindles" were part of a consignment of furniture David Alling shipped from Newark, New Jersey, in March 1819 to Nathan Bolles at New Orleans. Blossom probably is the same color described in paint recipes as "peach blow" or "peach blossom." To mix this color, Rufus Porter recommended adding small amounts of ultramarine blue and lake, a purplish red pigment, to white lead. Pink and rose represented minor variations of this recipe. James J. Skerrett's "6 Pink Chairs" purchased in 1818 at Philadelphia from Haydon and Stewart were comparable in price at $2.25 apiece to Alling's blossom-colored chairs. The price indicates that both groups were substantially ornamented. At the death in 1833 of Thomas Devor, a chairmaker of Shippensburg, Pennsylvania, chairs of both "rose" and "flesh" color stood in the shop. Appraisers distinguished between the two groups, suggesting there were noticeable differences in their basic pink hues. The blue cast of the rose was replaced by a yellow or orange cast in the flesh color. In a collection of recipes compiled in 1837, Waldo Tucker described flesh color as a mixture of white and "light ochre burnt," or roasted, to produce a light red color. Other painters chose vermilion as the tinting pigment. The flesh color of Devor's chairs likely was termed salmon color in other documents. As part of a shipment of three hundred fancy chairs received from New York in 1810, Nolen and Gridley of Boston offered "Salmon"-colored double-cross-back fancy chairs with "Grape Leaf" decoration.[101]

Blue Chairs

Among surface colors identified for Windsor and fancy seating in craft records, blue is mentioned least often, although documents provide several noteworthy highlights and general insights. An early reference of 1785 iden-

Figure 19   Tablet-top single-cross-back fancy side chair (one of five), Baltimore, Maryland, 1805–1815. Maple, butternut, and black walnut; cane. H. 32½", W. 19", D. 16". (Courtesy, Winterthur Museum.) Original decoration and surface paint in coquelicot red.

tifies "Windsor chairs painted blue" among auctioned furnishings of Major James Swan, a Boston merchant who had a temporary reversal of fortune. The pattern and origin of Swan's chairs are uncertain, although side chairs seem implied. Philadelphia was the design center for fan-back and bow-back Windsors of the late 1770s and mid-1780s, respectively, and the city was the source of new color options, including blue, to supplement the ubiquitous verdigris green. At the time of Major Swan's auction, Windsor chairmaking was in its infancy at Boston, the first notice dating only to 1786 and the color choice limited to one—green. The supposition is that Swan's Windsors originated at Philadelphia and were carried home in one of his own vessels. Given the auction date, his chairs likely were fan-backs. Seating described in 1802 as "6 Blue Fanback [Chairs]" was in the estate of Captain Hale Hilton at Beverly, Massachusetts. Valuation of the chairs at $1.10 apiece indicates they were in good condition and relatively new. A few records describe requests for dual surface colors, as recorded by Amos D. Allen of Windham, Connecticut, in 1800 when he sold a customer "6 fanback'd [Chairs] painted blue, bot[tom]s Mahog[any]" color.[102]

Ultimately, the newer bow-back Windsor proved to be the popular side chair of the late eighteenth century, principally because its compact rounded back was the perfect design for seating at a dining table. In the typically large eighteenth-century family, dining space was an important consideration. A few individuals with spacious rooms purchased bow-back armchairs for dining, although space remained a concern. Joseph Barrell, a wealthy Bostonian who built a handsome house in the 1790s at neighboring Charlestown, had household decor in mind when placing an order with his agents in New York for chairs: "18 of the handsomest windsor Chairs fit for Dining & my Hall. I would have them with arms, rather less in the Seat . . . , as they will thereby accomodate more at table. I would have them painted of light blue gray Colour, the same as my summer dining Room. . . . Let them be strong and neat." Dining chairs were at times repainted blue, whether that color was new or duplicated the original surface. In 1797 James Chase of Gilmanton, New Hampshire, noted a job of "painting four Dining Chairs Blue," the charge 2s., or 33¢, apiece.[103]

A few Windsor craftsmen, among them Amos D. Allen of Windham, Connecticut, offered Windsors with stuffed seats, an option that more than doubled the cost of a chair. Colonel Z. Swift acquired nine "Cushioned" chairs painted blue and "edged," or pinstriped, in 1798, the charge 16s. ($2.67) per chair. A year later Captain R. Ripley purchased "6 fancy [continuous-bow] Ch[air]s without braces—Cushions, Blue, edged." Having both arms and cushioned seats, these chairs likely were for use in a parlor. Stuffed-seat chairs, like plain chairs, occasionally needed refurbishing. Elizur Barnes of Middletown described a job he completed in 1822 for John Ledge: "Painting 8 Cheirs Blue & Covering Seets." The low charge of 50¢ per chair indicates the original stuffing was retained and only the show cover was changed. Customers with smaller pocketbooks could simulate the appearance of stuffed-seat chairs by directing the seats be painted a contrasting color. In 1803 David Russell of Winchester, Virginia, sold L. Lewis, possi-

Figure 20 Detail, bow-back Windsor side chair (one of six), Connecticut–Rhode Island border region, ca. 1797–1805. White pine (seat) with birch and ash. H. 38", W. 16¾", D. 16³⁄₁₆". (Courtesy, Winterthur Museum.) Original surface paint in Prussian blue on turned work, spindles, bow, and spindle platform; original "grained" paint on seat top in Venetian red and medium-light umber, with glazes of red and brown forming a looping pattern.

bly a retailer, two handsome chair lots with two-color paint described as "One Dozen [chairs] & 2 arms of a mazarine blue with mahogany bottoms" (fig. 20) and "Half a Dozen [Chairs] painted pale blue, yellow bottoms." The lot containing the armchairs perhaps was divided into two sets for retail. The mazarine blue of the chairs was a deep, rich color, probably compounded using the pigment Prussian blue.[104]

Several groups of blue Windsors sold by craftsmen date to the turn of the nineteenth century, making it difficult to determine the pattern. Bow-back chairs, new in the mid-1780s, continued to be made for a few years after 1800, particularly in New England. Square-back Windsors were introduced about 1800, the early patterns made with single or double cross rods forming the crest. Amasa Holden's six blue Windsors purchased from David Stowell at Worcester, Massachusetts, in 1801 for $1.33 the chair could have had either round or square backs. A purchase in 1804 of similarly priced Windsors by Josiah Walker from the shop of Oliver Wight at Sturbridge was described as "Dining Chares." Whereas the compact bow-back design initially elevated the Windsor to prominence for dining, the square-back styles of the early nineteenth century continued the momentum. When Silas E. Cheney of Litchfield, Connecticut, supplied a customer with Windsor side chairs in 1809 at $1.38 apiece, they were described as "6 sq[uare] Chairs Blue."[105]

Prussian blue was the pigment in blue paint used for vernacular seating in the period under study. Most other pigments were unsatisfactory for this purpose, except ultramarine, which was made from lapis lazuli and expensive for general use. Prussian blue was transparent and required mixing with white lead "where a body [was] wanted." Alternatively, the painter could brush Prussian blue "2 [twice] over the wood on A priming of lampblack and white lead." To obtain David Russell's "mazarine" and "pale" blues, Prussian blue and white lead were mixed in varying proportions. If not compounded properly, Prussian blue could "turn greenish or olive" over time.[106]

Information on fancy chairs painted blue is limited, although it is possible to describe the surface range and richness found in this construction form. Robert R. Livingston, chancellor of New York State, engaged Willam Challen of New York in 1798 to supply his household with "6 Blue Japan'd Chairs" at cost of $3.42 apiece. By the late eighteenth century, the practice of japanning using ground coats of size and whiting, as performed in the late seventeenth and early eighteenth centuries, had given way to a simpler, more stable ground consisting of several coats of chairmakers' varnish. Over this was applied japan made from shellac varnish and a paint pigment, in this case Prussian blue with white lead to make it opaque. Several japan coats, the last one polished, provided a lustrous surface.[107]

References to fancy chairs painted blue can describe basic to ornamental schemes. Fancy chairs in the Chester County, Pennsylvania, estate of Daniel Eachus in 1823 are described as "Pale blue" without further comment. Gilding was an expensive choice. James J. Skerrett's "8 Chairs Blue and Gilt" purchased in 1817 from James Mitchell at Philadelphia cost $5.00 apiece. The rich decoration suggests these were parlor chairs. William Cunningham of Wheeling, (West) Virginia, described another option in March 1839, when billing a Mr. A. Broadwell of Cynthiana, Kentucky, $40.00 for "1 Dozen of scroll post, cane seat chairs blue, black ornamented" ($3.33 each). Black may have identified an entire decorative scheme or striping only. The chairs were shipped boxed. The trip from Wheeling to Cynthiana, while long, was direct: down the Ohio River by steamboat for 350 miles to Licking River on the Kentucky shore opposite Cincinnati; up the Licking by steamer about 45 miles, and overland the short distance to Cynthiana, likely utilizing Kentucky's "splendid system of macadamized roads," as local rail transport was little developed. Mr. Broadwell's purchase raises a question, however. Why buy fancy chairs at Wheeling, when similar furniture was available at Cincinnati, a flourishing chairmaking center 66 miles north of Cynthiana opposite Licking River? Without further data, there is no satisfactory answer.[108]

Grained Chairs

Grain painting can be defined as "a process of painting furniture and woodwork by which the colour and figure of a more costly wood [or other material is] counterfeited in one of a cheaper kind." The practice of graining woodwork was established in England by the seventeenth century, whereas the first grain-painted interiors in America date from the early eighteenth century. Ornamented surfaces in early American furniture are found principally on joined rather than turned forms, with figures, foliage, and borders on plain-painted grounds more popular than grained surfaces. Grain painting became common for turned seating furniture only in the early nineteenth century, although the practice was well established by 1821, when David Bates, a chairmaker at the nation's capital, noted that "his imitations of the different woods in the European style are equalled by none in this District." By midcentury Rufus Porter reported substantial interest in "Imitation Painting": "Imitations or pretended imitations of oak, maple, mahogany, or marble, may be seen on three-fourths of the doors of houses in the cities, besides wainscoting, chimney pieces, and furniture."[109]

Beginning in the early 1810s, maple and rosewood were the usual grained surfaces on turned seating furniture. Simulated maple Windsors were known as "imitation maple chairs" (fig. 21) or simply "imitation chairs." Fancy seating painted in this manner probably led in the market. Focusing on the Windsor, David Alling recorded a shipment to Nathan Bolles at New Orleans in 1820 of "2 doz Imitation Curled maple square seat" chairs priced at $2.50 apiece. The price suggests the Windsors were richly ornamented, although that figure represented only 54 to 63 percent of the retail cost of Alling's maple-grained fancy chairs shipped to Bolles.[110]

By the mid-1830s, chair prices were significantly lower, patterns simpler, and turned work less detailed. Decoration still played a large role in pricing, from modest striping to detailed painted, stenciled (bronzed), and gilded ornament. The 83¢ Jason Williams paid Stephen Taylor at Providence, Rhode Island, for each of "12 square seat chairs Im[itation] maple" probably was in the shop's top pricing range for Windsor seating. Sullivan Hill of Spencer, Massachusetts, supplied "imitation Chairs" to Philemon Robbins

Figure 21   Shaped-slat-back Windsor side chair with flat sticks, northern Worcester County, Massachusetts, 1820–1830. White pine (seat). H. 34⅛", W. 17⅜", D. 15¼". (Present location unknown; formerly in an institutional collection; photo, Winterthur Museum.) Original decoration and surface paint in grained maple exhibiting a bird's-eye figure on the crest and a striped figure on the turnings and spindles.

at Hartford, Connecticut, for 50¢ apiece wholesale. Robbins's markup would have reflected his profit and the cost of ornamental work done in the shop. Hill was one of several suppliers patronized by Robbins, although his location required an overland trip of more than fifty miles with a team and wagon, whereas other Massachusetts suppliers were able to ship their chairs down the Connecticut River to Hartford. Hill probably made some, or all, of the trips himself, as suggested in an entry in Robbins's accounts for 1835 crediting the supplier with 217 chairs of several patterns. Hill's return trip to Spencer was made profitable by supplying Robbins with teamster services in "Carting wash stands & dress[ing] tables to Worcester."[III]

Luke Houghton of rural Barre, Massachusetts, a contemporary of Philemon Robbins, also acquired chair stock from suppliers, including David

West and Daniel Witt of Phillipston, a sister community of northern Worcester County. By the mid-1820s, this region had developed a thriving wholesale chair industry involving many local towns (see fig. 21). The optimal regional conditions that made this possible are described in a contemporary gazetteer: "Its surface is rather undulating than hilly. The soil is generally strong. . . . Its water power is abundant in almost every town, and perhaps in no section of New England are the interests of agriculture, commerce, and manufactures more completely blended." Of further significance to the flourishing state of the chair trade was the presence of raw materials close at hand. Among Houghton's customers was Joseph Osgood Jr., who in 1838 purchased "6 imitation chairs" of Windsor construction for 83¢ apiece, one of many sets of this description and price retailed by Houghton.[112]

When Charles Riley of Philadelphia died in 1842, appraisers faced a substantial task, since Riley had operated a large chairmaking facility. The inventory and the auctioneer's account of sales list Windsor chairs of several surface colors, including "Imitation Maple." Two construction patterns appear to be noted. The term "Baltimore" identifies ninety grained Windsors that likely had tablet-style crests mounted on the back posts. A single "Set Imitation Maple" chairs could well have been framed in a slat-back pattern. The chairs were valued low, a typical appraisal practice, although some may have lacked decoration on the grained ground. Standing in Riley's manufactory with the grained Windsors were "12 Imitation Rush Seat Maple" fancy chairs each valued at $1.25, about twice that of the Windsors.[113]

Prices obtained about 1810 at the introduction of maple-grained fancy seating were much higher than those realized at midcentury. Levi Hollingsworth, a leading Philadelphia merchant with interests in the Chesapeake Bay region, made two large purchases of "chairs with rush bottoms in imitation of maple" in 1812 from the firm of Haydon and Stewart. All told, there were forty side chairs and four armchairs priced at $4.25 and $6.50, respectively. Seven years later, David Alling's chair shipments from Newark, New Jersey, to New Orleans included three dozen "Curl'd Maple & Gilt" fancy chairs, some priced at $4.00 apiece. Chairs with a "pannel" in "back" cost $4.67.[114]

Craftsmen's estate records of the 1830s provide further insight on the currency of maple-grained fancy seating. Peter Peirce, a chairmaker of Templeton, Massachusetts, owned a homestead farm containing an extensive chair shop and mill at his death in 1836 at age forty-six. The "18 Fancy Imitation [Maple] Chairs" of low valuation in the estate inventory likely were part of his household and of some age. Business assets of the insolvent partnership of Parrott and Hubbel at Bridgeport, Connecticut, included framed and painted "imitation Curled Maple" seating. A dozen chairs had cane seats. Another dozen, identified as "Grecian," probably had ogee-profile sawed posts scrolling backward at the top, with front legs sawed to an ogee profile or fancy turned.[115]

Several records of the 1830s indicate that repainting fancy seating in imitation of maple was relatively common, whether to reflect an original surface or to introduce a new scheme. At Newark, New Jersey, David Alling recorded two jobs charged at 62½¢ per chair. The large number of chairs he repainted for Anthony Dye, Esq., twenty-eight in all, suggests the seating could have furnished Dye's home and place of business. At Providence, Rhode Island, Henry Barnard charged Albert C. Greene, Esq., slightly more at 75¢ per chair for "painting 12 chairs curl'd maple."[116]

The ground for maple graining was straw color, composed of white lead and a yellow pigment ground in linseed oil. Rufus Porter recommended a combination of chrome yellow and yellow ochre. When the ground was dry, the graining coat was brushed on and, while wet, manipulated to form the desired imitative figure. Some graining was executed in distemper, that is, a water-based medium, although painters usually employed an oil medium on seating furniture for greater durability. The coloring pigment for the graining coat was either terra di sienna or umber. A coat of varnish secured the finish. Craftsmen used various implements to execute the grained figure—graining combs, special brushes, cloth, feathers, and corks or stiff leather cut to special patterns. Both Rufus Porter and Nathaniel Whittock advised the novice painter to obtain a piece of wood or veneer "to guide him in forming the grains and shades." Maple graining in cheaper seating could be produced by applying striping over the ground, using a brush and darker paint.[117]

Craftsmen executed rosewood graining in two ways: with a red ground and graining coat of black or a black ground grained in red. Esther Stevens Brazer, who made an extensive study of painted surfaces and ornament on preindustrial American furniture, stated that a red ground with black graining was the more common of the two, noting, however, that Lambert Hitchcock's earliest chair work in Connecticut displays a black ground with red graining. This probably is the painted combination "black rose wood" that Sheraton made passing reference to in his *Cabinet Dictionary* (1803), when noting that a chair illustrated in one of the plates would "look well in painted black rose wood and gold." The popularity of black rosewood color in London probably stemmed from a familiarity with black rosewood timber first imported from India in the 1750s. Painters made the black coat from lampblack, and the brownish red coat, whether ground or graining, from red lead or Venetian red. Grained rosewood patterns were achieved using various implements at the pleasure of the grainer. Some graining was daubed, reminiscent of early-eighteenth-century japanned grounds. William G. Beesley of Salem, New Jersey, recorded a common pattern in the 1830s described as "streaking and ornamenting" or "streaking & shading," when working for craftsman Elijah Ware (fig. 22). In the finest rosewood graining, painters finished their work with a coat of plain or tinted varnish polished to a lustrous surface.[118]

In 1819, when Bates and Johnson advertised their chair facility at Albany, New York, where they finished Windsor and fancy chairs with rosewood grounds, David Alling, a chair manufacturer of Newark, New Jersey, shipped "Rose wood Winsor bent back" chairs to retailer Nathan Bolles at New Orleans, the price set at $2.25 the chair. In 1820 Bolles received rosewood Windsors with organ spindles or flat spindles, some with "Square

Figure 22 Detail, shaped-tablet-top Windsor side chair with stenciled identification of George Washington Bentley (b. ca. 1814; chair one of four), West Edmeston, New York, 1850–1860. Basswood (seat). H. 34⅝", W. 15", D. 15". (Courtesy, Fenimore Art Museum, Cooperstown, New York; photo, Winterthur Museum.) Original pinstriping and surface paint in grained rosewood exhibiting a "streaked" figure on the seat, crest, and mid-back slat and a daubed figure on the turnings.

seats," priced at $2.00 or $2.50 the chair. Two decades later, appraisers of Charles Riley's Philadelphia estate valued rosewood Windsors with "bent" backs and "Strait Backs" at low figures, an indication that the surfaces lacked decoration.[119]

Simulated rosewood fancy chairs were marketed successfully from the early nineteenth century. Notices by chairmakers and retailers covered the commercial community from Providence, Rhode Island, to Cleveland, Ohio, and from New York City to Charleston, South Carolina. The Providence firm of Sackett and Branch described its stock of fancy seating, which included rosewood-finish chairs with "flag seats," as "made by the best of workmen and choice stuff, and painted in Providence with the best of paints and finished by workmen that are second to none." Too often imported chairs arrived with surfaces bruised and scraped.[120]

Two prosperous entrepreneurs who successfully merchandised rosewood-painted fancy chairs in the 1810s were Stephen Girard, a Philadelphia merchant, and David Alling, a chairmaker of Newark, New Jersey, a location close to the style center at New York. When Girard's ship *North America* sailed from the Delaware River for Port Louis on the Isle of France (Mauritius), the vessel carried eighty-eight rosewood-grained chairs priced individually from $4.00 to $8.00. That price range indicates substantial differences in ornament and structural pattern, of which only a "Scrowl back" profile is identified. Decoration focused on gilded and bronzed ornament. More descriptive is Alling's record of nine dozen grained chairs, priced mostly between $4.00 and $5.00, shipped to Nathan Bolles at New Orleans. One dozen chairs had "bent front feet" (flaring outward). Other chairs had back features described as slats and oval or diamond frets (see fig. 13). Three dozen chairs were gilded; four dozen more were gilded and bronzed. A dozen chairs had a "pine apple in back," although the medium is unidentified. One group of gilded rush-seated chairs that differed from the others in its ground is described as "rose wood near a black walnut Couler," possibly Sheraton's black rosewood.[121]

Grain-painted chairs continued in fashion in the 1830s, when an Alling patron deposited seven fancy chairs at the shop to be refurbished by "pting m[at]ts yellow, wood rosewood." Painting rush seats probably was more common than records indicate. Sheraton encouraged the practice because it hardened and preserved the rushes, making the seats less vulnerable to wear and tear. Cane, the alternative material for fancy-chair seats, was identified in chairs of imitation rosewood appraised at Abraham McDonough's shop at Philadelphia.[122]

On occasion householders requested grain-painted chairs in surfaces other than curled maple or rosewood, the principal choices being imitation mahogany, satinwood, and marble, although examples are rare today. In 1845 Frederick Fox advertised "imitation . . . Mahogony Chairs" from his Reading, Pennsylvania, shop, and Abraham McDonough's Philadelphia estate of 1852 contained forty-eight "im[itation] mahog[any] Cain seat chairs." Though contemporary recipes for preparing grained mahogany grounds focus on finishes for woodwork, they were easily adapted for finishing fur-

Figure 23 Shaped-tablet-top Windsor side chair with splat and scroll seat, Baltimore, Maryland, or adjacent southern Pennsylvania, 1840–1850. Woods unknown. H. 33¼". (Courtesy, Abby Aldrich Rockefeller Folk Art Museum, The Colonial Williamsburg Foundation, Williamsburg, Virginia.) Original decoration and surface paint in mahogany graining.

Figure 24 Detail, shaped-tablet-top Windsor side chair with splat (one of six), Pennsylvania, 1850–1870. Yellow poplar (seat). H. 32¼", W. 18¼", D. 14½". (Present location unknown; formerly in a private collection; photo, Winterthur Museum.) Original decoration and surface paint, probably in satinwood graining.

niture. Painters began with a ground coat of either flesh color (white lead with red lead or Venetian red) or straw color (white lead with yellow ochre). The graining was one of several pigments, including Vandyke brown, burnt terra di sienna, and umber, sometimes applied in several coats varying in depth of color. A finish coat of copal varnish protected the surface. Graining tools included linen or cotton cloth, sponges, textured brushes, grainers, blenders, and "wash leather" (chamois?). A painter could supply himself with actual samples of mahogany to imitate (fig. 23).[123]

Sheraton noted in his *Cabinet Dictionary* the popularity of satinwood among English cabinetmakers and their clients. The straw-colored wood has an appealing satinlike quality that also was recognized among American consumers. Although grained imitations of satinwood seating (fig. 24) never achieved special interest among American families, a few records note its availability. William Haydon of Philadelphia advertised fancy japanned chairs in 1815 in imitations of rosewood, maple, and satinwood. When Haydon partnered with William H. Stewart in 1812, the prominent Quaker Reuben Haines visited their Walnut Street shop to order twenty-two side chairs and two armchairs identified as "Fancy rush bottomed chairs satinwood imitation plain" at $3.75 and $5.62½ the chair, respectively. In time, the chairs were transferred to Wyck, the Haines family ancestral home in Germantown. Several years after Haines purchased his chairs, David Alling of Newark, New Jersey, directed his painter, Moses Lyon, to grain a few dozen chairs in the same manner. Some, or all, of the chairs had slat backs. Decoration consisted of bronzework or striping, although one group received both types of ornament.[124]

To paint an imitation satinwood surface, Nathaniel Whittock recommended beginning with a buff ground, probably compounded from white lead and yellow ochre. Yellow ochre alone in a suitable medium was the graining coat. Further color and texture were achieved with a thin glaze of umber and raw sienna. Sheraton's recipe for this grained finish used a different selection of materials: "A fine tint of sattinwood may be imitated by gambouge, bister, and a little lake; and for shading furniture on the dark side, add more of the bister and lake." Gamboge is a bright yellow pigment made from tree resins; bister, a dark brown, is derived from soot. Lake is crimson red.[125]

Marbling was uncommon in vernacular seating furniture. This form of graining usually was reserved for tabletops, as advertised in 1815 by William Haydon at Philadelphia. An inventory of 1806 identifies "8 wooden Chairs painted like grey marble" in the Whitemarsh, Pennsylvania, home of Samuel P. Broome. The chairs stood in his "Yellow Hall or Eating room," the colors making a striking contrast. Furnishing his house with simulated marble chairs probably was a conceit on Broome's part, inasmuch as he was the proprietor of a marble quarry. Within two years, appraisers on Nantucket Island identified "½ dozen marblebottom Chairs" in the home of Jacob Chandler, a ship's carpenter. Chandler's chairs appear to have had a two-color surface scheme, the seats alone simulating marble. Rufus Porter, in discussing "Imitation Painting" in *Scientific American*, stated that "Imitations of marble are produced on white or light slate-colored grounds." Before the ground was dry, the painter applied the "shading colors," or graining, and immediately blended them into the ground with an appropriate tool. The common shading was a mixture of blue, black, and white, although green, yellow, and red also were in use. Like other grained surfaces, a varnish coat secured the work. On the subject of marbled seating furniture, Nathaniel Whittock had firm ideas, as expressed in his *Guide*: "In painting chairs it is sometimes the practice to marble them; nothing can be in worst taste, as no imitation should ever be introduced where the reality could not be applied if persons chose to go to the expense—and who would choose a marble chair?"[126]

ORNAMENTATION

The application of painted ornament to enhance the painted or japanned surfaces of vernacular seating gained a foothold in America in the early 1790s. Whereas Samuel Claphamson, a London immigrant, advertised "fancy" and "bamboo" chairs at Philadelphia by 1785, evidence supporting public interest in ornamented seating is thin before 1793, when Daniel Rea Jr., an ornamental painter of Boston, charged a client 18s. ($3.00) for "Painting, Varnishing, and Ornament'g Six Chamber Chairs" (fancy chairs). Two years later Rea recorded "painting seven winsor Chairs mehogony Colour, Varn[ishin]g &c, ornamented" at 18s. 8d. The mahogany color here was not a grained surface. By 1812 the craft of ornamental chair painting was well established, as indicated in a *Columbian Centinel* notice at Boston: "WANTED—a Journeyman PAINTER, one who understands ornamental Chair Painting, &c, will find constant employment and prompt pay."[127]

Several decorative forms made up the body of ornament. Lines and bands were basic. The next level introduced to the crest a prominent figure or composition. By 1810 bronzework executed with metallic powders in varnish was an alternative or enhancement to hand-painted decoration, and gilding was becoming fashionable as a rich embellishment in the best decorative work. Briefly, at the start of the nineteenth century, a visual option in Windsor seating was the use of dual-color surface paint, the general structure painted one color and the seat a second color.

In 1838 James C. Helme, a woodworker of Plymouth, Luzerne County, Pennsylvania, prepared a handwritten "Book of Prices for making Cabinet and Chair furnature," listing payments to journeymen for various tasks. Prices paid for "painting chairs fit for ornementing" were the same for Windsor and fancy chairs at 50¢ per half dozen. Pay by the half dozen for basic ornamental work and a finish coat of varnish depended on chair type and structure: straight-back chairs were 50¢ the half dozen, and bent-back chairs, 62¢ per half dozen, the shaved faces of the back posts creating additional flat surfaces for decoration. Pay for ornamenting ball-back chairs, with back slats and short ball-centered spindles, was the same as for bent-back chairs. Higher at 65¢ the half dozen were payments for ornamenting roll-top chairs, the crest a turned roll above two slats at mid-back. Highest priced at 81¢ the half dozen was elaborate ornament for "Stump Back" (fancy) chairs, framed with a tablet-type crest rabbeted to the upper faces of the back posts.[128]

As suggested by the interior view in figure 25, large shops were set up to handle all phases of chair manufacture, including ornamenting. At the back of the painting room in William Buttre's New York chair manufactory, a workman grinds pigment for paint using a large flat stone and a stone muller. A jug for oil used in grinding stands on the bench behind him; at the right is a spatula to gather the powdered material as it scatters on the

Figure 25 Detail, trade card of William Buttre (1782–1864), New York City, ca. 1813. Engraving. 5⅞" x 4¼". (Courtesy, Winterthur Museum Library, Joseph Downs Collection of Manuscripts and Printed Ephemera.) The scene is a painting room such as that found in a large manufactory producing painted vernacular seating furniture. Note the abundance of windows to admit natural light to the workplace.

stone. The specialist at the left ornaments a painted double-cross-back fancy chair using a fine brush. A third workman at the right front applies a finish, or varnish, coat to a similar chair. He uses a large round-headed brush as he balances one front chair leg on a block of wood, enabling him to turn the chair in any direction to coat all surfaces. The single-cross-back fancy chair at the center will doubtless receive a similar coating.

Once chairs were ornamented and varnished, it was critical to safeguard the surfaces from bruises, scratches, and abrasions. Craftsmen took various steps to protect their work. After "painting & ornamenting Six windsor Chairs" in 1831 for George Harvey, James Gere of Groton, Connecticut, undertook "Carting home" the chairs at a small charge to Harvey's residence at Preston, a town eighteen miles distant, thus ensuring the furniture was properly packed. Joel Brown of Raleigh, North Carolina, went a step further, offering to deliver chairs to a "distance of 30 or 40 miles either from Raleigh or Fayetteville [to] paint and ornament them at the house of the person ordering them, so as to suit the rooms and prevent their being injured by carriage over rough roads." Dockum and Brown of Portsmouth, New Hampshire, pursued another plan to avoid injury to finished surfaces during water travel: "just received ONE THOUSAND CHAIRS, of various kinds and colors, painted and gilded in this town by the first rate workmen from Boston" (see fig. 1).[129]

Striping

The simplest form of chair ornament was lines drawn on painted surfaces—from narrow pinstripes to broad bands. Craftsmen's records identify six terms relating to this type of decoration: creasing, penciling, stringing, edging, tipping, and striping. "Creasing" accented the grooves, or "creases," in bamboowork (see fig. 10). In 1797 Daniel Rea Jr., an ornamenter of Boston, painted "two Windsor Chairs Patent yellow & Creas'd in Green." "Penciling" probably identified the same process, the term having broader use to describe pinstriping as well. Amos Bradley of East Haven, Connecticut, recorded at least 140 chairs penciled in his shop in 1806 and 1807, including six painted white. A credit for Charles Stow, a shop workman, indicates he framed "54 Wooden Bottom Chairs" in 1807 over a period of 13½ days, spent another 6 days painting them, and 4½ days "penciling them." The penciling "tool" was a slim, long-tipped camel's-hair brush called a "pencil."[130]

"Stringing," "edging," and "tipping," terms current in the early 1800s, describe the process of applying fine lines, or pinstripes, to a surface (see fig. 33). The genesis of "stringing" as a painting technique was in the practice of inlaying cabinet work with fine lines. In 1804 Solomon Cole of Glastonbury, Connecticut, noted the sale of "6 fanback Chairs strung," the charge $1.50 per chair. Amos D. Allen of Windham preferred to describe the process as "edging," and, judging from his sales for 1798 through 1802, the decoration was popular with his clients. The introduction of fine painted lines was not confined to new chairs. Shubael Abbe paid Allen for "Edgeing Dineing Chairs" in his household. James Chase of New Hampshire and Ephraim Evans of Virginia used the term "tipping" to describe painting fine lines. Chase sold "6 fanback Chars tipt" in 1801 and later tipped half a dozen "Bambo Chars." Tipping bamboo chairs probably described creasing. In 1802 Evans advertised a reward for the return of a set of yellow round-back chairs purloined from his shop, described as "tip'd with black."[131]

In 1801, when using the term "striping" to identify detailing on Windsor furniture, Daniel Rea Jr. of Boston and Titus Preston of Wallingford, Connecticut, probably described pinstriping. Only when broad surfaces and thick elements, such as slats, tablets, shaved posts, fancy legs, and heavy rings, became part of vernacular chair design could craftsmen introduce a decorative stripe, or band, to form a line wider than a string or a crease. A requisite structure to accommodate striping appeared earlier in the fancy chair than in the Windsor by perhaps a decade. The first fancy chairs with stripes, or bands, probably were marketed shortly after 1800 (see fig. 19). Preston's bill of 1820 to George Wilnut for "6 green dining [Windsor] chairs striped" probably used the decorative term in its proper sense because by that date slat-type crests were common in Windsor seating. Concurrent evidence describes diffusion of the ornament. Tapping Reeve, founder of the Litchfield Law School, purchased "6 fancy [white] Doining striped Chairs" locally from Silas E. Cheney. Allen Holcomb, who worked briefly in Troy, New York, was paid for "painting the Seats & striping five fancy Chairs." When working in the shop of Thomas Boynton, at Windsor, Vermont, John Patterson striped chairs described as "B[road] top" and "narrow top," terms that identified either slat depth or tablet width. At Newark, New Jersey, David Alling embraced urban New York styles, represented by the "Single Cross [Back] Chair" striped by his workman Moses Lyon (see fig. 25).[132]

Striping was a decorative accent for vernacular seating through 1850, and activity by the 1830s was brisk (see figs. 11, 23). Imitation surfaces were still popular, as confirmed by Daniel Dewey of Hartford, Connecticut, who painted and striped eight "imitation Curl maple" chairs for Daniel Wadsworth. Striped Windsors of plain green ground were part of Thomas Devor's stock in Pennsylvania, whereas David Alling of New Jersey described fancy rush-bottom seating when "matting, moulding, pting, & striping 8 bell seat Ch[ai]rs." "Bell" seats were rounded in profile and broader at the front than back (see fig. 13). "Moulding," as identified by Alling, was a flexible strip of wood for casing the seat edges, held fast with small nails and often striped with a broad band. When records identify the color of banding or pinstriping, yellow and green are named. White is mentioned on occasion, and black less frequently. Other colors were selected from time to time.[133]

Several special decorative effects relate closely to the practices of striping and pinstriping vernacular seating. Titus Preston of Wallingford, Connecticut, identified one in 1804, when recording an order for Cornelius Cook: "6 green dining chairs striped, 8d. each for striping . . . the striping . . . to be a vine on the front of the bow & legs." The price per chair for this set of

Figure 26   Slat-back (or ball-back) Windsor side chair with "organ spindles," New York City, 1810–1815. Yellow poplar (seat) with maple. H. 32⅝", W. 17⅞", D. 15". (Courtesy, Winterthur Museum.) Original decoration and surface paint in pale blue.

bow-back Windsors with bamboo-style turnings was $1.28. Other references describe "sprigging," a contemporary technique. Written evidence here focuses on Connecticut, although the practice was more widespread (fig. 26). The device can consist of a triangular cluster of short, grasslike blades adjoining the creases in bamboo-style legs and back posts. Stephen Tracy and Nathaniel F. Martin, chairmaking neighbors at Lisbon and Windsor in eastern Connecticut, sold sprigged "Dining Chairs" in 1806 and 1809 for $1.33 the chair. The cost of painting sprigged decoration augmented by creasing was recorded as 14¢ the chair in 1811 by Oliver Avery of North Stonington. In western Connecticut, Silas E. Cheney of Litchfield made a charge of £2.11 in 1806 for "6 Doining Chars sprig," the price at $1.42 the chair comparable to that of his eastern colleagues.[134]

Ornamental Figures

The practice of applying ornamental figures to painted or japanned surfaces of vernacular chairs probably gained initial interest among American consumers in the 1790s as a market developed for fancy seating following its introduction from England about the mid-1780s. Before the 1790s, painted figures appeared occasionally on seating furniture associated with the ritual of fraternal organizations. On August 23, 1786, Daniel Rea Jr., an ornamental painter of Boston, entered in his accounts under the heading "Paul Revere Silversmith" a charge of 6s. ($1.00) for "painting the backs of Masonick chairs." Revere was a member of the Lodge of Saint Andrew and may already have become Master. The low charge for painting suggests the chairs were already part of the lodge furniture and were being newly ornamented or merely retouched.[135]

Evidence of a growing interest in ornamental figures on vernacular seating is indicated in notices dating from the mid-to-late 1790s. In 1795 both John Dewitt and Walter MacBride of New York advertised Windsor chairs "japann'd and neatly flowered," although the nature of their work is uncertain. William Haydon of Philadelphia, described in 1797 as a "Drawing Master from London," offered "all kinds of ornamental Painting, Flowers, Fruits, &c.," and soon expanded his services to include chairmaking. From their stand at Wilmington, North Carolina, Vosburgh and Childs advertised "Chairs . . . highly varnished any colour, and ornamented to any pattern." A New Yorker, Vosburgh probably was only a part-time resident of North Carolina. By 1803 the Baltimore firm of John and Hugh Finlay painted local views on furniture. An expanded selection of ornament two years later included "real Views, Fancy Landscapes, Flowers, Trophies of Music, War, Husbandry, Love, &c." (see fig. 19). Thomas S. Renshaw carried elements of the Baltimore style with him when he migrated to Chillicothe, Ohio, joined forces with Henry May, and advertised "gilt and plain chairs . . . Bent Backs, Broad Tops with landscapes" (see figs. 12, 33).[136]

Floral ornament is the most common figure on vernacular seating, and craft notices often mention "flowers," yet there is little record of specific plants (fig. 27; see also figs. 10, 24). More commonly identified are "fruits,"

Figure 27 Detail, roll-top Windsor side chair, Philadelphia or eastern Pennsylvania, 1830–1840. Yellow poplar (seat). H. 34⅞", W. 17⅜", D. 15⁵⁄₁₆". (Present location unknown; formerly in a private collection; photo, Winterthur Museum.) Original decoration and surface paint in creamy white.

Figure 28 Shaped-tablet-top Windsor side chair with pierced splat and stenciled identification of George Nees (act. 1850 and later), Manheim, Pennsylvania, 1850–1860. Yellow poplar (seat). H. 32¼", W. 19½", D. 14¼". (Collection of Dr. and Mrs. Donald M. Herr; photo, Winterthur Museum.) Original decoration and surface paint in bright green.

a term used at Newark, New Jersey, by David Alling, who at times was more specific (see fig. 35). In the mid-1810s his workman, Moses Lyon, stenciled "Peaches" on twelve scroll-back chairs, a "pine apple" on a dozen rosewood-grained chairs, and "Grapes," some in "Nat[ural] Coll[or]," on the crests of slat-back chairs (see fig. 9). Grapes proved popular. In 1810 the Boston firm of Nolen and Gridley imported assorted fancy chairs from New York, including salmon-colored double-cross-back chairs (see fig. 25) of "Grape Leaf" pattern. During the 1830s, Philemon Robbins of Hartford, Connecticut, sold "grape bush chairs." In Pennsylvania, an 1833 appraisal identified half a dozen new "Dining Chairs" ornamented with a "pair [pear] & peach" in Thomas Devor's shop at Shippensburg. Another shop design, described as a "Bowl patt'n," likely depicted a container filled with flowers or fruit (fig. 28; see also fig. 14).[137]

Figure 29 Tablet-top fancy side chair, Baltimore, Maryland, 1820–1830. Woods unknown; rush. H. 33½", W. 18½", D. 15⅞". (Courtesy, Fenimore Art Museum, gift of Stephen C. Clark, Sr.; photo, Winterthur Museum.) Original decoration and surface paint in dark rosewood graining. The paired-swan motif of the chair back was copied from an ornament in plate 21 of Thomas Hope's *Household Furniture and Interior Decoration* (London, 1807).

Figure 30 Ornamental design with squirrels from page 12 of a drawing or copy book kept by Christian M. Nestell (1793–1880), when a student at an unknown school in New York City, 1811–1812. Pencil and watercolor on laid paper. (Courtesy, Winterthur Library, Joseph Downs Collection of Manuscripts and Printed Ephemera.)

Images of birds and animals captured the attention of several shops. Fancy chairs shipped in 1810 from New York to Nolen and Gridley at Boston contained coquelicot-colored (orange-red) seating with double-cross backs and "Eagle Tops." Two decades later, half a dozen "Swan Back" chairs (fig. 29) stood in the Pennsylvania shop of Thomas Devor. The same year David Alling of New Jersey delivered "1 doz crown top, ball fret, scroll front" chairs with ornament described as "bird on fret" to the New York firm of Joseph W. Meeks and Company. The single mention of animal decoration in this study identifies a "Squirrell" on three chairs in Thomas Devor's estate. By coincidence, a design with two squirrels is among those in a copybook executed by Christian M. Nestell in 1811 and 1812, when he was a student at a drawing school in New York (fig. 30).[138]

Figure 31 Detail, slat-back (or ball-back) Windsor armchair (one of two), New York City, 1814–1820. Yellow poplar (seat) with maple. H. 34½", W. 19¼", D. 16⅞". (Courtesy, Winterthur Museum.) Original decoration and surface paint in yellow.

The vocabulary of ornament grew as craftsmen introduced new subjects for interpretation. The 1810s were particularly productive. The cornucopia, as a single or double motif, usually was accompanied by fruit or floral forms or a combination of the two, as shown in a painted example of New York origin (fig. 31). David Alling of neighboring New Jersey identified this motif in another medium, when describing fancy chairs: "[Bronzing] 12 Wide Tops & Scroll Backs (Cornucopia)." In Vermont Thomas Boynton named two other patterns, when crediting John Patterson with "Ornamenting feathers" (fig. 32) and "shells" (see figs. 15, 18). A shipment of fancy chairs

Figure 32 Ornamental design with feathers from page 79 of the Nestell drawing or copy book. (Courtesy, Winterthur Library, Joseph Downs Collection of Manuscripts and Printed Ephemera.)

from New York provided Nolen and Gridley of Boston with an opportunity to comment on the degree of elegance possible using simple patterns: one group of chairs was "White and gold [with] double shells and green Tops"; chairs painted coquelicot red had a "gold Grecian Border" in the crest.[139]

Busts of national figures were depicted at times in small medallions incorporated into other ornament on chair backs. The transfer-printed profile of Benjamin Franklin (1706–1790) in figure 33 is unusual for its medium. The

Figure 33   Detail, slat-back (or fret-back) fancy side chair, New York City, 1815–1825. Woods unknown; cane. Dimensions unknown. (Present location unknown; formerly in an institutional collection; photo, Winterthur Museum.) Original decoration and surface paint in light stone color (drab). The transfer-printed profile of Benjamin Franklin is based on a terracotta medallion cast in France in 1777 by Giovanni Battista Nini.

model for the bust was a terra-cotta bas-relief medallion cast in France in 1777 by Giovanni Battista Nini (1717–1786). Naval figures also caught the interest of the American public, particularly during the War of 1812 and immediately thereafter. Stephen Decatur (1779–1820) distinguished himself by capturing the British vessel *Macedonian* in October 1812, and patriotic fervor was still at a high pitch in 1815, when David Alling of Newark, New Jersey, credited Moses Lyon with decorating "12 Bronzed Double Cross (Decaturs)."[140]

Andrew Jackson (1767–1845), another hero of the War of 1812, achieved acclaim by routing the British on land at the battle of New Orleans. Prints of Jackson on horseback celebrated the event; however, the general's portrait bust on seating furniture dates after he left the office of president of the United States. In 1843 Nelson Talcott of Portage County, Ohio, noted the sale of "1 Set Jackson chairs." Two decades earlier, when the young nation began preparations to celebrate fifty years of independence, the U.S. Congress invited the marquis de Lafayette to be the nation's guest in a grand tour of the country for whose freedom he had fought. Lafayette was wined, dined, and feted in all twenty-four states. Souvenirs abounded—gloves, hats, ribbons, and more. Chairs were specially ordered to celebrate the great man's visit. Still in existence are several cane-seat fancy chairs of Baltimore origin, presumably used there in 1824 at a banquet in Lafayette's honor. The general's bust centered in the crest is surrounded by lavish gilding of neoclassical design.[141]

Bronzing

Evidence of bronze decoration on vernacular seating furniture before 1810 is rare. Nolen and Gridley's Boston advertisement of December 1810 for three hundred fancy chairs imported from New York is the earliest record noted for bronzework in American chairmaking. Many chairs offered by the firm were gilded; however, one group in the double-cross-back pattern had "Bronzed Tops." The term "bronzed" without explanation denotes general understanding of its meaning, although the medium was perhaps better known to the public at this date through imported fancy seating from England. Sheraton described the material in painted bronzework without providing a direct sense of its use on furniture: "BRONZE . . . denotes a prepared colour, wherewith to imitate bronze. There are two sorts, the red bronze, and the yellow or golden. The latter is made solely of copper dust, which must be the finest and brightest that can be got; the former is made of the same, with the addition of a little . . . red ochre well pulverized. Both these bronzes are laid on with varnish."[142]

Reinforcing the hypothesis that bronzework on American vernacular seating, whether painted or stenciled, was unknown much before 1810 are earlier notices of craftsmen. Samuel J. Tuck of Boston supplemented his chairmaking business by importing "PAINTS and COLOURS" from London in 1800 and later. He stocked metal leaf for work in gold, silver, brass, and white metal, although he made no mention of importing metallic powders. In 1808 Henry Beck of Portsmouth, New Hampshire, advertised "fancy gilt chairs of the newest fashion," followed a year later by Chapman and Merritt of Redding, Connecticut, who sold gold- and silver-gilt fancy chairs at "New-York prices." Neither shop appears to have offered bronzework. Nor was this type of work noted in 1809 by William Challen, a fancy chairmaker of London background who had worked for more than a decade in New York, when he resettled at Lexington, Kentucky, and offered a complete color range of fancy chairs ornamented in gold leaf.[143]

The records of Stephen Girard, a Philadelphia merchant, and David Alling, a Newark, New Jersey, chairmaker, describe the rise in marketing bronzed chairs by the mid-1810s. Fancy chairs loaded on Girard's ship *Montesque* in December 1810 for sale in South America comprised a range of colors with gilt decoration. A similar cargo placed on the *North America* in July 1816 for sale in the Far East was augmented by "rosewood" seating in "Bronze." In the mid-1810s Alling's painter, Moses Lyon, bronzed fancy seating with ornament such as flowers, fruits (grapes, peaches), portrait busts, and cornucopias on ground colors of green, nankeen (pale yellow), white, rosewood, and satinwood, the patterns including ball-, slat-, and scroll-backs. Lyon likely utilized shaded metallic powders. A New York ball-back Windsor of the 1810s with hand-painted cornucopias epitomizes chairmaking at the style center that influenced Alling's work (see fig. 31). The bow and outer crest leaves are painted in bronze, complemented by small leaves on the spindles and front legs.[144]

Bronze ornament of the late 1810s introduced the use of stencils, although craftsmen's accounts do not distinguish between painted bronzework and ornament utilizing patterns cut from stiff paper to produce shaded figures by manipulating metallic powders. Early stencil use is documented in a newspaper notice of 1819 by Rufus E. Shapley of Carlisle, Pennsylvania, who advertised chairs "bronzed with FRUIT PATTERNS" and compared the work with that made in New York and Philadelphia. Stencils were also used in other ways. In March 1819 Hugh Finlay, a Baltimore manufacturer of painted furniture, sent Humberston Skipwith a bill for a pair of card tables to furnish his neoclassical plantation house at Prestwould near Clarksville, Virginia. The neoclassical X-base tables have gilded decoration on a grained rosewood ground and a stenciled panel of fruit and foliage on the apron executed in painted polychrome colors rather than metallic powders.[145]

Some notices of the 1830s and 1840s likely identify stencilwork. At Baltimore Edward Needles offered chairs with "Landscape and Bronzed Tops," probably describing painted versus stenciled work. Bronzed chairs sold at the shops of Philemon Robbins and Isaac Wright at Hartford, Connecticut, had roll tops and rush or cane seats, whereas David Alling of Newark, New Jersey, offered bronzed crown-top chairs. The mid-back slats or crown-style crests of these chairs offered good surfaces for stenciled decoration. Of contemporary date is a set of ball-back chairs in "Drab" color enriched with "bronz bands" sold to a client at West Chester, Pennsylvania, by Joseph Jones. Simple painted metallic ornament also is suggested in a bill from Septimus Claypoole to the owners of the Baltimore Exchange Hotel for "painting 104 cane Chairs finished in Bronze."[146]

Gilding

References in craftsmen's records to gilding chairs outnumber those to bronzing. Actual use of gilding ranged from modest accents to lavish embellishments—probably the "Rich gilt" and "half rich gilt" identified in the 1830s in the records of Isaac Wright and Philemon Robbins at their Hartford, Connecticut, shops. An early reference to the decorative technique occurs in the accounts of Daniel Rea Jr., an ornamental painter of Boston, who in 1794 accommodated Andrew Craigie, Esq., of Cambridge by "Paint'g six Chamber Chairs ornamented with Gold." As used here, the word "chamber" is uncertain, as the term usually identified a bedroom, a space frequently furnished with modest or outmoded seating furniture. Perhaps Craigie's chairs were for a judge's chamber.[147]

Early references to gilding identify fancy chairs, the upscale painted or japanned seating introduced from England in the late 1780s. The Boston reference is followed in records by "8 Japan Black & Gold Chair[s]" bought at New York in 1799 by Stephen Arnold of East Greenwich, Rhode Island. Joshua Ward's "Six bamboo Chairs gilt & varnished" supplied by Robert Cowan of Salem, Massachusetts, followed in 1803 at $3.00 the chair. Other early references describe fancy seating in household use. In Samuel P. Broome's estate at Whitemarsh, Pennsylvania, in 1806 a dozen green-and-gold chairs were divided between the front entry hall and the northwest parlor. The nine parlor chairs had "horse hair Cushions" and "Chintz covers." Lydia Pinkham's estate itemized in 1810 on Nantucket Island included

Figure 34   Printed and inscribed bill from
William Buttre of New York City to Oliver
Wolcott of Connecticut, December 8, 1810, for
a large set of fancy chairs ornamented in gold.
(Courtesy, The Connecticut Historical Society,
Hartford.) The text of the billhead enumerates a
selection of chair colors and seating forms.

"6 white gilt Table Chairs" valued at $3.00 apiece with two matching arm-chairs, each appraised at $4.00, the valuations indicating almost new seating. Use of fancy seating for dining is unusual, since that function generally was reserved for the sturdier Windsor.[148]

To complement local business, many early fancy-chairmakers pursued a broader domestic market. New York craftsmen were particularly active in the early 1800s, among them William Palmer, a fancy-seating specialist. Locally, Palmer supplied a Mr. Cox and merchant Nicholas Low with white-and-gold fancy chairs. At $8.00 apiece, Low's elegant chairs were for drawing-room use. In an 1802 notice Palmer also identified his "highly finished black and gold . . . Fancy Chairs, with cane and rush bottoms" (see fig. 15), the same color seating he sold Stephen Arnold of East Greenwich, Rhode Island, and sent across New York Bay to a Mr. Bell at Perth Amboy, New Jersey. David Alling, a chairmaker of neighboring Newark, was a supplier of Palmer until he raised the craftsman's ire by requesting receipts for their business transactions. Charles Cluss, another New York craftsman associated with gilded seating, sent two dozen "Fancy gilt chairs" in 1808 to William Arnold of the East Greenwich family, and William Buttre supplied Oliver Wolcott, a Connecticut client, in 1810 (fig. 34). Alexander Patterson's patrons included Gerrit Wessel Van Schaick of Albany, who in 1814 paid $5.25 apiece for a dozen yellow-and-gilt chairs and a packing charge of $1.50 to ship them up the Hudson River on the sloop *Columbia*. Southern notices document a large trade in gilded fancy and Windsor chairs shipped from New York through middlemen to Charleston and Raleigh in the Carolinas, although the New York suppliers are unknown. The New York trade in gilded chairs also flowed north to Nolen and Gridley at Boston.[149]

Philadelphia craftsmen were equally active in distributing gilded furniture. Black-and-gold fancy seating was sold at Charleston, South Carolina. In 1801 Salem, Massachusetts, merchant John Derby engaged John Stille Jr., merchant-factor of Philadelphia, to acquire two sets of gilded chairs, half a dozen in black and a like number in green. The chairs were put up in six "packs" for shipping, each pack containing a pair of chairs. Surfaces were wrapped with haybands or cloth and each pair of chairs nested seat-to-seat and was enclosed in a woven mat secured with cord. In 1815 Zaccheus Collins, a Philadelphia merchant, used mats to pack a dozen fancy chairs for shipment to his brother-in-law Richard Bland Lee of Virginia, having acquired the chairs from William H. Stewart. Three years later the same shop, then a partnership between Stewart and William Haydon, furnished "Six Urn spindle Black & Gold Chairs" locally at $4.50 apiece to James J. Skerrett, who earlier had acquired "8 Chairs Blue and Gilt" from James Mitchell, paying $5.00 the chair.[150]

Stephen Girard also patronized Mitchell, acquiring in 1809 six black-and-gold side chairs and two armchairs, although whether for his own use or his business enterprises is not indicated. The merchant's further purchases of gilt chairs from unknown shops describe the colors available. For a voyage of the ship *Montesque* in December 1810, Girard acquired eighteen brown-and-gilt fancy side chairs and two armchairs, with an additional one dozen red-gilt chairs. The supercargo disposed of the chairs at Valparaiso, Chile, en route to China. A cargo on Girard's ship *North America* in July 1816 contained seventy-two gilded chairs with rosewood grounds, one group having "Scrowl backs." The chairs, with other seating furniture, were destined for Port Louis on the Isle of France (Mauritius) in the Indian Ocean.[151]

Gilded chairs were an attractive product to other entrepreneurs, whether merchants or craftsmen, for foreign and domestic markets. Early in 1800 merchants Brown and Ives of Providence, Rhode Island, prepared for a voyage to Buenos Aires, Argentina. When the *George and Mary* cleared port in April, it carried a large furniture cargo worth $2,800, of which $1,000 represented fancy and Windsor seating, including gilded fancy chairs of both white and brown ground. Brown and Ives bypassed local suppliers and acquired their furniture in New York, as per payment for "Truckage [of] furniture to the packet in New York," labor, and freight on the packet from New York to Providence. "Matting chairs" cost $10.00, although with 666 chairs on board, the fee covered mats for only expensive seating, such as the gilded chairs.[152]

As the chair trade expanded, business-oriented craftsmen saw the advantages in making quantities of chairs available to shippers "at short notice" and appropriately packaged. Business was particularly brisk by the 1820s, when Samuel G. Bodge of Providence advertised "400 Chairs prepared purposely for shipping, suitable for the West India or South American markets, and will be painted to suit the purchaser." Shipping preparations included matting some chairs, although quantity dealers, like Bodge, also offered "knock-downs," or disassembled chairs packed in cases for assembly at their destination. Cases were easier to handle and took less shipping space, making them cheaper to transport. Levi Stillman of New Haven, Connecticut, utilized boxes for furniture when shipping nineteen containers in 1826 to associate Horace A. Augur at Lima, Peru. Chairs, some gilded, formed the bulk of the furniture and were shipped assembled, the surfaces protected by most of the 517¾ yards of cotton sheeting listed on the invoice. The item "Freight of Boxes to New York" sheds further light on travel arrangements. The furniture was transferred to the brig *Rio* at New York for the voyage to South America. Boxes also figured in the overland transport of furniture, as recorded by Thomas Boynton of Windsor, Vermont. In 1818 Robert Davis paid $2.50 apiece for "12 gilt f[an]cy Bb [bent-back] Chairs," with an additional $2.00 for "Boxing ditto" and $1.50 for "Transportation of d[itt]o to Hanover," New Hampshire.[153]

A large domestic market for David Alling of Newark, New Jersey, was the American South, where he made four consignments of Windsor and fancy chairs to Nathan Bolles at New Orleans in 1819–1820. Of the 868 items shipped, most were side chairs supplemented by 14 rockers and 38 high and low chairs for children. Prices ranged from $1.50 to $7.00 an item. Although Alling did not identify the packaging, he provided a clue indicating that the furniture was boxed. The left margins of the invoices bear consecutive numbers next to the merchandise, the usual method of identifying shipping containers. Reinforcing the idea that the chairs were packed is the high value of the chairs. Those with gilded accents varied in structure: slat-backs, ball-backs (see fig. 31), and oval or diamond fret-backs (see fig. 13); specialty spindles were shaved flat and shaped with ovals, urns, or arrows (see figs. 18, 31), or turned to simulate organ pipes (see fig. 26); front stretchers were diamond- or slat-shaped (see figs. 13, 23) or cylindrical. Colors included rosewood and maple graining, green, yellow, and red augmented by white, coquelicot, brown, drab, nankeen, and cane.[154]

By 1811 shops everywhere sold painted seating furniture enriched with gilt decoration. The urban centers of Boston, New York, Philadelphia, and Baltimore probably led the way, although the migration of craftsmen and the coastal and overland trade in chairs carried the fashion far and wide   from Vermont to West Virginia, from Georgia to Kentucky. Thomas Sheraton and Rufus Porter, among other authors, commented on the mechanics of chair gilding. Of the two methods, oil gilding was more suitable than water gilding for chair work because it was more durable.[155]

Gilding occurred after a chair was painted or japanned. The areas to be gilded were brushed over with japanner's gold size or, as preferred by Porter, dilute copal varnish, to produce a quick-drying, tacky surface to secure the gold (or silver) leaf. Thomas Boynton of Vermont noted the process in 1815 in crediting John Patterson with "Sising and gilding 19 fancy chairs." As most gilded chair ornament formed narrow bands, or "fillets," Sheraton recommended cutting the fillets on a gilder's cushion, the gold leaf sandwiched between blank sheets from a book of leaf and one sheet retained to transfer the gold to the work. In 1827 James Gere of Connecticut recorded the cost of a "Book Gold Leaf" as 3s. (50¢). Sheraton advised making a complete application of leaf to a chair before using a cotton cloth to smooth the work and press the thin metal into the tacky sizing. Irregularities at the edges of the gilding could be "trimmed" using a slim brush and the ground color. Metallic ornament, especially silver leaf, could be tinted with transparent color or lacquer. Both Sheraton and Porter suggested "the gold in chair work ought to be varnished to secure it, and the best varnish for this purpose is copal."[156]

PAINTED SEATS

Woven Seats

Thomas Sheraton advocated preserving rush-woven seats in fancy furniture by painting the material, which hardened the fibers. Without some type of coating, rush dried out over time and became brittle. When brittle, the seats were vulnerable even to the normal pressures of sitting and soon collapsed, making a chair unfit for use until the seat was replaced. At times, frugal householders renewed the paint on their chair seats with a fresh coat, as when Henry Mason paid William G. Beesley of Salem, New Jersey, in 1831 for "varnishing 14 fancy Chairs [and] painting the seats of the same."[157]

Records identify white, as named by Sheraton, and yellow as the paint colors preferred for coating rush seats. White probably was more common. Judge Bruce, a client of Philemon Robbins at Hartford, Connecticut, likely deposited most of his household seating with the craftsman in 1835, when he paid $1.80 for "painting 24 chair seats white." Some householders elected to do the work themselves, as indicated by Charles Dyer, who in 1824 purchased "white Paint for Cheir Seets" at 25¢ from Elizur Barnes of Middletown. Two years earlier Barnes recorded a job of "Painting 8 Seats yellow." William Beesley of New Jersey provided some idea of the amount of paint needed to coat the seats of a set of chairs, when he charged a customer 19¢ for "1 lb yellow for Chair seats."[158]

Wooden Seats

References to Windsor chairs painted in two colors pose problems. Unless seats, or "bottoms," are named as one color, the second color likely identified ornament—pinstripes, bands, or figures. Two probate inventories of New York origin contain illustrative examples. In 1813 appraisers listed "5 Yellow & Green chairs" and "5 Yellow & White D[itt]o" in the home of Ezra Hounsfield. What did the second color in each entry represent—seats or ornament? A tentative answer can be found in an item from the estate of Whitehead Fish, cashier of the Merchants' Bank in the city: "14 White & Green fancy chairs." White was the color on the wood, and green probably was the color of the decoration, as there is no evidence of the use of dark paint on rush seats. Greater clarity occurs in a record from Salem, Massachusetts, where Richard Austin made chairs for the export business of Elijah and Jacob Sanderson. One item reads, "6 White [Chairs] Stript [striped] Green." References to two-color chairs without further explanation probably identify surface coats and ornament.[159]

The practice of painting Windsor chair seats in a color contrasting with that of the rest of the chair was of limited duration, ranging from about the mid-1790s into the next decade. A record of 1808 made by Stephanus Knight of Enfield, Connecticut, identifies refurbished work in describing "Painting 5 Chares green and Bottoms Black." Two-color references in probate records are noted as late as 1826, when the home of William Chappel of Lyme contained "½ Doz Green, Chocolate bottom windsor Chairs," probably purchased about two decades earlier. Some early references also need interpretation. The "6 Green [Chairs] with Red Bottoms" in the Nantucket inventory of Oliver Spencer in 1794 may have had stuffed bottoms with cloth covers rather than painted seats. This expensive option in Windsor seating was current from the 1780s through the 1790s. The vogue for painting Windsor chair seats in a contrasting color imitated stuffed work at a modest cost.[160]

Limited information prevents definite assessment of the popularity of particular two-color paint combinations. A separate analysis of seat and back colors reveals that seats usually were painted in dark colors—mahogany favored, black a second choice. Yellow was chosen for backs and bases, followed by green. Amos D. Allen's customers at Windham, Connecticut, preferred mahogany-colored seats combined with backs of yellow, green, or blue. A black bottom with a green back was another option. A similar set of chairs "ornamented with yellow" disappeared in 1804 from the auction room of Christian and Paxton at New York. Of bright color were

"6 [Cream Colored chairs] with green bottom[s], striped" sold by Titus Preston at Wallingford. David Russell of Winchester, Virginia, painted chairs cream color with mahogany bottoms besides retailing two uncommon selections—"mazarine blue with mahogany bottoms" and pale blue with yellow seats.[161]

SPECIALIZED SEATING FORMS

Minor markets existed for seating furniture designed to fill specialized needs not met by standard adult side and armchairs. Rocking chairs, settees, stools, and children's seating were the principal forms. Although each could be purchased independent of other furnishings, rocking chairs, settees, and children's furniture often were acquired as part of a suite of seating furniture of similar pattern, surface color, and decoration. Of these named forms, the rocking chair was the most common.

ROCKING CHAIRS

The rocking chair was part of American furniture production by the 1730s, although it was uncommon until the 1790s, when Windsor chairs with rockers began to supplement common rush-bottom examples. Interest in the form increased steadily after 1800 until by the 1820s the furniture industry was poised to install at least one rocking chair in every domestic household (fig. 35).

During the 1740s, Solomon Fussell, a chairmaker of Philadelphia, had occasional calls for rush-bottom rocking chairs, the surfaces either black or "white" ("in the wood," or without paint). White chairs were about a shilling less than those with paint. Later, in 1774, William Barker of Providence, Rhode Island, recorded "mend[ing] & Colloring [a] rocking chare" with a rush seat. "Coloring" likely identified a coating of pigment in size, a gelatinous solution. Amos D. Allen's records of the 1790s at Windham, Connecticut, serve to identify the introduction of the Windsor rocking chair, the cost twice or more that of Fussell's woven-bottom rockers.[162]

Color choices for Windsor rocking chairs paralleled those for standard seating. Usually named are green, yellow, browns, and imitation wood grounds. Black was chosen occasionally; white probably was uncommon. Imitation maple and rosewood were popular grained surfaces, although imitation satinwood and oak are named. Regarding ornamental maple, the shop inventory of Charles Riley of Philadelphia makes a cogent comparison. The appraised value of an "Imitation [bird's eye Rocking Chair]" was $2.25, whereas that of a true "bird eye Rocking chair" was $6.75. At Hartford, Connecticut, Philemon Robbins introduced "quaker" gray to rocking chairs in the mid-1830s, as he did on occasion to standard seating. A special-order "quaker" rocker made in 1834 had a "maple top" of natural finish. Other records hint that by the second quarter of the century chairmakers with large businesses stockpiled a few specialized chairs without finish or ornament to be completed when sold. For example, in 1836 after Elijah Ware took over William G. Beesley's shop at Salem, New Jersey, Beesley recorded "making & priming a highback Rocking Chr" for Ware. Chair-

Figure 35 Shaped-slat-back Windsor rocking armchair, southern New Hampshire, 1820–1830. White pine (seat). H. 35", W. 20¼", D. 17⅞" (seat). (Present location unknown; formerly in a private collection; photo, Winterthur Museum.) Original decoration and surface paint in light stone color (drab).

makers sometimes sold rocking chairs without finish to professional painters and handymen. In 1842 D. Burton purchased "1 L[arge] R[ocking] chair in the white" for $2.50 from Henry F. Dewey of Bennington, Vermont, and covered his debt by "painting 9 cott[age] Chr." When Launcelot Jenkins, probably a handyman, acquired a rocker at Philadelphia from Charles C. Robinson in 1815, he purchased paint to finish it, his total out-of-pocket expenses being $2.25.[163]

Rocking chairs were ornamented in fashions similar to standard seating. Fairly basic were tipping with pinstripes and striping with bands. Gilding enhanced some surfaces, and Philemon Robbins of Hartford, Connecticut, at times employed "rich gilt" decoration. Bronzing introduced painted or stenciled metallic ornament. Other records identify a "swan" and a "squirrel" as featured motifs. Nelson Talcott of Ohio included a portrait bust of Andrew Jackson in the crest of a rocking chair.[164]

Records at times identify structural features of the rocking chair, some of a special nature. Like those on standard seating, crests were principally of three types: a plain or fancy slat mounted between the back posts; a rectangular or rounded-end tablet mounted in mortise-and-tenon or rabbet joints at the tops of the back posts; and a turned "roll top" framed in rabbet joints at the post tips. Tall backs were common in the rocking chair, although the descriptive language might vary from place to place. In 1815 Thomas Boynton recorded "painting a high *top* rocking chair" at Windsor, Vermont, whereas William Beesley of Salem, New Jersey, identified similar work as "painting a high *back* Rocking Chair." Many rocking-chair seats imitated those in standard seating, often with increased dimensions. Almost exclusive to the rocking chair was a Boston-style seat with an ogee curve in the side profile, although its production was not limited to Boston or even to New England. Two alternative terms identify the same seat. When working for Franklin Howe, Thomas Boynton painted, ornamented, and varnished "55 raised seat rocking chairs" for which he was paid 50¢ apiece. The "rise" of the Boston seat occurs at the back and consists of several shaped and stacked blocks of wood. At Hartford, Connecticut, Philemon Robbins recorded a credit of $12.00 in the account of Sullivan Hill, a supplier who constructed "6 painted scroll seat Rocking Chairs." The term "scroll" pinpoints the half roll fixed to the underside of the rounded seat front to form a full scroll.[165]

Retail prices for rocking chairs varied widely, depending on date of construction, structural pattern, ornamentation, and special features, although the data can be reasonably qualified. Priced under $1.00 were "common" chairs with rush seats, slat backs, and plain painted surfaces, dating principally in the eighteenth century. Chairs in the $1.00 to $1.99 range were a step up in design and surface and represented the lower of the two common price groups. Rocking chairs in the second large group, priced from $2.00 to just under $3.00, were made for a more affluent market. Of the few chairs priced over $3.00, the record provides insights. In 1834 Philemon Robbins of Hartford, Connecticut, sold a "quaker [colored] large rocking chair" for $3.50 to E. Hooker, Esq., of Farmington. There followed a chair of similar color for Adam Miner priced at $4.00 and described as "First rate." A chair sold early in the century by Richard Austin of Salem, Massachusetts, to cabinetmaker Jacob Sanderson for $3.83 had simulated bamboo turnings "With Rockers [and] Gold leaf." Gilding enhanced two imitation rosewood sewing chairs (with rockers), each priced at $3.50, shipped in 1820 by David Alling of Newark, New Jersey, to Nathan Bolles at New Orleans. The chairs, however handsome, apparently were no match for two rockers priced at $11.00 apiece. In 1840 Alling recorded the sale to Frederick T. Frelinghuysen Jr., Esq., of a "black . . . cane b[a]ck & seat rock[ing] chr." Earlier, Philemon Robbins credited Horace Lee, a Springfield, Massachusetts, supplier, for delivery of a "Large green Can[e]d R[ocking] chair" to Hartford for commission sale. To achieve their high prices, both chairs had to have been substantially ornamented and gilded.[166]

Records identify two specialized rockers—the nurse, or nursing, chair and the sewing chair. Both chairs could be armless on occasion. Short legs, placing seats lower to the floor, appeared at times, and seats in sewing chairs could be of large size. Solomon Fussell listed "nurse" chairs in his Philadelphia accounts in the 1740s, whereas chairs dedicated to sewing were unnamed before the early nineteenth century. Several seating materials occur, as noted in sewing-chair records. David Alling of New Jersey identified wooden seats in the item "[Tipping] 5 Windsor Sewing Chs" (1816) and rush seats in "matting, moulding, p[ain]t'g, gilding, & bronzing sewing Chr" (1840). Standing in Alling's shop at his death were "3 Rosewood [cane seat] Sewing chairs."[167]

Like other seating, the rocking chair required periodic repair and refurbishing. By far the most common call was for a fresh coat of paint. Records at times note the application of ornament, although a finish coat of varnish is seldom mentioned. Both tasks may have been part of the general painting process. The specifics of repair work are seldom identified, with the exception of replacing rockers or adding them to the bottoms of stationary chairs. Rush-bottom chairs required periodic seat replacement, and cased seats at times needed new "molding" pieces painted to match the ground color of the chair. Some newly rushed seats were painted to better preserve them.[168]

SETTEES

Unlike the rocker, which after 1790 frequently was a wooden-bottom chair, settee construction employed wood, rush, or cane for the seat. Wood was the most durable and cane the most expensive. Of the specialized seating forms, the settee was most likely to be framed and purchased as part of a suite of furniture containing a set of side chairs or side chairs and armchairs.

Popular colors for the settee were those prominent in the rocking chair, although variants within color groups are more frequent in records naming the settee. Settees of verdigris green complemented eighteenth-century chairs of similar color. Dark olive was a nineteenth-century option, as itemized in the 1842 Philadelphia shop inventory of Charles Riley. Yellow, a popular choice, included pale variants. Joseph Burden of Philadelphia sold "cane coulered" chairs with settees to match to Stephen Girard in 1810 for his overseas trade, and the pale hue was still viable for settees three decades later, as recorded in Riley's inventory. "Nankeen," a color named for a cotton textile of pale, light brownish yellow, described the surface of a "sofa," probably of woven bottom, ornamented by Moses Lyon in 1817 in David Alling's shop at Newark, New Jersey.[169]

A notice of March 7, 1798, by Hopkins and Charles, Charleston, South Carolina, importers, for Philadelphia Windsor furniture lists chairs and settees in "Mahogany" and "Chocolate" color. Both colors were reddish brown, the mahogany of bright hue, the chocolate a deep, dark shade. The pattern likely was the bow-back current at that date. The "brown" settees sold in 1809 by William Challen of Kentucky probably reflected a continuing use of chocolate color. The "light Colour" settees in Charles Riley's Philadelphia shop in 1842 were a brownish yellow often equated with drab or stone color (fig. 36). In sharp contrast was Riley's settee of "blossom" color, a pink with a bluish purple cast. Equally brilliant were coquelicot settees advertised by Challen.[170]

Figure 36 Detail, roll-top Windsor settee with scroll arms, south-central Pennsylvania, 1835–1845. Woods unknown. H. 33⅛", W. 76½", D. 21". (Present location unknown; formerly in a private collection; photo, Winterthur Museum.) Original decoration and surface paint in light stone color (drab).

Black probably was uncommon for either Windsor or fancy furniture before 1800. By 1807 and 1808, however, public notices at Charleston, South Carolina, describe a popular market for chairs and settees of this color imported from Philadelphia and New York. There followed in 1810 work for Stephen Girard of Philadelphia by an unnamed chairmaker who produced black chairs and settees for the merchant's South American trade. Black furniture, in particular, looked well enhanced with gold, a fashion William Challen carried with him when he migrated from New York to Kentucky. The chairmaker's fancy production in the "West" also included white seating enriched with gold, which, compared with black, had an early introduction in the market. In 1793 appraisers listed "1 Round Top Settee painted white" (a sack-back or bow-back Windsor) in the Philadelphia estate of chairmaker John Lambert, victim of a yellow fever epidemic in the city. White again was chosen two years later by General Henry Knox, when he ordered a large suite of "Oval Back'd" furniture in the city from William Cox, comprising thirty-six side chairs, thirty-six armchairs, four long settees, and two short settees. The armchairs and settees had mahogany arms in a natural finish.[171]

David Alling of New Jersey credited Moses Lyon in 1817 with "Graining 1 Sofa." By 1818 Sass and Gready, merchants of Charleston, South Carolina, identified "Cane and Rush Seat Fancy CHAIRS and SETTEES, Rosewood colors" in one of many advertisements. Rosewood graining was still a viable settee finish in 1842, when appraisers listed the contents of Charles Riley's shop at Philadelphia. Supplementing this furniture were several "Imitation Maple" settees.[172]

When Silas Cheney of Litchfield, Connecticut, undertook a refurbishing job for Oliver Wolcott in 1815, he identified and classified the project's scope: "Painting & gilding Settee Euquel to 5 Chairs," the charge being $3.54. Settees "richly ornamented" with metallic leaf were widely available soon after 1800, not merely in urban and rural centers of the East but in the "West" at Lexington, Kentucky, where William Challen offered gilded ornament by 1809. Martin Kearns of Martinsburg, (West) Virginia, hinted in 1811 that both a customer's taste and pocketbook could be accommodated, when advertising "Windsor Chairs, Settees . . . finished plainly, or elegantly varnished and ornamented with gold and silver leaf." Bronzing, applied as paint or as a powder in stencilwork, offered another option in metallic decoration. Moses Lyon, who worked occasionally as a painter and ornamenter for David Alling at Newark, New Jersey, in the mid-1810s, bronzed both woven-bottom "Sofas" and wooden-bottom "Settees" framed in a variety of patterns and painted in various colors. Lyon provided alternative ornament by "tipping," or pinstriping, the long seats. At Middletown, Connecticut, the accounts of Elizur Barnes indicate that the craftsman spent almost two days in August 1822 "Stripping [striping] Sophas," judging by the $2.00 charge.[173]

Because long seats, such as settees and sofas, were made to accompany sets of chairs, their decoration was similar, although few references to ornament name the long seat. David Alling identified a dozen bronzed chairs and a sofa in a "Fruit" pattern. John and Hugh Finlay, painted furniture specialists of Baltimore, described a variety of ornament for chairs and long seats more typical of high-end than common furniture: "real Views, Fancy Landscapes, Flowers, Trophies of Music, War, Husbandry, Love, &c." Identification of structural design is somewhat more common. Earliest are patterns produced in the 1790s at Philadelphia. John Lambert framed a "Round Top Settee," identifying a sack- or bow-back Windsor, and William Cox constructed "Oval Back'd," or bow-back, settees. Several craftsmen identified bamboowork, whose creases simulate the character of the tropical plant. William Dutilh, a Philadelphia merchant, ventured seating of this type in 1800: "an elegant sett of 12 bamboo chairs ornamented and highly finished, 2 ditto armchairs . . . and two settees ditto." Other patterns are of later date. David Alling of Newark, New Jersey, whose work paralleled that of New York, noted special turned work of the mid-1810s in identifying a Windsor settee with "Organ Spindles," the short sticks of the lower back simulating the pipes of an organ in their rounded tops and sharply tapered bodies (see fig. 26). Settee styles from other shops included the slat-back, double-cross back, and ball-back patterns. The "Baltimore"-style tablet top was still current in 1842, when appraisers listed the contents of Charles Riley's Philadelphia shop.[174]

The price of a vernacular settee was substantial, even if the structure was plain and the ornament minimal. Retail prices might vary from $5.00 to $15.00, reflecting differences in pattern, size, and decoration. Henry Wilder Miller, entrepreneur-owner of a chair factory in the 1820s at Worcester, Massachusetts, provided a few general insights into production costs and retail prices for settees, suggesting a base for figuring a hypothetical profit range in merchandising this form. Miller obtained most of his furniture in the wood from area suppliers. Factory workmen, principally Smith Kendall, Miller's brother-in-law, framed stock as necessary but spent the majority of their time painting and ornamenting furniture for direct sale or distribution to retailers. In June 1827 Miller paid $1.66 apiece for "2 Unpainted Settees" from supplier W. and S. Barber. David Partridge earlier deposited two frames at the factory priced individually at $1.25, the same price recorded for painting a settee. A further account describes a job of "ornamenting 1 Settee" at a cost of 42¢ to the client. Miller's combined charge of $1.67 for painting and ornamenting a settee was considerably less than the $3.54 recorded by Silas Cheney at Litchfield, Connecticut, a few years earlier. However, Cheney's work involved gilding, an expensive process because of labor and material. With the complete cost of a settee at Miller's factory tallied at either $2.92 or $3.34, and a retail price quoted at $5.00 in one instance, the entrepreneur might realize a 50 to 71 percent profit for the sale of this form.[175]

STOOLS

Although stools of one type or another were relatively common in early households, indications of their surface finishes are elusive. Most stools had wooden tops or seats, as woven fibers were less practical in meeting the sometimes rugged use of this form. Records describe stools of several heights, either directly or by inference, and they occasionally identify stools of specialized function.

Crickets, or low stools, had several uses (fig. 37). They served as seats for small children, as footrests to elevate the feet above cold drafts at floor level, and as low platforms for standing or extending one's reach. Within this

Figure 37 Windsor cricket, or low stool, northern New England, 1825–1840. Basswood (top) with birch. H. 7⅛", W. 13", D. 8". (Courtesy, Winterthur Museum.) Original decoration and surface paint in yellow.

frame of function, surface refurbishing was a principal call, with repair work perhaps less in demand. Paint was the most common surface coating, and in 1800 Daniel Rea Jr., an ornamental painter of Boston, recorded "Painting a cricket green." True Currier, a woodworker of Deerfield, New Hampshire, undertook more extensive work in 1834 for Peter Jenness when "putting legs to crickets & painting them." Charges were in the 30¢ to 40¢ range.[176]

Medium-high stools for use at tables, workbenches, and the like are rarely identified by size, although they form the bulk of general references and provide the most insight into color choices. When William Beekman of New York died in 1795, his counting room included a "green painted square Writing Table" and "3 Stools" probably of similar finish. Other stools duplicated the color, if not the character, of various species of wood. A job that engaged William Gray at Salem, Massachusetts, in 1793 noted as "Painting Stool Seder Colour," probably only replicated the hue of red cedar, a timber used in case furniture as both a secondary and a primary wood. Work of later date imitated the actual grain of several popular cabinet woods. In 1839 David Alling of Newark, New Jersey, supplied a customer with "18 winsor rosewood stools," charging 62½¢ apiece. Charles Riley's shop at Philadelphia held a number of small seats three years later described as eleven "Imitation Maple Stools," each valued at 62¢. The "27 red seats or stools" at Lewis Bancel's school for young ladies in lower Manhattan in 1828 may have been a brilliant red poppy color (coquelicot) or merely a dark reddish brown. Of light brownish yellow was the "stone [colored] stool" returned in 1852 to the Otsego County, New York, shop of Chauncey Strong at Laurens.[177]

The absence of finish on a stool opens the door to speculation. In 1837 chairmaker Josiah P. Wilder of New Ipswich, New Hampshire, recorded the purchase of "4 Stools without paint" at 25¢ each by "Miss" Elisa Bachelder. The following year Maria Ryan paid 25¢ for "½ lb Blue Paint," which Wilder's accounts suggest was made with the pigment Prussian blue. Perhaps the rise in cottage industries of this period encouraged these women to try their hands at basic painting tasks. By the early 1830s, the flourishing chair industry in neighboring Worcester County, Massachusetts, employed almost two hundred women for simple jobs inside and outside the manufactories.[178]

David Alling had calls in the late 1830s at his Newark, New Jersey, facility for high stools, a useful form for business purposes from the eighteenth century. In 1837 the firm of Hay and Agens acquired "1 high winsor stool painted" for $1.12½. The same stool probably was back in Alling's shop in 1839, when Jonas Agens paid 38¢ for "mending & pting green high stool." Another client paid the same as Hay and Agens for a tall Windsor stool "stained & varnished." When Henry W. Miller listed a "White Desk Stool" in his accounts for 1829 at Worcester, Massachusetts, he may have identified a similar stool, one used at the high writing desk common to counting rooms or offices. The low price of 40¢ leaves in doubt whether "white" described paint or bare wood.[179]

Some records describe stools of highly specialized function. During the 1810s and 1820s, Thomas Boynton of Windsor, Vermont, and Henry Wilder Miller of Worcester, Massachusetts, and others identified "painting a Musick Stool," probably for use at a pianoforte. The cost of repainting varied from 33¢ to $1.00, suggesting that the highest prices included ornamentation. The presence of a long screw mounted on the seat bottom to permit adjusting the height may have been the element that distinguished a music stool from other stools of standard seat height.[180]

Figure 38   Child's sack-back Windsor armchair, New York City, 1785–1795. Yellow poplar (seat) with maple and oak. H. 25", W. 18", D. 11⅜". (Courtesy, Winterthur Museum.) A multilayered surface with coral red on the outside over white over a deteriorated dark color. Given the date and origin of this chair, the original surface paint probably was verdigris green. As demonstrated here, in the absence of an exposed original surface or the presence of a surface cleaned to the bare wood, a surface that retains many layers of paint (and resin) reflecting various surface renewals over time is typical.

CHILDREN'S SEATING FURNITURE

Records identify seating furniture for children (fig. 38) by one of three terms: "childs," "little," and "small." The last-named term, "small," introduces some ambiguity because it also appears at times to identify a slightly larger chair sometimes called a "youth's" or "half-size" chair. In still other instances, "small" may describe the lesser in size of two or more adult chairs. A few specialized seats round out the discussion.

Solomon Fussell, a Philadelphia chairmaker of the 1740s, offered a "childs" rush-bottom chair in white, black, or brown. White identified a chair "in the wood" without finish, such as that bought by Benjamin Franklin in 1744 for 2s. 6d. By contrast, the "2 Childrens Green Chairs" bought at New York for 12s. apiece in 1762 by James Beekman likely were Windsor armchairs because when Dinah Jenkins of Nantucket Island died in 1788, her estate contained "one Childs Green Arm'd Chair" valued at 8s. ($1.33). Green also described ornament on "12 little winsor Childrens Chairs brown & Green" sold by David Alling in 1819. Some children's low chairs in Alling's New Jersey shop were "tipped" with fine lines or striped with broad bands. At Boston, Thomas Boynton's records for 1811 note "a childs chair gilt," the quality reflected in the $1.75 price. Like adult seating, children's chairs were periodically repaired, refurbished, or reseated.[181]

A reference of 1753 to a "little chare" in William Barker's Providence, Rhode Island, accounts describes the surface finish as "coloring Black," that is, pigment suspended in a size base. Unusual because of the color's rare mention is James Chase's construction of "1 Little Char painted Blue" in 1799 at Gilmanton, New Hampshire. Several years later, the shop of Daniel and Samuel Proud at Providence filled two orders for a "Littel Green Chair," probably a Windsor. By the 1830s little chairs painted in drab and dark brownish earth pigments were made by Philemon Robbins at Hartford, Connecticut. Oliver Avery of North Stonington described ornament when making a "little Chair Sprigged," probably in the bamboo Windsor style. The sprigging likely was a narrow vine or grasslike tufts adjacent to creases in the bamboowork. Woven bottoms in little chairs, as recorded in 1822 by Elizur Barnes of Middletown, could be painted for preservation and contrast.[182]

A few records give credence to the word "small" in identifying seats for children. Charles C. Robinson of Philadelphia recorded a "Childs Small Windsor Chair" in 1817, having earlier painted another "small" Windsor. David Alling penned a more cogent description in 1820, when he shipped "10 Small Childrens Chairs Yellow [slats]" from New Jersey to New Orleans. Two "Small Coquelico Ch[air]s" painted in Alling's shop may have been similar in size. Of alternative surface treatment were thirty-five "Stain'd Small [Chairs Flagg'd]," or rush-bottomed, priced at 20¢ and 25¢ apiece in 1819, when appraisers made an accounting of Benjamin Bass's shop at Boston.[183]

Craftsmen's records make note of special seating for children. Prominent is the highchair, also known in records as a "table chair" and a "dining chair." At Philadelphia, Solomon Fussell recorded "matting and Colouring a table Chair" in 1742, the cost at 1s. 6d. describing a refurbished chair.

Later, in 1795, John Letchworth, a local Windsor chairmaker, completed a "Round top table Chair Mahogany colour" of sack- or bow-back pattern for Jonathan Williams at the high price of $2.53. The popular "quaker" gray used for furniture by Philemon Robbins in the mid-1830s at Hartford, Connecticut, covered the surface of at least one "Childs High chair." A few records identify "childrens dining" chairs with striped ornament. Thomas Boynton of Windsor, Vermont, engaged John Patterson in 1814 to stripe six chairs of this description.[184]

Specialty seats for children included other forms. Dating to 1774 is "a Grien Settee for Miss Nancy" made by William Cox, a Windsor chairmaker of Philadelphia, for Anne Cadwalader (b. 1771), the young daughter of General John and Elizabeth Lloyd Cadwalader. Some families with young children used a furniture form recorded in 1795 by Job E. Townsend at Newport, Rhode Island: "Painting a Standing stool." This small baby cage, at times fitted with a seat, was pushed along the floor, with or without wheels, as a child learned to walk. Essential in early childhood was the "small ch[ai]r with hole" (potty chair) noted by David Alling of New Jersey, who painted one in 1836 in imitation maple. Other forms were made for childhood pleasure. Daniel Rea Jr. of Boston charged Samuel Parkman 6s. ($1.00) in 1791, when "paint'g a Childs Rocking Horse." Producing related movement was a "yellow little chair, role [top] & rocker" that cost 75¢ in 1835 at Philemon Robbins's Hartford, Connecticut, shop.[185]

As demonstrated throughout this study, a comprehensive investigation of the written evidence of painted surfaces in seating furniture draws from a large body of documents, given the incomplete and sometimes fragmentary nature of original material. In a great measure, those same documents also supply complementary material that provides a framework for interpreting the data in a sociocultural context to illuminate furnishing practices in the home, business enterprise, price structuring, dissemination of products and design, packaging, and the important role of color in daily life.

1. Jacob Bigelow, *The Useful Arts*, 2 vols. (Boston: Thomas H. Webb, 1840), 1: 163–64.

2. Silas E. Cheney Daybook, Litchfield, Connecticut, 1813–1821, account with Orin Judd, May 18, 1821, Litchfield Historical Society, Litchfield, Connecticut (hereafter LHS).

3. Advertisements of Joseph Very, *Eastern Argus* (Portland, Maine), October 28, 1813; George Dame, *New-Hampshire Gazette* (Portsmouth), March 10, 1807; Reuben Sanborn, *Columbian Centinel* (Boston), January 1, 1806; anonymous, *Columbian Centinel*, April 17, 1802; James Always, *Weekly Museum* (New York), February 28, 1801.

4. Allen Holcomb Account Book, New Lisbon, New York, 1809–ca. 1828, account with Simon Smith, 1809, Metropolitan Museum of Art, New York; True Currier Account Book, Deerfield, New Hampshire, 1815–1838, account with Enos Sandborn Jr., April 1828, Joseph Downs Collection of Manuscripts and Printed Ephemera, Winterthur Museum Library, Winterthur, Delaware (hereafter DCM); Nathaniel Bangs Account Book, Amherst, Massachusetts, 1788–1799, account with Capt. Oliver Allen, June 1789, DCM.

5. Joseph Brown Jr., Account Book, Newbury, Massachusetts, 1726–1741, account with Joseph Lowell, May 14, 1741, Peabody Essex Museum, Salem, Massachusetts (hereafter PEM); Isaiah Tiffany Account Book, Norwich, Connecticut, 1746–1767, account with Elijah Bliss, August 25, 1756, Connecticut Historical Society, Hartford (hereafter CHS); Solomon Fussell Account Book, Philadelphia, 1738–1748, accounts with Joseph Marshall, 1741, Stephen Collins Papers, Library of Congress, Washington, D.C. (hereafter LC); Jacob Merrill Jr., Ledger, Ply-

mouth, New Hampshire, 1784–1812, account with Daniel Wyatt, August 10, 1797, New Hampshire Historical Society, Concord.

6. Advertisements of Lawrence Allwine, *Aurora* (Philadelphia), May 3, 1800, and Oliver Goodwin, *Times* (Charleston, South Carolina), April 7, 1801.

7. Cheney Daybook, account with Jonathan Buel, October 17, 1820; Christopher Clark, "The Diary of an Apprentice Cabinetmaker: Edward Jenner Carpenter's 'Journal,' 1844–1845," in *Proceedings of the American Antiquarian Society* (Worcester, Mass.: by the Society, 1989), vol. 98, pt. 2 (1988): 335–36; Nelson Talcott Daybook, Nelson and Garrettsville, Ohio, 1839–1848, account with William B. Payne, February 1, 1841, DCM.

8. Jacob S. Van Tyne Journal, Niles, New York, 1836–1839, entries for May 30 and June 9, 1838, DCM.

9. Talcott Daybook, account with Sylvester Taylor Jr., October 12, 1840; James Gere Ledger, Groton, Connecticut, 1822–1852, account with John Ashley Willet, September 1824, Connecticut State Library, Hartford (hereafter CSL).

10. William Lycett Bill to Robert R. Livingston, New York, 1794, Robert R. Livingston Papers, New-York Historical Society, New York (hereafter N-YHS); Benjamin Bass Estate Records, Boston, 1819, Suffolk County Probate Court, Boston (hereafter SCPC).

11. Advertisements of Vosburgh and Childs, *Hall's Wilmington Gazette* (North Carolina), February 9, 1797; Thomas Henning Sr., *Lewisburg Chronicle* ([West] Virginia), February 12, 1852; Silas Cooper, *Republican and Savannah Evening Ledger* (Savannah, Georgia), November 9, 1811; and Dockum and Brown, *New-Hampshire Gazette*, December 11, 1827.

12. Fussell Account Book; John Durand Account Book, Milford, Connecticut, 1760–1783, Milford Historical Society, Connecticut.

13. Robert F. Trent, *Hearts and Crowns: Folk Chairs of the Connecticut Coast, 1720–1840* (New Haven, Conn.: New Haven Colony Historical Society, 1977), figs. 37, 51–53; Durand Account Book, account with Deacon Joseph Treat, February 5, 1776.

14. Fussell Account Book, accounts with Abraham Linkcorn, 1743, Richard Tyson, 1741, and William Moss, 1744 and 1748.

15. The Fussell-Savery connection is discussed in Benno M. Forman, "Delaware Valley 'Crookt Foot' and Slat-back Chairs," *Winterthur Portfolio* 15, no. 1 (Spring 1980): 46; William Savery Bill to Gen. John Cadwalader, Philadelphia, 1770, Gen. John Cadwalader Section, Cadwalader Collection, Historical Society of Pennsylvania, Philadelphia (hereafter HSP); Nicholas B. Wainwright, *Colonial Grandeur in Philadelphia: The House and Furniture of General John Cadwalader* (Philadelphia: Historical Society of Pennsylvania, 1964).

16. Miles Ward Ledger, Salem, Massachusetts, 1717–1753, PEM; John II and Thomas Gaines Account Book, Ipswich, Massachusetts, 1725/56–1755, DCM; Tiffany Account Book, miscellaneous accounts, 1755–1756; David Haven Account Book, Framingham, Massachusetts, 1785–1800, DCM; John Baker, lists of goods, 1760 and 1766, as quoted in Joseph K. Ott, "More Notes on Rhode Island Cabinetmakers and Their Work," *Rhode Island History* 28, no. 2 (May 1969): 49.

17. Fussell Account Book, accounts with John Hammer, 1743/44, and Sarah Hogg, 1747.

18. Ward Ledger, accounts with Thomas Gould, April 11, 1727, David Foster, January 29, 1721/22, and John Low, June 25, 1737; Elisha Hawley Account Book, Ridgefield, Connecticut, 1781–1805, CHS; Jacob Hinsdale Ledger, Harwinton, Connecticut, 1723–1774, account with Elizabeth Hinsdale, April 2, 1728, Sterling Memorial Library, Yale University, New Haven, Connecticut (hereafter Yale); Durand Account Book, account with John Sanford, June 14, 1774.

19. Ward Ledger, 1717–1753; Gaines Account Book, 1725/56–1755; Hinsdale Account Book, 1723–1774; Fussell Account Book, 1738–1748, and account with Isaac Knight Sr., September 27, 1748.

20. Hezekiah Reynolds, *Directions for House and Ship Painting* (1812; reprint, Worcester, Mass.: American Antiquarian Society, 1978), p. 17; Nathaniel Whittock, *The Decorative Painters' and Glaziers' Guide* (London: Isaac Taylor Hinton, 1827), pp. 9–11.

21. Advertisements of James Claypoole, *Pennsylvania Gazette* (Philadelphia), June 14, 1750, and John McElwee, *Federal Gazette* (Philadelphia), May 7, 1800; Kenneth McKenzie Estate Records, New York, 1804, DCM.

22. Durand Account Book; Trent, *Hearts and Crowns*, pp. 48–66; Titus Preston Ledger, Wallingford, Connecticut, 1795–1817, account with Cornelius Cook, July 27, 1804, Yale.

23. Moody Carr Account Book, Rockingham County, New Hampshire, 1800–1815, account with Ezekiel Robinson, October 16, 1800, Old Sturbridge Village, Sturbridge, Massachusetts (hereafter OSV); Estate Records, Nantucket, Massachusetts, 1781–1806, Nantucket County

Probate Court, Nantucket, Massachusetts (hereafter NCPC); James Chestney Bill to Madame Schuyler, New York, May 14, 1793, Schuyler Papers, New York Public Library (hereafter NYPL).

24. Gaines Account Book, account with Francis Sayer, August 1730; Fussell Account Book; "Account of the House Furniture of B H Hathorne," Boston, March 14, 1800, Ward Family Manuscripts, PEM; Mary Pease Estate Records, Nantucket, Massachusetts, 1793, NCPC; William Jones Inventory, Birmingham Township, Chester County, Pennsylvania, 1789, as quoted in Margaret B. Schiffer, *Chester County, Pennsylvania, Inventories, 1684–1850* (Exton, Pa.: Schiffer Publishing, 1974), p. 328.

25. John Avery Sr., Estate Records, Preston, Connecticut, 1794, Genealogical Section, CSL; Hawley Account Book, accounts with Thomas Hawley, December 30, 1789, Ebenezer Hawley, January 5, 1793, and Abraham Lockwood, February 20, 1793; John Wheeler Geer Account Book, Preston, Connecticut, 1776–1781, account with John Tyler, July 20, 1781, CHS.

26. Oliver Moore Account Book, East Granby, Connecticut, 1808–1821, account with Erastus Holcomb, May 15, 1820, CHS; William Barney and Samuel Neil Estate Records, Baltimore, 1774 and 1776, Baltimore County Probate Records, Baltimore, Maryland (hereafter BCPR); Inventories of Thomas Pim, East Caln Township, 1786, and Elijah Funk, Charlestown Township, 1823, Chester County, Pennsylvania, as quoted in Schiffer, *Chester County Inventories*, pp. 325–26, 344–45; Samuel Beal Bill to Capt. Nathaniel Kinsman, Boston, May 5, 1824, Kinsman Manuscripts, PEM; James Chapman Estate Records, Ellington, Connecticut, 1838, Genealogical Section, CSL. Blue paint for chairs, especially common rush-bottom examples, appears to have been reasonably popular in Chester County, Pennsylvania. Recorded, in part, are "Six Blew Cheers" in the home of Philip Taylor (1754), a blue armchair owned by Joseph Struk (1805), and "10 Blew Rush Bottom'd Chairs" in the household of James Batten (1811); Philip Yarnall owned a yellow armchair in 1758 (all as quoted in Schiffer, *Chester County Inventories*, pp. 104–6).

27. William Fifield Ledger, Lyme, New Hampshire, 1810–ca. 1826, recipe for "Orange Colour" [ca. 1820], DCM; W. Jones Inventory; Fussell Account Book, accounts with Joseph Wall, 1747 (orange), John Thomas, 1746 (best dyed), and Patrick Ogilby, 1747 (arch back); Daniel Jones Estate Records, Philadelphia, 1766, Register of Wills, City and County of Philadelphia, Pennsylvania (hereafter RWP).

28. John Brown Advertisement, London, April 1730, as quoted in M. Harris and Sons, *The English Chair* (London: by the authors, 1937), p. 173; John F. Watson, *Annals of Philadelphia and Pennsylvania in the Olden Time*, rev. Willis P. Hazard, 3 vols. (1830; reprint, Philadelphia: Leary, Stuart, 1927), 1: 203n.

29. James Bentham Advertisement, *South Carolina and American General Gazette* (Charleston), March 10, 1775; Aaron Lopez Outward Bound Invoice Book, Newport, Rhode Island, 1767–1768, entries for August 21, September 28, and December 24, 1767, and July 20 and November 20, 1768, Newport Historical Society, Rhode Island (hereafter NHS); Stephen Girard Accounts, Philadelphia, 1786–1787, William Cox Bills to Girard, October 1786, November 10, 1786, and September 5, 1787, and Bills of Lading to Girard for schooner *Carolina* for Haiti, October 14, 1786, brig *Kitty* for Charleston, South Carolina, November 10, 1786, and brig *Kitty* for Cape Français, Haiti, April 28 and July 29, 1787, Girard Papers, American Philosophical Society (microfilm; originals, Girard College), Philadelphia.

30. Samuel Barrett Letter, Boston, April 1, 1779, to Samuel Salisbury at Worcester, Massachusetts, Salisbury Papers, American Antiquarian Society, Worcester, Massachusetts; Ebenezer Stone Advertisement, *Independent Chronicle* (Boston), April 13, 1786; Haven Account Book, account with Isaac Fisher, May 4, 1789; Claypool Advertisement; Obed Faye Paint Recipe, Nantucket, Massachusetts, n.d., sent to Samuel Wing, Sandwich, and Ebenezer Swift Letter, Barnstable, Massachusetts, May 18, 1799, to Samuel Wing, Samuel Wing Papers, OSV.

31. List of household furnishings, New York, June 1772, the property of Elizabeth Rutgers in the care of Anthony Rutgers, White-Beekman Papers, N-YHS; John Curry Advertisement, *South Carolina State Gazette and Timothy and Mason's Daily Advertiser* (Charleston), October 17, 1797, as quoted in Bradford L. Rauschenberg and John Bivins Jr., *The Furniture of Charleston, 1680–1820*, 3 vols. (Winston-Salem, N.C.: Old Salem and the Museum of Early Southern Decorative Arts, 2003), 2: 559; Girard Accounts, William Cox Bill to Stephen Girard, Philadelphia, October 12, 1787, Girard Papers; Joseph Stone Bill to William Arnold, East Greenwich, Rhode Island, January 6, 1795, A. C. and R. W. Greene Collection, Rhode Island Historical Society, Providence (hereafter RIHS); Daniel Rea Jr., Daybook, Boston, 1789–1793, account with Capt. James Magee, May 10, 1791, and Daybook, 1794–1797, accounts with Brad-

dock Loring, May 15, 1794, and David Townsend, March 25, 1795, Baker Library, Harvard University, Cambridge, Massachusetts (hereafter BL).

32. Andrew Huntington Ledger, Norwich, Connecticut, 1780–1794, account with Ebenezer Tracy Sr., March 29, 1788, Leffingwell Inn, Norwich, Connecticut; Amos D. Allen Order (or Memorandum) Book, Windham, Connecticut, 1796–1803, CHS.

33. Allen Order Book, accounts with William Wales, February 6, 1802 (black bottoms), and J. Clark, Esq., April 1800 (mahogany-colored bottoms); Stephen Tracy Ledger, Lisbon Township, New London County, Connecticut (and Plainfield, New Hampshire), 1804–1827, account with Joel Hyde, May 9, 1806, privately owned; John Avery Jr., Account Book, Preston, Connecticut, 1780–1814, accounts with Capt. Elijah Tracy, November 22, 1799, and April 26, November 1, and December 23, 1800, and with Elias Woodward, January 2, 1801, Honeyman Blanchard, January 19, 1801, and Daniel Morgan, Esq., February 24, 1801, CHS.

34. Estate Records, Nantucket, Massachusetts, 1781–1810, NCPC.

35. Ibid., for Oliver Spencer, 1794, Henry Clark, 1801, Jonathan Burnell, 1799, and Peter Coffin, 1800, NCPC.

36. Elias Hasket Derby Estate Records, Salem, Massachusetts, 1800, Essex County Probate Court, Salem, Massachusetts; Johannah Beekman Estate Records, New York, 1821, DCM; Capt. Jonathan Dalton Estate Records, Newburyport, Massachusetts, 1803, Papers of James Locke, PEM; Daniel Danforth Estate Records, Hartford, Connecticut, 1808, Genealogical Section, CSL.

37. William Chappel Estate Records, Lyme, Connecticut, 1826, Genealogical Section, CSL; Rufus Porter, "The Art of Painting," *Scientific American* 1, no. 6 (October 2, 1845): 2; Eneas Munson Estate Records, New Haven, Connecticut, 1826, Genealogical Section, CSL; Thomas Devor Estate Records, Shippensburg, Pennsylvania, 1833, Registry of Probate, Cumberland County, Pennsylvania (photocopy courtesy of Merri Lou Schaumann); Gerrit Wessel Van Schaick Estate Records, Albany, New York, 1816, Van Schaick Papers, Gansevoort-Lansing Collection, NYPL; Gen. George Mason Estate Records, Lexington, Virginia, 1797, Registry of Probate, Rockbridge County, Lexington, Virginia.

38. Ebenezer P. Rose Estate Records, Trenton, New Jersey, 1836, Archives and History Bureau, New Jersey State Library, Trenton; Thomas Sheraton, *The Cabinet Dictionary*, 2 vols. (1803; reprint, New York: Praeger Publishers, 1972), 2: 248. Several inventories of Chester County, Pennsylvania, origin also itemize sage-colored chairs. Records identify Windsors of this color in the household of Nathan Sharpless in 1833, and that construction probably applies to "8 Sage Coulered Chairs" listed in 1809 in the possession of Mary Rogers, as quoted in Schiffer, *Chester County Inventories*, pp. 104, 108.

39. Charles Riley Estate Records, Philadelphia, 1842, RWP; Porter, "Painting" (October 2, 1845), 2; Reynolds, *House and Ship Painting*, pp. 10–11.

40. Samuel Claphamson Advertisement, *Pennsylvania Packet* (Philadelphia), January 8, 1785, as quoted in Alfred Coxe Prime, comp., *The Arts and Crafts in Philadelphia, Maryland, and South Carolina, 1721–1785* (Philadelphia: Walpole Society, 1929), p. 162; William Challen Advertisement, *New-York Gazette and General Advertiser*, February 22, 1797, as quoted in Rita Susswein Gottesman, comp., *The Arts and Crafts in New York, 1777–1799* (New York: New-York Historical Society, 1954), p. 113.

41. Lambert Hitchcock Estate Records, Unionville, Connecticut, 1852, as quoted in John Tarrant Kenney, *The Hitchcock Chair* (New York: Clarkson W. Potter, 1971), p. 326; Sheraton, *Dictionary*, 2: 424.

42. Thomas Howard Advertisement, *Providence Patriot* (Rhode Island), June 29, 1822; David Alling Ledger, Newark, New Jersey, 1815–1818, accounts with painter Moses Lyon, January–March 1816, New Jersey Historical Society, Newark (hereafter NJHS); Nolen and Gridley Advertisement, *Columbian Centinel*, December 12, 1810.

43. John Lambert Estate Records, Philadelphia, 1793, RWP.

44. Allwine Advertisement; Harmon (Herman) Vosburgh Advertisement, *American Citizen* (New York), June 6, 1804, as quoted in Rita Susswein Gottesman, comp., *The Arts and Crafts in New York, 1800–1804* (New York: New-York Historical Society, 1965), p. 273; William Palmer Advertisement, *Longworth's New-York Register and City Directory* (New York: Thomas Longworth, 1818), advertising section.

45. James Chase Account Book, Gilmanton, New Hampshire, 1797–1807, account with Reuben Morgan, April 2, 1804, privately owned, as quoted in Charles S. Parsons, "New Hampshire Notes," Visual Resources Collection, Winterthur Museum Library (hereafter VRC); Allen Order Book, account with Dr. Samuel Lee, August 20, 1800; Samuel Lee Estate Records, Windham, Connecticut, 1815, Genealogical Section, CSL; Solomon Cole Account

Book, Glastonbury, Connecticut, 1794–1809, accounts with John Hall, June 9, 1800, widow Hannah Hale, June 23, 1800, and Capt. Moses Forbes, October 28, 1800, CHS; Estate Records, New York, New York, for Charles Ward Apthorpe (merchant), 1797, Alexander S. Gordon (silversmith), 1803, William Walton (lawyer), 1806, Capt. Joseph Dobell (shipmaster), 1811, Peter Coruth (blacksmith), 1812, Ezra Hounsfield (gentleman), 1813, and Thomas Marston (gentleman), 1814, DCM; Daniel Rea Jr., Daybook, 1772–1800, account with Samuel Bradford, Esq., May 18, 1797, and Daybook, 1789–1802, account with Capt. William Williams, March 10, 1801, BL; Ephraim Evans Advertisement, *Alexandria Advertiser and Commercial Intelligencer* (Virginia), June 12, 1802; Samuel Loomis Estate Records, Saybrook, Connecticut, 1814, Genealogical Section, CSL; Allen Order Book, account with Jonathan M. Young, February 5, 1802.

46. John Dutch Jr., Bill to John Derby, Salem, Massachusetts, April 1, 1802, Derby Family Papers, PEM; Cole Account Book, accounts with Gideon Hale Jr., December 16, 1803, and Stephen Shipman, May 7, 1805; Allen Order Book, account with Col. T. Dyer, June 20, 1799; Anthony Steel Bill of Lading, Philadelphia, December 1, 1801, Society Miscellaneous Collection, HSP; ship *George and Mary* Invoice of Cargo, Providence, Rhode Island, April 7, 1810, as quoted in Joseph K. Ott, "Still More Notes on Rhode Island Cabinetmakers and Allied Craftsmen," *Rhode Island History* 28, no. 4 (November 1969): 121; David Alling Invoice Book, Newark, New Jersey, 1819–1820, account of chairs shipped to Nathan Bolles at New Orleans, March 13, 1819, NJHS.

47. Sheraton, *Dictionary*, 2: 424 (recipes; yellow orpiment is a trisulfide of arsenic), and 1: 126 (canes); Reynolds, *House and Ship Painting*, p. 10; Porter, "Painting" 1 (October 2, 1845), 2. A general discussion of yellow pigments available in the period under study can be found in Richard M. Candee, "Housepaints in America: Their Materials, Manufacture, and Application," part 3, section 5, Yellows, *Color Engineering* (March–April 1967): 38–40.

48. Sheraton, *Dictionary*, 1: 29.

49. Girard Accounts, William Cox Bill to Girard, March 12, 1791, Girard Papers; Luke Houghton Ledger A, Barre, Massachusetts, 1816–1827, accounts with Seth Caldwell, March 30, 1818, Eliphalet How, December 28, 1819, Seth Winston, November 9, 1824, and Constant Brown, November 23, 1825, and Ledger B, 1824–1851, account with Miss Adaline Babbit, November 1, 1832, Barre Historical Society, Massachusetts; Philemon Robbins Account Book, Hartford, Connecticut, 1833–1836, account with Eliab Pratt, December 7, 1836, CHS.

50. Stephen Girard Accounts, Joseph Burden Bill to Stephen Girard, Philadelphia, December 12, 1810, and Invoice of Goods on ship *Rousseau*, December 22, 1810, Girard Papers; Verree and Blair Advertisement, *Charleston Courier* (South Carolina), February 18, 1807; Alling Ledger, account with painter Moses Lyon, April 1815–July 1816.

51. Robbins Account Book, account with Thomas C. Perkins, April 30, 1834; Reynolds, *House and Ship Painting*, pp. 9–10; Elijah Eldredge, "Book of Receipts for Painting and Staining Wood," Willington, Connecticut, ca. 1821–1829, DCM.

52. Ebenezer B. White Estate Records, Danbury, Connecticut, 1817, Genealogical Section, CSL; Thomas Safford Account Book, Canterbury, Connecticut, 1807–1835, accounts with John Safford, April 2, 1811, and Rufus Hubbard, August 1813, CSL; Cheney Daybook, account with William Brown, January 18, 1819; Preston Ledger, account with Polly Scovel, February 2, 1801; David Russell Account Book, Winchester, Virginia, 1796–1806, account with L. Lewis, ca. March 1803, Handley Library, Winchester, Virginia; Riley Estate Records.

53. Alling Ledger, accounts with painter Moses Lyon, August–November 1815 and February–October 1816; Florence M. Montgomery, *Textiles in America, 1650–1870* (New York: W. W. Norton, 1983), s.v. "Nankeen" (p. 308).

54. Elizur Barnes Account Book, Middletown, Connecticut, 1821–1825, account with Arthur W. Magill, April 9, 1822, Middlesex Historical Society, Middletown, Connecticut; Sheraton, *Dictionary*, 2: 423 and 1: 126.

55. Robbins Account Book, accounts with Mr. Churchill, September 7, 1835, and John A. L[?] t, June 2, 1834; William N. Hosley Jr., "Wright, Robbins, and Winship and the Industrialization of the Furniture Industry in Hartford, Connecticut," *Connecticut Antiquarian* 35, no. 2 (December 1983): 12–19; Kenney, *Hitchcock Chair*, p. 305 (store in Hartford).

56. Alexander Patterson Bill to Gerrit Wessel Van Schaick, New York, June 1, 1814, Van Schaick Papers, Gansevoort-Lansing Collection.

57. Alling Invoice Book, accounts of chairs shipped to Nathan Bolles at New Orleans, October 18, 1819, and ca. October 1820; Stephen Girard Accounts, Invoice Book, Philadelphia, 1811–1824, invoice of goods on ship *North America*, July 9, 1816, Girard Papers.

58. Joseph Walker Invoice Book, Philadelphia, 1784, "Remarks on Savannah Trade," Maritime Documents: Cargo Papers, Independence Seaport Museum, Philadelphia.

59. Franklin, "Chronology," in Page Talbott, ed., *Benjamin Franklin: In Search of a Better World* (New Haven, Conn.: Yale University Press, 2005), p. 363; Benjamin Franklin Estate Records, Philadelphia, 1790, RWP; William Cox Bills to Gen. Henry Knox, Philadelphia, July 29, 1794, and May 19, 1795, Papers of Henry Knox, Maine Historical Society, Portland.

60. John Letchworth Bill to William Meredith, Philadelphia, May 1, 1796, as illustrated in Alfred Coxe Prime, comp., *The Arts and Crafts in Philadelphia, Maryland, and South Carolina, 1786–1800* (Topsfield, Mass.: Walpole Society, 1932), opp. p. 240.

61. Bill from unknown craftsman to William Dutilh, Philadelphia, May 1800, as quoted in Carl Drepperd, *Handbook of Antique Chairs* (Garden City, N.Y.: Doubleday, 1948), p. 58; John B. Ackley Bill to Samuel Coates Jr., Philadelphia, November 26, 1800, Reynell and Coates Collection, BL; Girard Accounts, Taylor and King Bill to Stephen Girard, Philadelphia, 1799, Girard Papers.

62. Amos Bradley Ledger, East Haven, Connecticut, 1802–1815, account with Charles Stow, June 1, 1808, DCM; Silas E. Cheney Daybook, Litchfield, Connecticut, 1807–1813, account with Tapping Reeve, August 31, 1810, LHS; Lydia Pinkham Estate Records, Nantucket, Massachusetts, 1810, NCPC; Chase Account Book, account with Daniel Avery, October 8, 1804; John Doggett Daybook, Roxbury, Massachusetts, 1802–1809, account with Capt. Tribbs, August 9, 1806, DCM; Tracy Ledger, account with John Coit, August 23, 1805. For evidence of white Windsor chairs in bedchambers, see Samuel Broome Estate Records, Whitemarsh Township, Montgomery County, Pennsylvania, 1806, DCM; Susan Ward Estate Records, Dorchester, Massachusetts, 1835, DCM; and Barnes Account Book, account with Charles Dyer, September 14, 1822.

63. Alling Ledger, accounts with painter Moses Lyon, August 1816; Nolen and Gridley Advertisement.

64. William Palmer Bill to George Brewerton, New York, April 28, 1803, Brewerton Family Papers, DCM; Whitehead Fish Estate Records, New York, 1819, DCM; William Palmer Bill to Nicholas Low, New York, January 4, 1804, Nicholas Low Collection, LC; Sheraton, *Dictionary*, 2: 201.

65. Sheraton, *Dictionary*, 2: 222, 231–32; Samuel Gridley Bill to Joshua Ward, Boston, February 5, 1810, Ward Family Manuscripts.

66. Alling Ledger, accounts with painter Moses Lyon, 1815–1817; Nolen and Gridley Advertisement; William Challen Advertisement, *Kentucky Gazette and General Advertiser* (Lexington), May 9, 1809; Barnes Account Book, account with Charles Dyer, March 1824.

67. Walker Invoice Book; Allen Order Book, accounts with Jabez Clark, April or May 1801, Rogers Downer, December 9, 1801 (edged), Patty Parish, April or May 1801 (cloth), Jeptha Fitch, May 28, 1802, Jerusha Fitch, July 10, 1802, and Capt. Stephen Payne, December 2, 1799; Stephen Payne Estate Records, Lebanon, Connecticut, 1815, Genealogical Section, CSL.

68. Preston Ledger, accounts with Polly Scovel, January 1801, and Cornelius Cook, August 21, 1805; Titus Preston Ledger, Wallingford, Connecticut, 1811–1842, account with Amos Bristol, October 5, 1814, Yale; Ebenezer Knowlton Estate Records, Boston, 1811, SCPC; Girard Accounts, Invoice Book, account of sales for ship *Montesque*, December 4, 1811, Girard Papers.

69. Lewis Bancel Estate Records, New York, 1828, DCM; Ohio scene described in Alice Cary, *Clovernook, or Recollections of Our Neighborhood in the West* (New York, 1854), as quoted in "Clues and Footnotes," ed. Wendell Garrett, *Antiques* 108, no. 3 (September 1975): 456.

70. Tracy Ledger, accounts with John Coit, August 23, 1805, and John Corning, March 23, 1806; Bradley Ledger, account with Ezariah Bradley, November 13, 1802; Cole Account Book, account with Thomas Stevens, February 4, 1807; Samuel Barrett Estate Records, Concord, Massachusetts, 1825, Concord Free Public Library, Massachusetts (hereafter CFPL).

71. Sheraton, *Dictionary* 2: 424 and 1: 55; Porter, "Painting" (October 2, 1845), 2.

72. *Encyclopaedia, or Dictionary of Arts, Sciences, and Miscellaneous Literature*, 18 vols. (Philadelphia, 1798), 13: 653; Eldredge, "Book of Receipts," p. 3; Broome Estate Records; John Oldham Estate Records, Baltimore, 1835, BCPR; Robbins Account Book, cash sale, October 3, 1834 (with rocking chair), and accounts with H. Grant, December 18, 1834 (with rocking chair), Ogden M. Alden, April 15, 1834, and Colton and Williams, May 15, 1834; Riley Estate Records.

73. James Chestney Bill to Catherine Gansevoort, Albany, New York, June 22, 1815, Papers of Catherine Van Schaick (Gansevoort), Gansevoort-Lansing Collection; Sheraton, *Dictionary*, 2: 425–26.

74. William Palmer Advertisement, *Republican Watch-Tower* (New York), February 27, 1802, as quoted in Gottesman, comp., *Arts and Crafts in New York, 1800–1804*, p. 150; William Palmer Bill to Stephen Arnold, New York, May 24, 1799, Greene Collection; Sheraton, *Dictionary*, 2: 424; William Palmer Bill to Andrew Bell, New York, May 6, 1814, Mercantile Papers-New Jersey, NYPL.

75. Samuel Gridley Advertisement, *Columbian Centinel*, April 22, 1807; Thomas Boynton Ledger, Boston (and Vermont), 1810–1817, account with Isaac Averil, June 21, 1811, Dartmouth College Library, Hanover, New Hampshire (hereafter DCL); Girard Accounts, John Mitchell Bill to Stephen Girard, Philadelphia, December 28, 1809, Girard Papers; Anonymous Advertisements from 146 Broad Street, Charleston, South Carolina, *Charleston Courier*, December 13, 1807, and February 3, 1808; Stibbs and Stout Advertisement, *Liberty Hall and Cincinnati Gazette* (Ohio), September 30, 1816, as illustrated in Jane E. Sikes, *The Furniture Makers of Cincinnati, 1790–1849* (Cincinnati, Ohio: by the author, 1976), p. 230.

76. Haydon and Stewart Bill to James J. Skerrett, Philadelphia, March 17, 1818, Loudoun Papers, HSP; David Alling Account Book, Newark, New Jersey, 1801–1839, accounts with Smith and Morgan and T. and M. Evans, both August 1833, NJHS. Information on access to Columbus, Georgia, from a coastal location is derived from *A Complete Pronouncing Gazetteer or Geographical Dictionary of the World* (Philadelphia: J. B. Lippincott, 1888), s.v. "Appalachicola River," "Chattahoochee River," and "Columbus, Georgia."

77. John Minnick Advertisement, *City Gazette, or the Daily Advertiser* (Charleston, South Carolina), November 13, 1789; Solomon Maxwell Letter to Lawrence Allwine, Christiana, Delaware, August 25, 1794, Business Papers, Hollingsworth Collection, HSP

78. Girard Accounts, Taylor and King Bill to Girard, May 21, 1799, Girard Papers; Bill from unknown craftsman to Dutilh, 1800, as quoted in Drepperd, *Handbook*, p. 58; Steel Bill of Lading; Ackley Bill to Coates, Reynell and Coates Collection.

79. Russell Account Book, account with L. Lewis, ca. March 1803; Sarah B. Mason Estate Records, Prince William City, Virginia, 1815, Prince William County Probate Court, Manassas, Virginia; Rea Daybook (1794–1797), account with Henry Merkell, March 25, 1795; George Davidson Waste Book, Boston, 1793–1799, account with John Hayward, February 2, 1796, OSV; Allen Order Book, account with J. Clark, Esq., April 1800; Estate Records, Nantucket, Massachusetts, for Alexander Gardner, 1803, John Clasby, 1805, Davis Coleman, 1805, John H. Swain, 1808, Peter Folger, 1808, Wicklief Chadwick, 1809, Phillips Fosdick, 1809, George Fitch, 1809, and Uriah Swain, 1810, NCPC.

80. Recipes for imitation mahogany in Rufus Porter, "The Art of Painting," *Scientific American* 1, no. 17 (January 8, 1846): 2, and Reynolds, *House and Ship Painting*, p. 18.

81. *Smith's Art of House Painting*, rev. William Butcher (London: Richard Holmes Laurie, 1821), p. 27; A. Otis, "Every Man His Own Painter: A Collection of Receipts," n.p., 1836, s.v. "Chocolate," DCM.

82. Hopkins and Charles Advertisement, *City Gazette and Daily Advertiser* (Charleston, South Carolina), March 7, 1798; Isaac A. Kip Estate Records, New York, 1805, DCM; Francis Barrett Estate Records, Concord, Massachusetts, 1819, CFPL.

83. Cox Bill to Knox, May 19, 1795, Papers of Henry Knox; Sheraton, *Dictionary*, 1: 102–3.

84. Boynton Ledger, accounts with Bryant and Loud, June 29, 1811, and Rufus Norton, October 25, 1814; Alling Ledger, accounts with painter Moses Lyon, April 1815–July 1816; Houghton Ledger (1816–1827), accounts with Miss Candice Allen, November 3, 1817, and Seth Caldwell, March 30, 1818; John H. Piatt Account Book, Cincinnati, Ohio, dates unknown, order to Roll and Deeds for B. V. Hunt, October 16, 1818, as illustrated in Sikes, *Furniture Makers of Cincinnati*, p. 206; Robbins Account Book, accounts with Josiah Dewey, September 16, 1834, and an anonymous cash customer, April 7, 1835; Oldham Estate Records.

85. Joseph Jones Bill for "drab stone Colour" chairs to Benjamin Sharpless, West Chester, Pennsylvania, May 13, 1842, as quoted in Margaret Berwind Schiffer, *Furniture and Its Makers of Chester County, Pennsylvania* (Philadelphia: University of Pennsylvania Press, 1966), p. 134; recipes for "drab, or light stone colour" and "stone brown" in Porter, "Painting" (October 2, 1845), 2; recipes for "Light Stone Color" and "Dark Stone Color" in Reynolds, *House and Ship Painting*, pp. 15, 17; recipe for "Stone Colour" in Fifield Ledger, n.d.; recipe for "stone yellow" in Eldredge, "Book of Receipts," n.d.; recipe for "Portland-Stone Colour" in *Smith's Art of House Painting*, p. 27.

86. Lambert Estate Records; Jones Bill to Sharpless, as quoted in Schiffer, *Furniture and Its Makers of Chester County*, p. 134.

87. Alling Ledger, accounts with painter Moses Lyon, April–September 1815, January–March and October 1816; 1830s chair prices in David Alling Daybook, Newark, New Jersey, 1836–1854, NJHS; Robbins Account Book, general accounts for 1834 and 1835 and account with Sage and Birge, March 26, 1835, for secondhand chairs.

88. Peter Peirce Estate Records, Templeton, Massachusetts, 1829–1836, Worcester County Probate Court, Worcester, Massachusetts; Houghton Ledger B (1824–1851), account with Earl Rice, August 27, 1830; Robbins Account Book, account with R. Bidwell, December 21, 1835; Riley Estate Records; Talcott Daybook, accounts with Edwin Cadwell, December 25, 1840, and Sylvester Taylor, January 1, 1841.

89. Robbins Account Book, accounts with F. H. Huntington, July 25, 1835 (rocking chair), Curtis Elmer, March 7, 1836 (5-rod Windsors), Joseph Langdon, May 26, 1835 (dressing table), Thomas C. Perkins, September 12, 1835 (bureau and dressing glass), and Mrs. B. Fowler, March 3, 1836 (washstand). Tea-colored chairs of both Windsor and fancy construction are named in Chester County, Pennsylvania, estate records for 1826, as quoted in Schiffer, *Chester County Inventories*, pp. 105, 108.

90. Rose Estate Records; Riley Estate Records; Otis, "Collection of Receipts," p. 1. "Fawn colour" chairs are recorded in a Chester County, Pennsylvania, inventory of 1847, as quoted in Schiffer, *Chester County Inventories*, p. 104.

91. Alling Ledger, accounts with painter Moses Lyon, 1815–1817, and Invoice Book, Southern accounts, 1819–1820.

92. Ship *George and Mary* Invoice of Cargo in Ott, "Still More Notes," p. 121; Stephen Girard Accounts, Invoice Book, Philadelphia, 1802–1811, invoice of goods on ship *Montesque*, December 13, 1810, and Invoice Book (1811–1824), account of sales for ship *Montesque*, December 4, 1811, Girard Papers.

93. Congdon and Tracy Advertisement, *Norwich Courier* (Connecticut), October 27, 1830; Jones Bill to Sharpless, as quoted in Schiffer, *Furniture and Its Makers of Chester County*, p. 134; Robbins Account Book, accounts with Walter Clap, May 23, 1834, and Deming and Bulkley, November 20, 1835; Isaac Wright Account Book, Hartford, Connecticut, 1834–1837, account with Charles Goodwin for "Hitchcock drab chairs," February 23, 1834, CSL.

94. Benjamin Branson Estate Records, New York, 1835, DCM; Riley Estate Records; Robbins Account Book, accounts with Dr. Beresford, October 3, 1835 (dark-colored and tea-colored chairs), Edward Merrium, January 17, 1835 (dark-colored chairs), Sheldon and Colton, June 14, 1834 (drab-colored chairs), Lambert Hitchcock, July 29, 1834 (tea-colored chairs), and Hitchcock, Alford and Co., November 17, 1835 (gilt tea-colored chairs).

95. Robert Casey Estate Records, Baltimore County, Maryland, 1796, BCPR.

96. Burnell Estate Records; Allen Order Book, account with Charles Taintor, October 25, 1798.

97. Chase Account Book, accounts with Asa D. Ager, September 1, 1811, and Stephen Perley, April 2 and September 4, 1811 (including great chair); William Hemphill Estate Records, West Chester, Pennsylvania, 1817, as quoted in Schiffer, *Chester County Inventories*, p. 338; Bancel Estate Records.

98. Alling Invoice Book, account with Nathan Bolles, March 1820. Samuel Gridley of Boston advertised "Coclico" chairs, probably imported from New York, in the *Columbian Centinel*, April 22, 1807. Ship *George and Mary*, in Ott, "Still More Notes," p. 121; Stibbs and Stout Advertisement.

99. Reynolds, *House and Ship Painting*, p. 17; Whittock, *Guide*, pp. 9–10; Eldredge, "Book of Receipts," p. 4; Anonymous Collection of Receipts for coating wooden surfaces, n.p., ca. 1800, DCM; Boynton Ledger, account with James Stimson, 1812.

100. Gridley Advertisement; Nolen and Gridley Advertisement; Patterson and Dennis Advertisement, *New-York Evening Post*, January 2, 1810; Challen Advertisement; Girard Accounts, Invoice Book (1802–1811), invoice of goods on ship *Voltaire*, December 28, 1809.

101. Alling Invoice Book, account with Nathan Bolles, March 1819; Porter, "Painting" (October 2, 1845), 2; Haydon and Stewart Bill to Skerrett, Loudoun Papers; Devor Estate Records; Waldo Tucker, *The Mechanic's Assistant* (Windsor, Vt., 1837), p. 19; John Smith, *The Art of Painting in Oyl*, 5th ed. (London, 1723), as quoted in Candee, "Housepaints in America," 26; Nolen and Gridley Advertisement. Both rose- and flesh-colored chairs stood in the Chester County, Pennsylvania, home of James Hawthorne at his death in 1827, as quoted in Schiffer, *Chester County Inventories*, pp. 104, 108.

102. Maj. James Swan Auction Notice, *Massachusetts Centinel* (Boston), April 23, 1785; Ebenezer Stone Advertisement, *Independent Chronicle* (Boston), April 13, 1786; Hale Hilton

Estate Records, Beverly, Massachusetts, 1802, Nathan Dane Papers, Massachusetts Historical Society, Boston (hereafter MHS); Allen Order Book, account with Mrs. Polly Lathrop, April 16, 1800.

103. Joseph Barrell Letter Book, Boston, 1791–1797, letter to John Atkinson, New York, March 1, 1795, MHS; Chase Account Book, anonymous account, June 1, 1797.

104. Allen Order Book, accounts with Col. Z. Swift, May 4, 1798, and Capt. R. Ripley, June 14, 1799; Barnes Account Book, account with John Ledge, June 1822; Russell Account Book, account with L. Lewis.

105. David Stowell Account Book, Worcester, Massachusetts, 1794–1802, account with Amasa Holden, February 16, 1801, DCM; Oliver Wight Bill to Josiah Walker, Sturbridge, Massachusetts, November 2, 1804, Walker Family Collection, OSV; Cheney Daybook (1807–1813), account with Stephen Mars, December 12, 1809.

106. Whittock, *Guide*, p. 11; Eldredge, "Book of Receipts," p. 5; Reynolds, *House and Ship Painting*, p. 16 (recipe); Tucker, *Mechanic's Assistant*, p. 100.

107. William Challen Bill to Chancellor Robert R. Livingston, New York, April 26, 1798, Livingston Papers; "Japanning," in Bigelow, *Useful Arts*, 1: 175; "Japaning," in Robert D. Mussey Jr., *The First American Furniture Finisher's Manual* (*The Cabinet-Maker's Guide*, 1827; reprint, New York: Dover Publications, 1987), p. xxv.

108. Daniel Eachus Inventory, West Goshen, Chester County, Pennsylvania, 1823, as quoted in Schiffer, *Chester County Inventories*, p. 105; James Mitchell Bill to James J. Skerrett, Philadelphia, December 19, 1817, Loudoun Papers; William Cunningham Bill to Mr. A. Broadwell, Wheeling, (West) Virginia, March 23, 1839, facsimile in W. Graham Arader III, *Newsletter*, New York, October 1989; *Lippencott's Gazetteer*, s.v. "Cynthiana," "Licking River," and "Kentucky."

109. Percy Macquoid and Ralph Edwards, *The Dictionary of English Furniture*, 2nd rev. ed. Ralph Edwards, 3 vols. (1924–1927; reprint, Woodbridge, Eng.: Barra Books, 1983), 2: 250; David Bates Advertisement, *Daily National Intelligencer* (Washington, D.C.), March 13, 1821, as quoted in Anne Castrodale Golovin, "Cabinetmakers and Chairmakers of Washington, D.C., 1791–1840," *Antiques* 107, no. 5 (May 1975): 906; Porter, "Painting" (January 8, 1846), 2.

110. Alling Invoice Book, account with Nathan Bolles, ca. October 1820.

111. Stephen Taylor Bill to Jason Williams, Providence, Rhode Island, October 3, 1833, as quoted in Joseph K. Ott, "Recent Discoveries among Rhode Island Cabinetmakers and Their Work," *Rhode Island History* 28, no. 1 (February 1969): 23; Robbins Account Book, account with Sullivan Hill, December 25, 1835.

112. Houghton Ledger B (1824–1851), accounts with David West, February 1838–February 1839, and Daniel Witt, February 1838, and Ledger A (1816–1827), account with Joseph Osgood Jr., October 1838; John Hayward, *The New England Gazetteer* (Boston: John Hayward, 1839), s.v. "Worcester County, Mass."

113. Riley Estate Records.

114. Haydon and Stewart Bills to Levi Hollingsworth, Philadelphia, April 22 and June 27, 1812, Harrold Gillingham Collection, HSP; Alling Invoice Book, accounts with Nathan Bolles, March and October 1819.

115. Peirce Estate Records; Parrott and Hubbel Insolvency Records, Bridgeport, Connecticut, 1835, Genealogical Section, CSL.

116. David Alling Ledger, Newark, New Jersey, 1803–1853, account with John Taylor, May 29, 1837, NJHS, and Alling Daybook, account with Anthony Dye, Esq., August 23, 1836; Henry Barnard Bill to Albert C. Greene, Esq., Providence, Rhode Island, March 22, 1834, Greene Collection.

117. Porter, "Painting" (January 8, 1846), 2; Whittock, *Guide*, pp. 20, 40, 43.

118. Esther Stevens Brazer, *Early American Decoration* (Springfield, Mass.: Pond-Ekberg, 1947), pp. 128–29; Mussey, *Furniture Finisher's Manual*, "To imitate black Rose-wood," pp. 45–46; Sheraton, *Dictionary*, 1: 16, pl. 3; Adam Bowett, "Furniture Woods in London and Provincial Furniture, 1700–1800," in *Regional Furniture* (England), 22 (2008): 102; Whittock, *Guide*, p. 40; William G. Beesley Daybook, Salem, New Jersey, 1828–1836, accounts with Elijah Ware for "streaking and ornamenting," August 15, 1834, and "streaking and shading," November 17, 1834, Salem County Historical Society, New Jersey.

119. Bates and Johnson Advertisement, *The Albany Directory* (Albany, N.Y.: E. and E. Hosford, 1819), n.p.; Alling Invoice Book, accounts with Nathan Bolles, October 1819 and March and ca. October 1820; Riley Estate Records.

120. Sacket and Branch Advertisement, *Providence Patriot and Columbian Phenix* (Rhode Island), November 11, 1829; D. A. Shepard Advertisement, *Cleveland Herald* (Ohio), Septem-

ber 3, 1845, as quoted in Jane Sikes Hageman and Edward M. Hageman, *Ohio Furniture Makers*, 2 vols. (Cincinnati, Ohio: by the authors, 1989), 2: 192; Abraham D. Montayne Advertisement, New York, source unknown, 1825 (photocopy, courtesy of Michael Dunbar); Sass and Gready Advertisement, *City Gazette and Commercial Daily Advertiser* (Charleston, South Carolina), January 21, 1818, as quoted in Rauschenberg and Bivins, *Furniture of Charleston*, 3: 1212.

121. Girard Accounts, Invoice Book (1811–1824), invoice of goods on ship *North America*, July 9, 1816, Girard Papers; Alling Invoice Book, accounts with Nathan Bolles, March and October 1819 and ca. October 1820.

122. Alling Daybook, account with Daniel D. Benjamin, November 27, 1839; Sheraton, *Dictionary*, 2: 422–23; Abraham McDonough Estate Records, Philadelphia, 1852, DCM.

123. Frederick Fox Advertisement, *Berks and Schuylkill Journal* (Reading, Pennsylvania), April 26, 1845; McDonough Estate Records; Tucker, *Mechanic's Assistant*, pp. 156–57; Whittock, *Guide*, pp. 34–35; *Smith's Art of House Painting*, p. 28; Reynolds, *House and Ship Painting*, pp. 18–19.

124. Sheraton, *Dictionary*, 2: 314; Anthony A. P. Steumpfig, "William Haydon and William H. Stewart: Fancy-Chair Makers in Philadelphia," *Antiques* 104, no. 3 (September 1973): 452–57; Alling Ledger (1815–1818), accounts with painter Moses Lyon, 1815–1816.

125. Whittock, *Guide*, pp. 21, 38; Sheraton, *Dictionary*, 2: 315.

126. William Haydon Advertisement, *United States Gazette* (Philadelphia), June 20, 1815; Broome Estate Records; Jacob Chandler Estate Records, Nantucket, Massachusetts, 1808, NCPC; Porter, "Painting" (January 8, 1846), 2; Whittock, *Guide*, p. 77.

127. Samuel Claphamson Advertisement, *Pennsylvania Packet*, January 8, 1785, as quoted in Prime, comp., *Arts and Crafts in Philadelphia, 1721–1785*, p. 162; Rea Daybook (1789–1793), accounts with Andrew Craigie, Esq., August 27, 1793, and Henry Merkell, March 25, 1795; Anonymous Advertisement, *Columbian Centinel*, January 29, 1812.

128. James C. Helme, "Book of Prices for Making Cabinet & Chair furnature," Plymouth, Luzerne County, Pennsylvania, August 20, 1838, DCM.

129. James Gere Ledger, account with George Harvey, September 30, 1831; Joel Brown Advertisement, *North Carolina Star* (Raleigh), March 29, 1822, as quoted in James H. Craig, *The Arts and Crafts in North Carolina, 1699–1840* (Winston-Salem, N.C.: Museum of Early Southern Decorative Arts, 1965), p. 202; Dockum and Brown Advertisement, *New-Hampshire Gazette*, December 11, 1827.

130. Rea Daybook (1772–1800), account with Samuel Bradford, Esq., May 18, 1797; Bradley Ledger, account with Charles Stow, October 8, 1807.

131. Cole Account Book, account with Pardon Brown, July 19, 1804; Allen Order Book, accounts with Shubael Abbe, August 15, 1801, and April 10, 1802, Charles Taintor, October 25, 1798, Col. T. Dyer, June 20, 1799, and Rogers Downer, December 10, 1801; Chase Account Book (1797–1807), account with Stephen Parley, November 4, 1801, and James Chase Account Book, Gilmanton, New Hampshire, 1807–1812, account with Capt. Elisha Smith, March 29, 1810, privately owned, as quoted in Charles S. Parsons, "New Hampshire Notes," VRC; Evans Advertisement.

132. Rea Daybook (1789–1802), account with Capt. William Williams, March 10, 1801; Preston Ledger (1795–1817), account with Polly Scovel, January 1801, and Preston Ledger (1811–1842), account with George Wilnut, February 1820. Fancy seating furniture in the classical mode with striped and banded ornament, dating between 1800 and 1810, is illustrated in Lance Humphries, "Provenance, Patronage, and Perception: The Morris Suite of Baltimore Painted Furniture," in *American Furniture 2003*, ed. Luke Beckerdite (Hanover, N.H.: University Press of New England for the Chipstone Foundation, 2003), pp. 138–212, and Beatrice B. Garvan, *Federal Philadelphia: The Athens of the Western World* (Philadelphia: Philadelphia Museum of Art, 1987), pp. 90–93. Cheney Daybook (1807–1813), account with Tapping Reeve, August 31, 1810; Holcomb Account Book, account with Simon Smith, April [1810]; Boynton Ledger, account with John Patterson, December 1814; Alling Ledger (1815–1818), account with painter Moses Lyon, December 27, 1816.

133. Daniel Dewey Bill to Daniel Wadsworth, Esq., Hartford, Connecticut, August 30, 1831, Daniel Wadsworth Papers, CHS; Devor Estate Records; Alling Daybook, account with Thomas Peney, March 1, 1837.

134. Preston Ledger (1795–1817), account with Cornelius Cook, July 27, 1804; Tracy Ledger, accounts with Joel Hyde, May 9, 1806, and William Lord, April 1, 1809; Nathaniel F. Martin Account Book, Windham, Connecticut, ca. 1784–1833, account with Philip Pearl, February 1806, CHS; Oliver Avery Account Book, North Stonington, Connecticut, 1789–1813, account

with Capt. Stephen Avery, August 1811, DCM; Silas E. Cheney Daybook, Litchfield, Connecticut, 1802–1807, account with Elisha Mason, June 1806, LHS.

135. Daniel Rea Jr., Ledger, Boston, 1773–1794, account with Paul Revere, August 23, 1786, BL.

136. Advertisements of John Dewitt, *New-York Weekly Chronicle*, June 18, 1795, and Walter MacBride, *Weekly Museum* (New York), July 18, 1795, both as quoted in Gottesman, comp., *Arts and Crafts in New York, 1777–1779*, pp. 115, 123–24; William Haydon Advertisement, *Gazette of the United States* (Philadelphia), January 9, 1797, as quoted in Prime, comp., *Arts and Crafts in Philadelphia, 1786–1800*, p. 14; Vosburgh and Childs Advertisement; John and Hugh Finlay Advertisements, *Federal Gazette and Baltimore Daily Advertiser*, January 31, 1803, and November 8, 1805, as quoted in William Voss Elder III, *Baltimore Painted Furniture, 1800–1840* (Baltimore: Baltimore Museum of Art, 1972), p. 11; May and Renshaw Advertisement, *Scioto Gazette and Fredonian Advertiser* (Chillicothe, Ohio), February 29, 1816.

137. Alling Ledger (1815–1818), accounts with painter Moses Lyon, 1815–1817, and Invoice Book, account of chairs shipped to Nathen Bolles at New Orleans, October 18, 1819; Nolen and Gridley Advertisement; Robbins Account Book, account with Levi J. Waters, April 3, 1834; Devor Estate Records.

138. Nolen and Gridley Advertisement; Devor Estate Records; Alling Account Book, account with J. W. Meeks and Co., September 18, 1833.

139. Alling Ledger (1815–1818), account with painter Moses Lyon, September 1817; Boynton Ledger, account with John Patterson, March 24, 1815; Nolen and Gridley Advertisement.

140. Alling Ledger (1815–1818), account with painter Moses Lyon, November 25, 1815.

141. Talcott Daybook, account with Sylvester Taylor Jr., March 11, 1843, a Lafayette banquet chair is illustrated in Elder, *Baltimore Painted Furniture*, p. 69.

142. Nolen and Gridley Advertisement; Sheraton, *Dictionary*, 2: 102.

143. Samuel J. Tuck Advertisements, *Columbian Centinel*, July 12, 1800, October 15, 1803, and May 25, 1808; Henry Beck Advertisement, *New-Hampshire Gazette*, September 20, 1808; Chapman and Merritt Advertisement, *Connecticut Herald* (New Haven), April 18, 1809; Challen Advertisement.

144. Girard Accounts, Invoice Book (1802–1811), invoice of goods on ship *Montesque*, December 13, 1810, and Invoice Book (1811–1824), invoice of goods on ship *North America*, July 9, 1816; Alling Ledger (1815–1818), accounts with painter Moses Lyon, 1815–1817.

145. Rufus E. Shapley Advertisement, *American Volunteer* (Carlisle, Pennsylvania), September 16, 1819, as illustrated in Merri Lou Schaumann, *Plank Bottom Chairs and Chairmakers: South Central Pennsylvania, 1800–1880* (Carlisle, Pa.: Cumberland County Historical Society, 2009), p. 32. For the Humberston Skipwith table and explanation, see Gregory R. Weidman, "The Furniture of Classical Maryland, 1815–1845," in *Classical Maryland, 1815–1845* (Baltimore: Maryland Historical Society, 1993), fig. 121, pp. 103–5, and Cynthia V. A. Schaffner and Susan Klein, *American Painted Furniture, 1790–1880* (New York: Clarkson Potter, 1997), pp. 69–70.

146. Edward Needles Advertisement, *Baltimore Patriot and Mercantile Advertiser*, January 11, 1830; Robbins Account Book, account with Charles Bartlett, April 29, 1835; Wright Account Book, credit for Lambert Hitchcock, February 12, 1834; Alling Daybook, account with David B. Crockett, August 19, 1839; Jones Bill to Benjamin Sharpless; Septimus Claypoole Bill to Jerome N. Bonaparte, president, Baltimore Commercial Exchange Co., March 10, 1843, Baltimore Exchange Hotel Collection, Maryland Historical Society, Baltimore.

147. Wright Account Book, credit for Lambert Hitchcock, February 2, 1834; Robbins Account Book, account with Mrs. Williams, September 10, 1835; Rea Daybook (1794–1797), account with Andrew Craigie, Esq., May 12, 1794.

148. William Palmer Bill to Arnold, May 24, 1799, Greene Collection; Robert Cowan Bill to Joshua Ward, October 11, 1803, Ward Family Manuscripts; Broome Estate Records; Pinkham Estate Records.

149. William Palmer Bill to Mr. Cox, New York, June 15, 1805, White-Beekman Papers; Palmer Bill to Low, January 4, 1804, Low Collection; Palmer Advertisement; Palmer Bill to Arnold, May 24, 1799, Greene Collection; Palmer Bill to Bell, May 6, 1814, Mercantile Papers; David Alling, Receipt Book, Newark, New Jersey, 1803–1824, receipts from William Palmer, June 25 and July 12, 1803, NJHS; Charles Cluss Bill to William Arnold, New York, 1808, as quoted in Ott, "Recent Discoveries," p. 15; Patterson Bill to Van Schaick, Gansevoort-Lansing Collection; Charleston Newspaper Notices, *Charleston Courier*, December 13, 1807, and February 3, 1808; A. Clark advertisement, *Raleigh Minerva* (North Carolina), April 16, 1819; Nolen and Gridley Advertisement.

150. Charleston Newspaper Notices, *Charleston Courier*, January 16 and December 13, 1807, and February 3, 1808; John Stille Jr., Shipping Manifest listing chairs consigned to John Derby, Philadelphia, December 10, 1801, Derby Family Papers; William H. Stewart Bill to Richard Bland Lee via Zaccheus Collins, Philadelphia, May 13, 1815, Daniel Parker Papers, HSP; Haydon and Stewart Bill to Skerrett, March 17, 1818, and Mitchell Bill to Skerrett, December 19, 1817, Loudoun Papers.

151. Girard Accounts, Mitchell Bill to Girard, December 28, 1809, and Invoice Book (1802–1811), invoice of goods on ship *Montesque*, December 13, 1810, and Invoice Book (1811–1824), account of sales for ship *Montesque*, December 4, 1811, and invoice of goods on ship *North America*, July 9, 1816.

152. Ship *George and Mary* Invoice of Cargo.

153. Samuel G. Bodge Advertisement, *Providence Patriot and Columbian Phenix*, October 20, 1827; Levi Stillman Account Book, New Haven, Connecticut, 1815–1834, invoice of furniture shipped to Lima, Peru, on brig *Rio*, September 20, 1826, Yale; Thomas Boynton Ledger, Windsor, Vermont, 1817–1847, account with Robert Davis, June 7, 1818, DCL.

154. Alling Invoice Book, accounts of chairs shipped to Nathen Bolles, 1819–1820.

155. Daniel Rea Jr., Daybook (1794–1797), Boston, account with Andrew Craigie, Esq., May 12, 1794; William Palmer Advertisement, New York, February 27, 1802; John Mitchell Bill to Stephen Girard, Philadelphia, December 28, 1809; John and Hugh Finlay Advertisement, Baltimore, January 31, 1803; Thomas Boynton Ledger (1810–1817), Vermont, account with Isaac Averil, June 21, 1811; George Kearns Advertisement, *Martinsburgh Gazette* ([West] Virginia), April 5, 1811; Silas Cooper Advertisement, *Columbian Museum and Savannah Advertiser* (Savannah, Georgia), December 18, 1801; William Challen Advertisement, Kentucky, May 9, 1809; Sheraton, *Dictionary*, 2: 231–32; Rufus Porter, "The Art of Painting," *Scientific American* 1, no. 9 (November 13, 1845): 2.

156. Porter, "Painting" (November 13, 1845), 2; Boynton Ledger (1810–1817), credit for John Patterson, March 24, 1815; Sheraton, *Dictionary*, 2: 231–32; James Gere Ledger, Groton, Connecticut, 1809–1829, credit for Isaac Treby, March 12, 1827, CSL.

157. Sheraton, *Dictionary*, 2: 422–23; Beesley Daybook, account with Henry Mason, August 19, 1831.

158. Sheraton, *Dictionary*, 2: 422–23; Robbins Account Book, account with Judge Bruce, November 1835; Barnes Account Book, accounts with Charles Dyer, March 1824, and Arthur W. Magill, April 9, 1822; Beesley Daybook, account with William N. Jeffers, April 13, 1832.

159. Hounsfield Estate Records; Fish Estate Records; Jacob Sanderson in account with Richard Austin, Salem, Massachusetts, April 1805–May 1806, item recorded April 12, 1805, Papers of Elijah Sanderson, PEM.

160. Stephanus Knight Account Book, Enfield, Connecticut, 1795–1809, account with Zebulon Pease, January 12, 1808, CHS; Chappel Estate Records; Spenser Estate Records.

161. Allen Order Book, accounts with Mr. Story, September 18, 1800 (yellow backs), Ezra Chapman, September 15, 1800 (green backs), John Lathrop, April 16, 1800 (blue backs), and Mr. N. Simons, May 28, 1801 (green with black bottoms); Christian and Paxton Advertisement, *American Citizen* (New York), August 11, 1804; Preston Ledger (1795–1817), account with Polly Scovel, February 2, 1801; Russell Account book, account with L. Lewis, March 1803.

162. Fussell Account Book, accounts with Richard Tyson 1740/41, Joseph Hart, 1744, and Sarah Hogg, 1747; William Barker Account Book, Providence, Rhode Island, 1750–1772, account with Ephraim Bowen, February 1774, RIHS; Allen Order Book, account with Miss Chandler, November 1796.

163. Riley Estate Records; Robbins Account Book, accounts with E. Hooker, Esq., July 17, 1834, and William C. Andrews, March 22, 1834 (maple top); Beesley Daybook, account with Elijah Ware, August 5, 1836; Henry F. Dewey Account Book, Bennington, Vermont, 1837–1864, account with D. Burton, 1842, Shelburne Museum, Shelburne, Vermont; Charles C. Robinson Daybook, Philadelphia, 1809–1825, account with Launcelot Jenkins, November 25, 1815, HSP.

164. Robbins Account Book, account with Norman Hubbard, March 25, 1834; Devor Estate Records; Talcott Daybook, credit for Sylvester Taylor Jr., May 29, 1843.

165. Boynton Ledger (1810–1817), credit for John Parker, November 17, 1815, and Ledger (1817–1847), credit with Franklin Howe, 1836; Beesley Daybook, account with Joseph E. Brown, September 12, 1831; Robbins Account Book, credit for Sullivan Hill, March 6, 1835.

166. Robbins Account Book, accounts with E. Hooker, Esq., July 17, 1834, and Adam Miner, February 19, 1835, and credit for Horace Lee, September 4, 1835 (green caned rocker); Jacob

Sanderson in account with Richard Austin, 1805–1806, item recorded February 1806, Sanderson Papers; Alling Invoice Book, account of chairs shipped to Nathen Bolles, ca. October 1820, and Alling Daybook, account with Frederick T. Frelinghuysen Jr., Esq., May 25, 1840.

167. Fussell Account Book, accounts with Abraham Griffith, 1742, and Joseph Addis, 1747; Alling Ledger (1815–1818), account with painter Moses Lyon, February 13, 1816, and Alling Ledger (1803–1853), account with Fitch Smith, April 1, 1840; David Alling Estate Records, Newark, New Jersey, 1855, Archives and History Bureau, New Jersey State Library, Newark.

168. For further information on nurse and sewing chairs, see Nancy Goyne Evans, *American Windsor Furniture: Specialized Forms* (New York: Hudson Hills Press, 1997), pp. 55–57.

169. Riley Estate Records; Girard Accounts, Burden Bill to Girard, December 12, 1810, and Invoice Book (1802–1811), invoice of goods on ship *Rousseau*, December 22, 1810, Girard Papers; Alling Ledger (1815–1818), account with painter Moses Lyon, September 27, 1817.

170. Hopkins and Charles Advertisement; Challen Advertisement; Riley Estate Records.

171. Charleston Newspaper Notices, January 16 and December 13, 1807, and February 3, 1808; Girard Invoice Book (1802–1811), invoice of goods on ship *Rousseau*, December 22, 1810, Girard Papers; Challen Advertisement, May 9, 1809; Lambert Estate Records; Cox Bill to Knox, May 19, 1795, Knox Papers.

172. Alling Ledger (1815–1818), account with painter Moses Lyon, February 3, 1817; Sass and Gready Advertisement; Riley Estate Records.

173. Cheney Daybook (1813–1821), account with Oliver Wolcott, September 16, 1815; richly ornamented settees in Samuel Gridley Advertisement, April 22, 1807; Challen Advertisement; Kearns Advertisement; Alling Ledger (1815–1818), account with painter Moses Lyon, November 1815–July 1817 (bronzing) and 1816 (tipping); Barnes Account Book, account with Jonathan Barnes, August 23, 1822.

174. Alling Ledger (1815–1818), account with painter Moses Lyon, January 14, 1817 (fruit pattern); Finlay Advertisement, November 8, 1805; Lambert Estate Records; Cox Bill to Gen. Henry Knox, May 19, 1795, Knox Papers; Bill from unknown craftsman to Dutilh; Alling Ledger (1815–1818), accounts with painter Moses Lyon, March 19, 1816 (organ spindles), June 30, 1817 (slat backs), November 25, 1818 (double-cross backs), March 23, 1816, and January 14, 1817 (ball backs); Riley Estate Records.

175. Henry Wilder Miller Account Book, Worcester, Massachusetts, 1827–1831, accounts with W. and S. Barber, June 2, 1827, David Partridge, May 26, 1817, Scott and Smith, June 16, 1827 (painting settee), Warren Bowen, July 28, 1828 (ornamenting settee), and William Stowell, September 5, 1827 (purchase of a settee), Worcester Historical Museum, Massachusetts; Cheney Daybook (1813–1821), account with Oliver Wolcott, September 16, 1815.

176. Rea Daybook (1789–1802), account with William Bradford, October 26, 1800; Currier Account Book, account with Peter Jenness, November 1834.

177. William Beekman Estate Records, New York, 1795, DCM; William Gray Ledger, Salem, Massachusetts, 1774–1814, account with Samuel C. Ward, December 26, 1793, PEM; Alling Daybook, account with Thomas V. Johnson, August 31, 1839; Riley Estate Records; Bancel Estate Records; Chauncey Strong Daybook, Laurens, New York, 1852–1869, account with George and Edgar Holcomb, November 8, 1852, New York State Historical Association, Cooperstown.

178. Josiah P. Wilder Daybook and Ledger, New Ipswich, New Hampshire, 1837–1861, accounts with Miss Elisa Bachelder, November 22, 1837, and Maria Ryan, May 16, 1838, private collection (transcript, VRC). Further data on women in the furniture labor force can be found in Nancy Goyne Evans, *Windsor-Chair Making in America: From Craft Shop to Consumer* (Hanover, N.H.: University Press of New England, 2006), p. 16.

179. Alling Daybook (1836–1854), account with Hay and Agens, April 22, 1837, and Ledger (1803–1853), accounts with Jonas Agens, June 8, 1839, and C. W. Badger, July 19, 1838; Miller Account Book, account with anonymous purchaser, March 26, 1829.

180. Boynton Ledger (1810–1817), account with Samuel Barrett, October 16, 1816, and Ledger (1817–1847), account with William Savage, January 16, 1826; Miller Account Book, account with Joseph T. Turner, August 1, 1827; Stephen Girard Accounts, Joseph Burden Bill to Stephen Girard, Philadelphia, July 28, 1827, Girard Papers (painting music stool).

181. Fussell Account Book, accounts with Benjamin Franklin, 1744, John Smith, 1745 (black chair), and John Rush, 1748/49 (brown chairs); James Beekman Account Book of Personal Affairs, New York, 1761–1796, account entry dated October 27, 1762, White-Beekman Papers; Dinah Jenkins Estate Records, Nantucket, Massachusetts, 1788, NCPC; Alling Invoice Book, account of chairs shipped to Nathan Bolles at New Orleans, October 18, 1819, and Ledger

(1803–1853), accounts with Fitch Smith, April 1, 1840 (tipping), and William Garthwaite, March 25, 1841 (striping); Boynton Ledger (1810–1817), account with Stephen Child, July 24, 1811.

182. William Barker Account Book, Providence, Rhode Island, 1753–1766, account with John Power, September 2, 1753, RIHS; Chase Account Book (1797–1812), anonymous purchase, September 12, 1799; Daniel and Samuel Proud Ledger, Providence, Rhode Island, 1782–1825, accounts with Amos Atwell, December 8, 1803, and William Colegrow, April 14, 1807, RIHS; Robbins Account Book, account with Francis Pellomes (sp.?), November 14, 1835; Oliver Avery Account Book, account with Edward Stuart, May 1812; Barnes Account Book, account with William Scranton, April 16, 1822.

183. Robinson Account Book, accounts with David Hoopes, April 20, 1817, and Richard McIlvain, April 29, 1812; Alling Invoice Book, account of chairs shipped to Nathan Bolles, ca. October 1820, and Ledger (1815–1818), account with painter Moses Lyon, May 6, 1815; Bass Estate Records.

184. Fussell Account Book, account with George Emlen, 1742; John Letchworth Bill to Jonathan Williams, Philadelphia, 1795, Jonathan Williams Collection, DCM; Robbins Account Book, account with John A. Taintor, July 31, 1834; Boynton Ledger (1810–1817), credit for John Patterson, December 1814.

185. William Cox Bill to John Cadwalader, Philadelphia, October 29, 1774, Gen. John Cadwalader Section, Cadwalader Collection; Job E. Townsend Daybook, Newport, Rhode Island, 1778–1803, account with Joshua Crandel, September 28, 1795, NHS; Alling Daybook, account with David Tichenor, August 26, 1836; Rea Daybook (1789–1793), account with Samuel Parkman, June 10, 1791; Robbins Account Book, account with Nathan Pratt, August 26, 1835.

Book Reviews

Philip D. Zimmerman. *Harmony in Wood: Furniture of the Harmony Society*. Ambridge, Pa.: Friends of Old Harmony Village, 2010. x + 214 pp.; numerous color and bw illus., bibliography, index. Distributed by University Press of New England. $60.00.

This work is the first in a series of scholarly catalogues to focus on the material culture of the Harmony Society, a separatist religious sect that established a utopian community north of Pittsburgh in 1805. It sets the bar high for the studies that will follow. *Harmony in Wood* provides the first comprehensive look at the wide range of documented furniture made or used in the Harmonist communities, of which Economy (now Old Economy Village, a property of the Pennsylvania Historical and Museum Commission) was the last settlement. The author's stated goal, "to provide a detailed report on a highly select and refined group of the Harmonists' finest and best documented pieces" (vii), is capably and fully achieved.

The very nature of the Harmony Society's communal lifestyle presents a challenge for furniture historians accustomed to researching documentary evidence for provenance. No personal property means no probate records. It also means that the traditional understanding of an object's context, ownership, and use does not necessarily apply. Philip D. Zimmerman, undaunted by this situation, wisely allows the objects to speak for themselves. Through careful and methodical study and analysis, he has successfully defined and described Harmonist furniture and presents a carefully chosen group in ninety detailed catalogue entries. The inclusion of furniture from other public and private collections in addition to that of Old Economy Village allows him to make a richer and much more complete statement.

The book begins with three essays, which provide the context for the catalogue that follows. The first gives a brief history of the Harmony Society from the 1804 immigration of about five hundred followers of George Rapp, the leader of this pietistic millennialist group, from Germany into the wilderness north of Butler County, Pennsylvania. There they established their first settlement, Harmonie (as it was sometimes spelled), which prospered over time by successfully engaging in commerce with the outside world but still staying relatively isolated from worldly society. This economic success led to the decision in 1810 to move the entire community to a new location that offered access to a navigable river. Property was purchased in Indiana for this venture, and New Harmony was built on the Wabash River. In 1824 a third move was made, back to Pennsylvania, where they chose the name "Economy" for their final home, and "this time they got everything right" (p. 7). The second essay chronicles the long road taken by the Old Economy Village furniture collection from its transfer to the State of Pennsylvania in 1937 and its subsequent adoption as a WPA project, through multiple cataloguing campaigns and the gradual reacquisition of furniture that had made its way out of the community. The third section outlines "the essentials of Harmonist furniture," and here Zimmerman successfully and convincingly identifies distinctive styles, construction details, and craft practices that define the group. While there are many variables and not necessarily one distinctive commonality across all furniture forms, it is apparent that "Harmonists made furniture their own way," with a preference for Germanic forms, and that they "prized practicality over fashion" (p. 37).

The real story of Harmonist furniture is revealed in all of its complicated and sometimes contradictory glory within the catalogue entries. The majority of furniture shown might be described as sturdy, practical, or plain, with only a few very notable exceptions. The serene bobbin-shaped portrait bust that graces the cover of the book surmounts an elaborately carved and decorated shadow box (cat. no. 80) that stands out as a masterpiece among Harmonist work. A family history suggests a connection to one of Economy's known craftsmen, a turner, but Zimmerman correctly stops short of making that attribution based solely on a note that accompanied the object, tempting though it may have been. Another singular item is a pyramidal mahogany dish cupboard with carved paw feet (cat. no. 51), which can only be described as eccentric in the extreme. The individual creativity and expressiveness of this cupboard's design are not particularly in character with Harmonist furniture or thought, but the author is able to point out the reasons why it may have been a special piece made for a special person within the community.

Wide variations in skill, style, and craftsmanship suggest that a number of hands were at work over time; however, no pieces are signed or can be positively attributed to any of the six furniture makers who are known by name through society records. Their anonymity, while frustrating to us, seems well in keeping with their own culture and belief system. The craftsmen had access to wood from the community's active sawmills, but records show that they also purchased plank and supplies from the outside. Harmonist philosophy favored self-sufficiency first with surplus to be sold for the benefit of the community, but rules within this society were not always hard and fast.

The majority of furniture in the catalogue dates between 1805 and 1840, and the catalogue entries are organized by form. Types of furniture forms that survive reveal a great deal about the Harmonists' lives, from the numerous long feast tables that were used for group meetings and celebrations to the general preference for a clothespress in which to hang articles of clothing over a chest of drawers in which clothing would have to be folded flat. The latter is a convention that Zimmerman identifies with German culture. Fragments and tools from the Old Economy Village collection are also included in the catalogue, providing the opportunity to delve deeper into the Harmonist craftsmen's practices and methods. Ornament in the form of inlay was not commonly used, but not out of the question, appearing on several small tables and on chests of drawers showing style influence from outside contacts. Sometimes the influence of outside style may have been quite strongly felt, as in a chest of drawers (cat. no. 50) that illustrates the "ambiguity and uncertainty" in distinguishing work done by Harmonist craftsmen or Pittsburgh-area makers.

In fact, not all furniture used in the Harmonist community was made there, and several entries illustrate that anomaly within the self-sufficient community. A Connecticut shelf clock is a case in point (cat. no. 67), and the author takes the opportunity in that entry to discuss society records that document the purchase of "1 Yankee Clock" in 1830 as well as many other similar clocks in successive years (p. 173). We learn a little more about the society and its members from another clock made by John Hoff of Lancaster, Pennsylvania (cat. no. 64). It was purchased in 1809 as a gift to the society by a patron, Jacob Neff, also of Lancaster, who later moved to Harmony and became a member. The case was made after the clock arrived in Harmony, either by a cabinetmaker in the Pittsburgh area or possibly in Harmony itself.

A few pieces of furniture can be identified with an owner, a rarity in a communal society and outside the situation of the average Harmonist. An example is a blanket chest bearing the initials "C F" (cat. no. 27). Zimmerman identifies the owner as Conrad Feucht, who left the society, which espoused celibacy, in 1829 to marry another member, Heldegart Mutschler. They were later allowed to return as husband and wife, over the objections of some in the community, which is how the chest returned to Economy. The author weaves Feucht's story into the catalogue entry seamlessly and to good effect.

Zimmerman is to be congratulated on bringing what initially appears to be a moving target into focus as a cohesive group. While questions were consciously left unanswered in some of the entries, they are presented honestly as grist for future research. Other elusive details, like an explanation of the iconography on a watercolor panel over a charming small mirror (cat. no. 68), will, with luck, be revealed in subsequent studies in the series.

Zimmerman states in his introduction, "a talented team produced a beautiful book" (p. x). This volume and its content are of the highest quality in design and production, enhanced by superb photography by Will Brown. It merits a place on the bookshelf of anyone interested in American furniture of the early nineteenth century for its content as well as for its methodology. As the field of furniture study progresses, the value of this type of locally focused, in-depth research is becoming recognized as key to understanding the whole picture.

Lee Ellen Griffith
Monmouth County Historical Association

Brock Jobe, Gary R. Sullivan, and Jack O'Brien. *Harbor and Home: Furniture of Southeastern Massachusetts, 1710–1850.* Hanover, N.H., and London: University Press of New England, 2009. xviii + 435 pp.; numerous color and bw illus., maps, catalogue, appendix, bibliography, index. $75.00.

The earliest students of American material culture, such as Esther Single-ton, George Francis Dow, Clair Franklin Luther, and William Macpherson Hornor Jr., initiated the regional analysis of American furniture. Their detailed and thoughtful examination of inventories, provenance, and furniture design has been the model for much furniture scholarship throughout the twentieth and twenty-first centuries. When Brock Jobe completed his first regional study of American furniture with the publication of the indispensable *Portsmouth Furniture: Masterworks from the New Hampshire Seacoast* in 1993, the internet was in its infancy. Today material culture research can be performed at a speed unthinkable a mere eighteen years ago. As seen in *Harbor and Home: Furniture of Southeastern Massachusetts, 1710–1850*, these new technologies have permitted the analysis of material culture in a region that previously appeared too daunting to tackle, given its size and disparate communities. Even so, it took great courage and conviction of purpose by the authors to tackle the broad expanse chosen for this regional study. Here, in less than seven years of production, Jobe, Gary Sullivan, and Jack O'Brien have written an authoritative book that concisely presents the variety of furniture used throughout southeastern Massachusetts before 1850.[1]

As defined in *Harbor and Home*, the southeastern Massachusetts region comprises Barnstable, Bristol, Dukes (Martha's Vineyard), Nantucket, and Plymouth counties. Only two maps, an 1802 regional map and an 1854 map of New Bedford, are illustrated in the book. For individuals unfamiliar with the region, the lack of more detailed maps makes understanding the relation of the different towns to the coast or other communities difficult. Because this is a regional study, a simple, concise, modern map of each of the counties researched would have been of great assistance. This approach has been applied with good results in other regional studies, for example, *The Best the Country Affords: Vermont Furniture, 1765–1850* by Kenneth Joel Zogry.[2]

Jobe begins the book with an insightful discussion of the social conditions within the varying communities and how they influenced a resident's choices between locally made furniture or imported pieces from the well-established urban centers of Boston or Newport. As might be suspected, southeastern Massachusetts furniture design is based largely on the products emanating from urban New England cabinetmaking shops. Certainly, over a period of more than a century and a half, a number of urban-trained craftsmen settled in southeastern Massachusetts, bringing their training with them. Moreover, local cabinetmakers assimilated furniture designs from urban pieces to which they were exposed. They, in turn, produced items that the local population would desire and could afford.

Although southeastern Massachusetts had its share of wealthy families, the majority of residents were lower-income farming or fishing families. Therefore, the objects that they lived with were relatively simple in design and generally crafted from indigenous woods. Few of the examples of locally made objects compare favorably with urban pieces in their level of craftsmanship, complexity of construction, or quality of woods. It is these poor economic conditions that Jobe could have delved into with greater detail, since the area's economy explains the prevalence of simple furniture produced by local craftsmen.

Robert Blair St. George's *Wrought Covenant: Source Material for the Study of Craftsmen and Community in Southeastern New England, 1620–1700* was a comprehensive analysis of this region's seventeenth-century furniture. During the thirty years since its publication, several new discoveries have been made. While *Harbor and Home* focuses on material produced between 1710 and 1850, the inclusion of a few recently discovered late seventeenth-century objects recently discovered would have added greater breadth and depth to this book.[3]

The furniture-making trade in southeastern Massachusetts is wonderfully analyzed in detail here through the lives of Lemuel Tobey and Simeon Doggett of Middleborough, Ebenezer Allen Jr. and Cornelius Allen of New Bedford, Abiel White of Weymouth, and Samuel Wing of Sandwich. O'Brien and Derin Bray offer a thorough scrutiny of cabinetmaking in rural eighteenth- and early nineteenth-century America through the study of the surviving account books of Tobey, White, and Wing, and Wing's surviving tools. As was often the case, few cabinetmakers could survive from selling woodwork alone; many cabinetmakers also relied on farming for financial support. Margaret Hofer, who was one of the first scholars to perform intensive research on a southeastern Massachusetts cabinetmaker, Simeon Doggett, formulated many of these initial economic analyses.[4]

Clock making in southeastern Massachusetts, as Sullivan aptly notes, was primarily a nineteenth-century endeavor. Nearly all of the clocks present in southeastern Massachusetts before this time were imported from larger urban centers or from Europe, as in the instance of William Rotch, a Nantucket whaling merchant who owned a Dutch tall-case clock. Sullivan's excellent chapter on clock making focuses on the Bailey family as representative of the 115 clockmakers active in southeastern Massachusetts between 1750 and 1850. Since twelve other clockmakers are discussed in the catalogue entries, the reader would have gained additional understanding of the southeastern Massachusetts clock-making community if information about these other local clockmakers were interwoven with the discussion of the Baileys. That being said, Sullivan does provide important facts on the Bailey family. An interesting discovery noted by Sullivan is the retailing of clocks not only by such clockmakers as Calvin Bailey but in almost the same number by cabinetmakers such as Abiel White. As Sullivan states, "the business of selling clocks was more complicated than often portrayed" (p. 40). It would have added greater depth to the chapter if Sullivan had probed deeper into this complex issue. It is a tantalizing taste of what still needs to be researched in postcolonial American clock production.

Harbor and Home's catalogue entries present a broad diversity of rural- and urban-produced objects used in southeastern Massachusetts homes. It should be understood that the majority of furniture made in this region was mundane. As noted above, this was a direct result of the socioeconomic conditions of the region. The entries do not all focus, however, on the locally made pieces. Excluding the clocks, several of the catalogue entries discuss the imported urban object as the primary object and then examine the locally produced southeastern Massachusetts pieces as the ancillary objects. Unfortunately, many of the local pieces are illustrated with significantly smaller images than the urban piece. A plethora of publications already treat similar urban objects in detail; this book would have benefited if its approach were reversed and the focus was retained on local products, the ostensible subject of the book.

An exceptional example of the simpler furniture local craftsmen produced is the red-painted roundabout chair (cat. no. 5). The chair has been attributed to Plymouth County based on its provenance. However, a nearly identical roundabout chair that has been published was identified as originally belonging to a Lieutenant Benjamin Vassal (1742–1828), a Scituate, Massachusetts, cabinetmaker. It is likely that Vassal may be responsible for all of the roundabout chairs with double-cyma-shaped slats. The chair in catalogue number 5 descended in the Curtis family of Norwell, a mere five miles from Scituate.[5]

The banner or "tombstone" text is several times too unequivocal and does not always convey the uncertainty inherent in much furniture scholarship. Catalogue number 32, for instance, discusses a drop-leaf (or "tuckaway") table that descended through the Bonney family of Duxbury. The supposition based on the table's provenance is that the table is therefore from Duxbury. Although the turnings are not as proportional as those found on the best Boston turnings, the possibility of the object's being a Boston product perhaps should not be excluded. The table might better be identified as being "possibly from" Duxbury. As the research on late baroque seating furniture from Boston shows, provenance is not always the best indicator of origin.[6]

As the adage states, "a picture is worth a thousand words." Detail images of turnings, labels, and joinery are very helpful to curators, collectors, researchers, and dealers, and although the inclusion of more illustrations would have significantly increased the cost of the publication, the limited number of detailed pictures of salient aspects of different objects in *Harbor and Home* is regrettable. The one section that excels in this respect is the entries on the clocks. Many entries have multiple images of the clockworks, inscriptions, fretwork, and inlay, all of which are very useful for a comparative analysis. Another impediment to the reader is that the book designer (apparently) decided to place the notes at the rear of the book, necessitating a constant flipping back and forth. The unused space on the concluding page of many of the entries underlines this poorly chosen arrangement.

Furniture-focused scholarship is intrinsically limited and depicts only a finite aspect of a society. As recent publications and exhibitions have revealed, the juxtaposition of a variety of disparate objects such as fine art, textiles, ceramics, metalware, and furniture can greatly elucidate our understanding of a community. Taken as a whole, *Harbor and Home* brings to light a group of furniture that has been little understood for a century. The book is successful at reemphasizing furniture scholarship's grasp of the versatile trade and commerce present in early America and the varying quality of furniture used within a given population. While the book does not provide readers with a comprehensive study of the material culture of southeastern Massachusetts, it does present an important survey of the various cabinetmakers, clockmakers, and overall furniture traditions present in the region before the industrial revolution.

Erik Gronning
Sotheby's

1. Esther Singleton, *The Furniture of Our Forefathers* (New York: Doubleday, 1900), George Francis Dow, ed., *The Arts and Crafts in New England, 1704–1775: Gleanings from Boston Newspapers Relating to Painting, Engraving, Silversmiths, Pewterers, Clockmakers, Furniture, Pottery, Old Houses, Costume, Trades and Occupations* (Topsfield, Mass.: Wayside Press, 1927); Clair Franklin Luther, *The Hadley Chest* (Hartford, Conn.: Case, Lockwood and Brainard, 1935); William Macpherson Hornor Jr., *Blue Book, Philadelphia Furniture: William Penn to George Washington, with Special Reference to the Philadelphia-Chippendale School* (Philadelphia, Pa.: Hornor, 1935); *Portsmouth Furniture: Masterworks from the New Hampshire Seacoast*, organized and edited by Brock Jobe (Boston, Mass.: Society for the Preservation of New England Antiquities, 1993).

2. Kenneth Joel Zogry, *The Best the Country Affords: Vermont Furniture 1765–1850* (Bennington, Vt.: Bennington Museum, 1995).

3. Several examples of seventeenth-century furniture from southeastern Massachusetts have appeared in the marketplace since the publication of Robert Blair St. George, *The Wrought Covenant: Source Material for the Study of Craftsmen and Community in Southeastern New England, 1620–1700* (Brockton, Mass.: Brockton Art Center–Fuller Memorial, 1979). The new discoveries include a Marshfield carved and joined document box (Christie's, *Fine American Furniture, Silver and Decorative Arts*, New York, October 2, 1982, lot 315); a Plymouth County joined court cupboard (Christie's, *Important American Furniture, Silver, Folk Art and Decorative Arts*, New York, June 23, 1993, lot 141); an elaborately turned Tinkham armchair (Skinner, *American Furniture & Decorative Arts*, Boston, Mass., November 6, 2005, lot 623); the four-drawer Richard Bourne Plymouth County joined chest (Sotheby's, *Important Americana: Furniture, Folk Art, and Decorations*, New York, October 15, 1999, lot 90, and illustrated in Peter Follansbee, "Unpacking the Little Chest," *Old-Time New England* 78, no. 268 [spring/summer 2000]: 5–23); a Plymouth County two-drawer unornamented joined chest (Skinner, Bolton, Mass., June 11, 1995, lot 65, and also illustrated by Peter Follansbee); a Plymouth County two-drawer joined chest (offered at Sotheby's, *Important Americana Silver, Porcelain, Prints, Folk Art and Furniture*, New York, January 21, 2000, lot 552, and sold at Skinner, *American Furniture & Decorative Arts*, Boston, Mass., November 1, 2003, lot 101); Plymouth County six-board chests with serrated molding (first discussed in Brian Cullity, *A Cubberd, Four Joyne Stools & Other Smalle Thinges: The Material Culture of Plymouth Colony* [Sandwich, Mass.: Heritage Plantation of Sandwich, 1994]; one example sold at Sotheby's, *Important Americana from the Collection of James O. Keene*, New York, January 16, 1997, lot 35).

4. Margaret K. Hofer, "The Tory Joiner of Middleborough, Massachusetts: Simeon Doggett and His Community, 1762-1792" (master's thesis, University of Delaware, 1991).

5. Singleton, *The Furniture of Our Forefathers*, pp. 392–93. "Katherine Mansfield married Benjamin Vassal, a cabinet maker and possessed of a good home," from Elijah Comins's manuscript written in 1881, when he was seventy-four years old. See www.archive.org/stream/cominsfamilydescoocon/cominsfamilydescoocon_djvu.txt. Another nearly identical chair is discussed in Bruce Millar, "Two Centuries of Comfort," *American Collector* (October 1941): fig. 4.

6. Leigh Keno, Joan Barzilay Freund, and Alan Miller, "The Very Pink of the Mode: Boston Georgian Chairs, Their Export, and Their Influence," *American Furniture 1996*, edited by Luke Beckerdite (Milwaukee, Wis.: Chipstone Foundation, 1996), pp. 266–306; and Joan Barzilay Freund and Leigh Keno, "The Making and Marketing of Boston Seating Furniture in the Late Baroque Style," *American Furniture 1998*, edited by Luke Beckerdite (Hanover, N. H.: University Press of New England for the Chipstone Foundation, 1998), pp. 1–40.

Patricia Phillips Marshall and Jo Ramsay Leimenstoll. *Thomas Day: Master Craftsman and Free Man of Color*. The Richard Jenrette Series in Architecture and the Decorative Arts. Chapel Hill: University of North Carolina Press, in association with the North Carolina Museum of History, 2010. xii + 289 pp.; numerous color and bw illus., 2 appendixes, bibliography, index. $40.00.

It is now hard to remember that in the middle of the twentieth century it was still believed that the American Southeast had produced little in the way of distinctive early American furniture. Charleston Museum director E. Milby Burton's *Charleston Furniture, 1700–1825* (Charleston Museum, 1955) finally brought attention to the emergence of individualized styles of such master craftsmen as Thomas Elfe and to the high-style furniture designed and made in the eighteenth and nineteenth centuries by Southern craftsmen for clients who, owing to a slavery-based agrarian economy, made the region the richest in the colonies.

We have learned much about Southern material culture and decorative arts during the past half century, thanks largely to research and collecting engendered by Winston-Salem's Museum of Early Southern Decorative Arts (MESDA) and the Colonial Williamsburg Foundation. Jonathan Prown and Ronald L. Hurst's *Southern Furniture, 1680–1830* (Colonial Williamsburg, 1997) classifies the objects into the Chesapeake/Low Country/Back Country regional categories popularized by MESDA and documents the Colonial Williamsburg collection in ways that focused on a large group of relatively unknown furniture artisans. Brad Rauschenberg and John Bivins's towering achievement, *The Furniture of Charleston, 1680–1820* (MESDA, 2003), extended Burton's work by bringing together a thorough examination of styles and forms along with the microscopic analysis of woods and descriptions of regional commercial patterns to cast light on the furniture produced in what was then the wealthiest community in America. Other regional styles across the South have now been explored, in such works as Wallace Gusler's *Furniture of Williamsburg and Eastern Virginia* (Virginia Museum, 1979), Gregory Weidman's *Maryland Furniture* (Maryland Historical Society, 1984), Derita Coleman Williams and Nathan Harsh's *Art and Mystery of Tennessee Furniture* (Tennessee Historical Society, 1988), Pamela Wagner's *Hidden Heritage: Recent Discoveries in Georgia Decorative Art, 1735–1915* (High Museum, 1990), and Jack Holden, H. Parrott Bacot, and Cybele Gontar's *Furnishing Louisiana: Creole and Acadian Furniture, 1735–1835* (Historic New Orleans Collection, 2010).

Bivins and Rauschenberg worked together on a number of projects and employed MESDA's research resources as a base for their deep analyses of furniture styles and traditions across the South. Bivins's *The Furniture of Coastal North Carolina* (MESDA, 1988) set a standard for the assessment of regional, largely rural, work that by the middle of the eighteenth century had combined conservative British tastes with vernacular influences. Many of the small planters and farmers in this area were artisans themselves, and they combined idiosyncratic ethnic tastes, and often isolated commercial relationships with urban centers, to create an "industry" of small-scale furniture makers and architectural artisans that ultimately became the largest area of furniture manufacturing in the United States today. Bivins and Rauschenberg's work at MESDA drew together scores of students researching Southern decorative arts, including Patricia Phillips Marshall, whose *Thomas Day: Master Craftsman and Free Man of Color*, written with architectural historian Jo Ramsay Leimenstoll, sets a new standard for the treatment of a single artisan and marks an extraordinary achievement for research into the life and commercial activities of a free man of color in the antebellum South.

Thomas Day is one of a small handful of antebellum free people of color to have left behind enough documentary material to enable scholars to interpret his life, work, and business relationships. His father, John Day, was born in North Carolina in 1779 as the illegitimate mulatto grandson of a South Carolina family that supported his rearing in a white Quaker family whose beliefs ran counter to those of South Carolinian slaveholders. John learned cabinetmaking from a western piedmont craftsman and set up shop in a Southside Virginia community of free people of color. He married the daughter of a well-respected free mulatto doctor and landowner and had two sons, John Jr. (b. 1797) and Thomas (b. 1801). His financial circumstances enabled him to purchase, and subsequently lose, a plantation early in the nineteenth century and to begin to educate his sons outside their home, while teaching them the "art and mystery" of cabinetmaking at home.

The Day family became peripatetic during the sons' teens and by 1820 had relocated to Warren County in North Carolina to improve its business circumstances and to avoid Virginia's more repressive race laws. In 1821 John Jr. and Thomas moved to the vicinity of Milton, North Carolina, in Caswell County on the Virginia border. The area's residents were descendants of European, African, and Native American forebears, and mixed-race interactions were not uncommon. Light-skinned with wavy dark hair, the Days were able to avoid some of the stigmas attached to darker-skinned mulattos then living in North Carolina.

John Jr. had experienced a religious conversion that could be better pursued in Milton, while Thomas likely moved to be closer to the commercial transportation for manufactured goods that was readily accessible down the nearby Dan River. Both opened furniture-making shops. John Jr. left his furniture making in 1825 to become a Baptist missionary, while Thomas continued to produce furniture made of stylish walnut and imported Santo Domingo mahogany. The brothers continued to communicate by mail, even as John Jr. did missionary work in Africa. By 1827, through the cultivation of local business connections and clients, Thomas had become the leading supplier of custom-made cabinetry and case furniture in Milton. His popularity among his artisan and commercial peers was so great that by the time he married in 1830, more than sixty local white citizens and the attorney general successfully petitioned the General Assembly for the passage of a special act permitting the entry of his mulatto wife into North

Carolina, contravening an 1826 law banning the migration of free people of color into the state.

Thomas Day's maternal grandparents had owned up to nineteen slaves, one of whom had been bequeathed to Thomas's older brother, John Jr. In 1830, the year of Thomas's marriage, he owned two slaves, a man aged between twenty-four and thirty-six, and a woman between thirty-six and fifty-five. A decade later, he owned eight slaves; by 1850 he owned fourteen. These slaves were not, as some would hope, members of his immediate family whom he had benevolently purchased in order to set free. Ten were identified as black, four as mulatto, and none bore names indicating kinship with Day. He employed these enslaved workers within his furniture-making business as craftspeople and porters, and in his home as domestic help for his wife and three children. By 1850 26.8 percent of North Carolina's population was enslaved, and Day's workforce remarkably included black slaves, free people of color, and whites, working as journeymen, apprentices, and day laborers. Slavery and complex class relations based on skin color were commonplace, yet it will remain a mystery as to how Thomas Day, as a mulatto, could have owned so many human beings who shared his African origins.

Day was an expansive and pragmatic entrepreneur. He built custom domestic furniture, coffins, furnishings for churches and public buildings, and designed and produced distinctive curvilinear architectural embellishments for local homes, the state capitol, and North Carolina University interiors. He purchased extensive real estate holdings, including the local Union Tavern. He utilized technically advanced steam-powered mechanized tools, sought to vertically integrate his production to control his costs, and subcontracted portions of the work to specialists. His clients included some of the wealthiest white patrons in the region, and by 1850 he had become the largest furniture-maker in North Carolina. Day sent his children to a private boarding school in Massachusetts, violating North Carolina restrictions while exposing them to strong Northern abolitionist sentiments. Yet his prominent economic position and investments in capital and people in North Carolina apparently precluded him from relocating his business away from the slave-holding South, and, by 1857, as the national economy trended sharply downward, he began to experience economic difficulties. Creditors closed in on his assets. A North Carolina petition requested that the entire free black population be sent to Liberia. Day's health declined, and his property began to be transferred to his son Thomas Jr., who by 1860 had assumed full financial responsibility for the cabinet-making shop, architectural woodwork, and burial services. Thomas Day died in 1861 as the Confederacy was being formed.

Day's work, while emerging from the empire period of American furniture-making, has many distinctive curvilinear elements that some have attributed to an inclination on Day's part to include Africanisms among his improvisational design motifs. Many of the extensive black-and-white photographs in this volume certainly raise questions about the origins of Day's unique motifs. His bold fireplace surrounds and staircase embellishments were dramatically more expressive than was typical for the unprepossessing rural North Carolina homes of that era. (See, for example, those illustrated in Catherine Bishir, *North Carolina Architecture* [University of North Carolina Press, 1990].) The asymmetrical S-curved muntins on his glazed secretary doors were thought by collectors such as Derrick Joshua Beard to be references to West African "Sankofa" signs for well-being. Hopes were expressed that lost correspondence between Thomas and his brother John Jr., who became a missionary in Liberia, might have contained sketches of West African motifs. Both Days were trained as cabinetmakers, and such graphic image exchanges cannot be ruled out. But Patricia Phillips Marshall, following the lead of Jonathan Prown, indicates that there is no hard evidence of Day's having sought to incorporate references to African decorative embellishments in his work. Unlike the functional design transmissions Dale Rosengarten found in the evolution of Low Country baskets (see *Grass Roots: African Origins of an American Art* [Museum of African Art, 2008]) or the functional references John Michael Vlach attributes to connections between West African building forms and Southern American plantation vernacular architecture in *Back of the Big House* (University of North Carolina Press, 2003), Marshall sees no clearly identifiable Africanisms in Day's work.

At the beginning of Marshall's research, a number of articles had been written about Day, but most of his work was privately held by owners who cherished the pieces as family heirlooms. Knowledgeable Southern antiques pickers alerted collectors of individual pieces that came to the market through estate sales. By the early 1990s the North Carolina Museum of History had begun to document and collect his work, and when Marshall joined that staff as curator of furnishings and decorative arts and expanded her work with MESDA, the collecting activity accelerated. Jo Ramsey Leimenstoll joined the documentation project as a preservation architect at the University of North Carolina at Greensboro, where she was working to restore the fire-damaged Union Tavern. Grants to expand the research were provided by the National Endowment for the Arts, the North Carolina Department of Cultural Resources, the Andy Warhol Foundation, the Mary Duke Biddle Foundation, and a number of private donors.

A comprehensive exhibition of Day's work, "Behind the Veneer: Thomas Day, Master Cabinetmaker," has been installed at the North Carolina Museum of History. The exhibition includes about eighty varied pieces of his furniture and displays examples of the tools he would have used. The semipermanent exhibition also raises useful educational questions about Day's role as an entrepreneur of color in the antebellum South. Other museums, such as the Telfair Museum in Savannah and the Museum of Fine Arts, Boston, are also collecting and displaying Day's work.

This is a spectacular piece of research into an individual artisan. It provides insights into the narrative history of the man's life and family, details his business and public dealings, analyzes his stylistic distinctiveness within the larger furniture-making and architectural trends of his time, raises social and ethical questions about how the work came into being and was supported by clients, addresses the racial complexities of being a free entrepreneur of color in a highly restrictive antebellum South, and is accompanied by a lasting catalogue of the artisan's work that came into being concurrently with the development of the research. It is a towering achievement, as it explores both the life and work of a free man of color and what many artisans would have experienced in the antebellum South. It is an insightful corollary to other recent researches into early Southern artisanry. MESDA supported cabinetmaking research for Thomas Newbern and Jack Melchor's *WH Cabinetmaker: A Southern Mystery Solved* (Legacy Ink, 2009) and Elizabeth A. Davison's *The Furniture of John Shearer, 1790–1820* (Altamira, 2011), also reviewed in this volume. Leonard Todd's *Carolina Clay: The Life and Legend of the Slave Potter Dave* (Norton, 2008) explores the enigma of Dave Drake, the exact contemporary of Thomas Day who was producing equally eloquent poetic pottery only three hundred miles farther south, in Edgefield, South Carolina. One might hope for a similarly thorough exploration into the life of the African American freed slave tool-maker Cesar Chelor, who in mid-eighteenth-century Massachusetts made the hand tools that produced some of America's greatest New England cabinetry masterpieces.

Tragically, Patricia Phillips Marshall passed away just as this book was published and as her magnum opus exhibition was opening at the North Carolina Museum of History. Raleigh's *News and Observer* quoted her on the interconnected artistic, social, and historical impacts of her research into Day's legacy. "In order to understand the one you have to know the other. . . . As a curator, I recognize that people learn in different ways. Some will come through and read all the plaques and everything; some will come just to look at the furniture. Some people react better to visual information, and some better to tactile things. . . . This is why I got into museum work. I'm fascinated with objects and how they tell a story."

Patricia Phillips Marshall and I were fellows together at MESDA. As an African American researcher into the early roots of black material culture, I had heard of Thomas Day and the slave potter Dave, and it was Marshall's passion for the subject and the thorough research she undertook that inspired me to complete my doctorate. She and Liemenstoll dedicated *Thomas Day: Master Craftsman and Free Man of Color* to the great North Carolina African American historian John Hope Franklin and, in fact, to all of us who would have wished to have contributed to such a brilliant and insightful study of African American artisanry in the antebellum South. We now have this beautiful and comprehensive text as a testament to distinctive artisanry and to outstanding scholarship.

Ted Landsmark
Boston Architectural College

Kevin W. Tucker, with essays and contributions by Beverly K. Brandt, David Cathers, Joseph Cunningham, Beth Ann McPherson, Tommy McPherson, and with contributions by Sally-Anne Huxtable. *Gustav Stickley and the American Arts and Crafts Movement*. New Haven: Yale University Press, in association with Dallas Museum of Art, 2010. 271 pp.; numerous color and bw illus., catalogue, bibliography, index. $60.00.

Nearly forty years after the first exhibition on the Arts and Crafts movement to include the work of Gustav Stickley (1858–1942), held at the Princeton University Art Museum in 1972, and on the heels of several monograph exhibitions of other American architect-designers of the movement, it indeed seems a fitting moment to publish a full discussion of the words and work of a man who was both mediator and mouthpiece for the American Arts and Crafts movement. Stickley embodied the spirit and opinions of the movement. He was an entrepreneur with the aspirations of a master craftsman, beginning his work in the furniture industry at eighteen, finally working for himself at forty. He promoted himself and his designs to the new American middle class (though not without the assistance of a staff of talented writers and designers), marketing his simple and affordable furniture to complement the house designs he published from 1903 in his magazine, *The Craftsman* (1901–1916). The magazine remains a key resource for understanding the Arts and Crafts movement in America.

Within the pages of the *Craftsman*, Stickley was an early proponent of integrated design, and this new publication, edited by Kevin W. Tucker, is a tribute to that idea. Tucker, the Margot B. Perot Curator of Decorative Arts and Design at the Dallas Museum of Art and curator of the related exhibition, is keen to delineate Stickley's work as something apart from the "superficially promotional" or simply as Stickley's personal vision. As he rightly points out in his introduction, very little about Gustav Stickley can be gleaned from his personal correspondence. Instead, his publications and public interviews are the sources of information about him. It is appropriate, then, to consider discovering his position within the movement from an examination of the social and commercial context of the time, from his designs and practices, from an analysis of the work of one of his first and most significant advocates-interpreters, Irene Sargent, and from an examination of his own homes.

Having published his own monograph on Stickley in 2003, it is fitting that author David Cathers begins the book with his essay "'The Moment'—Gustav Stickley from 1898 to 1900." Cathers brings us up to "the moment" of Stickley's formal entry into the American Arts and Crafts movement with his exhibition of furniture at the Grand Rapids exposition in 1900. From an interest in furniture that was simple to clean and care for, to the economic bust and boom of the late nineteenth century, as well as the influence of the burgeoning middle class, Cathers capably gives us a sense of the furniture industry of the time and Stickley's evolution within it. He emphasizes the importance for Stickley as well as for the middle classes of separating themselves from the past and beginning the century and life itself afresh. Stickley captured this spirit, crafting his message in the *Craftsman* as he did his furniture, by slowly reshaping public taste and demand.

In his essay "Art from Industry: The Evolution of Craftsman Furniture," Tucker addresses Stickley's business, processes, and products. He stresses the importance of the *Craftsman* magazine in shaping Stickley's approach to industrialization, as he walked a fine line between the ideal of the craftsman and running a practical business—a challenge that even William Morris was never able successfully to overcome. One of the most interesting aspects of Tucker's chapter is his detailed discussion of Stickley's factory, its staffing, and the creative touches that Stickley was able to add to his furniture through choice of material, finishes, and techniques like fuming, the process that uses ammonia to alter the color of wood. Tucker is also keen to emphasize the collaborative nature of the firm's designs, further debunking the myth that Harvey Ellis was sole designer for the lighter inlaid furniture produced in 1903–1904. He concludes by again positioning Stickley as a kind of bridge, not just between art and industry but also between Arts and Crafts and modernism, reaching after the new while simultaneously wishing for the simple life. It further underscores the notion that achieving a simple style or a simple life was nothing if not complicated.

In the third and central essay of the volume, "Irene Sargent and the Craftsman Ideology," Joseph Cunningham, curatorial director of the American Decorative Art 1900 Foundation, examines Sargent's role in her five years as editor and contributor to the *Craftsman*, during which time she contributed eighty-four articles to Stickley's magazine. It is not difficult to argue Sargent's influence on Stickley or her usefulness as his mouthpiece and advocate. Yet in analyzing her very first contribution to the enterprise (pre-*Craftsman*), "A Revival of Old Arts and Crafts," Cunningham argues the significance of Sargent's strategic presentation of the Craftsman ideology, beginning with her statement "all things have become new." With but a few strokes of her pen, she allied Stickley's work with the design reform movement in England, with primitive cultures, the House Beautiful movement in America, and with American philosophical movements like Transcendentalism. It was Sargent, also, who possessed the rhetorical skill to help Stickley navigate the waters between socialist ideals and commercialism. Cunningham argues compellingly the importance of Sargent's ideas and influence in crafting Stickley's persona and the mission of his firm, so much so that his argument calls for further study of Sargent herself, her background, and the evolution of her ideas (though, as with Stickley, we are left with little personal correspondence to make such elucidation an easy matter).

With the discussion of Sargent and the *Craftsman* at the center of this collection of essays, it is appropriate that it should be framed by treatments of Stickley's furniture and architecture—together they form his Craftsman trident, so to speak, the three areas of his greatest influence on the Arts and Crafts movement. Beverly Brandt, professor in the Herberger Institute for Design and the Arts at Arizona State University, addresses "The Paradox of the Craftsman Home," explaining how these published house designs were both essential to the new way of living promulgated by the *Craftsman* magazine as well as literally becoming homes for Craftsman furniture. In examining a number of the house designs, Brandt illustrates the paradox that although the houses were unified in principle, their styles could vary widely. Bound together by common Arts and Crafts ideas such as the use of local materials and attention to natural surroundings, they could still be distinctive enough to suit varying individual tastes. Indeed, she posits their model as one for sustainable housing in the twenty-first century.

While Brandt identifies Stickley's own homes in Syracuse and Craftsman Farms as deliberate and effective models for the Craftsman way of life, Beth Ann and Tommy McPherson take this one step further in their chapter, "Gustav Stickley at Home." They bring together discussions of Craftsman furniture and the Craftsman home, noting the importance of examining this furniture in its intended context, as well as its suitability to that context. Specifically, they examine the furniture and interior decoration in Stickley's homes in Syracuse and at Craftsman Farms, where they served as executive director and curator. The McPhersons draw on contemporary photographs and accounts of these interiors (as published in the *Craftsman*) and recent analyses in Historic Structure Reports, which provide a wealth of documentary, graphic, and physical information about a property's history and physical condition. While their own analysis is compelling, it is sometimes hampered by the lack of comparative photographs within the chapter (one must delve into the catalogue for images of the corner cupboard and sideboard discussed), and by the small size of the photos of interiors. New color photographs are shown side by side and to scale with contemporaneous black-and-white photos (the latter are presumably scans from the magazine itself, preventing them from being shown at a higher resolution and larger format). However, it seems a shame that, given the topic, it was decided to deprive the reader of the opportunity to appreciate the details of interiors and furniture writ large and in color, since newer photos of restored interiors are available.

Throughout the essays there is a consistent emphasis on the fact that Stickley was influenced by the Arts and Crafts movement in England (especially by the work of architect-designers M. H. Baillie Scott and C. F. A. Voysey)—whether from his various visits to the country, through contemporary art periodicals, or his own exhibitions in Syracuse and Rochester, in which he exhibited English examples alongside the work of his own firm. Nonetheless, when direct comparison is made with English work there are rarely any photos to substantiate the point (only one comparative image of a Liberty piece is shown). One fully expects the majority of images in the publication accompanying a monographic exhibition to be of the artist's work, and yet, as Tucker himself emphasizes in his introduction and essay, Stickley by no means worked alone or in isolation. The intent of this exhibition and catalogue, as expressed by their shared title, is to examine Stickley's position within the larger Arts and Crafts movement, and it seems somewhat unjust not to have fleshed this out more fully with illustrations. Additionally, given that Stickley is positioned as mediator between the English and American movements, it would have been helpful if there had been a more substantial comparison between the works of Stickley and, say, Voysey, Baillie Scott, C. R. Ashbee (who visited America on several occasions), or C. R. Mackintosh in Britain; and Greene and Greene or Frank Lloyd Wright in America.

Following the essays, the second half of the book is composed largely of catalogue entries, examining individual works in the exhibition alongside beautiful full-page color photographs of furnishings and designs. Entries are contributed by the various essayists and by Sally-Anne Huxtable (project researcher at the Dallas Museum of Art), elucidating details about the designers, influences, and the history of the particular design. Tucker and Cathers are especially adept at incorporating relevant entries from the *Craftsman*, allowing Stickley to speak for himself where possible, and further enhancing the context for discussion of the object. While analysis in some entries is occasionally uneven, the photographs remain important documents of the objects in the exhibition and as examples of Stickley's most definitive work.

As well as a checklist of objects, the appendixes further elucidate important details related to Stickley's business history and practices—including a "tree" or time line of Stickley family companies, a listing of marks and labels used by Stickley's firm, a list of retailers of Craftsman products (compiled from advertisements and lists published in the *Craftsman*), and especially a list of employees and associates, along with approximate dates they were active in Stickley's firm (recalling Anita Ellis's seminal work on Rookwood Pottery artists in *Rookwood Pottery: The Glaze Lines* [1995]). For these compilations alone, this publication makes a valuable addition to Stickley scholarship, while its essays raise important points (and further questions) as to Stickley's influence within the Arts and Crafts movement in America. The quality of both this publication and its accompanying exhibition make it difficult to believe that this is the first nationally touring exhibition to address Stickley's work, and Kevin Tucker and the Dallas Museum of Art are to be applauded for their vision and efforts in bringing it together. In thus readdressing the work of Gustav Stickley, both exhibition and publication cannot fail to inspire further discussion and, one hopes, future exhibitions on Stickley's contribution to the Arts and Crafts movement and to the history of decorative arts in America.

Anne E. Mallek
The Gamble House

Wendy A. Cooper and Lisa Minardi. *Paint, Pattern & People: Furniture of Southeastern Pennsylvania, 1725–1850*. A Winterthur Book. Winterthur, Del.: Henry Francis du Pont Winterthur Museum, 2011. xxv + 277 pp.; numerous color and bw illus., checklist, bibliography, index. Distributed by University of Pennsylvania Press. (Also vol. 45 in the annual volume series of the Pennsylvania German Society.) $55.00.

Paint, Pattern & People: Furniture of Southeastern Pennsylvania, 1725–1850 is an important addition to the scholarship of American decorative arts. The publication differs in several respects from earlier studies in that it looks at the full range of English and Germanic populations in southeastern Pennsylvania during the eighteenth and first half of the nineteenth centuries. The well-documented objects they produced are presented as evidence of the continuation of European traditions in the decorative arts and, more important, as evidence of the cross-fertilization of design between neighboring groups and the creation of a distinct, local, and "American" aesthetic.

Examples of such "Americanizations" appear throughout the book. In the introduction, for instance, the authors discuss the Philadelphia high chest form. While the high chest of drawers is, in effect, an "American" form—American craftsmen altered and popularized an English design—there were further "Americanizations" by German craftsmen who, "instead of copying the Philadelphia style, took inspiration from it, transforming the technique and design conventions to fit their perceptions of beauty" (p. xvii).

The methodology used for this study is also outstanding. To this author's knowledge, few other publications present such thorough and complete research of such a large number of objects to provide a clear picture of the environment in which they were made. This book examines the European origins of the population of southeastern Pennsylvania, its ethnic composition, stylistic preferences in the arts, migration within America, occupations, social mobility, and any number of other factors that influenced their choices in the decorative arts. With respect to the objects themselves, the authors analyzed construction, finishes, materials used, descent in families, as well as the history and, when possible, even the training of the maker, his or her ethnic ties, religion, and the cost of the object. In other words, this study is based on an amazing amount of research and information, which permitted the authors to attribute objects to very specific and sometimes small regions of southeastern Pennsylvania. Such an impressive study in these financial times is a tremendous achievement and one that most institutions cannot afford to duplicate but can only strive toward with limited means and limited success.

The stated goal of the publication and exhibition at Winterthur Museum (April 2, 2011, to January 8, 2012) was to identify distinct local interpretations, "localisms" in the words of the authors, "based on well-documented examples in which the maker or family history is known" (p. xxiv). This approach enabled the authors to "go beyond loose attributions to one county or another and vague classifications that have long prevailed." According to the authors, this is "not a comprehensive survey of the furniture of southeastern Pennsylvania, but rather one based on furniture with histories and the people associated with those objects" (p. xxiv–xxv). In the process the authors also debunk myths about the furniture and people of the region. Among these, for instance, are the misconceptions about the ownership of "dower" chests, which were in fact owned by both men and women and were not necessarily "dower" chests. They also dismiss the frequent association of Quakers with "plainness." Noting that Germans were only one of many groups in the region, they reject the attribution of countless objects to the "Pennsylvania Dutch." They prove that southeastern Pennsylvania included members of many different faiths and nationalities—Quakers of English, Welsh, and Irish origin, as well as Scots-Irish Presbyterians, German Lutheran and Reformed groups, and nonconformist German minorities such as the Mennonites and Moravians, among others.

Although an exhibition accompanies this publication, it is not organized as a typical exhibition catalogue in which one can easily find text relating to a numbered, exhibited object. Instead, the book, which includes a checklist, is organized around three foci—color, pattern, and people—in four chapters: "People: A Great Mixed Multitude"; "Places: Regional Forms and Local Expressions"; "Families: Owners and Inheritors"; and "Makers: From Cradle to Coffin."

The first chapter, "People: A Great Mixed Multitude," focuses primarily on the history and immigration patterns of southeastern Pennsylvania. The authors begin by looking at settlers to the region from Wales, Scotland, Ireland, and England and make clear that religious affiliation, socioeconomic status, geographic location, and local craftsmanship practices were factors that influenced what a patron bought and what that object looked like. In the process, items are identified by histories of ownership in particular regions including, when possible, when the objects were purchased in relation to the date of the owner's, and even the maker's, immigration and settlement. Specific regional characteristics of construction and decoration, such as the line-and-berry inlay found primarily on objects made for Quakers in Chester County, Pennsylvania, are points of discussion in this chapter. In some instances, it was possible for the authors to posit the significance of objects as signs of "membership in the highest levels of Quaker society" (p. 19). Similar examinations and histories are presented when scrutinizing furniture and other decorative arts, including architectural contributions, of other ethnic groups in differing regions. The German-speaking peoples, for instance, including the Mennonites, Moravians, Swenkfelders, and the Ephrata community, all receive attention, and objects known to have been produced by them and owned by them are analyzed in detail.

Chapter two, "Places: Regional Forms and Local Expressions," treats specifically painted, carved, and inlaid decorations. Under the subtitle "Regionalisms: Common Furniture Forms," slat-back chairs, benches, dry sinks, dough troughs, tables, and cupboards are examined. Specific local preferences for types of furniture and decoration are discussed under "Settles" and "Rush Bottom Couches." The line-and-berry inlay of Chester County and the forms on which it appears is described in greater detail than in the previous chapter, as is the sulfur inlay of Lancaster County. Last, the chapter includes sections on painted and carved decoration. Under "Painted Decoration," the so-called Compass Artist, who decorated boxes and chests from 1775 to 1820 in Lancaster County, is considered, as are the chests made by the Jonestown School northwest of Lancaster and a group of objects from Wythe County, Virginia, which resemble those from Jonestown and suggest migration from the Lancaster area to Virginia. The Schwaben Creek and Mahantogo Valley of Northumberland County, Pennsylvania, also come into focus with the analysis of various objects and the identification of individual construction characteristics, paint colors, and techniques, including stamps and stencils used to create decorations on chests of drawers, chests, kitchen cupboards, and hanging cupboards.

The "Carved Decoration" section of chapter two looks at objects by the region in which they were created: Chester and Berks Counties, Lancaster County, the Nottingham School of Chester County, and, last, Cumberland County. The authors note the strong influence of Philadelphia rococo furniture and the impact it had on the production of related furniture throughout the region. Yet, they also identify the manner in which regional craftsmen altered designs in ways that suited local tastes and preferences. The objects made in these four regions changed just enough in proportion, construction, and extent and quality of carving, which was sometimes exaggerated and overly abundant, to qualify as local preferences, the "localisms" on which the publication focuses.

Chapter three, "Families: Owners and Inheritors," illustrates and analyzes numerous objects with very firm provenances and cites the great importance of history of ownership as crucial to "identifying distinctive localisms of form, ornament, and construction" (p. 118). It is also essential for an understanding of the objects in their original context. In this section a number of objects, including decorated paper fraktur with firm provenances to individual families are examined, including those owned by the Lanborn, Miller, and Hottenstein families. They are analyzed as groups of objects with specific histories, along with the houses and even the rooms of the structures that sheltered them. Clocks are also examined with reference to local characteristics in design and also in the works themselves. Further, the chapter looks at objects whose maker and original owner are known, and also again at paint-decorated chests, dispelling the myth of the "dower" chest as having been made only for women and only as "dower" objects, as well as the myth that the decorations on these chests were either religious or symbolic.

The final chapter, "Makers: From Cradle to Coffin," describes the practices of a number of identified cabinetmakers, noting that coffins were frequently a mainstay of business for many in the field. Such subjects as the master-apprentice relationship, the design of the shops in which they worked, the ways makers marked their furniture, and specific construction details, some associated with an ethnic tradition or as the innovation of a specific shop, are discussed in detail.

The chapter also studies fancy goods and the appearance of multiple colors and patterns in house interiors and on furniture produced by craftsmen identified and studied throughout the region. Others subjects examined in this last chapter are the work of John Fisher of York, Pennsylvania, with a discussion of his clocks, sculpture, and painted decoration; the relationship of architecture and furniture through the analysis of Tulpehocken Manor (near Myerstown, Jackson Township, Lebanon County, Pennsylvania), its interiors and the documented objects that furnished the house originally. This is followed by an analysis of the Deyers of Manheim, who made clocks, case furniture, and designed and built architecture. In the words of the authors, "such versatility, a necessity for many woodworkers faced with increasing competition, also reinforced the development of distinctive localisms in which details of form, construction, and ornament took on the specifics of maker and place" (p. 188).

Last, the authors point to the slow rate at which industrialization and mechanization affected southeastern Pennsylvania and list reasons for this. They cite "a strong ethnic and artisanal consciousness; a conservative tendency; and thriftiness that valued tried-and-true hand-tool technologies over unproven new machinery" (p. 192). They also note that the cost of new mass-produced forms was a factor in the pervasive conservatism of the region.

Unfortunately, the methodology employed here—aggressive research into the minutiae of individual shops, regions, ethnic groups, and craftsmen—is difficult to duplicate if only because of the time commitment and associated costs that most museums, independent scholars, and research institutions simply cannot afford. There is no doubt, however, that the methodology pursued for *Paint, Pattern & People: Furniture of Southeastern Pennsylvania, 1725–1850* will remain the ideal for scholars for years to come.

Overall, the book reads well and easily. Some might have preferred a different organization to the publication, a more typical catalogue format, for instance, that would make it easier to find and retrieve information on a specific craftsman, ethnic group, object, or subject. As it is, the reader is forced to read the entirety of the book to fully understand the region and its "localisms." In some cases, the information presented in one chapter might seem to fit more comfortably within the parameters and subject matter of another chapter, leading to some confusion. One might wonder, for example, why we read about regional forms and local expressions in the chapter titled "Makers: From Cradle to Coffin." Nevertheless, the writing style is comfortable to read, and the book is well researched, well documented (frequently providing specific information for the first time), and also well illustrated and supremely interesting. This is a wonderful publication and is well worth the purchase price to anyone interested in the decorative arts.

Francis J. Puig
Sarasota, Florida

Elizabeth A. Davison. *The Furniture of John Shearer, 1790–1820: "A True North Britain" in the Southern Backcountry*. Lanham, Md.: Altamira Press, 2011. xix + 217 pp.; numerous color and bw illus., tables, appendixes, bibliography, index. $90.00.

The Furniture of John Shearer by Elizabeth Davison brings to life the maker of quirky, overbuilt furniture made in the northern Shenandoah Valley and in the backcountry of Virginia in the late eighteenth and early nineteenth centuries. Using his inscriptions and characteristic inlay as diagnostic features, Davison identifies a Lowland Scot with fierce dual loyalty to England and Scotland as the maker of distinctive chests, desks, tables, clocks, and a dressing glass—fifty-two pieces so far. It wasn't easy. John Shearer never owned property and never paid taxes, so there is no paper trail. He did, however, write long inscriptions on his furniture, and Davison has not only deciphered their meaning but has identified the significance of some of his puzzling inlays.

We have known about John Shearer since 1970, when John Snyder, the Harrisburg collector and scholar, acquired a chest of drawers thinking it was made in Lancaster, Pennsylvania, and then discovered it was signed by John Shearer of Martinsburg, Virginia (now West Virginia). Snyder presented his findings in the May 1979 issue of the *Journal of Early Southern Decorative Arts* published by the Museum of Early Southern Decorative Arts (MESDA). He wrote the introduction to Davison's new book, conceding he had identified the wrong John Shearer. Snyder's John Shearer (1765–1810), the son of Archibald Shearer, was a wealthy planter who lived in Falling Waters, eight miles north of Martinsburg, and died in 1810. Davison's John Shearer, the furniture maker, was still signing and dating furniture in 1818. Although Shearer wrote "from Edinburgh 1775" on several pieces, Davison, working with Scottish genealogists, has found neither a record of his birth nor evidence of his immigration. She did find a third John Shearer (ca. 1737–1777) in Frederick County, Virginia, who lived too early to be the joiner. Davison believes that Shearer the furniture maker was born in Edinburgh circa 1760 and probably came to America in 1775 before he served his apprenticeship. His furniture does not look like anything made in Scotland!

Davison was not the first to publish the fact that John Snyder's Shearer was not the right guy. In 1997 Ronald L. Hurst and Jonathan Prown, writing about the three pieces of Shearer furniture at Colonial Williamsburg in *Southern Furniture, 1680–1830: The Colonial Williamsburg Collection*, noted that there was a John Shearer piece dated 1816, so he was not Snyder's John Shearer, son of Archibald Shearer, who died in 1810, though he may have been a relative.

Using his furniture as documents, Davison introduces us to a newspaper-reading, itinerant craftsman who probably spent some time at taverns. She gives us a reference book that catalogues and illustrates in color thirty-two of the fifty-two pieces of Shearer furniture that are known. The book also served as the catalogue for the exhibition of Shearer furniture at the DAR Museum in Washington, D.C. (October 8, 2010, to March 4, 2011), that then traveled to Colonial Williamsburg (April 2, 2011, to March 2012).

Davison was an intern at the DAR Museum for two semesters while in graduate school at the Smithsonian/Parsons/New School of Design Program in the History of Decorative Arts and Design, where she was encouraged to pursue the study of Shearer by her professor, Oscar P. Fitzgerald. Fitzgerald contributed an essay here, in the appendix, called "Shear Madness: The Shearer Collectors," identifying the collectors of this idiosyncratic furniture. Martinsville collector Linda Quynn Ross, who owns at least ten pieces of Shearer's work, was an early inspiration. Gary Heimbuch, a Boonsboro, Maryland, dealer and collector of American furniture, has handled more Shearer work than any other dealer. Heimbuch inspected forty-five of the fifty-two pieces known, sold seven of them, and kept one, a dressing glass. He also made his photographs available for this book and was generous with his time as a consultant.

Davison has not been able to find the date of John Shearer's birth or death. Tax lists are not helpful because Shearer did not own anything taxable: no land, slaves, or livestock. His earliest inscription is dated 1798, and he identifies himself as "John Shearer from Edinburgh." On an undated desk that Davison believes is earlier he calls himself a carpenter. He inscribed a chest of drawers "May 2, 1804 by me Shearer Martinsburg." By 1810 John Shearer the joiner was living in Loudoun County, where he made a desk for Samuel Luckett. He was still living in Loudoun County in June 9 and 13, 1812, when he obtained a restraining order against John Smith, a schoolmaster; he was afraid Smith might beat him and do him bodily harm. After that he disappears from public records. Davison believes two pieces dated 1818 were made in Loudoun County, but nothing is known of him after that date. She thinks he may have left the state during the economic panic of 1819, when farming became unprofitable in Virginia owing to falling prices for corn, wheat, and tobacco. Perhaps he moved to Ohio.

From his inscriptions we know he came from Edinburgh, Scotland, probably as a young boy in 1775. One of the inscriptions on the secretary desk at MESDA reads "John Shearer [illegible] from Edinburgh 1775" (p. 131). It is not known where Shearer trained. On the interior back of a case drawer in an undated desk, made circa 1790 to 1803, is "Shearer Carpenter," visible only with infrared photography. Davison uses this as evidence that he was trained in the house-building trade. In all other inscriptions but one he calls himself a joiner. On one bedroom table he calls himself "Joiner & Cabinetmaker." In 1805 he incised "By Shearer Joiner" on the arched-hood door of a tall-case clock. An 1812 court record lists him as a joiner. Davison thinks he may have been a house joiner and worked as a carpenter in the house-building trades and that he learned his skills from an English joiner using English tools and an English-style workbench. Her evidence includes his use of glue-soaked linen, an English custom. She believes he had his own carving tools.

Shearer moved between three counties: Berkeley County, Virginia (now West Virginia); Frederick County, Maryland; and Loudoun County, Virginia, where he moved circa 1808–1810, probably drawn by the prosperity arising from the county's primary exports, wheat and flour.

Davison thinks Shearer got his joiner's and carver's tools by barter. His inscriptions show he could read and write and was interested in current events and the theater. He was never attracted to the rebelling American colonists. Inscriptions from his days in Martinsburg and Berkeley County are pro-federalist and pro-British. Shearer's earliest known loyalist inscription is on a bedroom table in the Linda Ross collection. It reads, "Made by Shearer from Edinburgh, July 27th, 1798 / I am a true frind [sic] to my King + / country . . . and tell the Whole World Round Grate [sic] Gorge [sic] is King Hurah" (p. 21). Davison explains that Shearer is referring to the Irish Rebellion, an uprising of Roman Catholics and the Society of United Irishmen living in Northern Ireland who wanted religious freedom for Catholics in that Protestant country.

On the desk and bookcase at MESDA, one of the twenty inscriptions is a hidden message on the back of the desk's large top drawer along with a drawing of a man being stabbed with a pitchfork by the devil reading "Down with the Cropper of Ireland / Cropper is Repenting, and his Master is Angry" (p. 131). The man being stabbed is shouting "Never Rebel." Davison says it, too, relates to the Irish Rebellion of 1798 and that Shearer meant "Croppy," a derogatory term for Irish Rebels because they wore their hair cropped short, a sign of unity with the French government (p. 23). On the back of the long drawer to the fitted interior Shearer wrote, "By Shearer to Mr. Pendleton / 1801" of Winchester. It is unclear who Mr. Pendleton was, but he liked his desk, dated 1801, well enough to have Shearer add the bookcase in 1806. On it he carved a fouled anchor, with a chain wrapped around it, alluding to the October 21, 1805, Battle of Trafalgar. Although Admiral Nelson was wounded at that battle and later died, the news did not reach Martinsburg until December. On other pieces of furniture Shearer again referred to Nelson. On the bottom of a drawer of a bureau table made in January 1804 he wrote, "Huz(z)ah for Admiral Nelson / for vanquishing the Enemies of his / Country" (p. 28).

Davison believes Shearer got the news of Nelson's victories and his death from local newspapers, and she quotes accounts he might have read. His incised inscription on a slant-lid desk made circa 1808–1810 for Mr. and Mrs. Emely Dixon reads, "Neptune Gave the Sea to England Now the world must Obay [*sic*]" (p. 38). Davison says Shearer refers to British naval supremacy here: *Neptune* was not only the Roman god of the sea but also the name of the ship that towed Nelson's badly damaged flagship back to the British base at Gibraltar, and, after it was repaired, the *Neptune* served as Commander-in-Chief Cochrane's flagship during his exploits in the West Indies. As he had done on a chest he made for Mrs. Elizabeth Richards in 1808–1814, Shearer inlaid four Indian faces on the fall board of the Dixon desk. Davison contends these are a reference to the Indian problems reported in the local newspapers.

On a desk he made for Samuel Luckett, Shearer inlaid an American eagle and the word "Liberty," his only use of American iconography. He generally used pro-British imagery: a rampant lion with a crown, a thistle, or an anchor for the Royal Navy. Davison illustrates several political prints Shearer used as his sources. Politically he would have sided with the federalists because they were pro-British, anti-Jeffersonian Republicans. When nationalism became firm in America, after the War of 1812, Shearer used more subtle British naval imagery, but he continued to use anchors with chains and ropes.

In a note hidden in the section of Alfred Belt's desk into which the tambour recedes, Shearer wrote, "this Desk for Alfred Belt / the meanest know [*sic*] man / I Worked for the Greatest scoundrel in Loudoun County" (p. 146). Davison discovered that Belt was a slave owner and wealthy planter who "was hated by his neighbors and loved by nobody" (p. 149); Shearer added those words in red pencil to the desk. Belt's Quaker abolitionist neighbors would have had no use for him.

Shearer's inscriptions on his latest piece, a table stand for Mary Piles, are touching: "To love Intire, is my desire. (Who My Mary Piles)" and "September, A free Gift to Mary Piles" (p. 189). Who was Mary Piles? Davison has found no trace of her.

Shearer generally used walnut as a primary wood and occasionally cherry and small pieces of oak. He sometimes mixed woods in a single piece, for example, two drawers of cherry and one of walnut. Yellow pine, tulip poplar, and oak were his secondary woods. He often used crotched graining for drawer fronts. He often signed his name multiple times: on a chest he made in 1804, fourteen times; on a desk-and-bookcase, twenty. Davison believes he signed some of his boards before he used them to keep them separate from other cabinetmakers' lumber in storage.

Shearer always nailed his backboards vertically. Some fall boards on his desks were mitered and some have batten ends. Davison thinks he may have learned some Pennsylvania shop practices from Henry Klinger, a house carpenter and cabinetmaker who went from Reading, Pennsylvania, to Williamsport, Maryland, and married the daughter of Archibald Shearer, plantation owner in Falling Water, possibly a relative of John Shearer. She speculates that John Shearer could have worked as a journeyman for Klinger and there learned some of his woodworking skills. The fact that Shearer used the entire fall board of a desk rather than just the center as his artistic canvas may be an influence of desks made in Reading, Lancaster, and York, Pennsylvania (pp. 12, 58). Shearer's drawers are supported by a mortise-and-tenoned frame. The rear rails are further secured by nails driven through the backboard, an example of Shearer's overengineered construction.

Another example of his overconstruction is his use of additional leather and brads to reinforce tambour slides. He sometimes secured inlay with countersunk screws and covered them with wax. A Shearer characteristic is exaggerated large-scale feet, either ogee bracket feet or carved ball-and-claw feet. He did his own carving.

One of Shearer's favorite motifs is a pierced quatrefoil, an interlacing knot in an oval frame, a motif that appears in William Ince and John Mayhew's *Universal System of Household Furniture* (London, 1762). On only one piece, a chest made in 1809, he incised the words "The Federal Knot." Hurst and Prown alluded to the popular backcountry perception that the Federal Knot stands for the hopelessly entangled and ineffective new federal government, an anti-Jeffersonian point of view. Davison says Shearer was an outsider in American politics and that he used this design to poke fun at the American government in crisis after Jefferson's Embargo and Nonimportation Act led to the severe economic downturn of 1808 and 1809.

Shearer also carved convex shells with alternating convex and concave lobes. He used engaged quarter-columns, some with stop fluting, and some with bay-leaf motifs. The distinctive shapes of Shearer's spade feet with deep cove moldings at the top help attribute some tables and stands to his hand. In the beginning of his career Shearer made case pieces with flat façades and drawer pulls where you would expect them to be, but circa 1800 he made bold blocked serpentine chests of drawers and desks with variations in the top and base moldings, boldly swelled feet, and unconventionally placed pulls in vertical or diagonal positions.

Brian Coe, in a thoughtful article in the appendix, speculates on what might have been in John Shearer's tool kit, circa 1800 to 1806. By studying what he made, Coe came up with a list of tools Shearer must have owned: planes, chisels, saws, mallets, screwdrivers, awls, a brace and bit, a square, a ruler, marking gauges, scribing knives, dividers, trammel points, and a bevel gauge, plus carving tools, notably a stippling tool, turning saw, and a rasp. He may have had an English-style workbench and likely had some patterns. He used hide glue, files, sharpening stones, scrapers, finishing tools, and pencils and crayons. His turnings may have been done by others. And of course he had to have had a tool chest, one that would fit into a small buck-board or wagon.

Elizabeth Davison continues to pursue Shearer's message-laden furniture, hoping she will learn more about this enigmatic, eccentric, rural crafts-man, a house-carpenter-turned-joiner who catered to his like-minded backcountry clientele. Davidson marvels that Shearer made thirty-two large case pieces and left one of the largest bodies of signed and attributed work of any craftsman working in the late eighteenth and early nineteenth centuries, even though he never owned a shop. Here she has fully cata-logued those thirty-two pieces, and she hopes others will turn up. Since the exhibition at the DAR Museum, a tall-case clock has surfaced, and she is pursuing a lead for a table.

Lita Solis-Cohen
Maine Antique Digest

Mansfield Bascom. *Wharton Esherick: The Journey of a Creative Mind*. New York: Abrams, 2010. 275 pp.; numerous color and bw illus. $80.00.

Paul Eisenhauer and Lynne Farrington, eds., with an essay by Paul Eisenhauer. *Wharton Esherick and the Birth of the American Modern*. Atglen, Pa.: Schiffer in cooperation with Penn Libraries, 2010. 160 pp.; numerous color illus., bibliography. $29.99.

Andrew Spahr, with an introduction by Wendell Castle. *Jon Brooks: A Collab-oration with Nature*. Manchester, N.H.: Currier Museum of Art, 2011. 56 pp.; color illus., checklist. $18.00 (pb).

Wharton Esherick was a nudist. Who knew? I didn't, although given the innovative spirit and adventurous nature of this important Pennsylvania artist, I perhaps should not have been surprised.

Esherick's penchant for answering the front door in the altogether is only one of many personal insights provided by Mansfield Bascom in *Wharton Esherick: The Journey of a Creative Mind*, the first full-length biography of this major twentieth-century artist. Bascom has been married for more than fifty years to Wharton's daughter Ruth and as Wharton's son-in-law has enjoyed a unique perspective on the life and times of the man generally acknowledged as the founder of the American studio furniture movement. Moreover, until his recent retirement, he has also served as the director and later the curator of the Wharton Esherick Museum in Paoli, Pennsylvania, founded in the 1970s as a means of preserving the artist's home and studio as a shrine to his career. More than forty years in the works, Bascom's biography was undertaken with the reluctant blessing of Esherick, who preferred to let his work speak for itself but who eventually assented to the project.

Utilizing his full access to the Esherick papers, interviews, and works, as well as his lengthy personal relationship with the artist, Bascom leads us chronologically through Esherick's long and rich life, starting with his upbringing in a well-to-do Philadelphia family early in the twentieth century to his eventual standing as the grand old man of studio furniture in the 1960s, before his death in 1970. Elegantly written and beautifully illustrated, Bascom's text presents Esherick as a human being as well as a craftsman. Given Bascom's matchless personal knowledge and long familiarity with his subject, his biography will undoubtedly remain the starting point for all future research.

Bascom's biography can be read in conjunction with *Wharton Esherick and the Birth of the American Modern*, the catalogue of an exhibition at the Kamin and Kroiz Galleries at the University of Pennsylvania (September 7, 2010–February 13, 2011). Paul Eisenhauer, current curator of the Esherick Museum, organized the show with Lynne Farrington, Curator of Printed Books in the Rare Book and Manuscript Library at Penn. The bulk of the attention here is to Esherick's "flat" work—drawings, paintings, woodcuts, book illustrations, and the like—with his furniture receiving less attention. In his lengthy introduction, Eisenhauer firmly places Esherick within the modernist art movement, seeing him as a vigorous, active participant, rather than as a nearly hermetic Thoreau-like figure laboring away in the wilderness. This is a healthy perspective to maintain, and it anchors Esherick in the context of his time in an invaluable way, seeing Esherick and his circle of artistic and literary friends as part of America's contribution to modernism as it unfolded in all its ramifications. The introduction is followed by illustrations of some 267 objects accompanied by what appear to be the gallery labels and text panels.

Both of these Esherick-centered works, however, as detailed as they are, do not deal with Esherick's furniture qua furniture, for the most part, in the detailed manner that many readers of *American Furniture* get pleasure from. But they do provide an enormous amount of material that furniture historians can sink their teeth into for many years to come, as Esherick's furniture will inevitably continue to be better understood and as his reputation grows. They have laid down a baseline of research and cleared the way for scholars in the future to develop and refine more specific areas of investigation.

The world of studio furniture, like all aspects of the art world, is a tangled skein of relationships and bonds both personal and professional, linking masters with apprentices, teachers with students. Wendell Castle, himself an acknowledged leader of the field today, provides a thread that ties Esherick together with Jon Brooks, a New Hampshire furniture maker whose life and art were recently surveyed in an exhibition at the Currier Museum of Art in Manchester organized by Andrew Spahr. Castle, who "discovered" Esherick in 1958, once observed, "Esherick taught me that the making of furniture could be a form of sculpture; Esherick caused me to come to appreciate inherent tree characteristics in the utilization of wood; and, finally, he demonstrated the importance of the entire sculptural environment" (as quoted by Bascom, 255). Castle, in turn, had his own impact on Brooks, who early in his career served as Castle's "first paid help" in his studio in Rochester, New York, in the mid-1960s. Castle, as he notes in his introduction to the Currier exhibition catalogue, recognized Brooks's talent when Brooks was still quite young.

Those elements that Castle found appealing in Esherick's work—specifically the attention to sculptural form and the deft handling of wood—are also reflected in Brooks's furniture, as revealed in Spahr's text and in the illustrations of many of the forty-three objects included in the exhibition. For more than forty years, Brooks has created impressive, often colorful objects that take advantage of the properties of wood, utilizing both large, trunklike pieces to create massive seating furniture, for example, and smaller branchlike members, often painted, to fashion table legs, ladder-back chairs, and other forms. Combining his passion for art and for nature, Brooks, as Spahr notes, "has produced a body of work that balances craftsmanship with poetry and humor, function with imagery and dynamic abstract forms, and natural wood finishes with colorfully decorated surfaces" (p. 37). This retrospective at the Currier is a most fitting tribute to one of New Hampshire's finest grand masters, one made more poignant in that Brooks, a Manchester native, first studied art as a young boy at the Currier Museum Art Center.

Gerald W. R. Ward
Museum of Fine Arts, Boston

Compiled by
Gerald W. R. Ward

Recent Writing on American Furniture: A Bibliography

This year's list includes works published in 2010 and roughly through September 2011. As always, a few earlier publications that had escaped notice are also included. The short title *American Furniture 2010* is used in citations for articles and reviews published in last year's edition of this journal, which is also cited in full under Luke Beckerdite's name.

Once again, many people have assisted in compiling this list. I am particularly grateful to Luke Beckerdite, Fronia W. Simpson, Jonathan Fairbanks, Nicholas R. Bell, Dennis Carr, Michelle Finamore, Nonie Gadsden, Kelly H. L'Ecuyer, Johanna McBrien, Steven M. Lash, and Barbara McLean Ward, as well as to the scholars who have prepared reviews for this issue. I am also indebted to the librarians of the Museum of Fine Arts, Boston, the Portsmouth Athenaeum, and the Portsmouth Public Library for their ogoing assistance.

I would be glad to receive citations for titles that have been inadvertently omitted from this or previous lists. Information about new publications and review copies of significant works would also be much appreciated.

Ackermann, Daniel Kurt. "Google Goes Antiquing." *Antiques* 178, no. 3 (May–June 2011): 114–23. Color illus.

———. "Living with Antiques: The Kentucky Collection of Sharon and Mack Cox." *Antiques* 178, no. 4 (July–August 2011): 122–29. 17 color illus.

Albrecht, Donald, and Thomas Mellins. "American Revivalism." *Antiques* 178, no. 3 (May–June 2011): 96–105. Color illus.

Allman, William, and Melissa C. Naulin. *Something of Splendor: Decorative Arts from the White House*. Washington, D.C.: White House Historical Association, 2011. 93 pp.; color and bw illus.

American Period Furniture: Journal of the Society of American Period Furniture Makers 10 (2010): 1–108. Numerous color and bw illus. (See also individual articles cited separately.)

Ames, Kenneth L. Review of Briann G. Greenfield, *Out of the Attic: Inventing Antiques in Twentieth-Century New England*. In *American Furniture 2010*, 241–48.

Andrews, Gail C., et al. *Birmingham Museum of Art: Guide to the Collection*. London: Giles, 2010. 286 pp.; numerous color illus., index. (Includes a Belter sofa and several examples of English, European, and African furniture.)

Barquist, David L. "Touch Wood." *Antiques* 178, no. 5 (September–October 2011): 128–35. 10 color illus.

Beach, Laura. "Living with Antiques: No Velvet Ropes." *Antiques* 178, no. 5 (September–October 2011): 96–105. 16 color illus.

Beckerdite, Luke, ed. *American Furniture 2010*. Milwaukee, Wis.: Chipstone Foundation, 2010. ix + 290 pp.; numerous color and bw illus., bibliography, index. Distributed by University Press of New England, Hanover and London.

Bell, Nicholas R. "Matthias Pliessnig." In Nicholas R. Bell, Ulysses Grant Dietz, and Andrew Wagner, *History in the Making: Renwick Craft Invitational 2011* (Washington, D.C.: Smithsonian American Art Museum; London:

Scala Publishers, 2011), 74–91. 14 color and bw illus.

Bernhard, Virginia. *Ima Hogg: The Governor's Daughter*. Denton, Tex.: Texas State Historical Association, 2011. ix + 144 pp.; color illus.

Brandt, Beverly K. Review of Joseph Cunningham, *The Artistic Furniture of Charles Rohlfs*. In *American Furniture 2010*, 248–52.

Burt, Owen H. "Walter H. Durfee and His Curtis Girandole Clocks." *Watch & Clock Bulletin* 53 (February 2011): 4–12. 23 color and bw illus.

Callahan, W. Mickey. "Steven Lash: 2010 Cartouche Award Recipient." *American Period Furniture: Journal of the Society of American Period Furniture Makers* 10 (2010): 2–6. 10 color and bw illus.

[Carnegie Museum of Art]. "Carnegie Museum of Art Makes Decorative Arts Acquisitions." *Antiques and the Arts Weekly* (July 29, 2011). 34. 2 bw illus. (Re rocking chair by Sam Maloof, Monkey Settee by Judy Kensley McKie, Architect's Valet chair by Alphonse Mattia, and other gifts from the collection of Deena and Jerome Kaplan.)

Carr, Dennis. "Period Rooms in the New Art of the Americas Wing at the Museum of Fine Arts, Boston." *Antiques and Fine Art* 10, no. 6 (2011): 312–19. Color illus.

Castillo, Greg. *Cold War on the Home Front*. Minneapolis: University of Minnesota Press, 2010. 312 pp.; 97 bw illus.

Çevik, Gülen. "American Style or Turkish Chair: The Triumph of Bodily Comfort." *Journal of Design History* 23, no. 4 (December 2010): 367–85. Illus.

Charleston Museum, S.C. "Discoveries from the Field: Soulfully Sold; Catalogue of Genuine Antique Furniture from Eminent Families of South Carolina, Published in 1894 by the Fifth Avenue Auction Rooms, New York City." *Antiques and Fine Art* 10, no. 6 (2011): 298–99. 2 color illus.

Clancy, Jonathan. "Elbert Hubbard, Transcendentalism and the Arts and Crafts Movement in America." *Journal*

of Modern Craft 2, no. 2 (July 2009): 143–60. 11 bw illus.

Connors, Michael. *British West Indies Style: Antigua, Jamaica, Barbados, and Beyond*. New York: Rizzoli, 2010. 200 pp.; numerous color illus., index.

———. "Caribbean Cool: Caned Furniture of the Colonial British West Indies." *Antiques* 177, no. 6 (November–December 2010): 150–55. Color illus.

[Cook, Claire, Collection]. *Important Auction of the Claire Cook Collection from Winnetka, Illinois*. Portsmouth, N.H.: Northeast Auctions, August 6, 2011. 72 pp.; color illus. (With introductory statements by Ron Bourgeault and by Steve and Beverly White.)

Cooper, Wendy A., and Lisa Minardi. *Paint, Pattern & People: Furniture of Southeastern Pennsylvania, 1725–1850*. A Winterthur Book. Winterthur, Del.: Henry Francis du Pont Winterthur Museum, 2011. xxv + 277 pp.; numerous color and bw illus., checklist, bibliography, index. Distributed by University of Pennsylvania Press. (Also vol. 45 in the annual volume series of the Pennsylvania German Society.)

———. "Paint, Pattern & People." *Antiques* 178, no. 3 (May–June 2011): 160–69. 17 color illus.

———. "Paint, Pattern & People: Furniture of Southeastern Pennsylvania, 1725–1850." *Antiques and Fine Art* 11, no. 1 (spring 2011): 170–77. 13 color illus.

Corrales, Juan Manuel. "Viceregal Furniture from Oaxaca Carried Out in *Zumaque*: The Marquetry of Villa Alta." *Revista de Dialectologia y Tradiciones Populares* 66, no. 1 (January–June 2011): 57–88. 18 illus., bibliography. (In Spanish, with summary in English.)

Davison, Elizabeth A. *The Furniture of John Shearer, 1790–1820: "A True North Britain" in the Southern Backcountry*. Lanham, Md.: Altamira Press, 2011. xix + 217 pp.; numerous color and bw illus., tables, appendixes, bibliography, index.

Dervan, Andrew. "Daniel J. Steele's Legacy." *Watch & Clock Bulletin* 53, no. 3 (June 2011): 306–10. Color illus. (Re a twentieth-century ornamental glass painter.)

Dietz, Ulysses Grant, and Sam Watters. *Dream House: The White House as an American Home*. New York: Acanthus Press, 2009. 304 pp.; 350+ color and bw illus., drawings, plans, bibliography, index.

Dion, Arthur, and Judy Kensley McKie. *Judy Kensley McKie: Conversation with Arthur Dion*. Boston: Gallery NAGA, 2010. 28 pp.; color illus., bibliography.

Douglas, Ed Polk. Review of Jack D. Holden et al., *Furnishing Louisiana: Creole and Acadian Furniture, 1735–1835. Maine Antique Digest* 39, no. 6 (June 2011): 38B–39B. 5 bw illus., bibliography.

Eastberg, John C. *The Captain Frederick Pabst Mansion: An Illustrated History*. Milwaukee: Captain Frederick Pabst Mansion, 2009. 28 pp.; illus. Distributed by University of Wisconsin Press.

[Eckel, John R., Jr., Collection]. *The Collection of John R. Eckel, Jr.* Chicago: Wright, June 28, 2011. Unpaged; numerous color illus. (Auction of part of the modernist collection of Eckel [1951–2009] of Houston; other parts were bequeathed to the Museum of Fine Arts, Houston, and the Whitney Museum of American Art in New York.)

Edwards, Jason, and Imogen Hart. *Rethinking the Interior, c. 1867–1896: Aestheticism and Arts and Crafts*. Aldershot, U.K.: Ashgate, 2010. 294 pp.; 65 bw illus.

Ehrenpreis, Diane C. "The Seat of State: Thomas Jefferson and the Campeche Chair." In *American Furniture 2010*, 28–53. 27 color illus.

Eisenhauer, Paul, and Lynne Farrington, eds., with an essay by Paul Eisenhauer. *Wharton Esherick and the Birth of the American Modern*. Atglen, Pa.: Schiffer in cooperation with Penn Libraries, 2010. 160 pp.; numerous color illus., bibliography.

[Esherick, Wharton]. *Wharton Esherick's Illuminated and Illustrated Song of the Broad-Axe by Walt Whitman*. Atglen, Pa.: Schiffer Publishing, 2010. Unpaged; bw illus. (A facsimile edition with introductory essay by Paul Eisenhauer.)

Falino, Jeannine, and Jennifer Scanlan. "Crafting Modernism: Midcentury American Art and Design." In [Catalogue of] *The 14th Annual Sculpture Objects and Functional Art Fair, April 14–17, 2011*. New York: SOFA New York, 2011. 18–23. 9 color illus.

Falk, Cynthia G. *Architecture and Artifacts of the Pennsylvania Germans: Constructing Identity in Early America*. University Park: Pennsylvania State University Press, 2008. xiv + 241 pp.; 103 bw illus., appendixes, index.

Follansbee, Peter. Review of Paul Fitzsimmons, Robert Tarule, and Donald P. White III, *Discovering Dennis: The Search for Thomas Dennis among the Artisans of Exeter*. In *American Furniture 2010*, 256–70.

Follansbee, Peter, and Robert F. Trent. "Reassessing the London-Style Joinery and Turning of Seventeenth-Century Boston." In *American Furniture 2010*, 194–240. 41 color and bw illus., appendixes.

[Georgia Museum of Art]. "Acquisitions." *Decorative Arts Society Newsletter* 20, no. 1 (spring 2011): 3. 1 bw illus. (Re chest of drawers, ca. 1825–1860, from Virginia or North Carolina.)

Gere, Charlotte. *Artistic Circles: Design and Decoration in the Aesthetic Movement*. London: V&A Publishing, 2010. 160 pp.; 160 color illus.

Gieben-Gamal, Emma. Review of Penny Sparke, Anne Weallens, Trevor Keeble, and Brenda Martin, *Designing the Modern Interior: From the Victorians to Today*. In *West 86th: A Journal of Decorative Arts, Design History, and Material Culture* 18, no. 1 (spring/summer 2011): 111–14. 1 bw illus.

Giles, Leah. "Music in Washington, D.C., 1800–1825." *Decorative Arts Trust* [Newsletter] 20, no. 1 (summer 2011): 6–7. 6 color illus.

Gómez, Edward M. "Design for Living." *Art & Antiques* 33, no. 8 (September 2010): 64–75. Color illus.

Gontar, Cybèle T. "A Federal Campeche Chair Restored." *American Period Furniture: Journal of the Society of American Period Furniture Makers* 10 (2010): 22–27. 21 color illus.

Grandeur Preserved: Masterworks Presented by Historic Charleston Foundation; The Loan Exhibition for the 57th Annual Winter Antiques Show, January 21–30, 2011. No place: no publisher, 2011. 64 pp.; color illus.

Gray, Edward G. *Colonial America: A History in Documents*. 2nd ed. New York: Oxford University Press, 2011. ix + 211 pp.; numerous bw illus., timeline, bibliography, index. (Textbook including some furniture and other objects.)

Gustafson, Eleanor H. "End Notes." *Antiques* 178, no. 3 (May–June 2011): 176. 3 color illus. (Re tall-case clock with works by John Heiling, Montgomery County, Pennsylvania, ca. 1789.)

Hanus, Julie K. "Curves Ahead." *American Craft* 71, no. 3 (June–July 2011): 32–39. Color illus. (Re studio furniture maker Vivian Beer.)

Hazlewood, Karolee R. *Remembering Grand Rapids*. New York: Trade Paper Press, 2010. x + 134 pp.; illus.

Hershon, Marissa. "The Egyptian Revival Reception Room at Cedar Hill." *Nineteenth Century* 31, no. 1 (spring 2011): 3–12. 6 color and 2 bw illus.

Hewett, David. "That Gothic Bench in the Garden: How Old Is It?" *Maine Antique Digest* 39, no. 6 (June 2011): 24B–25B. 9 bw illus.

Hinds, Hilary. "Together and Apart: Twin Beds, Domestic Hygiene, and Modern Marriage, 1890–1945." *Journal of Design History* 23, no. 3 (September 2010): 275–304. Illus. (With a focus on England.)

Hobbs, Matthew. "An Introduction to Cabinetmaker Thomas White." *American Period Furniture: Journal of the Society of American Period Furniture Makers* 10 (2010): 54–57. 9 color illus. (See also Ben Hobbs, "The Drawer Construction of Thomas White," 58–59.)

Holden, Jack D., H. Parrott Bacot, Cybèle T. Gontar, with Brian J. Costello and Francis J. Puig. *Furnishing Louisiana: Creole and Acadian Furniture, 1735–1835*. New Orleans:

Historic New Orleans Collection, 2010. xiv + 538 pp.; numerous color and bw illus., three appendixes, glossary, bibliography, index.

Hudgins, Carter C. "The Material World of John Drayton: International Connections to Wealth, Intellect, and Taste." *Antiques and Fine Art* 10, no. 6 (2011): 289–95. Color illus.

Johnson, Don. "Equal in Goodness: Ohio Decorative Arts, 1788–1860." *Maine Antique Digest* 39, no. 5 (May 2011): 14B–15B. Bw illus.

Jones, Leslie. "The Bellangé Furniture of the White House." *Decorative Arts Trust* [Newsletter] 20, no. 1 (summer 2011): 4–5. 5 color illus.

Kane, Patricia E. "A High Point of Americana." *Yale Alumni Magazine* 74, no. 4 (March–April 2011): 58. 1 color illus.

Katcher, Jane, David A. Schorsch, and Ruth Wolfe, eds. *Expressions of Innocence and Eloquence: Selections from the Jane Katcher Collection of Americana, Volume 2*. Seattle: Marquand Books, 2011. 452 pp.; 417 color illus. Distributed by Yale University Press, New Haven and London.

[Kaufman Collection]. "National Gallery of Art to Receive the Kaufman Collection." *Antiques and Fine Art* 10, no. 6 (2011): 102. 5 color illus.

[Kellogg, Helen, and Steven Kellogg Collection]. *A Product of Passion: The American Folk Art Collection of Helen and Steven Kellogg*. Portsmouth, N.H.: Northeast Auctions, August 6, 2011. 119 pp.; numerous color illus., index. (With introduction by Patrick Bell.)

Kenny, Peter M. "Museum Accessions." *Antiques* 178, no. 3 (May–June 2011): 86. 1 color illus. (Re cupboard, ca. 1680–1685, from northern Essex County, Massachusetts, acquired by the Metropolitan Museum of Art, New York City.)

Kinchin, Juliet, and Aidan O'Connor. *Counter Space: Design and the Modern Kitchen*. New York: Museum of Modern Art, 2011. 88 pp.; 75 color and bw illus.

Kirtley, Alexandra Alevizatos. "Fit for Any Amusement." *Antiques* 178, no. 3

(May–June 2011): 154–59. 6 color illus. (Re reed organ, ca. 1837, by Emilius Nicolai Scheer, recently acquired by the Philadelphia Museum of Art.)

Kolbe, Regina. "Frank Lloyd Wright: Organic Architecture for the Twenty-first Century." *Antiques and the Arts Weekly* (February 18, 2011): 1, 40–41. 14 bw illus.

Kuykendall, Erin. "Report on Thomas Newell, Master Builder." [Newsletter of] *The Decorative Arts Trust* 18, no. 3 (fall 2010): 6–7. 4 color illus.

LaFond, Edward F., Jr. "Thomas Crow of Wilmington, Delaware." *Watch & Clock Bulletin* 53, no. 3 (June 2011): 264–66. 6 bw illus.

Lash, Steven M. "The Green Man in the Duke's Closet: An Ancient Motif Crafted with Contemporary Techniques." *American Period Furniture: Journal of the Society of American Period Furniture Makers* 10 (2010): 7–11. 20 color and bw illus.

Lasser, Ethan W. "The Cane Chair and Its Sitter." In *American Furniture 2010*, 54–75. 20 color illus.

Latta, Steve. "Rural Inlay." *American Period Furniture: Journal of the Society of American Period Furniture Makers* 10 (2010): 40–44. 8 color and bw illus. (See also pp. 45–47.)

[Levine, Barbara, and Bob Levine Collection]. *American Furniture and Decorative Arts*. Sale 2558M. Marlborough, Mass.: Skinner, August 14, 2011. 182 pp.; numerous color illus., bibliography. (Re Vermont furniture.)

Lucas, June. "'The Neat[est] Pieces of Any Description': Piedmont North Carolina Furniture, 1780–1860." *Antiques and Fine Art* 11, no. 1 (spring 2011): 186–92. Color illus.

MacKay, Keith D. "Victorian Revival in Wisconsin: Neo-Rococo Surrealism at Ten Chimneys." *Nineteenth Century* 31, no. 1 (spring 2011): 31–36. 5 color and 1 bw illus.

[Maloof, Sam]. "Current and Coming: Maloof and Friends at the Huntington." *Antiques* 178, no. 5 (September–October 2011): 30. 1 color illus.

Marzio, Peter, et al. *American Art and Philanthropy: Twenty Years of Collecting*

at the Museum of Fine Arts, Houston. Houston: Museum of Fine Arts, Houston, 2010. 388 pp.; numerous color and bw illus., index.

Mascolo, Frances McQueeney-Jones. "Paint, Pattern, and People: Furniture of Southeastern Pennsylvania, 1725–1850." *Antiques and the Arts Weekly* (April 8, 2011): 1, 40–41. Bw illus.

———. "Rudy Ciccarello and the Two Red Roses Foundation: Preserving the American Arts and Crafts Movement." *Antiques and the Arts Weekly* (August 5, 2011): 1, 30–31. 12 bw illus.

———. Review of Jack D. Holden and H. Parrott Bacot et al., *Furnishing Louisiana: Creole and Acadian Furniture, 1735–1835*. In *Antiques and the Arts Weekly* (May 20, 2011): 1, 30–31. bw illus.

Massey, Anne. *Chair*. London: Reaktion Books, 2011. 224 pp.; numerous color and bw illus., bibliography, index.

May, Stephen. "A Centennial Celebration at Gustav Stickley's Craftsman Farms." *Antiques and the Arts Weekly* (July 8, 2011): 1, 30–31. 13 bw illus.

———. "Something of Splendor: Decorative Arts from the White House." *Antiques and the Arts Weekly* (October 7, 2011): 1, 40–41. 12 bw illus.

Mayer, Roberta, and Mark Sfirri. "Early Expressions of Anthroposophical Design in America: The Influence of Rudolf Steiner and Fritz Westhoff on Wharton Esherick." *Journal of Modern Craft* 2, no. 3 (November 2009): 299–323. 20 bw illus.

McBrien, Johanna. "Lifestyle: Charleston Calling." *Antiques and Fine Art* 10, no. 6 (2011): 236–47. Color illus.

———. "Lifestyle: Devotion." *Antiques and Fine Art* 10, no. 6 (2011): 210–21. Color illus.

———. "Lifestyle: 'A Rare Opportunity for a Residence.'" *Antiques and Fine Art* 10, no. 6 (2011): 222–35. Color illus.

McDonald, Gay. "The Modern American Home as Soft Power: Finland, MoMA, and the 'American Home 1953' Exhibition." *Journal of Design History* 23, no. 4 (December 2010): 387–408. Illus.

Miller, Marla R., ed. *Cultivating a Past: Essays on the History of Hadley, Massachusetts*. Amherst: University of Massachusetts Press, 2009. 384 pp.; 46 illus., bibliography, index. (Includes reprint of Laurel Thatcher Ulrich, "Hannah Barnard's Cupboard: Female Property and Identity in Eighteenth-Century New England," 154–90.)

Moore, Patti. "Patti Moore's Observations about Her Collection of United Clock Company Clocks." *Watch & Clock Bulletin* 53 (February 2011): 13–29. 67+ color illus.

Morris, Philip E., Jr. *American Wooden Movement Tall Clocks, 1712–1835*. Hoover, Ala.: Heritage Park Publishing, 2011. 511 pp.; numerous color illus., biographies, appendixes, glossary, bibliography, index.

Moses, Meredyth Hyatt. *Furniture Divas: Recent Work by Contemporary Makers*. Brockton, Mass.: Fuller Craft Museum, 2011. Unpaged; color illus. (Small brochure accompanying exhibition held February 19–October 30, 2011.)

Mr. Stickley's Home: 1911. Morris Plains, N.J.: Craftsman Farms, 2011. 44 pp.; color and bw illus, checklist, bibliography. (Accompanies an exhibition produced by the Stickley Museum at Craftsman Farms, February 2011, at the 24th Annual Arts and Crafts Conference, Grove Park Inn, Asheville, North Carolina; includes contributions by Mark E. Weaver, Heather E. Stivison, David Cathers, Mark Alan Hewitt, Peter K. Mars, and A. Patricia Bartinique.)

Muller, Charles. "Equal in Goodness." *Antiques and the Arts Weekly* (April 22, 2011): 1, 40–41. bw illus. (Re exhibition of the early material culture of Ohio.)

[Museum of Early Southern Decorative Arts]. "Current and Coming." *Antiques* 177, no. 6 (November–December 2010): 26. 1 color illus. (Re exhibition "'The Neatest Pieces of Any Description': Furniture of Piedmont North Carolina, 1780–1860," organized by Jane Lucas.)

Mussey, Robert, and Christopher Shelton. "John Penniman and the Ornamental Painting Tradition in Federal-Era

Boston." In *American Furniture 2010*, 2–27. 36 color and bw illus.

Neuhart, Marilyn, with John Neuhart. *The Story of Eames Furniture*. Vol. 1, *The Early Years*. Vol. 2, *The Herman Miller Age*. Berlin: Gestalten Verlag, 2010. 2 vols. 798 pp.; 2,500 color and bw illus., bibliography, index.

[Newport Historical Society]. "Found: Newport Desk." *Newport Historical Society* [newsletter and annual report] (spring 2011): 4. 3 color illus. (Re desk attributed to John or Thomas Goddard.)

Olivares, Jonathan. *A Taxonomy of Office Chairs*. New York and London: Phaidon Press, 2011. 224 pp.; numerous color and bw illus., line drawings, appendix, index. (Described as a study of "the evolution of the office chair, demonstrated through a catalogue of seminal models and an illustrated taxonomy of their components.")

Palmer, Arlene. "'A breath of the far distant East' in Maine: The Restoration of Victoria Mansion's Turkish Room." *Antiques* 178, no. 4 (July–August 2011): 130–37. 16 color and bw illus.

Pierce, Donna, ed. *The Arts of South America, 1492–1850: Papers from the 2008 Mayer Center Symposium at the Denver Art Museum*. Denver: Denver Art Museum, 2010. 224 pp.; color and bw illus.

Piña, Leslie A. *Furniture in History, 3000 B.C.–2000 A.D.* 2nd ed. Boston: Prentice-Hall, 2010. xiv + 409 pp.; numerous color illus., glossary.

Pennington, Kate. Review of Elizabeth A. Davison, *The Furniture of John Shearer, 1790–1820: "A True North Britain" in the Southern Backcountry*. In *Maine Antique Digest* 39, no. 7 (July 2011): 7B. 1 bw illus.

Pérez de Salazar Verea, Francisco, ed. *El mobiliario en Puebla: Preciosismo, mitos y cotidianidad de la carpintería y la ebanistería*. Puebla de los Angeles, Mexico: Fundación Mary Street Jenkins, 2009. 192 pp.; numerous color illus., appendix, glossary, bibliography.

Pochoda, Elizabeth, et al. "Fortunate Son: Reading the Memoirs, Albert Sack (1915–2011)." *Antiques* 178, no. 4

(July–August 2011): 104–13. Color illus.

Porter, David. *The Chinese Taste in Eighteenth-Century England*. Cambridge: Cambridge University Press, 2010. x + 210 pp.; numerous bw illus., bibliography, index.

Priddy, Sumpter, and Ann Steuart. "Seating Furniture from the District of Columbia, 1795–1820." In *American Furniture 2010*, 76–139. 93 color and bw illus.

Rector, Rebecca. "Researching Art and Craft: Allen Holcomb and His Daughter Collata Holcomb." *American Ancestors* 12, no. 1 (winter 2011): 37–39. 2 bw illus.

Richmond, Andrew, and Hollie Davis. *Equal in Goodness: Ohio Decorative Arts, 1788–1860*. Lancaster, Ohio: Decorative Arts Center of Ohio, 2011. 128 pp.; color illus.

Richmond, Andrew, and Hollie Davis. "Highlights from Equal in Goodness: Ohio Decorative Arts, 1788–1860." *Antiques and Fine Art* 11, no. 1 (spring 2011): 218–20. 4 color illus.

[Rivers Collection]. "The Rivers Collection, Charleston, South Carolina." *Antiques and Fine Art* 10, no. 6 (2011): 300–301. 4 color illus.

Roberts, Ellen E. Review of Edward R. Bosley and Anne E. Mallek, *A New and Native Beauty: The Art and Craft of Greene and Greene*. In *American Furniture 2010*, 252–56.

Robinson, Katharine S. "Winter Antiques Show Loan Exhibit: Charleston's Master Works Presented by Historic Charleston Foundation." *Antiques and Fine Art* 10, no. 6 (2011): 272–79. Color illus.

Rudolph, William Keyse, and Alexandra Alevizatos Kirtley. *Treasures of American and English Painting and Decorative Arts from the Julian Wood Glass, Jr., Collection*. Winchester, Va.: Museum of the Shenandoah Valley, 2010. 248 pp.; numerous color and bw illus., glossary, bibliography, index. Distributed by Skira Rizzoli, New York.

Russell, David R., assisted by Robert Lesage. *Antique Woodworking Tools: Their Craftsmanship from the Earliest*

Times to the Twentieth Century. Cambridge, U.K.: John Adamson in association with Bernard J. Shapero Rare Books, London, 2010. 527 pp.; numerous color illus., bibliography, index.

Savage, David. *Furniture with Soul: Master Woodworkers and Their Craft.* Tokyo and New York: Kodansha International, 2011. 231 pp.; color and bw illus.

Schaumann, Merri Lou Scribner. *Plank Bottom Chairs and Chairmakers: South Central Pennsylvania, 1800–1880.* Carlisle, Pa.: Cumberland County Historical Society, 2009. viii + 136 pp.; color and bw illus., maps.

Seagrave, Ronald Roy. *The Early Artisans and Mechanics of Petersburg, Virginia, 1607–1860: The Building of a Multi-Cultural Maritime Community.* Denver: Outskirts Press, 2010. viii + 541 pp.; illus., maps.

Shales, Ezra. "Corporate Craft: Constructing the Empire State Building." *Journal of Modern Craft* 4, no. 2 (July 2011): 119–45. 13 bw illus.

Shaykett, Jessica. "Jere Osgood: Deliberate Design." *American Craft* 71, no. 4 (August–September 2011): 112. 2 color illus.

Shields, David S., ed. *Material Culture in Anglo-America: Regional Identity and Urbanity in the Tidewater, Lowcountry, and Caribbean.* Columbia: University of South Carolina Press, 2009. xvi + 272 pp.; 300 color and bw illus., 3 maps, appendixes, bibliography, index.

Simpson, Tommy. *Totally Tommy: The Art of Tommy Simpson, April 29–May 28, 2011.* Boston: Gallery NAGA, 2011. 16 pp.; color illus.

Solis-Cohen, Lita. "Fernside Cottage: A Collection of Collections." *Antiques and Fine Art* 11, no. 1 (spring 2011): 138–51. Color illus.

———. Review of Luke Beckerdite, ed., *American Furniture 2010.* In *Maine Antique Digest* 39, no. 6 (June 2011): 28B–30B. 1 bw illus.

Spahr, P. Andrew, with an introduction by Wendell Castle. *Jon Brooks: A Collaboration with Nature.* Manchester, N.H.: Currier Museum of Art, 2011. 56 pp.; color illus., checklist.

[Speed Art Museum]. "Speed Art Museum Receives Donation of More than 100 Objects of Kentucky Art." *Antiques and the Arts Weekly* (September 9, 2011): 13. 2 bw illus. (Includes Kentucky furniture from the Noe Collection.)

Sperling, David. "Joseph Ives and Abel Stowell: In Search of Lost Time." *Maine Antique Digest* 39, no. 10 (October 2011): 28C–29C. 17 bw illus.

———. "A Summary of the Egerton Family and Their Furniture: What's Attributable and What's Not!—Part 1." *Watch & Clock Bulletin* 52 (December 2010): 666–76. 22+ color and bw illus. (Previously published in slightly different form in *Maine Antique Digest*, in October, November, and December 2009.)

———. "A Summary of the Egerton Family and Their Furniture: What's Attributable and What's Not!—Part 2." *Watch & Clock Bulletin* 53 (February 2011): 33–39. 11+ bw illus., bibliography.

———. "Will the Real John Adams Please Stand Up?" *Watch & Clock Bulletin* 53, no. 4 (August 2011): 390–98. Color and bw illus.

Stapleton, Annamarie, et al. "The Aesthetic Movement." *Decorative Arts Society: 1850 to the Present* 34 (2010): 1–144. Numerous color illus.

Taylor, Snowden, ed. "Research Activities and News." *Watch & Clock Bulletin* 53, no. 3 (June 2011): 353–64. bw illus. (Short notes on a variety of topics related to clockmaking.)

Trent, Robert F., Erik Gronning, and Alan Anderson. "The Gaines Attributions and Baroque Seating in Northeastern New England." In *American Furniture 2010*, 140–93. 91 color and bw illus., appendix.

Trexler, Adam. "Crafting a *New Age*: A. R. Orage and the Politics of Craft." *Journal of Modern Craft* 4, no. 2 (July 2011): 161–82. 2 bw illus. (See also, in the same issue, "Primary Text: Politics for Craftsmen [by] A. R. Orage," 183–92.)

"The Virginia Safe Project." *Maine Antique Digest* 39, no. 3 (March 2011): 10A. 1 bw illus.

Van Aalst, Lock, and Annigje Hofstede. *Noord-Nederlandse meubelen van renaissance tot vroege barok, 1550–1670.* Houten, the Netherlands: Hes en De Graaf, 2011. 518 pp.; numerous color illus., glossary, bibliography, index.

Vernimb, Bryan, and Snowden Taylor. "The Hopkins Clockmakers of Litchfield and Harwinton, CT: Part 1A, Asa Hopkins, Litchfield." *Watch & Clock Bulletin* 53, no. 3 (June 2011): 278–301. Color and bw illus., tables. Part 1B, "Asa Hopkins, Litchfield." *Watch & Clock Bulletin* 53, no. 4 (August 2011): 421–33. Bw illus., bibliography.

Ward, Gerald W. R. "Little Green Men: A Note on the Masked Men of Massachusetts." *American Period Furniture: Journal of the Society of American Period Furniture Makers* 10 (2010): 12–16. 3 color and bw illus.

Ward, Gerald W. R., comp. "Recent Writing on American Furniture: A Bibliography." In *American Furniture 2010*, 271–79.

West 86th: A Journal of Decorative Arts, Design History, and Material Culture 18, no. 1 (spring/summer 2011): 1–136. Numerous color and bw illus. (This is the first issue of the revamped *Studies in the Decorative Arts*, published by Bard between 1993 and 2010, now to be published semiannually by the Bard Graduate Center, New York, and the University of Chicago Press.)

Wilk, Christopher. Review of Marilyn Neuhart with John Neuhart, *The Story of Eames Furniture.* In *The Furniture History Society Newsletter*, no. 183 (August 2011): 10–12.

Wood, Robin. "Statement of Practice: Technology and Hand Skill in Craft and Industry." *Journal of Modern Craft* 4, no. 2 (July 2011): 193–202. 5 bw illus.

Wroth, William, Robin Farwell Gavin, Keith Bakker, et al. *Converging Streams: Art of the Hispanic and Native American Southwest.* Santa Fe, N.Mex.: Museum of Spanish Colonial Art, 2010. 283 pp.; color and bw illus.

Index

Abbe, Shubael, 249

Ache, Christina, 40, 41(fig. 60), 44, 107*n*19, 110*n*27

Ache, Henry, 40, 43, 110*n*27

Ache, Henry, Jr., 40, 41

Ache, Hermannus, 43–44, 110*n*28

Ache, Jacob, 43, 45

Ache, Johannes, 49

Ache, Johann Jacob, 110*n*28

Ache, Johann Ludwig, 110*n*28

Ache, Maria Catharina, 110*n*27; birth and baptismal certificate, 40–41(&fig. 61)

Ache, Mary, 44(fig. 65)

Ache, Peter, 43

Ache, Samuel, 42–46(&figs. 63 & 64), 58, 72

Ache, Sophia, 41, 42(fig.), 44, 107*n*19, 110*n*27

Ache, Thomas, 41

Ache (Achey, Aughe), Henry, 40, 43, 110*n*27

Achey, Filbert, 44(fig. 65)

Achey's Corner (Pennsylvania), 42

Ackley, John B., 225, 231

Adam and Eve motif, 98(fig. 143), 99(&fig.), 119*n*63

Africanisms, Thomas Day and, 295–96

Agens, Jonas, 270

Albany Chronicle, 212(fig.)

Albrecht (Albright), Elisabeth, 42

Alexander, Hugh, desks, 123–25(&figs. 4 & 5), 150, 160*n*6

Alexander, James, 160*n*6

Allen, A. D., 203*n*46

Allen, Amos D.: black chairs and, 227; bow-back Windsor chairs and, 215–16; edging on chairs and, 249; mahogany-colored chairs and, 231, 262; red chairs and, 236; stuffed seats and, 221, 239; Windsor rocking chairs and, 263; yellow chairs and, 220

Allen, Cornelius, 290

Allen, Ebenezer, Jr., 290

Allen, Oliver, 205

Allen, Simeon, 202*n*31

Alling, David: blossom-colored chairs and, 238; bronzed chairs and, 257, 258; brown chairs and, 232; children's seating and, 271, 272; drab-colored chairs and, 233; export of fancy chairs, 224, 230; fancy chair prices, 234–35; gilded furniture and, 260–61, 265, 266; grained chairs and, 241, 243–44, 245, 246; green chairs and, 219; imitation maple chairs and, 241, 243–44; ornamentation and, 250, 253, 254, 255, 256; Palmer and, 259; red chairs and, 236; settees and, 266, 267, 268; stools and, 270; white chairs and, 226, 227; yellow chairs and, 221, 222, 223, 224

Allwine, Lawrence, 206, 220, 230

Allyn, Stephen Billings, 194, 196

Alsace Township (Pennsylvania), tulip poplar chest, 61(fig. 88)

Always, James, 205

American arts and crafts movement, 297–301

American Mercury, 199*n*11

American studio furniture movement, 310–12

Andy Warhol Foundation, 296

Angel heads, 103*n*6; earthenware, 9, 10(fig. 14); fraktur, 92, 93(fig. 134); pine, 21, 22(fig.)

Angel motif, 94(figs.), 95, 96(fig. 138), 106*n*17

Animal feet, 230

Animals, as ornament on chairs, 254

Anna (ship), 202*n*42

Antimony, 220

Antiques (magazine), 61

Appliques: foliate, 145, 146(&figs.); rosettes, 150

Architectural context, for Nottingham furniture, 125–31

Armchairs: fan-back Windsor, 216(fig.); slat-back, 213(fig.); slat-back Windsor, 255(fig. 31)

Arnold, Stephen, 229, 258, 259

Arnold, William, 215, 259

Arons, Harry, 200*n*20

Art and Mystery of Tennessee Furniture (Williams & Harsh), 293

Art Institute of Chicago, 181

"Art of Painting, The" (Porter), 217

Arts and crafts movement, 297–301

Ash: banister-back side chair, 210(fig.); as secondary wood on chair, 214(fig.), 216(fig.), 240(fig.)

Ashbee, C. R., 300

Augur, Horace A., 260

Austin, Richard, 262, 265

Avery, Jabez, 194

Avery, John, Jr., 194, 197, 203*n*46, 216

Avery, John, Sr., 212

Avery, Oliver, 194, 251

Avery, Richard, 194

Ayer, Joseph, 194